1989-90 GUINNESS SPORTS RECORD BOOK

EDITORS

Editor-in-Chief
David A. Boehm

Assistant Editors
Jim Benagh   Cyd Smith

Contributing Editors
Robert Obojski   Gene Jones
Peter J. Matthews

 Sterling Publishing Co., Inc.   New York

CONTENTS

The Sports World *5*
Aerobatics *9*
Archery *9*
Auto Racing *10*
Badminton *17*
Baseball *18*
Basketball *31*
Boardsailing (Windsurfing) *38*
Bobsledding, Luging and Tobogganing *39*
Bodybuilding *40*
Bowling *41*
Boxing *45*
Canoeing and Kayaking *53*
Croquet *55*
Cross-Country Running *56*
Curling *57*
Cycling *58*
Equestrian Sports *64*
Fencing *66*
Field Hockey *68*
Fishing *69*
Footbag *72*
Football *72*
Games *82*
   Backgammon *82*
   Blackjack *82*
   Bridge (Contract) *82*
   Checkers *83*
   Chess *84*
   Cribbage *85*
   Darts *85*
   Marbles *86*
   Monopoly® *87*
   Poker *87*
   Pool and Billiards *87*
   Roulette *88*
   Scrabble® Crossword Game *88*
   Table Soccer *88*
   Throwing *88*
   Twister® *89*
   Video Games *89*
Gliding *90*
   Hang Gliding *90*
Golf *91*
Greyhound Racing *105*
Gymnastics *106*
Handball *113*
   (Team) *114*
Harness Racing *114*

Hockey *116*
Horse Racing *120*
Horseshoe Pitching *124*
Ice and Sand Yachting *124*
Ice Skating *125*
Jai-Alai (Pelota) *128*
Joggling *129*
Judo *130*
Karate *131*
Lacrosse *131*
Marathons (Running) *132*
Modern Pentathlon *133*
Motorcycling *135*
Mountaineering *139*
Olympic Games *141*
Orienteering *148*
Polo *149*
Powerboat Racing *150*
Racquetball *153*
Rodeo *153*
Roller Skating *156*
Rowing *158*
Shooting *162*
Skateboarding *164*
Skiing *165*
   Biathlon *171*
Snowmobiling *172*
Snowshoe Racing *172*
Soccer *173*
Softball *175*
Squash *177*
Surfing *179*
Swimming *180*
Table Tennis *193*
Tennis *195*
Track and Field *208*
Trampolining *228*
Triathlon *230*
Volleyball *232*
Walking *233*
Water Polo *237*
Water Skiing *238*
Weightlifting and Powerlifting *242*
Wrestling *247*
Yachting *249*
Latest Verified Sports Records *250*
Sports and Games Endurance Marathons *251*
Index *253*

IS IT A RECORD?

From the American Editors of *Guinness*

Categories

We are *likely* to publish only those records which improve upon previously published records or which are newly significant in having become the subject of widespread and, preferably, worldwide competition. Records in our sense essentially have to be both measureable and comparable to other performances in the same category.

It should be stressed that unique occurrences, interesting peculiarities and the collecting of everyday objects, are not themselves necessarily records. Records which are *qualified* or limited in some way—for example, by age, handicap, day of the week, etc.—cannot be accommodated in a reference work like *Guinness*.

We do not publish records in gratuitously hazardous categories, such as the lowest starting height for a handcuffed, free-fall parachute jump, or the thinnest burning rope suspending a man in a straitjacket from a helicopter. World records claimed on TV specials are not always set according to Guinness rules. Certain innately dangerous but historically significant activities, such as tightrope walking, are included but are best left to professionals. Other categories which have reached the limits of safety, such as sword swallowing and Volkswagen stuffing, have been retired and either are so marked or have been deleted. No further claims will be considered for publication.

We reserve the right to determine in our sole discretion the record to be published and the use of the name of the record holder for purposes of inclusion in the book.

Rules and Procedures

A record attempt should compete *exactly* with the record in the book and the conditions under which it was set. Where there is doubt about the rules, it is recommended that the strictest interpretation be adopted. Contact with the Guinness editorial offices at 2 Cecil Court, London Road, Enfield, Middlesex, England (01-441-367-4567) for clarification should be made well in advance of a planned attempt.

If there is a recognized world or national governing body for an activity, that body should be consulted for rules and one of its representatives, whenever possible, should be involved in officiating. For any attempt, expert officiating by impartial witnesses is desirable.

In marathon events, five-minute rest intervals are permitted, but only AFTER each *completed* hour, except for a few "non-stop" categories in which minimal intervals may be taken only for purposes other than for resting. These rest breaks are optional and may be accumulated (for example, 3 hours of activity earns 15 minutes of rest time, etc.). Violation of the rest-interval rules will disqualify an attempt. The accepted record will be the gross time (that is, the total elapsed time, including rest intervals, from start to finish). However, unused accumulated rest break time cannot be added to the final figure.

In recent years there has been a marked increase in efforts to establish records for sheer endurance in many activities. In the very nature of record-breaking, the duration of such "marathons" will tend to be pushed to greater and greater extremes, and it should be stressed that marathon attempts are not without possible dangers. Those responsible for marathon events would be well counseled to seek medical advice before, and surveillance during, marathons which involve extended periods with little or no sleep.

Documentation and Verification

■ We do *not* normally supply personnel to monitor, invigilate or observe record attempts, but reserve the right to do so. In any case, the burden of proof rests with the claimant. No particular form is required, and no entry fee is payable. Guidelines for documentation are provided below. We cannot accept as accurate any claim that is insufficiently documented.

■ Claimants should obtain independent corroboration in the form of local or national newspaper, radio or TV coverage. Newspaper clippings must be annotated with the name of the newspaper, its place of publication and the date of the issue in which the article appeared. When possible, the name of the reporter and black-and-white and/or color action photographs should also be supplied. Videotapes and audio cassettes should not be sent, but held in reserve in the event further documentation is requested.

■ Claimants should send signed authentication by independent, impartial adult witnesses or representatives of organizations of standing in their community. Where applicable, a signed document showing ratification by a governing body should be supplied (see above). A claim is naturally enhanced by a witness with a high degree of expertise in the area of endeavor.

■ Signed log books should show there has been unremitting surveillance in the case of endurance events. These log books must include, in chronological order, the times of activity and the times and durations of all rest breaks taken. The log books must be legible and readily decipherable. They must include signatures of witnesses with times of entering and leaving (at least two *independent* witnesses must be on hand at all times). Where applicable, scoresheets must be kept to demonstrate a satisfactory rate of play.

All submissions become the property of the publishers. The publishers will consider, but not guarantee, the return of material, only if a self-addressed stamped envelope or wrapper is supplied *with sufficient postage*.

Revisions

Notwithstanding the best efforts of the editors, errors in the book, while rare, may occur. In the event of such errors, the sole responsibility of the publishers will be to correct such errors in subsequent editions of the book.

If there are discrepancies between entries in one edition and another, it may be generally assumed that the *later* entry is the product of up-to-date research.

Editorial Offices

Please consult the latest edition of the book before phoning or writing the editorial offices, which are primarily concerned with maintaining and improving the quality of each succeeding edition. We do not offer advice on choosing a record for anyone to attempt breaking. Also, we are unable to perform the function of a free general information bureau for quiz competitions and the like. However, we are always happy to hear about new record attempts.

The Sports World

Earliest

The origins of sport stem from the time when self-preservation ceased to be the all-consuming human preoccupation. Archery was a hunting skill in Mesolithic times (by *c.* 8000 BC), but did not become an organized sport until later, possibly as early as *c.* 1150 BC as an archery competition is described in Homer's *Iliad* and certainly by *c.* 300 AD among the Genoese. The earliest dated evidence for sport is *c.* 2750–2600 BC for wrestling. Ball games by girls, depicted on Middle Kingdom murals at Beni Hasan, Egypt, have been dated to *c.* 2050 BC.

Fastest

The highest speed reached in a non-mechanical sport is sky-diving, in which a speed of 185 mph is attained in a head-down free-falling position, even in the lower atmosphere. In delayed drops, a speed of 625 mph has been recorded at high rarefied altitudes. The highest projectile speed in any moving ball game is *c.* 188 mph in pelota (jai-alai). This compares with 170 mph (electronically timed) for a golf ball driven off a tee.

Slowest

In amateur wrestling, before the rules were modified toward "brighter wrestling," contestants could be locked in holds for so long that a single bout once lasted for 11 hours 40 min. In the extreme case of the 2-hour-41-min pull in the regimental tug o' war in Jubbulpore, India, Aug 12, 1889, the winning team moved a net distance of 12 ft at an average speed of 0.00084 mph.

Longest

The most protracted sporting contest was an automobile duration test of 222,621 miles (equivalent to 8.93 times around the equator) by Appaurchaux and others in a Ford Taunus at Miranas, France. This was contested over 142 days (July–Nov) in 1963. The car averaged 65.33 mph.

The most protracted human-powered sporting event is the *Tour de France* cycling race. In 1926 this was over 3,569 miles, lasting 29 days, but is now reduced to 23 days.

Youngest and Oldest Recordbreakers

The youngest age at which any person has broken a non-mechanical world record is 12 years 298 days for Gertrude Caroline Ederle (b Oct 23, 1906) of the US, who broke the women's 880-yd freestyle swimming world record with 13 min 19.0 sec at Indianapolis, Ind, Aug, 17, 1919.

The oldest person to break a world record is Gerhard Weidner (W Germany) (b Mar 15, 1933) who set a 20-mi walk record on May 25, 1974, aged 41 years 71 days.

Youngest and Oldest Champions

The youngest person to have successfully participated in a world title event was a French boy, whose name is not recorded, who coxed the winning Netherlands Olympic pair in rowing at Paris on Aug 26, 1900. He was not more than 10 and may have been as young as 7. The youngest individual Olympic winner was Marjorie Gestring (US) (b Nov 18, 1922), who took the springboard diving title at the age of 13 years 268 days at the Olympic Games in Berlin, Aug 12, 1936. Oscar G. Swahn (see below) was aged 64 years 258 days when he won the gold medal in the 1912 Olympic Running Deer team shooting competition.

Youngest and Oldest Internationals

The youngest age at which any person has won international honors is 8 years in the case of Joy Foster, the Jamaican singles and mixed doubles table tennis champion in 1958. It would appear that the greatest age at which anyone has actively competed for his country is 72 years 280 days in the case of Oscar Gomer Swahn (Sweden) (1847–1927), who won a silver medal for shooting in the Olympic Games at Antwerp on July 26, 1920. He qualified for the 1924 Games, but was unable to participate because of illness.

Largest Field

The largest field for any ball game is that for polo with 12.4 acres, or a maximum length of 300 yd and a width, without side-boards, of 200 yd (with boards the width is 160 yd).

VERSATILITY

ASHRITA FURMAN (b 1954) of Jamaica, NYC, holds 11 competitive stamina records (left top to right): pogo stick jumping (up Mt Fuji); pogo stick jumping underwater (in Peru); milk bottle balancing on head; skip-running (10 mi); juggling while jumping on pogo stick; and land rowing. Other records he holds (not shown) are joggling marathons, somersaulting continuously, juggling 3 balls continuously, stretcher bearing (with partner) and, now, versatility.

Biggest Sports Contract

In March 1982 the National Football League concluded a deal worth $2.1 billion for 5 years coverage of their games by the 3 major TV networks (ABC, CBS and NBC). This represents $14.2 million for each team in the league.

Largest Crowd

The greatest number of live spectators for any sporting spectacle is the estimated 2,500,000 who in 1986 and earlier years lined the route of the New York City Marathon. However, spread over 23 days, it is estimated that more than 10 million see the annual *Tour de France* along the route.

The largest crowd traveling to any single sporting event is "more than 400,000" for the annual *Grand Prix d'Endurance* motor race on the Sarthe circuit near Le Mans, France. The record stadium crowd was one of 199,854 for the Brazil vs Uruguay soccer match in the Maracaña Municipal Stadium, Rio de Janeiro, Brazil, July 16, 1950.

Most Participants

The *Bay-to-Breakers* footrace through San Francisco in 1986 (the 77th annual race) was estimated by police to have included 104,000 runners over the 7.6 mi. The 1983 WIBC Championship Tournament attracted 75,480 women bowlers (all of whom paid entry fees) for the 83-day event held Apr 7–July 1 at Showboat Lanes, Las Vegas, Nev.

The most runners in a marathon were an estimated 23,000 starters in Mexico City on Sept 28, 1986.

In May 1971, the "Ramblin' Raft Race" on the Chattahoochee River at Atlanta, Ga, attracted 37,683 competitors on 8,304 rafts.

Most Athletes

According to a report in 1978, 55 million people are active in sports in the USSR. The country has

3,282 stadiums, 1,435 swimming pools and over 66,000 indoor gymnasia. It is estimated that some 29 percent of the population of E Germany participate in sport regularly.

Most Versatile Athletes

Charlotte "Lottie" Dod (1871–1960) won the Wimbledon singles title (1887 to 1893) 5 times, the British Ladies Golf Championship in 1904, an Olympic silver medal for archery in 1908, and represented England at hockey in 1899. She also excelled at skating and tobogganing.

Mildred (Babe) Didrikson Zaharias (US) (1914–56) was an All-American basketball player, took the silver medal in the high jump, and gold medals in the javelin throw and hurdles in the 1932 Olympics. Turning professional, she first trained as a boxer, and then, switching to golf, eventually won 19 championships, including the US Women's Open and All-American Open. She holds the women's world record also for longest throw of a baseball—296 ft.

Jim Thorpe (US) (1887–1953) excelled at football, baseball, the 10-event decathlon, and the 5-event pentathlon. He won two gold medals in the 1912 Olympics and was declared "the greatest athlete in the world" by King Gustav of Sweden.

Most Versatile Record Holder

Ashrita Furman (b 1954) of Jamaica, New York, has earned 11 stamina world records in unrelated categories, more than any other person.

The records he has held are:
Continuous Somersaults
Skip Running
Joggling in a marathon
Juggling 3 Balls Continuously
Pogo Stick Jumping for Distance
Pogo Stick Jumping Underwater
Pogo Stick Jumping while Juggling 3 Balls
Milk Bottle Balancing
Stretcher Bearing
Land Rowing
and now for Versatility

Greatest Earnings

The greatest fortune amassed by an individual in sport is an estimated $69 million by the boxer Muhammad Ali Haj (US) to the end of 1981.

The highest-paid woman athlete is tennis player Martina Navratilova (b Prague, Czechoslovakia, Oct 18, 1956) (US) whose career earnings passed $12 million in 1987.

Heaviest Athlete

The heaviest sportsman of all time was the wrestler William J. Cobb of Macon, Ga, who in 1962 was billed as the 802-lb "Happy Humphrey." The heaviest player of a ball game was Bob Pointer, the 487-lb tackle on the 1967 Santa Barbara High School football team.

Longest Reign

The longest reign as a world champion is 33 years (1829–62) by Jacques Edmond Barre (France, 1802–73) at the rarely played real (royal) tennis.

Shortest Reign

Olga Rukavishnikova (USSR) (b Mar 13, 1955) held the pentathlon world record for only 0.4 sec at Moscow on July 24, 1980. That is the difference between her second place time of 2 min 04.8 sec in the final 800m event of the Olympic five-event competition, and that of the third-placed Nadezda Tkachenko (USSR), whose overall points came to more than Rukavishnikova's total—5,083 points to 4,937 points.

Most Prolific Recordbreaker

Between Jan 24, 1970, and Nov 1, 1977, Vasili Alexeyev (USSR) (b Jan 7, 1942) broke 80 official world records in weightlifting.

Worst Disasters

The worst disaster in recent history was when an estimated 604 were killed after some stands at the Hong Kong Jockey Club race course collapsed and caught fire on Feb 26, 1918. During the reign of Antoninus Pius (138–161 AD) the upper wooden tiers in the Circus Maximus, Rome, collapsed during a gladiatorial combat, killing 1,112 spectators.

Largest Stadiums

The largest stadium is the Strahov Stadium in Praha (Prague), Czechoslovakia. It was completed in 1934 and accommodates 200,000 spectators (capacity 240,000) for each of the 4 days of the annual Czechoslovak Spartakiad, where 180,000 participate in a gymnastics-Aerobics display. There are markers for 13,824 gymnasts at a time.

The largest football (soccer) stadium is the Mara

AEROBICS STADIUM: At the annual "Spartakiad" at the Strahov Stadium in Prague, Czechoslovakia, the field is marked off for 13,284 gymnasts to perform simultaneously. With as many as 200,000 spectators per day, the display goes on for 4 days and a total of about 180,000 participate.

caña Municipal Stadium in Rio de Janeiro, Brazil, which has a normal capacity of 205,000, of whom 155,000 may be seated. A crowd of 199,854 was accommodated for the World Cup final between Brazil and Uruguay on July 16, 1950. A dry moat, 7 ft wide and over 5 ft deep, protects players from spectators and *vice versa*.

The largest covered stadium in the world is the Azteca Stadium, Mexico City, opened in 1968, which has a capacity of 107,000, of whom nearly all are under cover.

The largest retractable roof is being constructed to cover the 60,000-capacity Toronto Blue Jays' new stadium near the CN Tower. It was to have been completed by Aug 1988. The diameter will be 679 ft.

The transparent acrylic glass "tent" roof over the Munich Olympic Stadium, W Germany, measures 914,940 sq ft in area. It rests on a steel net supported by masts. The roof of longest span is the 680-ft diameter of the Louisiana Superdome. The major axis of the elliptical Texas Stadium, Irving, Tex, completed in 1971 is, however, 784 ft 4 in.

The largest indoor stadium is the 13-acre $173-million 273-ft-tall Superdome in New Orleans, La, completed in May 1975. Its maximum seating capacity for conventions is 97,365 or 76,791 for football.

Box suites rent for $35,000, excluding the price of admission. A gondola with six 312-in TV screens produces instant replay.

MOST VERSATILE ATHLETE: Mildred (Babe) Didrikson Zaharias (US) was tops in basketball, high jump, javelin throwing, hurdling and golf (19 championships), besides having boxing and baseball talent.

AEROBATICS

Earliest

The first aerobatic maneuver is generally considered the sustained inverted flight in a Blériot of Célestin-Adolphe Pégoud (1889–1915) at Buc, France, Sept 21, 1913, but Lieut Peter Nikolayevich Nesterov (1887–1914), of the Imperial Russian Air Service, performed a loop in a Nieuport Type IV monoplane at Kiev, USSR, Aug 27, 1913.

World Championships

Held biennially since 1960 (excepting 1974), scoring is based on the system devised by Col José Aresti of Spain. The competitions consist of two compulsory and two free programs. Team competition has been won on 5 occasions by the USSR. No individual has won more than one title, the most successful competitor being Igor Egorov (USSR) who won in 1970, was second in 1976, fifth in 1972 and eleventh in 1968. The most successful in the women's competition has been Betty Stewart (US) who has won twice, 1980 and 1982. The US had a clean sweep of all the medals in 1980.

Inverted Flight

The duration record for inverted flight is 4 hours 9 min 5 sec by John "Hal" McClain in a Swick Taylorcraft on Aug 23, 1980 over Houston Raceways, Tex.

Loops

On June 21, 1980, R. Steven Powell performed 2,315⅝ inside loops in a Bellanca Decathlon over Almont, Mich. John McClain achieved 180 outside loops in a Bellanca Super Decathlon on Sept 2, 1978, over Houston, Tex. Ken Ballinger (GB) completed 155 consecutive loops in a Bellanca Citabria on Aug 6, 1983 over Staverton Airport, Cheltenham, Eng.

ARCHERY

Origins

Though the earliest evidence of the existence of bows is seen in the Mesolithic cave paintings in Spain, archery as an organized sport appears to have developed in the 3rd century AD. Competitive archery may, however, date back to the 12th century BC. The world governing body is the Fédération Internationale de Tir à l'Arc (FITA), founded in 1931.

Highest 24-Hour Scores

The record score at target archery over 24 hours by a pair of archers is 52,008 during 48 Portsmouth Rounds (40 arrows per round at 20 yd at 60-cm FITA targets) by Mick Brown and Les Powioi of Guilford (Eng) Archery Club May 14–15, 1987.

Phyllis Griffiths, 64, achieved a score of 31,000 in 76 Portsmouth Rounds in 24 hours at Holsworthy, Eng, Mar 30–31 1986.

LONG-LASTING RECORDS: 1984 Olympic Gold Medalist Darrell Pace (US) (left) in 1979 had set a target-shooting record of 1,341 out of a possible 1,440, a mark that still stands. In the 1988 Olympics, Pace scored 2,617 points out of a possible 2,880. (LA Times) FLIGHT-SHOOTING: April Moon (US) (right), using a handbow, set a women's record (over 1,039 yd) in 1981, and it still stands.

Highest Championship Scores

The highest scores achieved in either a world or Olympic championship for Double FITA rounds are: Men, 2,617 points (possible 2,880) by Richard McKinney (b Oct 20, 1963) (US) and Darrell Pace (b Oct 23, 1956) (US) and Women, 2,683 points by Kim Soo-nyung (S Korea) (b Apr 5, 1971) at the Olympic Games, Seoul, S Korea Sept 27-30, 1988.

Most Titles

The greatest number of world titles (instituted 1931) ever won by a man is 4 by Hans Deutgen (b Feb 28, 1917) (Sweden), 1947–50. The greatest number won by a woman is 7 by Mrs Janina Spychajowa-Kurkowska (b Feb 8, 1901) (Poland), 1931–34, 36, 39 and 47.

Oscar Kessels (Belgium) participated in 21 world championships.

Flight Shooting

The longest flight shooting records are achieved in the footbow class. In the unlimited footbow division, Harry Drake (b May 7, 1915) of Lakeside, Calif, holds the record at 1 mile 268 yd, shot at Ivanpah Dry Lake, Calif, Oct 24, 1971, at 3,000-ft altitude. He also holds the regular footbow record with 1,542 yd 34 in set on Oct 6, 1979.

The greatest distance that an arrow has been fired is 2,047 yd 2 in, the record for crossbow flight set by Harry Drake at Smith Creek Flight Range, Nev. The female footbow record is 1,113 yd 30 in by Arlyne Rhode (b May 4, 1936) at Wendover, Utah, on Sept 10, 1978. The flight record for the handbow is 1,336 yd 1 ft 3 in set by Don Brown (US) Aug 2, 1987 at Smith Creek, Nev. April Moon (US) set a women's record of 1,039 yd 13 in on Sept 13, 1981, at Ivanpah Dry Lake. The new compound bow records are held by Arlan Reynolds (US) at 1,030 yd 2 ft 11 in, and his wife Sherrie Reynolds at 704 yd 1 ft 9 in, both set at Bonneville Flight Range, Utah, in 1986.

Olympic Medals

Hubert van Innis (Belgium) (1866–1961) won 6 gold and 3 silver medals in archery events at the 1900 and 1920 Olympic Games.

In 1988, the men's individual gold medal was won by Jay Barrs (US) and the other 3 gold medals went to S Koreans.

Also in 1988, the US women's team which won a bronze medal included Denise Parker of S Jordan, Utah, a 14-year-old, the youngest Olympian archer.

Archery World Records

Single FITA rounds

These consist of 144 arrows. Archers shoot 36 arrows from each of four distances—30, 50, 70, and 90 meters (men) and 30, 50, 60, and 70 meters (women). A hit in the center gold (bull's-eye) is scored 10, so the highest possible score is 1440.

Event	Points	Name and Country	Possible	Year
MEN				
FITA	1341	Darrell Pace (US)	1440	1979
90 m	329	Vladimir Yesheyev (USSR)	360	1988
	329	Yuri Leontiev (USSR)	360	1988
70 m	343	Tomi Poikolainen (Fin)	360	1988
50 m	345	Richard McKinney (US)	360	1982
30 m	357	Takayoshi Matsushita (Jap)	360	1986
Team	3948	US (Richard McKinney, 1323; Jay Barrs, 1317; Darrell Pace, 1308)	4320	1987
WOMEN				
FITA	1352	Kim Soo-nyung (S Korea)	1440	1988
70 m	330	Yelena Marfel (USSR)	360	1987
60 m	342	Lessia Schah (USSR)	360	1988
50 m	336	Kim Soo-nyung (S. Korea)	360	1988
30 m	356	Kim Soo-nyung (S Korea)	360	1987
Team	3981	S Korea (Lee Hae-young, Kim Kyung-wook, Kim Soo-nyung)	4320	1988

Indoor Double FITA rounds at 25 m

	Points	Name and Country	Possible	Year
MEN	589	Darrell Pace (US)	600	1984
WOMEN	588	Elena Marfel (USSR)	600	1985

Indoor FITA round at 18 m

	Points	Name and Country	Possible	Year
MEN	590	Thierry Venant (France)	600	1987
WOMEN	583	Natalya Butuzova (USSR)	600	1983

Greatest Pull

Gary Sentman of Roseburg, Ore, drew a longbow weighing a record of 176 lb to the maximum draw on the arrow (28¼ in) at Forksville, Pa, Sept 20, 1975.

AUTO RACING

Earliest Races

There are various conflicting claims, but the first automobile race was the 201-mile Green Bay-to-Madison, Wis, run in 1878, won by an Oshkosh steamer.

In 1887, Count Jules Felix Philippe Albert de Dion de Malfiance (1856–1946) won the *La Velocipede* 19.3-mile race in Paris in a De Dion steam quadri-

HIGHEST EARNER: Darrell Waltrip of Franklin, Tenn, now age 39, won a record $8,674,062 in his career through 1988. Here he is posing with his Tide Chevrolet.

cycle in which he is reputed to have exceeded 37 mph.

The first "real" race was from Paris to Bordeaux and back (732 miles) June 11–13, 1895. The winner was Emile Levassor (1844–97) (France) driving a Panhard-Levassor two-seater with a 1.2-liter Daimler engine developing 3½ hp. His time was 48 hours 47 min (average speed 15.01 mph). The first closed-circuit race was held over 5 laps of a mile dirt track at Narragansett Park, Cranston, RI on Sept 7, 1896. It was won by A. H. Whiting, who drove a Riker electric.

The oldest auto race in the world still being regularly run is the R.A.C. Tourist Trophy, first staged on the Isle of Man on Sept 14, 1905. The oldest continental race is the French Grand Prix, first held June 26–27, 1906. The Coppa Florio, in Sicily, has been irregularly held since 1900.

Fastest Races

The fastest race in the world is the NASCAR Busch Clash, a 50-mi all-out sprint on the 2½-mile 31-degree-banked tri-oval at Daytona International Speedway, Daytona Beach, Fla. On Feb 8, 1987, Bill Elliott (b Oct 8, 1955) of Dawsonville, Ga, averaged 197.802 mph in a Ford Thunderbird to set the record. Elliott set the world record for a 500-mi race in 1985 when he won at Talladega, Ala, at an average speed of 186.288 mph. He also set the NASCAR qualifying record of 212.809 at Talladega's Alabama International Motor Speedway on Apr 30, 1987.

Fastest Runs

The highest average lap speed attained on any closed circuit test course is 257.123 mph by A. J. Foyt Jr. (b Jan 16, 1935) at Fort Stockton Test Center, Tex on Aug 27, 1987. The test vehicle was a specially developed super heavy duty turbocharged "RE" version of the Quad 4 engine in an Oldsmobile Aerotech 5 (short tail). It was based on a production double overhead camshaft, 16-valve, 4-cylinder Quad 4 powerplant to be used later in the 1988 Oldsmobile Cutlass Calais.

The highest average lap speed in an actual race on a closed circuit is 223.401 mph by Rick Mears of Bakersfield, Calif, driving a Chevrolet-powered March on the 2-mi Michigan International Speedway, Brooklyn, Mich, July 31, 1986, during the qualifying for the Michigan 500. Mears, in the same car on the same track Nov 17, 1986, was clocked at 233.934 under simulated race conditions and has applied for certification of that time to break his 223.401 record.

The fastest average lap speed on a closed-circuit track by a woman racer is 204.223 by Lyn St. James, (US), in a Mustang Probe on the 2.66-mi Alabama International Motor Speedway in Talladega, Ala, on Nov 26, 1985.

Grand Prix Victories

The most Grand Prix victories is 35 in 137 races by Alain Prost (France) (b Feb 24, 1955) 1981 through 1988. Jim Clark (1936–1968) of Scotland shares the

Indianapolis 500

Winners since 1946 (all US except where stated):

Year	Driver	Car	Speed (mph)
1946	George Robson	Thorne Engineering	114.820
1947	Mauri Rose	Blue Crown Special	116.338
1948	Mauri Rose	Blue Crown Special	119.814
1949	Bill Holland	Blue Crown Special	121.327
1950	Johnny Parsons	Wynn Kurtis Kraft	124.002
1951	Lee Wallard	Belanger	126.224
1952	Troy Ruttman	Agajanian	128.922
1953	Bill Vukovich	Fuel Injection	128.740
1954	Bill Vukovich	Fuel Injection	130.840
1955	Bob Sweikert	John Zink Special	128.209
1956	Pat Flaherty	John Zink Special	128.490
1957	Sam Hanks	Belond Exhaust	135.601
1958	Jimmy Bryan	Belond A. P.	133.791
1959	Rodger Ward	Leader Card Special	135.857
1960	Jim Rathmann	Ken-Paul Special	138.767
1961	A. J. Foyt	Bowes Seal Fast	139.130
1962	Rodger Ward	Leader Card Special	140.293
1963	Parnelli Jones	Agajanian Special	143.137
1964	A. J. Foyt	Sheraton-Thompson Special	147.350
1965	Jim Clark (GB)	Lotus-Ford	150.686
1966	Graham Hill (GB)	American Red Ball	144.317
1967	A. J. Foyt	Sheraton-Thompson Special	151.207
1968	Bobby Unser	Rislone Special	152.882
1969	Mario Andretti	STP Oil Treatment Special	156.867
1970	Al Unser, Sr.	Johnny Lightning Special	155.749
1971	Al Unser, Sr.	Johnny Lightning Special	157.735
1972	Mark Donohue	Sunoco McLaren	162.962
1973	Gordon Johncock	STP Double Oil Filter	159.036
1974	Johnny Rutherford	McLaren	158.589
1975	Bobby Unser	Jorgensen Eagle	149.213
1976	Johnny Rutherford	Hygain McLaren	148.725
1977	A. J. Foyt	Gilmore Coyote-Foyt	161.331
1978	Al Unser, Sr.	Lola-Chapparal Cosworth	161.363
1979	Rick Mears	Penske-Cosworth	158.899
1980	Johnny Rutherford	Chapparal Cosworth	142.862
1981	Bobby Unser	Penske-Cosworth	139.084
1982	Gordon Johncock	Wildcat-Cosworth	162.025
1983	Tom Sneva	March-Cosworth	162.117
1984	Rick Mears	March-Cosworth	163.612
1985	Danny Sullivan	March-Cosworth	152.982
1986	Bobby Rahal	March-Cosworth	170.722
1987	Al Unser, Sr.	March-Cosworth	162.575
1988	Rick Mears	Penske-Chevrolet	144.809

record of Grand Prix victories in one year with 7 in 1963; Prost had 7 in 1984. The most Grand Prix starts is 176 (out of a possible 184) between May 18, 1958, and Jan 26, 1975, by (Norman) Graham Hill (1929–1975); Jacques Laffite (France) (b Nov 21, 1943), likewise had 176 starts 1974–86.

The most Grand Prix points won is 511½ by Alain Prost 1980–88.

Ayrton Senna (Brazil) (b Mar 21, 1960) had a record 8 wins in a year in 1988.

Youngest and Oldest Grand Prix Winners and Drivers

The youngest Grand Prix driver was Michael Christopher Thackwell (b New Zealand, March 30, 1961) who took part in the Canadian Grand Prix on Sept 28, 1980, aged 19 years 182 days. The youngest Grand Prix winner was Bruce Leslie McLaren (1937–70) of New Zealand, who won the US Grand Prix at Sebring, Fla, on Dec 12, 1959, aged 22 years 104 days. The youngest world champion was Emerson Fittipaldi of Brazil (b Dec 12, 1946), who won the World Championship in 1972 at age 25 years 273 days.

The oldest Grand Prix winner was Tazio Giorgio Nuvolari (1892–1953) of Italy, who won the Albi Grand Prix at Albi, France, on July 14, 1946, aged 53 years 240 days. The oldest Grand Prix driver was Louis Alexandre Chiron (Monaco, 1899–1979), who finished 6th in the Monaco Grand Prix on May 22,

Le Mans 24-Hour Race

The world's most important race for sports cars was first held in 1923. Winners since 1949 when the race was revived after the Second World War:

	Driver	Car	Speed (mph)
1949	Luigi Chinetti/Lord Peter Selsdon	Ferrari	82.27
1950	Louis Rosier/Jean-Louis Rosier	Talbot	89.73
1951	Peter Walker/Peter Whitehead	Jaguar	93.50
1952	Hermann Lang/Fritz Riess	Mercedes	96.67
1953	Anthony Rolt/Duncan Hamilton	Jaguar	105.85
1954	José Froilan Gonzalez/Maurice Trintignant	Ferrari	105.15
1955	Mike Hawthorn/Ivor Bueb	Jaguar	107.07
1956	Ron Flockhart/Ninian Sanderson	Jaguar	104.46
1957	Ron Flockhart/Ivor Bueb	Jaguar	113.85
1958	Phil Hill/Olivier Gendebien	Ferrari	106.20
1959	Roy Salvadori/Carroll Shelby	Aston Martin	112.57
1960	Paul Frère/Olivier Gendebien	Ferrari	109.19
1961	Phil Hill/Olivier Gendebien	Ferrari	115.90
1962	Phil Hill/Olivier Gendebien	Ferrari	115.24
1963	Ludovico Scarfiotti/Lorenzo Bandini	Ferrari	118.10
1964	Jean Guichet/Nino Vaccarella	Ferrari	121.55
1965	Masten Gregory/Jochen Rindt	Ferrari	121.09
1966	Bruce McLaren/Chris Amon	Ford	126.01
1967	Anthony Joseph Foyt/Dan Gurney	Ford	132.49
1968	Pedro Rodriguez/Lucien Bianchi	Ford	115.29
1969	Jackie Ickx/Jackie Oliver	Ford	125.44
1970	Hans Herrmann/Richard Attwood	Porsche	119.29
1971	Helmut Marko/Gijs van Lennep	Porsche	138.142
1972	Graham Hill/Henri Pescarolo	Matra-Simca	121.47
1973	Henri Pescarolo/Gerard Larrousse	Matra-Simca	125.68
1974	Henri Pescarolo/Gerard Larrousse	Matra-Simca	119.27
1975	Jackie Ickx/Derek Bell	Gulf Ford	118.99
1976	Jackie Ickx/Gijs van Lennep	Porsche	123.50
1977	Jackie Ickx/Jurgen Barth/Hurley Haywood	Porsche	120.95
1978	Didier Peroni/Jean-Pierre Jaussaud	Renault Alpine	130.60
1979	Klaus Ludwig/Bill and Don Whittington	Porsche	108.06
1980	Jean-Pierre Jaussaud/Jean Rondeau	Rondeau	119.17
1981	Jackie Ickx/Derek Bell	Porsche	124.87
1982	Jackie Ickx/Derek Bell	Porsche	126.84
1983	Vern Schuppan/Hurley Haywood/Al Holbert	Porsche	130.70
1984	Klaus Ludwig/Henri Pescarolo	Porsche	126.88
1985	Klaus Ludwig/Paulo Barilla/John Winter	Porsche 956	131.74
1986	Hans Stuck/Al Holbert/Derek Bell	Porsche	128.74
1987	Hans Stuck/Al Holbert/Derek Bell	Porsche	124.087
1988	Johnny Dumfries/Andy Wallace/Jan Lammers	Jaguar XJR-9	137.718

1955, aged 55 years 292 days. The oldest world champion was Juan-Manuel Fangio, who won in 1957 at age 46 years 55 days.

Indianapolis 500

The Indianapolis 500-mile race (200 laps) was inaugurated on May 30, 1911. The most successful drivers have been Anthony Joseph ''A. J.'' Foyt, Jr (b Houston, Tex, Jan 16, 1935), who won in 1961, 64, 67 and 77, and Al Unser, Sr (b May 29, 1939) of Albuquerque, N Mex, who won in 1970, 71, 78 and 87.

The record time is 2 hours 55 min 42.48 sec (average speed 170.722 mph) by Bobby Rahal (US) on May 31, 1986, driving a March Cosworth.

The fastest one-lap record in practice is 221.565 mph by Mario Gabriele Andretti (US) (b Feb 28, 1940) in a Lola-Chevrolet on May 11, 1988. The fastest official qualifying lap is 220.453 by Rick Mears on May 14, 1988.

The qualifying 4-lap record average speed is 219.198 mph by Rick Mears (US) in a Penske-Chevrolet V8 on May 14, 1988.

The record prize fund is $5,016,959 for the 1988 race. The individual prize record is the $804,853 won by Rick Mears in 1988.

The first and only woman to qualify for and compete in the Indianapolis 500 is Janet Guthrie (b Mar 7, 1938). She passed her rookie test in May 1976, and earned the right to compete in the qualify-

Daytona 500

Year	Driver	Car	Average Speed
1959	Lee Petty	59 Oldsmobile	135.521
1960	Junior Johnson	59 Chevrolet	124.740
1961	Marvin Panch	60 Pontiac	149.601
1962	Fireball Roberts	62 Pontiac	152.529
1963	Tiny Lund	63 Ford	151.566
1964	Richard Petty	64 Plymouth	154.334
1965*	Fred Lorenzen	65 Ford	141.539
1966**	Richard Petty	66 Plymouth	160.627
1967	Mario Andretti	67 Ford	146.926
1968	Cale Yarborough	68 Mercury	143.251
1969	LeeRoy Yarborough	69 Ford	157.950
1970	Pete Hamilton	70 Plymouth	149.601
1971	Richard Petty	71 Plymouth	144.462
1972	A. J. Foyt	71 Mercury	161.550
1973	Richard Petty	73 Dodge	157.205
1974	Richard Petty	74 Dodge	140.894
1975	Benny Parsons	Chevrolet	153.649
1976	David Pearson	Mercury	152.181
1977	Cale Yarborough	Chevrolet	153.218
1978	Bobby Allison	Ford	159.730
1979	Richard Petty	Oldsmobile	143.977
1980	Buddy Baker	Oldsmobile	177.602
1981	Richard Petty	Buick	169.651
1982	Bobby Allison	Buick	153.991
1983	Cale Yarborough	Pontiac	155.979
1984	Cale Yarborough	Chevrolet	150.994
1985	Bill Elliott	Ford	172.265
1986	Geoff Bodine	Chevrolet	148.124
1987	Bill Elliott	Ford	176.263
1988	Bobby Allison	Buick	137.531

*332½ miles because of rain   **495 miles because of rain

MOST NASCAR VICTORIES: Richard Petty has won a total of 200 Winston Cup races 1958–88 in 1,073 starts, his best season being 1967 with 27 victories. He was the first driver to pass $1 million in career earnings.

ing rounds, but was unable to win a place on the starting line when the Vollstedt-Offenhauser she drove was withdrawn from the race after repeated mechanical failures. In the 61st running of the Indianapolis 500, in 1977, Guthrie became the first woman to compete, although her car developed mechanical problems which forced her to retire after 27 laps. In 1978, she completed the race, finishing in ninth place after 190 laps.

CART Leaders

The Indy cars, the fastest open-wheeled class of racing cars in the United States, are the American equivalent of the international Formula One series. They race under the auspices of CART (Championship Auto Racing Teams). A. J. Foyt holds the all-time record for victories with 67. Mario Andretti is the leader in earnings ($6,175,551), pole positions (64) and laps led (7,159) through 1988.

Most Successful Drivers

Based on the World Drivers' Championships, inaugurated in 1950, the most successful driver is Juan-Manuel Fangio (b Balcarce, Argentina, June

24, 1911), who won five times in 1951, 54–57. He retired in 1958, after having won 24 Grand Prix races (2 shared) in 51 starts.

The most successful driver in terms of earnings is Darrell Waltrip (b Feb 5, 1949) of Franklin, Tenn, whose career earnings reached $8,674,062 through 1988. Richard Lee Petty (b Randleman, NC, July 2, 1937) has 200 NASCAR Winston Cup wins, 1958–87. Petty's best season was 1967 with 27 wins. Geoff Bodine won 55 races in 1978. Bill Elliott holds the single year's record of $2,383,187 in NASCAR events in 1985. In 1988, Elliott won $1,411,567, marking the 4th straight year with more than $1 million in earnings.

Le Mans

The greatest distance ever covered in the 24-hour *Grand Prix d'Endurance* (first held May 26–27, 1923) on the old Sarthe circuit (8 miles 650 yd) at Le Mans, France, is 3,314.222 miles by Dr Helmut Marko (b Graz, Austria, Apr 27, 1943) and Jonkheer Gijs van Lennep (b Bloemendaal, Netherlands, March 16, 1942) driving a 4,907-cc flat-12 Porsche 917K Group 5 sports car June 12–13, 1971. The

FASTEST STOCK CAR: At 212 mph, Bill Elliott drove this Ford Thunderbird to a speed record at Talladega, Ala, Apr 30, 1987. Elliott has record earnings of over $2 million in one year. (NASCAR)

RECORD-SETTERS ALL: Bobby Rahal (left) won the 1986 Indy 500 in record time (2 hours 55 min 42.48 sec) at a speed of 170.722 mph. Rick Mears (center) has been victorious at Indy 3 times in the last 10 years. Alain Prost of France (right) has the most Grand Prix triumphs (35 in 137 races) 1981–88, and the most points (511½).

record for the current circuit is 3,161.938 miles (average speed 131.747 mph) in a Porsche 956 June 15–16, 1985 by Klaus Ludwig (W Ger), Paulo Barillo (Italy), and John Winter (W Ger). The race lap record (8.410-mile lap) is 3 min 25.1 sec (average speed 148.61 mph) by Jackie Ickx (Belgium) in a Porsche 962C in 1985. The practice lap record is 3 min 14.8 sec (av. speed 156.62 mph) by Hans Stuck (W Ger) in a Porsche 962C on June 14, 1985.

The most wins by one man is 6 by Jackie Ickx (b Belgium, Jan 1, 1940), who won in 1969, 75-77 and 81-82.

Fastest Pit Stop

Bobby Unser (US) took 4 sec to take on fuel on lap 10 of the Indianapolis 500 on May 30, 1976.

Closest Finishes

The closest finish to a World Championship race occurred when Ayrton Senna (Brazil) beat Nigel Mansell (GB) by 0.014 sec in the Spanish Grand Prix at Jerez de la Frontera Apr 13, 1986.

The closest finish in the Indianapolis 500 was in the 1982 race when the winner, Gordon Johncock, crossed the finish line just 0.16 sec before runner-up Rick Mears.

1988 WINNERS AT LE MANS: Lammers, Dumfries and Wallace raced the last few laps together and crossed the finish line 1-2-3 like this to win for Jaguar. (All Sport/Vandystadt)

DRAG RECORD: Eddie Hill (US) recorded the lowest elapsed time—4.936 sec Oct 9, 1988.

Duration Record

The greatest distance ever covered in one year is 400,000 km (248,548.5 miles) by François Lecot (1879–1949), an innkeeper from Rochetaillée, France, in a 1,900-cc 66-bhp Citroën 11 sedan mainly between Paris and Monte Carlo, from July 22, 1935 to July 26, 1936. He drove on 363 of the 370 days allowed.

Land Speed Records

The highest speed attained by any wheeled land vehicle is 739.666 mph or Mach 1.0106 (making it the only land vehicle to break the sound barrier) *in a one-way stretch* by the rocket-engined *Budweiser Rocket,* designed by William Frederick, and driven by Stan Barrett at Edwards Air Force Base, California, on Dec 17, 1979. The vehicle, owned by Hal Needham, has a 48,000-hp rocket engine with 6,000 lb of extra thrust from a sidewinder missile. The rear wheels (100-lb solid discs) lifted 10 in off the ground above Mach 0.95, acting as 7,500-rpm gyroscopes.

The official 1-mi land speed record, which is for the average of a two-way run, was set on Oct 4, 1983 when Richard Noble (GB) drove a jet-powered car, *Thrust 2,* at 633.468 mph at Black Rock Desert, Gerlach, Nev. The previous record, 622.287, was set by Gary Gabelich and had stood for 13 years.

The most successful land speed record breaker was Major Malcolm Campbell (1885–1948) (UK). He broke the official record nine times between Sept 25, 1924, with 146.157 mph in a Sunbeam, and Sept 3, 1935, when he achieved 301.129 mph in the Rolls-Royce-engined *Bluebird.*

Drag Racing

The lowest elapsed time recorded by a piston-engined dragster is 4.936 sec from a standing start for 440 yd by Eddie Hill at Ennis, Tex, on Oct 9, 1988. The highest terminal velocity recorded at the end of a 440-yd run is 288.73 mph by Hill at Gainesville, Fla, on Mar 18, 1988.

BADMINTON

Origins

A game similar to badminton was played in China in the 2nd millennium BC. The modern game may have evolved c. 1850 at Badminton Hall in Avon, England, the seat of the Dukes of Beaufort, or from a game played in India. The first modern rules were codified in Poona, India in 1876.

International Championships

The Men's International Championship or Thomas Cup (instituted 1948) has been won 8 times by Indonesia, in 1958, 61, 64, 70, 73, 76, 79, and 1984.

BADMINTON CHAMPION: Indonesian Rudy Hartono Kurniawan won the men's singles world title in 1980, captured 8 singles titles in the All-England championships and has been the mainstay of Indonesia's successful Thomas Cup teams.

Indonesians have also won All-England titles 12 times in the last 16 years. China won all 5 events at the 1987 world championships in Beijing, China.

The Ladies International Championship or Uber Cup (instituted 1956) has been won 5 times by Japan (1966, 69, 72, 78 and 81). China won the Uber Cup *and* the Thomas Cup in 1986 and 1988.

Most Titles

The record for men's singles in the All-England Championship is 8 by Rudy Hartono Kurniawan (b Aug 18, 1948) of Indonesia (1968-74, 76). The most, including doubles, is 21 by George Alan Thomas (Eng), between 1903 and 1928. The most, including doubles, by women is 17, a record shared by Muriel Lucas (later Mrs King Adams) (1899-1910) and Mrs G. C. K. Hashman (*née* Judy Devlin) (US) (b Oct 22, 1935), whose wins came from 1954 to 1967, including a record 10 singles titles. Judy Hashman also won 29 US titles.

A record of 211 victories without a defeat was set by the Miller Place High School girls' team of Miller Place, LI, NY, from 1972 through 1987.

Marathons

The longest singles match is 80 hours 21 min by Graham D. Nell and Jannie E. Vasloo at Komga, S Africa, June 26–29, 1987. This was tied by Stuart Dobbie and Paul Irvine at the Police Assembly Hall, Coventry, Eng, Oct 28–31, 1987. The longest doubles is 86 hours 22 min 44 sec by Cameron McMullen, Michael Pattison, Stephen Breuer, and Michael Bain, at Rhyl, Wales, July 18–21, 1987.

Shortest International Game

In the 1969 Uber Cup in Tokyo, Japan, Noriko Takagi (later Mrs Nakayama) (Japan) beat Poppy Tumengkol (Indonesia) in 9 min.

Longest Hit and Rally

Frank Rugani drove a shuttlecock 79 ft 8½ in in indoor tests at San Jose, Calif, Feb 29, 1964.

Morten Frost (Denmark) and Icuk Sugiarto (Indonesia) played two successive rallies of over 90 strokes in the 1986 All-England final.

BASEBALL

Earliest Games

The Reverend Thomas Wilson, of Maidstone, Kent, England, wrote disapprovingly, in 1700, of baseball being played on Sundays. The earliest game on record under the Cartwright (Alexander Joy Cartwright, Jr, 1820–92) rules was on June 19, 1846, in Hoboken, NJ, where the "New York Nine" defeated the Knickerbockers 23 to 1 in 4 innings. The earliest all-professional team was the Cincinnati Red Stockings in 1869, who had 56 wins and 1 tie that season.

Night Baseball

The first night game was played on June 2, 1883 (M.E. College vs professionals from Quincy, Ill). The major leagues were slow to adopt this change of program, then considered radical. The Cincinnati Reds were the first big-league team to play under lights when they hosted the Philadelphia Phillies on May 24, 1935. President Franklin D. Roosevelt pressed a button at the White House to flick the switch at Crosley Field. Wrigley Field, home of the Chicago Cubs, finally saw the light Aug 8, 1988. However, that game was rained out, and the first full night game was completed the next evening.

Home Runs

Henry L. (Hank) Aaron (b Feb 5, 1934, Mobile, Ala) broke the major league record set by George H. (Babe) Ruth of 714 home runs in a lifetime when he hit No. 715 on Apr 8, 1974. Between 1954 and 1974 he hit 733 home runs for the Milwaukee and Atlanta Braves in the National League. In 1975, he switched to the Milwaukee Brewers in the American League and in that year and 1976, when he finally retired, he hit 22 more, bringing his lifetime total to 755, the major league record.

MAJOR LEAGUE ALL-TIME RECORDS

Individual Batting

(including 1988 season)

Most years
25 Roderick (Bobby) Wallace, Cleve NL 1894–98; St L NL 1899–1901, 1917–18; St L AL 1902–16

Edward Collins, Phil AL 1906–14, 1927–30; Chi AL 1915–26

Highest percentage, lifetime (5,000 at-bats)
.367 Tyrus R. Cobb, Det AL, 1905–26; Phil AL, 1927–28

Highest percentage, season (500 at-bats)
.438 Hugh Duffy, Bos NL, 1894
Modern Record
.424 Rogers Hornsby, St L NL, 1924

Most games played
3,562 Peter Rose, Cin NL, 1963–78; Phil NL, 1979–83; Mont NL, 1984; Cin NL, 1984–86

Most consecutive games played
2,130 Henry Louis (Lou) Gehrig, NY AL, June 1, 1925 through Apr 30, 1939

Most runs batted in, season
190 Lewis R. (Hack) Wilson, Chi NL, 155 games, 1930

Most runs batted in, game
12 James L. Bottomley, St L NL, Sept 16, 1924

Most runs batted in, lifetime
2,297 Henry L. (Hank) Aaron, Mil NL, 1954–65; Atl NL, 1966–74; Mil AL, 1975–76

Most runs, lifetime
2,244 Tyrus R. Cobb, Det AL, 1905–26; Phil AL, 1927–28

Most runs, season
196 William R. Hamilton Phil NL 1894
Modern Record
177 George H. (Babe) Ruth NY AL 1921

Most runs, game
6 Held by 12 players. Most recent: Spike D. Owen, Bos AL Aug 21, 1986

Most base hits, lifetime
4,256 Peter Rose, Cin NL, 1963–78; Phil NL, 1979–83; Mont NL, 1984; Cin NL, 1984–86

Most base hits, season
257 George H. Sisler, St L AL, 154 games, 1920

Most hits in succession
12 M. Frank (Pinky) Higgins, Bos AL, June 19–21 (4 games), 1938
Walter Dropo, Det AL, July 14, July 15, 2 games, 1952

Most base hits, game
9 John H. Burnett, Cleve AL, July 10, 1932 (18 innings)

Most base hits, consecutive, game
7 Wilbert Robinson, Balt NL, June 10, 1892, 1st game (7-ab), 6-1b, 1-2b
Renaldo Stennett, Pitt NL, Sept 16, 1975 (7-ab), 4-1b, 2-2b, 1-3b
Cesar Gutierrez, Det AL, June 21, 1970, 2nd game (7-ab) 6-1b, 1-2b (12-inning game)

Most times at bat, lifetime
14,053 Peter Rose, Cin NL, 1963–78; Phil NL, 1979–83; Mont NL, 1984; Cin NL, 1984–86

Most consecutive games batted safely, season
56 Joseph P. DiMaggio, NY AL (91 hits—16-2b, 4-3b, 15 hr), May 15 to July 16, 1941

Most total bases, lifetime
6,856 Henry L. (Hank) Aaron, Mil NL, 1954–65; Atl NL, 1966–74; Mil AL, 1975–76

Most total bases, season
457 George H. (Babe) Ruth, NY AL, 152 gs (85 on 1b, 88 on 2b, 48 on 3b, 236 on hr), 1921

Most total bases, game
18 Joseph W. Adcock, Mil NL (1-2b, 4-hr), July 31, 1954

Most one-base hits (singles), season
202 William H. (Wee Willie) Keeler, Balt NL, 128 games, 1898
Modern Record
198 Lloyd Waner, Pitt NL, 1927

Most two-base hits, season
67 Earl W. Webb, Bos AL, 151 games, 1931

Most three-base hits, season
36 J. Owen Wilson, Pitt NL, 152 games, 1912

Most home runs, season
61 Roger E. Maris, NY AL (162-game schedule) (30 home, 31 away), 161 gs, 1961

HOME RUN HEROES: Josh Gibson (left) hit 800 homers in the Negro leagues, but died in 1947 just 3 months before the first black, Jackie Robinson, got into the major leagues. Mickey Mantle (right) can claim 3 "longest" major league home runs—one an officially measured 565 ft, another a trigonometrically measured 643 ft, and a third in an LA exhibition game that is claimed to have been 660-ft long. (NY Yankees)

HITTING IN EVERY GAME for 56 games is the record Joe DiMaggio (left) of the Yankees set in 1941, collecting 91 hits in those 2 months. HOME RUN KING Hank Aaron (right) did rewrite the record book. The great outfielder hit 755 homers in the major leagues and collected a lifetime record of 2,297 rbi's.

Most home runs, season (continued)
  60 George H. (Babe) Ruth, NY AL (154-game schedule) (28 home, 32 away), 151 gs, 1927

Most home runs, lifetime
  755 Henry L. Aaron, Mil NL, 1954 (13), 1955 (27), 1956 (26), 1957 (44), 1958 (30), 1959 (39), 1960 (40), 1961 (34), 1962 (45), 1963 (44), 1964 (24), 1965 (32); Atl NL, 1966 (44), 1967 (39), 1968 (29), 1969 (44), 1970 (38), 1971 (47), 1972 (34), 1973 (40), 1974 (20); Mil AL, 1975 (12), 1976 (10)

Most home runs, bases filled, lifetime
  23 Henry Louis (Lou) Gehrig, NY AL, 1923–1939

Most consecutive games hitting home runs
  8 R. Dale Long, Pitt NL, Don Mattingly, NY AL, 1987

Most home runs with bases filled, season
  6 Don Mattingly, NY AL, 1987

Most home runs, with bases filled, game
  2 Anthony M. Lazzeri, NY AL, May 24, 1936
     James R. Tabor, Bos AL (2nd game), July 4, 1939
     Rudolph York, Bos AL, July 27, 1946
     James E. Gentile, Balt AL, May 9, 1961 (consecutive at-bats)
     Tony L. Cloninger, Atl NL, July 3, 1966

James T. Northrup, Det AL, June 24, 1968 (consecutive at-bats)
     Frank Robinson, Balt AL, June 26, 1970 (consecutive at-bats)

Most home runs, one doubleheader
  5 Stanley F. Musial, St L NL, 1st game (3), 2nd game (2), May 2, 1954; Nathan Colbert, SD NL, 1st game (2), 2nd game (3), Aug 1, 1972

Most bases on balls, game
  6 James E. Foxx, Bos AL, June 16, 1938
     Andre Thornton, Clev AL, May 2, 1984 (16 inns)

Most bases on balls, season
  170 George H. (Babe) Ruth, NY AL, 152 games, 1923

Most hits, pinch-hitter, lifetime
  150 Manuel R. Mota, SF NL, 1962; Pitt NL, 1963–1968; Mont NL, 1969; LA NL, 1969–1980

Most consecutive home runs, pinch-hitter
  3 Delbert Unser, Phil NL, June 30, July 5, 10, 1979
     Leondaus (Lee) Lacy, LA NL, May 2, 6, 17, 1978 (one walk in between)

Most consecutive pinch hits
  9 David E. Philley, Phil NL, Sept 9, 11, 12, 13, 19, 20, 27, 28, 1958; Apr 16, 1959

Base Running

Most stolen bases, lifetime
  938 Louis C. Brock, Chi NL, 1961–64; St L NL, 1964–79

Most stolen bases, season since 1900
  130 Rickey Henderson, Oak AL, 149 games, 1982

BASE STEALER SUPREME: Rickey Henderson, while with the Oakland A's in 1982, stole 130 bases in 149 games. (Steve Babineau photo)

0102320

Major League All-Time Records (continued)

Most stolen bases, game
  7 George F. (Piano Legs) Gore, Chi NL, June 25, 1881
    William R. (Sliding Billy) Hamilton, Phil NL, 2nd game, 8 inn, Aug 31, 1894
    Modern Record
  6 Edward T Collins, Phil AL, Sept 11 and again Sept 22, 1912

Most times stealing home, lifetime
  46 Tyrus R. Cobb, Det AL, 1905–26; Phil AL 1927–28

Fewest times caught stealing, season (50+ attempts)
  2 Max Carey, Pitt NL, 1922 (53 atts)

Pitching

Most years
  25 James Kaat, Wash AL 1959–60; Minn AL 1961–73; Chi AL 1973–75; Phil NL 1976–79; NY AL 1979–80; St L NL 1980–83
    Tommy John, Cleve AL 1963–64; Chi AL 1965–71; LA NL 1972–78; NY AL 1979–82; Cal AL 1982–85; NY AL 86–88.

Most games, lifetime
  1,070 J. Hoyt Wilhelm, NY-St L-Atl-Chi-LA (448) NL, 1952–57, 69–72; Clev-Balt-Chi-Cal (622) AL, 1957–69

Most complete games, lifetime
  751 Denton T. (Cy) Young, Clev-St L-Bos NL (428); Bos-Clev AL (323), 1890–1911

Perfect game—9 innings
  1880 John Lee Richmond, Worcester vs Clev NL, June 12   1–0
    John M. Ward, Prov vs Buff NL, June 17 AM   5–0
  1904 Denton T. (Cy) Young, Bos vs Phil AL, May 5   3–0
  1908 Adrian C. Joss, Clev vs Chi AL, Oct 2   1–0
  †1917 Ernest G. Shore, Bos vs Wash AL, June 23 (1st g)   4–0
  1922 C. C. Robertson, Chi vs Det AL, Apr 30   2–0
  *1956 Donald J. Larsen, NY AL vs Bklyn NL, Oct 8   2–0
  1964 James P. Bunning, Phil NL vs NY, June 21 (1st g)   6–0
  1965 Sanford (Sandy) Koufax, LA NL vs Chi, Sept 9   1–0
  1968 James A. (Catfish) Hunter, Oak AL vs Minn, May 8   4–0
  1981 Leonard H. Barker II, Cleve AL vs Tor, May 15   3–0
  1984 Michael Witt. Cal AL vs Texas, Sept 9   1–0
  1988 Tom Browning, Cin NL vs LA, Sept 16   1–0

Special mention
  1959 Harvey Haddix, Jr, Pitt vs Mil NL, May 26, pitched 12 perfect innings, allowed hit in 13th and lost.

Most games, season
  106 Michael G. Marshall, LA NL, 1974

Most games won, season
  60 Charles Radbourn, Providence NL, 1884

Most complete games, season
  74 William H. White, Cin NL, 1879
    Modern Record
  48 John D. Chesbro, NY AL, 1904

Lowest earned run average, season
  0.90 Ferdinand M. Schupp, NY NL, 1916 (140 inn)
  1.00 Hubert B. (Dutch) Leonard, Bos AL, 1914 (222 inn)
  1.12 Robert Gibson, St L NL, 1968 (305 inn)

Most innings pitched, game
  26 Leon J. Cadore, Bklyn NL, May 1, 1920
    Joseph Oeschger, Bos NL, May 1, 1920

Most games won, lifetime
  511 Denton T. (Cy) Young, Clev NL (239) 1890–98; St L NL (46) 1899–1900; Bos AL (193) 1901–08; Clev AL (29) 1909–11; Bos NL (4) 1911

Most consecutive games won, lifetime
  24 Carl O. Hubbell, NY NL, 1936 (16); 1937 (8)

Most strikeouts, season
  383 L. Nolan Ryan, Cal AL, 1973 (Distance 60 ft 6 in)

Most strikeouts, career
  4,805 L. Nolan Ryan, NY NL, Cal AL, Houston NL, 1968–88

Most strikeouts, game (9 inn) since 1900
  20 Roger Clemens, Bos AL vs Seat, Apr 29, 1986

Most strikeouts, extra-inning game
  21 Thomas E. Cheney, Wash AL vs Balt (16 inn), Sept 12, 1962 (night)

Most no-hit games, lifetime
  5 L. Nolan Ryan, Cal AL, 1973 (2)–74–75; Hou NL, 1981

Most consecutive no-hit games
  2 John S. Vander Meer, Cin NL, June 11–15, 1938

Most consecutive games won, season
  19 Timothy J. Keefe, NY NL, 1888
    Richard W. (Rube) Marquard, NY NL, 1912

Most shutout games, season
  16 George W. Bradley, St L NL, 1876
    Grover C. Alexander, Phil NL, 1916

4,805 STRIKEOUTS is the record total achieved by Nolan Ryan in his career, begun in 1968 with the Mets, then the Angels, and in 1988 the Astros.

Most shutout games, lifetime
  113 Walter P. Johnson, Wash AL, 21 years, 1907–27

Most consecutive shutout games, season
  6 Donald S. Drysdale, LA NL, May 14, 18, 22, 26, 31, June 4, 1968

Most consecutive shutout innings
  59 Orel Hershiser, LA NL, Aug 30–Sept 28, 1988

Most saves, season
  46 Dave Righetti, NY AL, 1986

Most saves, lifetime
  341 Roland (Rollie) Fingers, Oak AL, 1968–76; SD NL 1977–80; Mil AL 1981–85

Fielding

Best percentage, season, by position

First Base: 1.000
Steven Garvey, SD NL, 1984

Second Base: .9966
Robert Grich, Cal AL, 1985

Third Base: .9894
Donald Money, Mil AL, 1974

Shortstop: .9912
Lawrence Bowa, Phil NL, 1979

---

†Starting pitcher, "Babe" Ruth, was banished from game by Umpire Brick Owens after an argument. He gave the first batter, Ray Morgan, a base on balls. Shore relieved and while he pitched to second batter, Morgan was caught stealing. Shore then retired next 26 batters to complete the "perfect" game.
*World Series game.

Fielding (continued)

Outfield: 1.000
Curtis Flood, St L NL, 1966 (based on most chances handled without an error—396)

Catcher: 1.000
Warren (Buddy) Rosar, Phil AL, 1946

Pitcher: 1.000
Randall Jones, SD NL, 1976 (based on most chances handled without an error—112)

Consecutive games, no errors, by position

First Base: 193
Steven Garvey, SD NL, 1983–85

Second Base: 91
Joe Morgan, Cin NL, 1977–78

Third Base: 97
James Davenport, SF NL, 1966–68

Shortstop: 72
Edwin Brinkman, Det AL, 1972

Outfield: 266
Donald Demeter, Phil NL–Det AL, 1962–65

Catcher: 148
Lawrence P. (Yogi) Berra, NY AL, 1957–59

Pitcher: 385
Paul Lindblad, KC-Oak AL, 1966–74

World Series Records

Most series played
14 Lawrence P. (Yogi) Berra, NY, AL, 1947, 49–53, 55–58, 60–63

Highest batting percentage (75 at bats, min), total series
391 Louis C. Brock, St L NL, 1964, 67–68 (g-21, ab-87, h-34)

Highest batting percentage, 4 or more games, one series
.625 4-game series, George H. (Babe) Ruth, NY AL, 1928

Most runs, total series
42 Mickey C. Mantle, NY AL, 1951–53, 55–58, 60–64

Most runs, one series
10 Reginald M. Jackson, NY AL, 1977

Most runs batted in, total series
40 Mickey C. Mantle, NY, AL, 1951–53, 55–58, 60–64

Most strikeouts, one series
23 in 4 game series
Sanford (Sandy) Koufax, LA NL, 1963
18 in 5 game series
Christy Mathewson, NY NL, 1905
20 in 6 game series
C. A. (Chief) Bender, Phil AL, 1911
35 in 7 game series
Robert Gibson, St L NL, 1968
28 in 8 game series
W. H. Dinneen, Bos AL, 1903

Most strikeouts, one pitcher game
17 Robert Gibson, St L NL, 1968

Most base hits, total series
71 Lawrence P. (Yogi) Berra, NY AL, 1947, 49–53, 55–58, 60–63

Most home runs, total series
18 Mickey C. Mantle, NY AL, 1952 (2), 53 (2), 55, 56 (3), 57, 58 (2), 60 (3), 63, 64 (3)

Most home runs, game
3 George H. (Babe) Ruth, NY AL, Oct 6, 1926; Oct 9, 1928
Reginald (Reggie) M. Jackson, NY AL, Oct 18, 1977

Most home runs, one series
5 Reginald (Reggie) M. Jackson, NY AL, 1977

Most runs batted in, game
6 Robert C. Richardson, NY AL, (4) 1st inn, (2) 4th inn, 1960

Most hits, 7-game Series
13 Martin Barrett, Bos AL, 1986
Louis Brock, St L NL, 1968
Robt Richardson, NY AL, 1960

Most Series Won
22 New York AL, 1923, 1927, 1928, 1932, 1936–39, 1941, 1943, 1947, 1949–53, 1956, 1958, 1961, 1962, 1977, 1978

Pitching in most series
11 Edward C. (Whitey) Ford, NY AL, 1950, 53, 55–58, 60–64

Most victories, total series
10 Edward C. (Whitey) Ford, NY AL, 1950 (1), 55 (2), 56 (1), 57 (1), 60 (2), 61 (2), 62 (1)

Most games won, one series
3 games in 5-game series
Christy Mathewson, NY NL, 1905
J. W. Coombs, Phil AL, 1910
Ten others won 3 games in series of more games.

Most victories, no defeats
6 Vernon L. (Lefty) Gomez, NY AL, 1932 (1), 36 (2), 37 (2), 38 (1)

Most shutout games, total series
4 Christy Mathewson, NY NL, 1905 (3), 1913

Most shutout games, one series
3 Christy Mathewson, NY NL, 1905

Most strikeouts, one pitcher, total series
94 Edward C. (Whitey) Ford, NY AL, 1950, 53, 55–58, 60–64

WORLD SERIES HERO: Reggie Jackson (left) got the name "Mr October" by hitting 5 home runs for the NY Yankees in the 1977 Series and attaining a record slugging average of .755.

Home Runs (continued)

A North American record of almost 800 in a lifetime has been claimed for Josh Gibson (1911–47), mostly for the Homestead Grays of the Negro National League, who was elected in 1972 to the Baseball Hall of Fame in Cooperstown, NY. Gibson is said to have hit 75 round-trippers in one season, in 1931, but no official records were kept.

The most officially recorded home runs hit by a professional player in the US in one season is 72, by Joe Bauman, of the Roswell, NM team, a minor league club, in 1954. The major league record is 61 in 161 games of a 162-game season by Roger Maris (1934–1985) of the NY Yankees, in 1961. George Herman ''Babe'' Ruth (1895–1948) hit 60 in a 154-game season in 1927.

The longest home run ''officially'' measured was 618 ft by Roy Edward ''Dizzy'' Carlyle (1900–56) in a minor league game at Emeryville Ball Park, Calif, July 4, 1929. Babe Ruth hit a 587-ft homer for the Boston Red Sox vs NY Giants in an exhibition game at Tampa, Fla, in 1919. The longest measured home run in a regular-season major league game is 565 ft by Mickey Mantle (b Oct 20, 1931) for the NY Yankees vs Washington Senators on Apr 17, 1953, at Griffith Stadium, Wash DC.

First 40 and 40

In 1988, Jose Canseco of the Oakland Athletics became the first ballplayer in major league history to hit 40 or more home runs and have 40 stolen bases in the same season. He had 42 homers and 40 steals.

8 BASEBALLS IN HAND: Robert Link of St Petersburg, Fla, shows how he held 8 baseballs in one hand without any adhesives in June 1987.

STRIKEOUT KING: Roger Clemens of the Boston Red Sox fanned 20 Seattle Mariners on Apr 29, 1986, to beat the record of 19 in a 9-inning game, jointly held by Nolan Ryan, Steve Carlton and Tom Seaver. (Boston Red Sox)

Finishing with a Flourish

In addition to setting a record of 59 consecutive innings without giving up a run, Orel Hershiser of the Los Angeles Dodgers in 1988 completed his season by giving up only 3 earned runs in his last 101⅓ innings, including playoffs and World Series.

Shortest and Tallest Players

The shortest major league player was surely Eddie Gaedel, a 3-ft-7-in, 65-lb midget, who pinch hit for the St Louis Browns vs the Detroit Tigers on Aug 19, 1951. Wearing number ⅛, the batter with the smallest

Mantle's homer in Detroit on Sept 10, 1960, which ascended over the right field roof and is said to have landed in a lumberyard, was measured trigonometrically in 1985 to have traveled 643 ft. He also hit a 660-foot homer in an exhibition game in Los Angeles in 1961.

One Day Wonder

John Paciorek of the Houston Colt '45s had a perfect day at bat in his only game in the majors in 1963 with 3 singles, 2 walks, 4 runs scored, and 3 rbi's, for a 1.000 average.

Fastest Base Runner

Ernest Evar Swanson (1902–73) took only 13.3 sec to circle the bases at Columbus, Ohio, in 1932, averaging 18.45 mph.

Most Stolen Bases

While Lou Brock holds the career record for most bases stolen with 938, this was topped in the Japanese league by Yubaka Kikomoto with 1,059.

Most Strikeouts

Bobby Bonds in 1970, right fielder for the San Francisco Giants, fanned 189 times in 157 games.

Fewest Strikeouts

Joe Sewell in 1929, while playing third base for the Cleveland Indians, played in 115 consecutive games, going to bat 437 times without once striking out. In his career stretching 14 years he only struck out 114 times.

ever major league strike zone walked on four pitches. Following the game, major league rules were hastily rewritten to prevent the recurrence of such an affair.

The tallest major leaguer of all time is Randy Johnson (b Sept 10, 1963) of Walnut Creek, Calif, the Montreal Expos' 6-ft-10-in pitcher, who played in his first game Sept 15, 1988.

Youngest and Oldest Players

The youngest major league player of all time was the Cincinnati pitcher Joe Nuxhall, who started his career in June 1944, aged 15 years 10 months 11 days.

Leroy "Satchel" Paige (1906?–82) pitched three scoreless innings for the Kansas City Athletics at approximately age 59 in 1965. Baseball's color barrier had kept him out of the major leagues until 1948, when he was a 42-year-old "rookie," and his record of 6 wins and 1 loss helped the Cleveland Indians win the pennant. His birthday is listed as July 7, 1906, but many believe he was born earlier. The Atlanta Braves carried Paige on their roster in 1968 to allow him to qualify for a pension.

Most Strikeouts in an Inning

Nineteen different pitchers hold the record of 4 in an inning. How? The catcher misses on a third strike and the batter gets on base, so the hurler has to fan another batter. The latest pitcher to have 4 K's (strikeouts) in one inning was Bobby Witt of the Texas Rangers, Aug 2, 1987.

Most Foul-Offs

Luke Appling, shortstop for the White Sox in the 1930's, fouled off 14 consecutive pitches from Dizzy Trout of the Tigers. On the 15th pitch, Trout threw his glove instead of the ball.

Hit by Pitch

Don Baylor, outfielder-first baseman and designated hitter, who played with 7 American League teams from 1970 through 1988 (most recently with the Oakland Athletics), holds the major league record for getting hit by pitch the most times: 267, including 12 times in 1988, when he performed as a designated hitter. The previous record of 243 was held by Ron Hunt, National League infielder from 1963 to 1974, who still holds the record of 50 in one season (1970). Hunt was hit hard so many times his career was shortened.

Baylor, a powerful righthanded batter, stands close to the plate and gets hit most frequently on the left

PITCHED 59 CONSECUTIVE SCORELESS INNINGS: Orel Hershiser ended the 1988 season with this record and led the Dodgers in the Playoffs and World Series to a World Championship. In his last 101⅓ innings he yielded just 3 earned runs. (LA Dodgers)

shoulder and arm. No matter how hard he gets hit, he never rubs the injured area.

Catcher's Interference

Steve Lombardozzi, Minnesota second baseman, set a probable major league record in 1986 in getting on base the most times in a single season because of catcher's interference, 11. (Records were not kept until fairly recently.)

When Connie Mack was a catcher in the National League with Washington and Pittsburgh from 1886 to 1896, he became so adept at tipping a bat that he would rarely be called for catcher's interference.

Consecutive Innings

Calvin Ripken, Jr, (b Aug 24, 1960) of the Baltimore Orioles set what is believed to be a record

MOST VALUABLE PLAYER: Kirk Gibson of the World Champion Dodgers earned this title in 1988 in spite of batting only .290. All year long he inspired his team, and despite injuries came through in the clutch with timely hits. (LA Dodgers)

MOST CONSECUTIVE INNINGS PLAYED: Cal Ripken, Jr., the Baltimore Oriole shortstop, played all of every inning for 910 games in a unique record of 8,243 innings, 1982–87. (Jerry Wachter)

for playing every inning of consecutive games, when he played 8,243 innings over 910 games, 1982–87. Ripken played the first six games at third base, beginning June 5, 1982, then moved to shortstop for the duration of the streak, which came to an end Sept 14, 1987, when the manager pulled him from a game because he felt the streak was distracting the slumping Orioles. The manager was his father, Cal Ripken, Sr. Young Ripken still had a streak of 927 consecutive games at the close of the 1987 season. The known previous best for consecutive innings had been no longer than 534 games by Buck Freeman, Boston Red Sox, 1901–05.

Fastest Pitcher

The fastest recorded pitcher is (Lynn) Nolan Ryan (b Jan 31, 1947) who, on Aug 20, 1974 (then of the California Angels, now of the Houston Astros) at Anaheim Stadium, Calif, was measured to pitch at 100.9 mph.

Unanimous Choice for Rookies of the Year

For only the second time in 40 years the Baseball Writers Association of America was unanimous in choosing Mark McGwire, the Oakland Athletics first baseman, as the 1987 American League Rookie of

the Year. McGwire set records with 49 homers breaking all rookie records in the majors, and also hit 5 homers and scored 9 runs in 2 games.

For the National League Rookie of the Year, the writers were again unanimous in selecting Benito Santiago, catcher for the San Diego Padres.

Do-Everything Record

Two major league ballplayers, Bert Campaneris (b Mar 12, 1942) and Cesar Tovar (b July 3, 1940), have the distinction of playing each of the nine field positions in a single major league game. Campaneris did it first, on Sept 8, 1965, when his team, the Kansas City Athletics, announced he would. He played one inning at each position, including the full eighth inning as a pitcher and gave up just one run. Tovar duplicated the feat on Sept 22, 1968, when he played for the Minnesota Twins. He pitched a scoreless first inning and retired the first batter, none other than Campaneris. On June 4, 1983, Mike Ashman, a minor league player for the Albany-Colonie A's of the Eastern League, improved upon the Campaneris-Tovar feat by playing 10 positions, including designated hitter, in a game against Nashua.

Do-Nothing Record

Toby Harrah of the Texas Rangers (AL) played an entire doubleheader at shortstop on June 26, 1976, without having a chance to make any fielding plays, assists or putouts.

MOST HITS, MOST AT-BATS, MOST GAMES: Pete Rose, spark plug of the Cincinnati Reds (with the Phillies for 5 years), now manager of the Reds, ended the 1986 season with 4,256 hits (65 more than Cobb) in 3,562 games and 14,053 times at the plate.

In 1893, there was an important rules change that must be considered when looking at batting records. In the early days of the game, pitching was viewed merely as a matter of trying to get the ball over the plate. Any outfielder might be called upon to pitch. But as managers discovered that there was a decisive advantage to having a pitcher who knew how to throw a spitball or a knuckleball, batting averages declined drastically. Thus in 1893 the distance between home plate and the pitcher's rubber was changed from 50 ft to the current 60 ft 6 in. Batting averages soared.

OLDEST IN BASEBALL: Satchel Paige (right) was about 59 (exact age in doubt) when he pitched for the Kansas City Athletics in 1959. He couldn't break into the majors before he was 42 because of the "color barrier." (UPI)

LEGENDARY PITCHER: Denton T. (Cy for "cyclone") Young (below) pitched 751 complete games in his 22-year career including 511 victories (one a perfect game), and averaged 24 wins per season. Now each year the outstanding pitcher in each league is given a Cy Young award.

HERO IN HIS ERA: Christy Mathewson, idol of the Giants, pitched 3 shutouts including 18 strikeouts in the 5-game 1905 World Series. His best pitch was a "fadeaway," a screwball-like pitch that broke away from left-handed batters.

→

KNUCKLEBALL PITCHER Hoyt Wilhelm (right) pitched in 1,070 games, 1952-72, and finished 651 games.

"BEST" SHORTSTOP Honus Wagner of the Pittsburgh Pirates in the early 1900's, noted for his base stealing, is renowned as much today for the baseball card issued in 1910 and called back by the cigarette company because Wagner, a nonsmoker, objected. Wagner never received any money for it, but the card sold for $100,000 in 1988.

(Card supplied by Tom Miceli and B & E Collectibles, Thornwood, NY. Photo by V. J. Holland)

9 Games Won by 9 Different Pitchers

The pennant-winning St. Louis Cardinals of 1985 established an unusual streak record, according to Paul Ferrell. In one stretch of 10 games, the Red Birds won 9, with those victories being recorded by 9 different pitchers.

Date	Winning Pitcher	Opposing Team
Sept 14	Bill Campbell	Chicago
Sept 15	Danny Cox	Chicago
Sept 16	John Tudor	Pittsburgh
Sept 16	Bill Perry	Pittsburgh
Sept 17	Joaquin Andujar	Pittsburgh
Sept 18	Bob Forsch	Philadelphia
Sept 19	Matt Keough (Lost)	Philadelphia
Sept 20	Todd Worrell	Montreal
Sept 21	Jeff Lahti	Montreal
Sept 22	Ken Dayley	Montreal

On Sept 23, Lahti defeated Pittsburgh, and on the 24th Rick Horton became the 10th Cards pitcher in 11 days to win a game when he throttled the Pirates. For September the Cardinals posted a 21–9 record and went 101–61 for the season.

Most Strikeouts, Career

Nolan Ryan of the Houston Astros pitched his 4,000th strikeout on July 11, 1985 against the NY Mets, his former team. By the 1988 season's end his total had risen to 4,805. Ryan was the first to eclipse Walter Johnson's (Wash AL) record of 3,508 which he set between 1907 and 1927 and which stood for 55 years until April 27, 1983.

Dwight Gooden (b Nov 16, 1964) of the Mets in the 1984 All-Star Game in San Francisco struck out 6 consecutive AL batters.

Gooden, in 1985, became the youngest pitcher to win the coveted Cy Young Award. He won it by unanimous vote of the 24 sportswriters who make the selection.

Longest Career in 3 Major Leagues

James "Deacon" McGuire (1865–1936), a catcher-infielder, played in 26 seasons for 12 different teams in three major leagues (American Association, National and American) 1884–1912. He also managed Washington in the National League (1898) and Boston (1907–08) and Cleveland (1909–11) in the American League.

Longest Throw

The longest throw of a 5–54-oz (regulation) baseball is 445 ft 10 in by Glen Gorbous (b Canada) Aug 1, 1957. Mildred "Babe" Didrickson (later Mrs George Zaharias) (1914–56) threw a ball 296 ft at Jersey City, NJ, July 25, 1931.

Longest Shutouts

Four pitchers have hurled 18-inning shutout games in the majors: Carl Hubbell, NY Giants, 1933; Walter Johnson, Wash Senators, 1918; Ed Summers, Det Tigers, 1908; John Montgomery Ward, Providence NL, 1882.

Managers

Connie Mack (1862–1956) managed in the major leagues for 53 seasons—3 with Pittsburgh (NL), 1894–96, and 50 with the Philadelphia Athletics (AL), the team he owned, 1901–50. He amassed a record 3,776 regular-season victories (952 victories ahead of John McGraw). Eddie Stanky managed the Texas Rangers (AL) for one day (June 23, 1977) before deciding he did not want the job—even though his team beat Minnesota, 10–8. It is believed to be the shortest term for anyone who signed a managerial contract (that is, excluding interim managers).

Charles D. "Casey" Stengel (1890–1975) set records by managing the NY Yankees (AL) in 10 World Series and winning 7 of them, including 5 in a row (1949–53).

Longest and Shortest Major League Games

The Brooklyn Dodgers and Boston Braves played to a 1–1 tie after 26 innings on May 1, 1920.

The NY Giants needed only 51 min to beat the

MOST CONSECUTIVE GAMES: Lou Gehrig played in 2,130 consecutive games, 1925–39, helping the NY Yankees to 6 of their record 22 championships. His 23 grand-slam homers is a career record.

YOUNGEST WINNER of Cy Young award was Dwight Gooden of the NY Mets who was only 20 in 1985 when he was unanimously selected. (AP/Wide World)

STRIKEOUT KING: Sandy Koufax (left) pitched a record 23 strikeouts in 4 World Series games in 1963 for the LA Dodgers.

MOST HITS: Ty Cobb (below) held the record of 4,191 career hits established in 1928 until Pete Rose broke it in 1985. (UPI-Bettmann Archives)

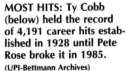

CARDINAL LEADER: Stan Musial got St Louis into 4 World Series within 5 years with feats like hitting 5 homers in one day. He was selected National League MVP 3 times.

SLUGGERS: Although his home run records have been surpassed, Babe Ruth (left) is unlikely to be forgotten. His .625 batting average in the 1928 World Series is the best ever, as is his career slugging percentage of .690. Roger Maris (right) watches his 60th home run fly into the seats at Yankee Stadium. Maris then hit his record-breaking 61st in the last game of the 1961 season.

Philadelphia Phillies, 6–1, in 9 innings on Sept 28, 1919. (A minor league game, Atlanta vs Mobile in the Southern Association on Sept 19, 1910, took only 32 min, it is claimed.)

The Chicago White Sox played the longest ballgame in elapsed time—8 hours 6 min—before beating the Milwaukee Brewers, 7–6, in the 25th inning on May 9, 1984 in Chicago. The game took 2 days, actually. It started on Tuesday night and was still tied at 3–3 when the 1 A.M. curfew caused suspension until Wednesday night.

Attendances

The World Series record attendance is 420,784 (6 games with total gate receipts of $2,626,973.44) when the Los Angeles Dodgers beat the Chicago White Sox 4 games to 2, Oct 1–8, 1959.

The single game record is 92,706 for the fifth game (gate receipts $552,774.77) at the Memorial Coliseum (no longer used for baseball), LA, Oct 6, 1959.

The all-time season record for attendance for both leagues has been 52,263,000 in 1988, with AL 28,090,964 and NL 24,172,036.

An estimated 114,000 spectators watched a game between Australia and an American servicemen's team in a "demonstration" during the Dec 1, 1956 Olympics in Melbourne, Australia.

An estimated 115,000 fans watched the Tellings Strollers play the Hanna Cleaners for the "Class A" amateur baseball championship at Cleveland's Brookside Stadium in Sept 1914. Brookside Stadium, shaped like a huge amphitheatre, had only a few thousand seats behind home plate, and so most of the fans sat along the bluffs directly above the playing field.

Ball Drop from a Dirigible

Joe Sprinz, later catcher for the Cleveland Indians, in 1939 was playing for the Seals of the Pacific Coast League, when Lefty O'Doul was his manager. The San Francisco World's Fair was drawing crowds to Treasure Island in the Bay when someone dreamed up the stunt of dropping baseballs from a dirigible from 1,200 ft up for the Seals' players to try to catch. Sprinz was the only one who had dared to try.

"I had to shade my eyes, I saw the ball all the way, but it looked the size of an aspirin tablet," he said later. "The ball hit me in the mouth, my lips were lacerated very badly, 12 cracks in my upper jaw, lost 5 teeth, was knocked out." And he dropped the ball.

Rained-Out Game in Covered Stadium

The only time in baseball history a game in a covered stadium was called because of rain was on

June 16, 1976, in Houston. Flooding around the Astrodome prevented anyone getting into the stadium and the game between Houston and Pittsburgh was called.

Running Bases in Reverse

Herman (Germany) Schaefer of the Washington Senators in 1910 stole first base. This was after he had stolen second with a runner on third. Dissatisfied because the catcher had not thrown to second to allow a double steal to begin, he stole first on the next pitch to try again. A new baseball rule (7.08 i) was instituted at once to prevent this happening again.

Baseball Memorabilia

The National Baseball Hall of Fame and Museum in Cooperstown, NY, to celebrate its 50th anniversary in 1989, dedicated a new exhibition building including a large multimedia theatre. This is in addition to its room devoted to Babe Ruth which includes a life-sized wood carving of him and his voice on records. Also it contains a wood sculpture of Ted Williams, and even razor blades used by Cy Young. In the ballparks room, there are turnstiles, lockers, dugout benches and grandstand seats from Ebbets Field, Polo Grounds and other defunct stadiums. In the library are 15,000 books and 150,000 photographs, as well as millions of press clippings, and audio and visual aids.

The greatest private collection is undoubtedly that of Barry Halper of Elizabeth, NJ, whose memorabilia is insured for over $10 million. It includes over 1 million different baseball cards, 900 uniform jerseys, nearly 5,000 autographed baseballs, over 1,000 bats, and at least 1,000 different examples of baseball sheet music. Among his newest acquisitions are 2 vintage Boston Red Stockings (NL) jerseys that belonged to Hall of Famers a century ago, as well as the fire hat that belonged to Alexander Joy Cartwright, the father of modern baseball, who served as fire chief in Honolulu in the 1850's.

The most valuable baseball cigarette card is still the Honus Wagner issued in 1910 which sold for $100,000 in 1988.

All Runs Unearned

The Mets scored 16 runs against the Houston Astros on July 27, 1985, winning 16–4, with all the Met runs unearned. Houston made 5 errors in the game.

Longest Game in Baseball History

The longest game was a minor league game in 1981 that lasted 33 innings. At the end of 9, the score was tied, 1–1, with the Rochester (NY) Red Wings battling the home team Pawtucket (RI) Red Sox. At the end of 21 it was tied, 2–2, and at the end of 32, the score was still 2–2, when the game was suspended. Two months later, play was resumed and 18 minutes later, Pawtucket scored one run and won. The winning pitcher was the Red Sox' Bob Ojida, whose teammates included Marty Barrett at 2B, Wade Boggs at 3B, and Rich Gedman catching. The Rochester cleanup batter was Cal Ripken, Jr. The 33rd inning was witnessed by 54 newspaper reporters, got a top-of-page headline in *The New York Times*, and was carried by the national TV networks!

BASKETBALL

Origins

Ollamalitzli was a 16th century Aztec precursor of basketball played in Mexico. If the solid rubber ball was put through a fixed stone ring placed high on one side of the stadium, the player was entitled to the clothing of all the spectators. The captain of the losing team often lost his head (by execution). Another game played much earlier, in the 10th century BC by the Olmecs in Mexico, called *Pok-ta-Pok*, also resembled basketball in its concept of a ring through which a round object was passed.

Modern basketball was devised by the Canadian-born Dr James Naismith (1861–1939) at the Training School of the International YMCA College at Springfield, Mass, in Dec 1891. The first game played under modified rules was on Jan 20, 1892. The first public contest was on March 11, 1892.

The International Amateur Basketball Federation (FIBA) was founded in 1932.

The Court

The professional 3-point shot is measured from the center of the hoop to the top of the key, namely 23 ft 9 in. This is 4 ft longer than the college 3-point distance. In the corners, the pro distance is 22 ft, or 2 ft 2 in longer than the college distance.

MAJOR-COLLEGE INDIVIDUAL RECORDS
(Through 1988 Season)

Points

Most in a Game	100	Frank Selvy (Furman)	1954
Most in a Season	1,381	Pete Maravich (Louisiana St)	1970
Best Average, Season	44.5	Pete Maravich (Louisiana St)	1970
Most in a Career	3,667	Pete Maravich (Louisiana St)	1968–70
Best Average, Career	44.2	Pete Maravich (Louisiana St)	1968–70

Field Goals

Most in a Game	41	Frank Selvy (Furman)	1954
Best Percentage, Season	74.6	Steve Johnson (Oregon St)	1981
Best Percentage, Career	67.8	Steve Johnson (Oregon St)	1976–81

Free Throws

Most in a Game	30	Pete Maravich (Louisiana St)	1969
Best Percentage, Season	95.9	Craig Collins (Penn St)	1985
Best Percentage, Career	90.9	Greg Starrick (Ky, So Ill)	1969–72
Consecutive	64	Joe Dykstra (W Ill)	1982

Rebounds

Most in a Game	51	Bill Chambers (Wm & Mary)	1953

3-Point Goals

Most in a Game	12	Gary Bossert (Niagara)	1987
		Darrin Fitzgerald (Butler)	1987

Assists

Most in a Game	22	Tony Fairly (Baptist)	1987

Blocked Shots

Most in a Game	14	David Robinson (Navy)	1986

Division I Tournament

Most Points in a Game	61	Austin Carr (Notre Dame)	1970
Most Points in a Tournament	177	Bill Bradley (Princeton)	1965
Most Points in a Career	358	Elvin Hayes (Houston)	1966–68
Most Rebounds in a Game	31	Nate Thurmond (Bowling Green)	1963
Most Field Goals in a Game	25	Austin Carr (Notre Dame)	1970
Most Free Throws in a Game	23	Bob Carney (Bradley)	1953
Most Blocked Shots in a Game	9	David Robinson (Navy)	1986
Most Assists in a Game	18	Mark Wade (Nev-Las Vegas)	1987
Most 3-Pt Goals in a Game	10	Freddie Banks (Nev-Las Vegas)	1987

From the backboard to the top of the key, the pro distance is 25 ft and the college distance 21 ft. The free-throw line has always been measured from the backboard and is 15 ft, both college and pro.

Rule Change

In the 1940's coaches devised a new tactic, "freezing the ball," in order to maintain a leading score. It consisted of dribbling the ball and avoiding shooting it at the basket in order to maintain possession. In a short time this strategy became part of the entire game resulting in slow play and low scores. The lowest ever was when the Fort Wayne Pistons beat the Minneapolis Lakers 19–18, Nov 22, 1950. As attendance dropped as a result of boring play,

Danny Biasone, a team owner, conceived of the "24-second rule" which requires a team to make a try at a basket within 24 seconds of gaining possession of the ball or turn possession over to the opposing team. In 1954, the NBA adopted the rule and scores increased dramatically—as did attendance. In international amateur play the 30-second rule is enforced. In college play the rule is 45 seconds.

End of an Era

The Univ of Dallas won a basketball game, 76-68, over John Brown Univ, on Feb. 6, 1988, ending its losing streak of 86 games, longest by a US college team. The streak began Nov 11, 1985.

Individual Scoring

Marie Boyd (Eichler) scored 156 points in a girls' high school basketball game for Central HS, Lonaconing, Md, in a 163–3 victory over Ursuline Academy, on Feb 25, 1924. The boys' high school record is 135 points by Danny Heater of Burnsville, W Va, on Jan 26, 1960.

In college play, Clarence (Bevo) Francis of Rio Grande College, Ohio, scored 113 points against Hillsdale on Feb 2, 1954. One year earlier, Francis scored 116 points in a game, but the record was disallowed because the competition was with a two-year school. In women's college basketball, Annette Kennedy of State Univ at Purchase, NY, scored 70 points vs Pratt Institute on Jan 22, 1984, with 34 field goals in 43 attempts.

Wilton Norman (Wilt) Chamberlain (b Aug 21, 1936) holds the professional record with 100 points for the Philadelphia Warriors vs NY Knicks, scored in one game on Mar 2, 1962. During the same season, Wilt set the record for points in a season (4,029).

Kareem Abdul-Jabbar (formerly Lewis Ferdinand Alcindor) (b Apr 16, 1947) has scored a professional career record of 37,639 points from 1970 through the 1988 season for the Milwaukee Bucks and Los Angeles Lakers. His streak of 787 consecutive games in which he scored in double figures was broken on Dec 4, 1987, after 10 seasons. Wilt Chamberlain holds the record average of 30.1 points per game for his total of 31,419.

Pearl Moore of Francis Marion College, Florence, SC, scored a record 4,061 points during her college career, 1975–79. The men's college career scoring record is 4,045 points by Travis Grant for Kentucky State, 1969–72.

Mats Wermelin (Sweden), 13, scored all 272 points in a 272–0 win in a regional boys' tournament in Stockholm, Sweden, on Feb 5, 1974.

Longest Field Goal

The longest *measured* field goal in a college game was made from a distance of 89 ft 10 in by Bruce Morris for Marshall Univ vs Appalachian St, Feb 7, 1985. In an AAU game at Pacific Lutheran University on Jan 16, 1970, Steve Myers sank a shot while standing out of bounds at the other end of the court. Though the basket was illegal, the officials gave in to crowd sentiment and allowed the points to count. The distance is claimed to be 92 ft 3½ in from measurements made 10 years later. The longest for a woman is one of 77 ft by Cheryl Myers of Lakeland (Ind)

MAGIC! Earvin Johnson ("magic" tactician of the LA Lakers) added to his record for assists in a career in 1987–88. Here "Magic" drives to a basket over the Boston Celtics' Greg Kite (#50) in the NBA finals. The Lakers broke the Celtics' streak of championships. (Nathaniel Butler/NBA).

Christian Academy in a 48–29 victory over Elkhart Baptist on Jan 20, 1987.

Most Accurate Shooting

The greatest goal-shooting demonstration was made by a professional, Ted St. Martin, now of Jacksonville, Fla, who, on June 25, 1977, scored 2,036 consecutive free throws. He also set a record of 169 free throws out of 175 in 10 min with a single ball

BUCKET BRIGADE: Bevo Francis (left) scored 113 points in one game for tiny Rio Grande College in 1954. That season, he averaged 46.5 points per game. Starring for Francis Marion College, Pearl Moore (right) topped all collegiate players with 4,061 career points, 16 more than the men's college record held by Travis Grant of Kentucky State.

and a sole rebounder during halftime at a game in Jacksonville, Fla, May 16, 1988.

In 24 hours, Robert Browning scored 16,093 free throws from a total of 23,194 taken (69.38%) at St. Mark's School, Dallas, Tex on Nov 21–22, 1987. Fred L. Newman of San Jose, Calif, made 88 consecutive free throws while blindfolded at the Central YMCA, San Jose, Calif, Feb 5, 1978. On Dec 17, 1986 he made 338 free throws out of 356 attempts in 10 min, for an average accuracy of 94.9%.

The longest reported string of consecutive free throws made at any level of organized game competition is 126 by Daryl Moreau over 2 seasons (Jan 17, 1978–Jan 9, 1979) of high school play for De La Salle in New Orleans, La. The best reported one-game free throw performance was by Chris McMullin who made all 29 of his foul shots for Dixie College (St. George, Utah) in the NJCAA National Finals on Mar 16, 1982.

Team Scoring

The highest game total in the NBA is 370 points in the Detroit Pistons' victory over the Denver Nuggets 186–184 in 1983. The highest in college play is 282,

Univ of Nevada—Las Vegas vs Utah State, 1985. Nevada won, 142–140.

The highest score recorded in a senior international match is 251 by Iraq against Yemen (33) at New Delhi in November 1982 at the Asian Games.

Olympic Champions

The US won all 7 Olympic titles from the time the sport was introduced to the Games in 1936 until 1972, without losing a single contest. In 1972, in Munich, the US run of 63 consecutive victories was broken when its team lost, 51–50, to the USSR in a much-disputed final game. The US regained the Olympic title in Montreal in 1976, again without losing a game. In 1980 Yugoslavia took the Olympic gold, when the US did not play, but the US came back once more in 1984 for a record 9th title. The Soviet Union defeated the US for only the second time in Olympic play in 1988, and went on to win the gold.

In women's Olympics, the USSR won in 1976 and 1980, but the US took the gold in 1984 and 1988.

World Champions

The USSR has won most titles at both the Men's World Championships (inst. 1950) with three (1967, 1974 and 1982) and Women's (inst. 1953) with six (1959, 1964, 1967, 1971, 1975 and 1983).

The National Basketball Association's Championship series was established in 1947. Prior to 1949, when it joined with the National Basketball League, the professional circuit was known as the Basketball Association of America.

SERVICE

Most Games, Lifetime
1,486 Kareem Abdul-Jabbar, Mil 1970–75, LA Lakers 1976–88

Most Games, Consecutive, Lifetime
906 Randy Smith, Buf-SD-Cleve-NY 1972–1983

Most Complete Games, Season
79 Wilt Chamberlain, Phil 1962

Most Minutes, Lifetime
55,751 Kareem Abdul-Jabbar, Mil 1970–75, LA Lakers 1976–88

Most Minutes, Season
3,882 Wilt Chamberlain, Phil 1962

Most Games, No Disqualifications
1,045 Wilt Chamberlain, Phil-SF-LA 1960–73 (Entire Career)

SCORING

Most Seasons Leading League
7 Wilt Chamberlain, Phil 1960–62; SF 1963–64; SF-Phil 1965; Phil 1966

Most Points, Lifetime
37,639 Kareem Abdul-Jabbar, Mil 1970–75, LA Lakers 1976–88

Most Points, Season
4,029 Wilt Chamberlain, Phil 1962

Most Points, Game
100 Wilt Chamberlain, Phil vs NY, Mar 2, 1962

Most Points, Half
59 Wilt Chamberlain, Phil vs NY, Mar 2, 1962

Most Points, Quarter
33 George Gervin, SA vs NO, Apr 9, 1978

Most Points, Overtime Period
14 Butch Carter, Ind vs Bos, March 20, 1984

Highest Scoring Average, Lifetime (400+ games)
30.1 Wilt Chamberlain, Phil-SF-LA 1960–73

Highest Scoring Average, Season
50.4 Wilt Chamberlain, Phil 1962

Field Goals Made

Most Field Goals, Lifetime
15,524 Kareem Abdul-Jabbar, Mil 1970–75; LA Lakers 1976–88

Most Field Goals, Season
1,597 Wilt Chamberlain, Phil 1962

Most Field Goals, Game
36 Wilt Chamberlain, Phil vs NY, Mar 2, 1962

NBA Championships

The most National Basketball Association titles have been won by the Boston Celtics with 16 championships between 1957 and 1988. They also hold the record for 8 consecutive championships (1959–66).

Most Field Goals, Half
22 Wilt Chamberlain, Phil vs NY, Mar 2, 1962

Most Field Goals, Quarter
13 David Thompson, Den vs Det, Apr 9, 1978

Most 3-Point Field Goals, Game
8 Rick Barry, Hou vs Utah, Feb 9, 1980
John Roche, Den vs Sea, Jan 9, 1982

Most 3-Point Field Goals, Season
148 Danny Ainge, Bos 1988

Field Goal Percentage

Most Seasons Leading League
9 Wilt Chamberlain, Phil 1961; SF 1963; SF-Phil 1965; Phil 1966–68; LA 1969, 72–73

Highest Percentage, Lifetime
.599 Artis Gilmore, Chi 1977–82; SA 1983–87; Chi, Bos 1988

Highest Percentage, Season
.727 Wilt Chamberlain, LA 1973

Free Throws Made

Most Free Throws Made, Lifetime
7,694 Oscar Robertson, Cin-Mil 1961–74

Most Free Throws Made, Season
840 Jerry West, LA 1966

Most Free Throws Made, Consecutive, Season
78 Calvin Murphy, Hou Dec 27, 1980–Feb 28, 1981

Most Free Throws Made, Game
28 Wilt Chamberlain, Phil vs NY, Mar 2, 1962
Adrian Dantley, Utah vs Hou, Jan 5, 1984

Most Free Throws Made (No Misses), Game
19 Bob Pettit, St L vs Bos, Nov 22, 1961
Bill Cartwright, NY vs KC, Nov 17, 1981
Adrian Dantley, Det vs Chi, Dec 15, 1987

Most Free Throws Made, Half
19 Oscar Robertson, Cin vs Balt, Dec 27, 1964

Most Free Throws Made, Quarter
14 Rick Barry, SF vs NY, Dec 6, 1966
Pete Maravich, At vs Buff, Nov 28, 1973
Adrian Dantley, Det vs Sac, Dec 10, 1986

Team Free Throws

Wash Bullets made 60 free throws in 69 attempts vs NJ Nets on Nov 13, 1987, to break a 38-year-old NBA record for one game.

Free Throw Percentage

Most Seasons Leading League
7 Bill Sharman, Bos 1953–57, 59, 61

Highest Percentage, Lifetime
.900 Rick Barry, SF-GS-Hou 1966–67, 73–80

Highest Percentage, Season
.958 Calvin Murphy, Hou 1981

REBOUNDS

Most Seasons Leading League
11 Wilt Chamberlain, Phil 1960–62; SF 1963; Phil 1966–68; LA 1969, 71–73

Most Rebounds, Lifetime
23,924 Wilt Chamberlain, Phil-SF-LA 1960–73

Most Rebounds, Season
2,149 Wilt Chamberlain, Phil 1961

Most Rebounds, Game
55 Wilt Chamberlain, Phil vs Bos, Nov 24, 1960

Most Rebounds, Half
32 Bill Russell, Bos vs Phil, Nov 16, 1957

Most Rebounds, Quarter
18 Nate Thurmond, SF vs Balt, Feb 28, 1965

Highest Average (per game), Lifetime
22.9 Wilt Chamberlain, Phil-SF-LA 1960–73

Highest Average (per game), Season
27.2 Wilt Chamberlain, Phil 1961

ASSISTS

Most Seasons Leading League
8 Bob Cousy, Bos 1953–60

Most Assists, Lifetime
9,887 Oscar Robertson, Cin-Mil 1961–74

Most Assists, Season
1,128 John Stockton, Utah, 1988

Most Assists, Game
29 Kevin Porter, NJ vs Hou, Feb 24, 1978

ASSISTS (continued)

Highest Average (per game), Lifetime
11.0 Earvin (Magic) Johnson, LA Lakers 1979–88

Highest Average (per game), Season
13.9 Isiah Thomas, Detroit 1985

PERSONAL FOULS

Most Personal Fouls, Lifetime
4,461 Kareem Abdul-Jabbar, Mil 1970–75, LA Lakers 1976–88

Most Personal Fouls, Season
386 Darryl Dawkins, NJ 1984

Most Personal Fouls, Game
8 Don Otten, TC vs Sheb, Nov 24, 1949

STEALS

Most Steals, Lifetime
1,837 Maurice Cheeks, Phil 1979–88

Most Steals, Season
301 Alvin Robertson, SA, 1986

Highest Steals Average, Season, per game
3.67 Alvin Robertson, SA, 1986

Most Steals, Game
11 Larry Kenon, SA vs KC, Dec 26, 1976

NBA PLAYOFF RECORDS
(Through 1988)

Most games played, lifetime
222 Kareem Abdul-Jabbar, Mil-LA Lakers, 17 years

Most points scored, lifetime
5,595 Kareem Abdul-Jabbar, Mil-LA Lakers, 17 years

Most points, game
63 Michael Jordan, Chi vs Bos, Apr 20, 1986 (2 overtimes)
61 Elgin Baylor, LA Lakers vs Bos, Apr 14, 1962

Most field goals, game
24 Wilt Chamberlain, Phil vs Syr, March 14, 1960
John Havlicek, Bos vs Atl, Apr 1, 1973
Michael Jordan, Chi vs Cleve, May 1, 1988

Best scoring average, lifetime
29.1 Jerry West, LA Lakers, 13 years

Most free throws, lifetime
1,213 Jerry West, LA Lakers, 13 years

Most free throws, game
30 Bob Cousy, Bos vs Syr, March 21, 1953 (4 overtimes)
21 Oscar Robertson, Cin vs Bos, Apr 10, 1963

Most assists, game
24 Earvin (Magic) Johnson, LA Lakers vs Phoenix, May 15, 1984
John Stockton, Utah vs LA Lakers, May 17, 1988

Most rebounds, lifetime
4,104 Bill Russell, Bos, 13 years

Most rebounds, game
41 Wilt Chamberlain, Phil vs Bos, Apr 5, 1967

Most assists, lifetime
1,800 Earvin (Magic) Johnson, LA Lakers, 9 years

Greatest Attendances

The Harlem Globetrotters played an exhibition to 75,000 in the Olympic Stadium, West Berlin, Germany, in 1951. The largest indoor basketball attendance was 67,596, including 64,682 tickets sold at the box office, for the Indiana Olympic Basketball Tribute at the Hoosier Dome, Indianapolis on July 9, 1984. They saw victories by the US men's and women's Olympic teams over all-star opposition. The record for a women's college game is 24,563 in Knoxville, Tenn, for a game between Univ of Tenn and Univ of Tex on Dec 9, 1987. The NBA record is 61,983 on Jan 29, 1988 in Pontiac, Mich, with the Boston Celtics vs Detroit Pistons. The Pistons also set records for largest attendance in a season (1,066,505 in 41 games, 1988) and largest attendance in a playoff game (41,732 on June 16, 1988).

Marathon

The longest game is 102 hours by two teams of five from the Sigma Nu fraternity at Indiana Univ of Pennsylvania, Indiana, Penn, Apr 13–17, 1983.

Tallest and Shortest Players

The tallest player of all time is reputed to be Suleiman Ali Nashnush (b 1943) who played for the

BULL'S EYE: Artis Gilmore formerly of the Chicago Bulls leads the NBA with a .599 field goal percentage. The 7-ft-2-in center raised his percentage by 22 points in 6 years.

TOP SCORERS: Kareem Abdul-Jabbar, Mil-LA, (left) compiled 37,639 points with 15,524 field goals 1970–88, beating the 31,419 point record of Wilt Chamberlain (above, #13 in Phila uniform) who scored 100 points in one game and never fouled out of his 1,045 games played. Here he is seen jumping for a rebound.

Libyan team in 1962 when he measured 8 ft tall. Aleksandr Sizonenko of the USSR national team is 7 ft 10 in tall. The tallest woman player is Iuliana Semenova (USSR) who played in the 1976 Olympics and is reputed to stand 7 ft 2 in tall and weigh 281 lb.

In the 1987 NBA season, the shortest player in league history was Tyrone Bogues, drafted by the Wash Bullets, at 5 ft 3½ in in bare feet. His teammate, Manute Bol, at 7 ft 6 in is the tallest in the League's history.

Youngest and Oldest NBA Players

Bill Willoughby (b May 20, 1957) made his NBA debut for the Atlanta Hawks on Oct 23, 1975, when he was 18 years 5 months 3 days old. The oldest NBA player was Bob Cousy (b Aug 9, 1928), who was 41 years 6 months 2 days old when he appeared in the last of seven games he played for the team he was coaching (Cincinnati Royals) during 1969–70.

College Coach

Richard E. Baldwin, coach at Broome Community College, Binghamton, NY, celebrated his 40th year of coaching in 1987, without ever having missed a game out of a total of 1,169 games played by his team. His record is 879 wins, 290 losses to Feb 28, 1987, his last game. He retired in June 1987.

BIATHLON (See Skiing)

BOARDSAILING (Windsurfing)

Windsurfing is a misnomer. If a surfboard with a sail and mast mounted is used as a surfboard the event is called *sailsurfing* (see Surfing), and if a surfboard with a sail and mast mounted is used like a boat this is called *boardsailing* or *sailboarding*.

The idea of adding a sail enabled surfriders to continue practicing their sport even when there were no waves.

The British High Court ruled on Apr 7, 1982 that Peter Chilvers (when aged 12) had devised a prototype of a boardsailer in 1958 in England. In 1968 Henry Hoyle Schweitzer and Jim Drake pioneered the sport, often termed windsurfing, in California. World Championships were first held in 1973 and the sport was added to the Olympic Games in 1984.

World Championships

The world championships (started in 1973) have been won five times, consecutively, by Stephan van den Berg (Neth) to 1983, who also won the 1984 Olympics.

The longest boardsail ever made was by Timothy John Batstone (b Apr 22, 1959) in circumnavigating 1,794 miles around Great Britain May 2–July 10, 1984. He did 70 miles in a single stretch, made 40 sail changes and had zero falls on eight days.

Highest Speed

The record speed for boardsailing is 38.861 knots in a wind of 50 knots by Pascal Maka (France) at Fuerteventura, Canary Islands, on July 21, 1986, on a Gaastra 4 sq m limited edition speed-trial sailboard.

The women's record of 33.77 knots was set by Britt Dunderbeke in the Canary Islands in July 1986 also.

BOARDSAILING SPEED RECORD of 38.86 knots in a 50-knot wind was achieved by Pascal Maka of France. (All Sport/Oli Tennant)

Longest Sail

Starting from Dakar, Senegal, Jan 23, 1986, two French boardsailors, Stéphane Peyron and Alain Pichavant, crossed the Atlantic unescorted on a 31-ft tandem sailboard in 24 days 12 hours 5 min, landing on the West Indies island of Guadeloupe, some 3,000 mi away. They then proceeded to Miami where they were joined by Carolyn Stalins, 18 (a US citizen living in France), and boardsailed to NYC to arrive on July 2 for the Statue of Liberty celebration. The men covered about 5,000 mi in all.

BOARDSAILING ACROSS THE ATLANTIC: These 2 Frenchmen, Stéphane Peyron and Alain Pichavant, traveled from W Africa to Guadeloupe in the West Indies, and then to NYC, on this 31-ft sailboard, covering 3,000 mi of the journey in 24½ days. They arrived in time for the July 4, 1986, celebration.

Endurance

Neil Marlow (GB) went 107 hours in Guernsey, Channel Is, Aug 4–8, 1987.

Longest Line and Board

The longest line of boardsails was achieved by 60 windsurfers in tandem at the International Windsurfing Week event in Balk, Holland, on July 2, 1985.

A board 165 ft long was constructed in Fredrikstad, Norway, and first sailed on June 28, 1986.

BOBSLEDDING, LUGING AND TOBOGGANING

Origins

The oldest known sled is dated *c.* 6500 BC and came from Heinola, Finland. The first known bobsled race took place at Davos, Switzerland, in 1889.

Bobs have two pairs of runners and streamlined cowls. Steering is by means of cables attached to the front runners, which are flexible. The International Federation of Bobsleigh and Tobogganing was formed in 1923, followed by the International Bobsleigh Federation in 1957.

Olympic and World Titles

The Olympic 4-man bob title (instituted 1924) has been won 5 times by Switzerland (1924, 36, 56, 72, 88). The US (1932, 36), Switzerland (1948, 80), Italy (1956, 68) W Germany (1952, 72) and E Germany (1976, 84) have won the Olympic 2-man bob event (instituted 1932) twice. The most gold medals won by an individual is 3 by Meinhard Nehmer (b June 13, 1941) (E Germany) and Bernhard Germeshausen (b Aug 21, 1951) (E Germany) in the 1976 two-man, 1976 and 1980 four-man events. The most medals won is 6 (2 gold, 2 silver, 2 bronze) by Eugenio Monti (Italy) (b Jan 23, 1928) from 1956 to 1968.

In Olympic years, the Olympic champion is also world champion.

The world 4-man bob has been won 17 times by Switzerland (1924, 36, 39, 47, 54–57, 71–73, 75, 82–83, 86–87, 88). Italy won the 2-man title 14 times (1954, 56–63, 66, 68–69, 71, 75). Eugenio Monti has been a member of 11 world championship crews, 8 two-man and 3 four-man.

MOST BOBSLED TITLES: Switzerland has won the 4-man bob title in the Olympics 5 times, including 1988, and 11 more times for the world title. (All Sport)

Tobogganing

In tobogganing, the rider lies prone on his (her) belly.

The word "toboggan" comes from the Micmac American Indian word *tobaakan.* The St Moritz Tobogganing Club, Switzerland, founded in 1887 is the oldest toboggan club in the world. It is unique in being the home of the Cresta Run, which dates from 1884, and for the introduction of the one-man skeleton racing toboggan. The course is 3,977 ft long with a drop of 514 ft and the record is 50.91 sec (av. 53.27 mph) by Franco Gansser of Switzerland on Feb 16, 1986. On Feb 21, 1986, Nico Bracchi (Switz) set a record from Junction (2,920 ft) of 41.58 sec. Speeds of 90 mph are sometimes reached.

The greatest number of wins in the Grand National (instituted 1885) is eight by the 1948 Olympic champion Nino Bibbia (Italy) (b Sept 9, 1924) in 1960–64, 66, 68, 73. The greatest number of wins in the Curzon Cup (instituted in 1910) is eight by Bibbia in 1950, 57–58, 60, 62–64, 69, who hence won the double in 1960, 62–64.

Luge

Official international luging (*loojing*) competition, in which the rider adopts a sitting, as opposed to a prone, position, began at Klosters, Switzerland, in 1881. The first European championships were at Reichenberg (now East) Germany, in 1914 and the first world championships at Oslo, Norway, in 1953. The International Luge Federation was formed in 1957. Luging became an Olympic sport in 1964.

The two most successful riders in the championships are Thomas Köhler (E Germany) (b June 25, 1940), who won the world single-seater title in 1962, 64 (Olympic), 66, and 67, and shared the two-seater title in 1967 and 68 (Olympic); and Hans Rinn (E Ger) (b Mar 19, 1953), world champion two-seater 1976 (Olympic), 1977 and 1980 (Olympic), and one-seater world champion 1973 and 1977. Margit Schumann (E Germany) (b Sept 14, 1952) has won the women's championship 5 times—in 1973, 74, 75, 76 (Olympic) and 77.

The highest recorded photo-timed speed is 85.38 mph by Asle Strand (Norway) at Tandådalens Linbane, Sälen, Sweden, on May 1, 1982.

BODYBUILDING

In this category, information on men's championships has been supplied by the International Federation of Bodybuilders (IFBB), Ben Weider, president, and honorary Doctor of Sport Science. Information on women's championships has been supplied by *Women's Physique World* magazine, Steve Wennerstrom, editor-in-chief.

In its efforts to eradicate drugs from the sport, the IFBB introduced steroid testing in 1985 and in the years since then has been conducting tests at each world championship, as well as at continental and national contests. In the US, steroid testing is done on a local and/or state level. At the international congress organized in Australia in 1988, the IFBB strengthened its suspension ruling with regard to athletes testing positive and the following rules are in effect: For a first offense for testing positive, a one-year suspension from the date of the contest; for a second offense, a 2-year suspension; and for a third offense, permanent suspension.

The Mr. Olympia competition has been dominated by Arnold Schwarzenegger (US) who won 7 titles, 1970–75 and 1980. Lee Haney (US), the current Mr. Olympia, won 5 times, 1984–88. Frank Zane (US) has also won 3 times, 1977–79.

In the Mr. Universe championships, various weight classes are contested. Lee Haney won the heavyweight title in 1982. Multiple winners are: Herman Hoffend (W Ger) who won 4 championships, 1983–6,

MR OLYMPIA: Lee Haney, the 1988 champion, has won this title 5 times.

and a 2nd place in 1982, his weight growing from bantamweight to lightweight; Renato Bertagna (Italy) won 1st place finally in 1979 as a lightweight, after having placed 2nd and 3rd in the short class in 1971, 75, 77 and 78; in the lightweight division, Heinz Sallmeyer (Austria) won once (1980) and took 2nd place once (1979) while Emmat Sadek (Egypt) took 3rd place 3 times (1984, 85, 86).

In the world championships in Queensland, Australia, Oct 15, 1988 where 44 countries competed, the winners were:

Bantamweight: Teufik Ulusogly (Turkey)
Lightweight: Juan Marquez (US)
Middleweight: Prem Chand (India)
Light Heavyweight: Renel Janvier (US)
Heavyweight: Pavol Jablonicky (Czech)

In women's contests held by the International

Federation of Bodybuilders, the current (1988) Ms. Olympia, Corinna Everson (US) also won that title in 1984, 85, 86 and 87 and the National Women's Championship in 1984. In the IFBB Pro World Championships, Bev Francis (Australia) is the 1987 winner. In the World Amateur Championship the winner in lightweight is Charla Sedacca, in middleweight, Renee Casella, and heavyweight, Janice Graser (all US).

In the world amateur championships for women, held in Puerto Rico, Oct 1988, the winners were Janet Tech (US), lightweight; Veronica Dahlen (Sweden), middleweight; and Laura Creavalle (Guyana), heavyweight.

In women's contests held by the National Physique Committee, the US Champion in 1987 is Jackie Paisley (Ariz) and the National Women's Champion is Charla Sedacca (Georgia). Multiple winners have been Carla Dunlap (US) who won 4 titles (1981, 82, 83), Rachel McLish (US) who also won 4 (1980, 82), Lori Bowen (US) who won 3 (1983, 84) and Corinna Everson 5 titles.

BOWLING

Origins

Bowling can be traced to articles found in the tomb of an Egyptian child of 5200 BC where there were nine pieces of stone to be set up as pins at which a stone "ball" was rolled. The ball first had to roll through an archway made of three pieces of marble. In the Italian Alps about 2,000 years ago, the underhand tossing of stones at an object is believed the beginnings of *bocci*, a game still widely played in Italy and similar to bowling. Martin Luther is credited with the statement that nine was the ideal number of pins. In the British Isles, lawn bowls was preferred to bowling at pins. In the 16th century, bowling at pins was the national sport of Scotland. Early British settlers probably brought lawn bowls to the US and set up what is known as Bowling Green at the tip of Manhattan Island in NY but perhaps the Dutch under Henry Hudson were the ones to be credited.

In 1841, the Connecticut state legislature prohibited the game and other states followed. Eventually, a tenth pin was added to what had all along been a 9-pin game, to evade the ban.

Organizations

The American Bowling Congress (ABC), established in NY on Sept 9, 1895, was the first body to

WOMEN CHAMPIONS: Corinna Everson (left) and Charla Sedacca (right) have been consistent contest winners. ("Women's Physique World" magazine)

standardize rules, and the organization now comprises 3,424,204 men who bowl in leagues and tournaments. The Women's International Bowling Congress (WIBC), founded 1916, has a membership of 3,351,411. The Young American Bowling Alliance (YABA) (inst 1982), the successor to the American Junior Bowling Congress and Youth Bowling Assn, has 646,203 youth and collegiate members. The Professional Bowlers Association (PBA), formed in 1958, comprises more than 2,800 of the world's best male bowlers. The Ladies Professional Bowlers Tour has 170 members.

Lanes

In the US there were 8,031 bowling establishments with 151,312 lanes in 1986–87 and about 68 million bowlers.

The world's largest bowling center (now closed) was the Tokyo World Lanes Center, Japan, with 252 lanes. Currently the largest center is Fukuyana Bowl, Osaka, Japan, which has 144 lanes.

Highest Score in 24 Hours

A 6-man team toppled 126,276 pins on 6 lanes in 24 hours, Nov 2, 1988, at Northland Bowl, Jennings, Missouri, beating the previous published record by 51,053 pins. The team consisted of Anthony White (23,572 pins), James Brauch (21,732), David Potts (20,963), Jim Spangler (20,662), Larry Morrow (19,856), and Paul Brandon (19,491). They bowled a total of 698 games, and averaged 181 pins per game.

MOST TITLES IN A SEASON: Mark Roth of N Arlington, NJ, was victorious in 8 PBA tournaments in one year. He has also beaten Earl Anthony's record for total earnings with $1,278,681.

Marathon Attempts

A record of 265 hours at a pace of 7½ games per hour was set by Bob Atheney Jr of St Petersburg, Fla, Nov 9–21, 1975, at a time when the event was sanctioned by the ABC, but the record and the event were later withdrawn.

Donnie Moore (b 1960), a US Navy petty officer stationed at the Jacksonville (Fla) Naval Air Station, bowled 2,028 games in 217 hours, 55 min, July 15–24, 1985, for an average of 9.3 games per hour. However, he was not awarded the record because he stopped for 24½ hours for medical reasons.

The best accepted record is 195 hours 1 min by Jim Webb at Gosford City Bowl, NSW, Australia in 1984.

Chrissy Wolking of Riva, Md, aged 14 (YABA) broke the female record on Nov 29, 1987 by bowling 173 games in 18 hours averaging 9.6 games per hour.

World Championships

The Fédération Internationale des Quilleurs world championships were instituted in 1954. The highest pinfall in the individual men's event is 5,963 for 28 games by Ed Luther (US) at Milwaukee, Wis on Aug 28, 1971. In the current schedule of 24 games, the men's record is 5,261 by Rick Steelsmith (US) and 4,894 by Sandra Jo Shiery (US) is the women's record, both set in 1987 at Helsinki, Finland.

ABC LEAGUE RECORDS

Highest Scores

The highest individual score for three games is 886 by Albert "Allie" Brandt of Lockport, NY, on Oct 25, 1939. Glenn Allison (b 1930) rolled a perfect 900 in a 3-game series in league play on July 1, 1982, at La Habra Bowl, LA, Calif, but the ABC could not recognize the record when an ABC inspector determined the lanes were improperly dressed. Highest 3-game team score is 3,858 by Budweisers of St Louis on Mar 12, 1958.

The 886 record (after 49 years) was tied by Pat Landry, 21, a student at Mich State Nov 22, 1988, who rolled 33 strikes in 36 balls with games of 298,300 and 288 in league play. He had never before rolled an 800 series, and averages 201 on his university team.

The highest season average attained in sanctioned competition is 242 by John Ragard of Susquehanna, Pa, for 66 games in 1981–82.

The all-time ABC-sanctioned 2-man single-game record is 600, held jointly by the team of John Crimmins (300) and Walter Schackett (300) of Detroit, Mich, on Oct 27, 1933; a team of John Cotta (300) and Steve Lanson (300) on May 1, 1981, at the Manteca, Calif, Bowling Assn Tournament; and Jeff Marz and Dave Roney of Canton, O, Nov 8, 1987 in the Ann Doubles Classic in Canton. The 2-man team series record is 1,642 by Joe Golden (865) and Frank Henberger (717) in Oakland, NJ, on Aug 10, 1987.

Consecutive Strikes

The record for consecutive strikes in sanctioned match play is 33 by John Pezzin (b 1930) at Toledo, Ohio, on March 4, 1976.

Most Perfect Scores

The highest number of sanctioned 300 games is 31 by Jim Johnson Jr of Wilmington, Del through July 18, 1988.

The maximum 900 for a three-game series has been recorded 6 times in unsanctioned competition—by Leo Bentley at Lorain, Ohio, on March 26, 1931; by Joe Sargent at Rochester, NY, in 1934; by Jim Murgie in Philadelphia, on Feb 4, 1937; by Bob Brown at Roseville Bowl, Calif, on Apr 12, 1980; by Glenn Allison at Whittier, Calif, on July 1, 1982, and by John Strausbaugh at Columbia, Pa, on July 11, 1987.

PBA RECORDS

Most Titles

Earl Anthony of Dublin, Calif, has won a lifetime total of 41 PBA titles through Oct 1986. The record number of titles won in one PBA season is 8, by Mark Roth of North Arlington, NJ, in 1978.

Consecutive Titles

Only three bowlers have ever won three consecutive professional tournaments—Dick Weber in 1959, 60, and 61, Johnny Petraglia in 1971, and Mark Roth in 1977.

Perfect Games

A total of 119 perfect (300-pin) games were bowled in PBA tournaments in 1979, the most ever for one year. Dick Weber rolled 3 perfect games in one tournament (Houston) in 1965, as did Billy Hardwick of Louisville, Ky (in the Japan Gold Cup competition) in 1968, Roy Buckley of Columbus, Ohio (at Chagrin Falls, Ohio) in 1971, John Wilcox (at Detroit), Norm Meyers of St Louis (at Peoria, Ill) in 1979, and Shawn Christensen of Denver (at Denver) in 1984.

Don Johnson of Las Vegas, Nev, bowled at least one perfect game in 12 consecutive seasons (1966–77). Guppy Troup, of Savannah, Ga, rolled 6 perfect games on the 1979 tour.

Highest Earnings

The greatest lifetime earnings on the Professional Bowlers Association circuit have been won by Mark Roth who has taken home $1,278,681 through 1987. Mike Aulby holds the season earnings record with $201,200 in 1985.

Television Bowling

Nelson Burton Jr, St Louis, rolled the best series, 1,050, for four games (278–279–257–236) at Dick Weber Lanes in Florissant, Mo, Feb 11, 1984.

ABC TOURNAMENT RECORDS

Highest Individual

Highest three-game series in singles is 801 by Mickey Higham of Kansas City, Mo, in 1977. Best three-game total in any ABC event is 833 by Fran Bax of Niagara Falls, NY, in team in 1983. Jim Godman of Lorain, Ohio, holds the record for a nine-game All-Events total with 2,184 (731–749–704) set in Indianapolis, Ind, in 1974. ABC Hall of Famers Fred Bujack of Detroit, Bill Lillard of Houston, and Nelson Burton Jr of St Louis, have won the most championships with 8 each. Bujack shared in 3 team and 4 team All-Events titles between 1949 and 1955, and also won the individual All-Events title in 1955. Lillard bowled on regular and team All-Events champions in 1955 and 1956, the Classic team champions in 1962 and 1971, and won regular doubles and All-Events titles in 1956. Burton shared in 3 Classic team titles, 2 Classic doubles titles and has won Classic singles twice and Classic All-Events.

Highest Doubles

The ABC national tournament record of 558 was set in 1976 by Les Zikes of Chicago and Tommy Hudson of Akron, Ohio. The record score in a doubles series is 1,453, set in 1952 by John Klares (755) and Steve Nagy (698) of Cleveland.

Perfect Scores

Les Schissler of Denver scored 300 in the Classic team event in 1967, and Ray Williams of Detroit scored 300 in Regular team play in 1974, the first two perfect games bowled in team competition. In all, there have been only 50 300 games in the ABC tournament through 1988.

Best Finishes in One Tournament

Les Schissler of Denver won the singles, All-Events, and was on the winning team in 1966 to tie Ed Lubanski of Detroit and Bill Lillard of Houston as the only men to win three ABC crowns in one year. The best four finishes in one ABC tournament were third in singles, second in doubles, third in team and first in All-Events by Bob Strampe, Detroit, in 1967, and first in singles, third in team and doubles and second in All-Events by Paul Kulbaga, Cleveland, in 1960.

Youngest and Oldest Winners

The youngest champion was Ronnie Knapp of New London, Ohio, who was a member of the 1963 booster team champions when he was 16 years old. The oldest champion was Joe Detloff of Chicago, Ill, who, at the age of 72, was a winner in the 1965 Booster team event. The oldest doubles team in ABC competition totaled 165 years in 1955: Jerry Ameling (83) and Joseph Lehnbeutter (82), both from St

Louis. The youngest bowler to score 300 is said to be John Jaszkowski of S Milwaukee, Wis, who performed this feat at age 11, on Mar 13, 1982. The oldest bowler to score 300 is Leo Sites of Wichita, Kans, who performed the feat on Apr 10, 1985 at age 80.

Strikes and Spares in a Row

In the greatest finish to win an ABC title, Ed Shay set a record of 12 strikes in a row in 1958, when he scored a perfect game for a total of 733 in singles. Most strikes in a row is 20 by Lou Viet of Milwaukee in 1977. The most spares in a row is 23 by Lt Hazen Sweet of Battle Creek, Mich, in 1950.

Most Tournament Appearances

Bill Doehrman of Fort Wayne, Ind, competed in 71 consecutive ABC tournaments, beginning in 1908. (No tournaments were held 1943–45.)

WIBC RECORDS

Highest Scores

Patty Ann of Bloomington, Ill, had a record 5-year composite average of 227.20 through the 1985–86 season. She also has the best one-season average, 232, in the 1983–84 season. Her record for the highest total in a three-game series was exceeded in 1986 by Jeanne Maiden (see photo) who rolled 864.

The highest 5-woman team score for a 3-game series is 3,379 by Freeway Washer of Cleveland in 1960. The highest game score by a 5-woman team is 1,210 by Sheraton Inn, Scranton, Pa in 1982 as well as Veltri & Sons Clothier, also of Scranton, in the 1984–85 season.

Championship Tournaments

The highest score for a 3-game series in the annual WIBC Championship Tournament is 737 by D. D. Jacobson in the 1972 singles competition. The record for one game is 300 by Lori Gensch of Milwaukee in the 1979 doubles event, by Rose Walsh of Pomona, Calif in the 1986 singles event, and by Linda Kelly of Union, Ohio, in the 1987 doubles event.

Mary Covell of Chicago participated in her 55th WIBC tournament in 1986. The oldest participant was Ethel Brunnick (b Aug 30, 1887) of Santa Monica, Calif, at age 99 in 1987. Mary Ann Keiper of St Louis was only 5 years old when she participated in the 1952 tournament. The youngest champion was Leila Wagner (b July 12, 1960) of Seattle, Wash,

SUPER BOWLER: Jeanne Maiden of Solon, Ohio, has rolled 13 perfect games to set the WIBC career record. She also set a record of 40 consecutive strikes in 1986. (WIBC)

who was 18 when she was a member of the championship 5-woman team in 1979.

Dorothy Miller of Chicago has won 10 WIBC Championship Tournament events, the most by an individual. Millie Martorella is the only one to have won 3 WIBC Queen Tournaments, 1967, 1970, and 1971.

The highest lifetime average is 199.14 by Dorothy Fothergill of Lincoln, RI, who has bowled for 10 years but is now inactive.

Perfect Games

The most 300 games rolled in a career is 13 by Jeanne Maiden of Solon, Ohio. The oldest woman to bowl a perfect game (12 strikes in a row) was Helen Duval of Berkeley, Calif, at age 65 in 1982. Of all the women who rolled a perfect game, the one with the lowest average was Diane Ponza of Santa Cruz, Calif, who had a 112 average in the 1977–78 season.

Consecutive Strikes, Spares and Splits

The record for most consecutive strikes is 40 by Jeanne Maiden (see above). Joan Taylor of Syracuse, NY, made 27 consecutive spares. Shirley Tophigh of

Las Vegas, Nev, holds the unenviable record of rolling 14 consecutive splits.

Hall of Fame (WIBC)

Four bowlers were inducted in 1988. Those selected for Superior Performance are Patty Costello, 41, of Scranton, Pa, who among other things captured 25 titles on the pro tour and was Bowler of the Year in 1980–82 and 1984; Mary Lou Graham, 51, of Chiefland, Fla, an amateur with a lifetime tournament average of 185, who has competed in many WIBC and international events, 1948–75; Lorrie Nichols, 36, who holds world, professional and WIBC titles, with a lifetime tournament average of 195.58 for 19 appearances, 1971–88, and a season high average of 203 in 1987–88. For Meritorious Service, Helen Baker of Cocoa Beach, Fla, was chosen after 23 years on the WIBC board of directors, and especially for being instrumental in bowling being recognized by the US Olympic Committee for the 1988 Games.

BOXING*

Boxing with gloves was depicted on a fresco from the Isle of Thera, Greece, which has been dated to 1520 BC. The earliest prize-ring code of rules was formulated in England, Aug 16, 1743, by the champion pugilist Jack Broughton (1704–89), who reigned from 1729 to 1750. Boxing, which had in 1867 come under the Queensberry Rules, formulated for John Sholto Douglas, 9th Marquess of Queensberry, was not established as a legal sport in Britain until after a ruling of Mr Justice Grantham following the death of Billy Smith (Murray Livingstone) due to a fight on Apr 24, 1901, at Covent Garden, London.

Longest Fights

The longest recorded fight with gloves was between Andy Bowen of New Orleans and Jack Burke in New Orleans, Apr 6–7, 1893. The fight lasted 110 rounds (7 hours 19 min from 9:15 p.m. to 4:34 a.m.) but was declared no contest (later changed to a draw) when both men were unable to continue. The longest recorded bare knuckle fight was one of 6 hours 15 min between James Kelly and Jack Smith at Fiery Creek, Dalesford, Australia, Dec 3, 1855. The greatest recorded number of rounds is 276 in 4 hours 30 min, when Jack Jones beat Patsy Tunney in Chesh-

* More boxing records may be found in "Guinness Boxing: The Records" by Ian Morrison (Sterling).

TITLE DEEDS: Joe Louis (left) kept the heavyweight title for over 11 years, the longest reign at any weight class. Known as "The Brown Bomber," Louis successfully defended his title a record 25 times. Louis' largest purse, earned in his 8th round KO of Billy Conn in 1946, was $625,916—a far cry from today's high-priced bouts. Ringside seats cost a then-record $100.

ire, England, in 1825. The longest world title fight was in 1906 when Joe Gans (US) beat Battling Nelson (Den) when Nelson was disqualified in the 42nd round of a scheduled 45-round contest.

Shortest Fights

There is a distinction between the quickest knockout and the shortest fight. A knockout in 10½ sec (including a 10-sec count) occurred on Sept 23, 1946, when Al Couture struck Ralph Walton while the latter was adjusting his mouthpiece in his corner at Lewiston, Me. If the time was accurately taken it is clear that Couture must have been more than half-way across the ring from his own corner at the opening bell.

The shortest *professional* bout occurred Apr 3, 1936 when Al Carr (Alfred Tramantano) stopped Lew Massey in 7 sec with one punch in New Haven, Conn.

The shortest world title fight was 45 sec, when Lloyd Honeyghan (b Apr 22, 1960) beat Gene Hatcher in an IBF welterweight bout on Aug 30, 1987. The shortest ever heavyweight world title fight was the James J. Jeffries (1875–1953)–Jack Finnegan bout on Apr 6, 1900, won by Jeffries in 55 sec.

MIKE TYSON, YOUNGEST HEAVYWEIGHT CHAMP

(Photos counterclockwise)

Mike Tyson snaps John Alderson's head back with an extraordinary left hook in his fifth professional fight.

Tyson, wearing his championship belt, with his manager, Bill Cayton.

Co-managers, the late Jim Jacobs and Bill Cayton, congratulate Tyson on unifying WBC and WBA championships.

Tyson, gloves on, with his managers.

Tyson, happy, in Cayton's office.

Tyson, fully adorned, arriving at Heathrow Airport, London, with Cayton.

TYSON FIGHTING HIS WAY TO THE TOP

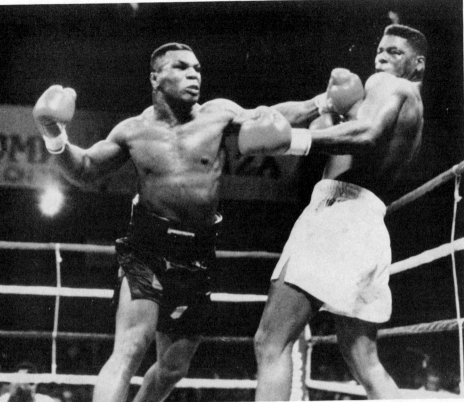

Tyson holds off Tyrell Biggs, Olympic gold medal winner (1984), with his left while readying his right for a knockout blow.

In a rare photo (below) Cus D'Amato unleashes the heavyweight fighter the world was waiting for.

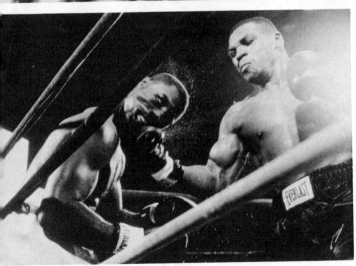

Tyson's devastating uppercut terminates Marvis Frazier in the first round, fastest KO (30 sec) in TV boxing history.

All photos from the Bill Cayton-Jim Jacobs files at Big Fights, Inc.

YOUNGEST BOXER to win a world title was Wilfred Benitez (right), who captured the light-welterweight title when he was only 17½ years old. Benitez is one of only a handful of fighters who have won world titles in 3 different weight classes. (Raymon Kopff)

Largest Receipts

The Mike Tyson–Michael Spinks fight which Tyson won in 91 sec brought in $12,150,000 at the gate in Atlantic City, NJ on June 27, 1988. Held at the Convention Center, it resulted in gross receipts that exceeded $74 million, a record for *any* sports event. The gross includes attendance live-at-site, closed circuit TV at theaters, home viewing, foreign and domestic delayed telecast.

Longest Career

The heavyweight Jem Mace (GB) (1831–1910), known as "the Gypsy," had a career lasting 50 years from 1855 to 1905, when he put on an exhibition bout with Tug Wilson, but his career is not fully documented. Kid Azteca (b Louis Villanueva Parano, 1915, Mexico City) started boxing professionally in 1929 and has a published record that includes at least one bout per year, 1932–61.

Tallest Boxer

The tallest boxer to fight professionally was Gogea Mitu (b 1914) of Rumania in 1935. He was 7 ft 4 in and weighed 327 lb. John Rankin, who won a fight in New Orleans in Nov 1967, also claimed 7 ft 4 in as

did Jim Culley, the "Tipperary Giant" who boxed and wrestled in the 1940's.

WORLD HEAVYWEIGHT CHAMPIONS

Earliest Title Fight

The first world heavyweight title fight, with 3-oz gloves and 3-minute rounds, was between John L. Sullivan (1858–1918) and Dominick McCaffrey on Aug 29, 1885 in Cincinnati, O. It went 6 rounds and Sullivan won.

Longest and Shortest Reigns

The longest reign of any world heavyweight champion is 11 years 252 days by Joe Louis (b Joseph Louis Barrow, 1914–81), from June 22, 1937, when he knocked out James J. Braddock in the 8th round at Chicago until announcing his retirement on March 1, 1949. During his reign Louis made a record 25 defenses of his title.

The shortest reigns were 83 days for WBA champion James "Bonecrusher" Smith (US) (b Apr 3, 1955), who ruled Dec 13, 1986 to Mar 7, 1987; Ken Norton (US) (b Aug 9, 1945) recognized by the WBC as champion for 83 days from Mar 18 to June 9, 1978; and 64 days for Tony Tucker (US) (b Dec 28, 1958), IBF champion May 30–Aug 2, 1987.

The longest-lived heavyweight champion was Jack Dempsey, who died May 31, 1983 aged 87 years 341 days.

Oldest and Youngest

The oldest man to win the heavyweight crown was Jersey Joe Walcott (b Arnold Raymond Cream, Jan 31, 1914, at Merchantville, NJ), who knocked out Ezzard Charles on July 18, 1951, in Pittsburgh, when aged 37 years 5 months 18 days. Walcott was the oldest title holder at 38 years 7 months 23 days when he lost to Rocky Marciano on Sept 23, 1952. The youngest age at which the world heavyweight title has been won is 20 years 145 days by Mike Tyson (b June 30, 1966), who won the WBC title by beating Trevor Berbick in the 2nd round on Nov 22, 1986, in Las Vegas, Nev.

Most Recaptures

Muhammad Ali Haj (b Cassius Marcellus Clay, in Louisville, Ky, Jan 17, 1942) is the only man to regain the heavyweight title twice. Ali first won the title on Feb 25, 1964, defeating Sonny Liston. He defeated George Foreman on Oct 30, 1974, having been stripped of his title by the world boxing author-

ities on Apr 28, 1967. He lost his title to Leon Spinks on Feb 15, 1978, but regained it on Sept 15, 1978 by defeating Spinks in New Orleans.

Heaviest and Lightest

The heaviest world champion was Primo Carnera (Italy) (1906–67), the "Ambling Alp," who won the title from Jack Sharkey in 6 rounds in NYC, on June 29, 1933. He scaled 260½ lb for this fight, but his peak weight was 270. He had the longest reach at 85½ in (finger tip to finger tip) and an expanded chest measurement of 53 in.

The lightest was Robert James Fitzsimmons (1863–1917), (b Helston, Cornwall, England) who, at a weight of 167 lb, won the title by knocking out James J. Corbett in 14 rounds at Carson City, Nev, March 17, 1897.

The greatest differential in a world title fight was 86 lb between Carnera (270 lb) and Tommy Loughran (184 lb) of the US, when the former won on points at Miami, Fla, March 1, 1934.

Tallest and Shortest

The tallest world champion was Primo Carnera, who was measured at 6 ft 5.4 in by the Physical Education Director at the Hemingway Gymnasium of Harvard, although he was widely reported and believed in 1933 to be 6 ft 8½ in tall. Jess Willard

(1881–1968), who won the title in 1915, was often described as being 6 ft 6¼ in tall, but was in fact 6 ft 5¼ in. The shortest was Tommy Burns (1881–1955) of Canada, world champion from Feb 23, 1906, to Dec 26, 1908, who stood 5 ft 7 in and weighed between 168 and 180 lb.

Olympic Gold Medals

In the 1984 Olympics, US boxers won a record total of 9 of the 12 gold medals, but in 1988 the US won only 3 golds. Here are the gold medal winners:

Light Flyweight (105.8 lb): Ivalio Khristov (Bulgaria)
Flyweight (112.5 lb): Kim Kwang-Sun (S Korea)
Bantamweight (119 lb): Kennedy McKinney (US)
Featherweight (126 lb): Giovanni Parisi (Italy)
Lightweight (132 lb): Andreas Zuelow (E Ger)
Light Welterweight (140 lb): Vyatcheslav Yanovskiy (USSR)
Welterweight (148 lb): Robert Wangila (Kenya)
Light Middleweight (157 lb): Park Si-Hun (S Korea)
Middleweight (165 lb): Henry Maske (E Ger)
Light Heavyweight (178.5 lb): Andrew Maynard (US)
Heavyweight (200.2 lb): Ray Mercer (US)
Super Heavyweight (over 200.2 lb): Lennox Lewis (Canada)

Only two boxers have won three Olympic gold

LORD OF THE RING: Rocky Marciano (left) is the only heavyweight champion to go through his entire professional career without a loss. Marciano won all 49 of his bouts, including 43 knockouts.

medals: southpaw László Papp (b 1926, Hungary), who took the middleweight (1948) and the light-middleweight titles (1952 and 56), and Cuban heavyweight Teofilo Stevenson (b Mar 23, 1952), who won the gold medal in his division for three successive Games (1972, 76 and 80). The only man to win two titles in one meeting was Oliver L. Kirk (US), who took both the bantam and featherweight titles at St Louis, Mo, in 1904, but he only needed one bout in each class.

The oldest man to win an Olympic gold medal in boxing was Richard K. Gunn (1871–1961) (GB), who won the featherweight title on Oct 27, 1908, in London, aged 38.

Heavyweight Champions through the Years

1882 John L. Sullivan (US)
1892 James J. Corbett (US)
1897 Bob Fitzsimmons (GB)
1899 James J. Jeffries (US)
1905 Marvin Hart (US)
1906 Tommy Burns (Can)
1908 Jack Johnson (US)
1915 Jess Willard (US)
1919 Jack Dempsey (US)
1926 Gene Tunney (US)
1930 Max Schmeling (Ger)
1932 Jack Sharkey (US)
1933 Primo Carnera (Ita)
1934 Max Baer (US)
1935 James J. Braddock (US)
1937 Joe Louis (US)
1949 Ezzard Charles (US)
1951 Jersey Joe Walcott (US)
1952 Rocky Marciano (US)
1956 Floyd Patterson (US)
1959 Ingemar Johansson (Swe)
1960 Floyd Patterson (US)
1962 Sonny Liston (US)
1964 Cassius Clay/Muhammad Ali (US)
1965 Ernie Terrell (US)—WBA only till 1967
1968 Joe Frazier (US)—NY State
1968 Jimmy Ellis (US)—WBA
1970 Joe Frazier (US)—undisputed
1973 George Foreman (US)
1974 Muhammad Ali (US)
1978 Leon Spinks (US)
1978 Muhammad Ali (US)—WBA
1978 Ken Norton (US)—WBC
1978 Larry Holmes (US)—WBC, IBF from 1983
1979 John Tate (US)—WBA
1980 Mike Weaver (US)—WBA
1982 Mike Dokes (US)—WBA
1983 Gerry Coetzee (So Afr)—WBA
1984 Tim Witherspoon (US)—WBC
1984 Pinklon Thomas (US)—WBC
1984 Greg Page (US)—WBA
1985 Tony Tubbs (US)—WBA
1985 Michael Spinks (US)—WBC, IBF
1986 Trevor Berbick (Canada)—WBC
1986 Tim Witherspoon (US)—WBA
1986 Mike Tyson (US)—WBC, WBA, IBF

WBC—World Boxing Council, headquartered in Mexico City. President: Jose Sulaiman, who has devoted himself to boxing for 20 years. A substantial portion of WBC's income has been spent furthering the sport, protecting the athletes and improving medical facilities. This is the most highly regarded organization.

WBA—World Boxing Association, headquartered in Panama City, Panama. President: Gilberto Mendoza.

IBF—International Boxing Federation, headquartered in NJ. President: Bob Lee.

These 3 bodies represent national federations of boxing commissions throughout the world, and have a variety of financial and political connections.

Undefeated

Rocky Marciano (b Rocco Francis Marchegiano) (1923–69) is the only heavyweight champion to retire undefeated after his entire professional career (1947–1956). His record was 49 wins (43 by KO) and no losses or draws.

TALLEST AND HEAVIEST CHAMPION (6 ft 5.4 in, 270 lb at the time) Primo Carnera shows off his strength before winning the heavyweight title in 1933.

WORLD CHAMPIONS (ANY WEIGHT)

Youngest and Oldest

The youngest at which any world championship has been won is 17 years 176 days by Wilfredo Benitez (b Sept 12, 1958) of Puerto Rico, who won the WBA junior-welterweight title, Mar 6, 1976.

The oldest world champion was Archie Moore (b Archibald Lee Wright, Collinsville, Ill, Dec 13, 1913 or 1916), who was recognized as a light-heavyweight champion up to Feb 10, 1962, when his title was removed. He was then between 45 and 48. Bob Fitzsimmons (1863–1917) had the longest career of any official world titleholder with over 31 years from 1883 to 1914. He had his last world title bout on Dec 20, 1905 at the age of 42 years 208 days.

Most Fights Without Loss

Edward Henry (Harry) Greb (US) (1894–1926), who was blind in one eye, was unbeaten in 178 bouts, but these included 117 "no decisions" 1916–23 and 5 were unofficial losses. Of boxers with complete records Packey McFarland (US) (1888–1936) had 97 fights (five draws) in 1905–15 without a defeat. Pedro

Carrasco (b Spain, Nov 7, 1943) won 83 consecutive fights from Apr 22, 1964 to Sept 3, 1970, and then drew once and had a further nine wins before his loss to Armando Ramos in a WBC lightweight contest on Feb 18, 1972.

Longest and Shortest Reigns

Joe Louis's heavyweight duration record of 11 years 252 days stands for all divisions.

The shortest reign was that of Tony Canzoneri who held the light-welterweight title for 33 days, May 21–June 23, 1933. By ruling Joe Burman was awarded the bantamweight title on Oct 19, 1923, when Joe Lynch pulled out of the championship contest at the last minute at 3 PM, and at 11 PM the same night Burman was knocked out and lost the title to Abe Goldstein in Madison Sq Garden, NYC.

Most Recaptures

The only boxer to win a world title five times at one weight is Sugar Ray Robinson (b Walker Smith, Jr, in Detroit, May 3, 1921) who beat Carmen Basilio (US) in the Chicago Stadium on March 25, 1958, to regain the world middleweight title for the fourth time. The other title wins were over Jake LaMotta (US) in Chicago on Feb 14, 1951; Randy Turpin (UK) in NYC on Sept 12, 1951; Carl "Bobo" Olson (US) in Chicago on Dec 9, 1955; and Gene Fullmer (US) in Chicago on May 1, 1957.

Most Titles Simultaneously

The only man to hold world titles at three weights simultaneously was Henry "Hammering Hank" Armstrong (1912–88) of the US, at featherweight, lightweight and welterweight from Aug to Dec 1938.

Thomas Hearns (b Oct 18, 1958) became the first man ever to hold world titles at 5 different weights. On Nov 5, 1988, he won the super-middleweight title recognized by a newly created World Boxing Organization (WBO) to add to his previous 4. He won the WBC middleweight title after holding WBA welterweight since 1980, WBC super-welterweight since 1982 and WBC light heavyweight in 1987.

Sugar Ray Leonard (US) (b May 17, 1956) won titles in his 4th and 5th weight categories recognized by the 2 senior authorities (WBA and WBC) when he beat Donny Lalonde (Canada) on Nov 8, 1988 to annex both WBC light heavyweight and super middleweight titles. He had previously won the WBC welterweight title (1977 and 1980), WBA junior middleweight (1981) and WCC middleweight (1987).

Amateur World Championships

Two boxers have won three world championships (instituted 1974): Teofilo Stevenson (Cuba), heavyweight 1974, 1978 and 1986, and Adolfo Horta (b Oct 3, 1957) (Cuba), bantam 1978, feather 1982 and lightweight 1986.

Longest and Shortest Title Fights

The longest world title fight (under Queensberry Rules) was between the lightweights Joe Gans (1874–1910), of the US, and Oscar "Battling" Nelson (1882–1954), the "Durable Dane," at Goldfield, Nev, Sept 3, 1906. It was terminated in the 42nd round when Gans was named winner on a foul.

The shortest title bout was 40 sec from the starting bell when welterweight champion Lloyd Honeyghan knocked out Gene Hatcher on Aug 30, 1987, at Marbella, Spain, to retain his WBA and IBF titles. This beat the previous mark of 52 sec when Sugar Ray Robinson on Aug 25, 1950, defended his middleweight title against Jose Basora.

Most Title Bouts

The record number of title bouts in a career is 37, of which 18 ended in "no decision," by 3-time world welterweight champion Jack Britton (US) (1885–1962), from 1915 to 1922.

Most Frequent Championship Fights

Henry Armstrong (US) between Oct 9 and Oct 30, 1939, fought 5 times for the welterweight title and won each time.

Most Knockdowns in Title Fights

Vic Toweel (South Africa) knocked down Danny O'Sullivan of London 14 times in 10 rounds in their world bantamweight fight at Johannesburg, Dec 2, 1950, before the latter retired.

George Foreman is the only US champion in any weight class to have won, defended, and lost his crown all outside the US. To win his title he defeated Joe Frazier in Kingston, Jamaica, Jan 22, 1973. He defended it against Jose Roman in Tokyo, Japan, Sept 1, 1973, and against Ken Norton in Caracas, Venezuela, Mar 26, 1974. He lost it to Muhammad Ali in Kinshasa, Zaire, Oct 30, 1974. As world champion, this native of Marshall, Tex never fought in his own country.

ALL FIGHTS

Highest Earnings in Career

The largest known fortune ever made in a fighting career is an estimated $69 million (including exhibitions) amassed by Muhammad Ali from Oct 1960 to Dec 1981, in 61 fights comprising 551 rounds.

Most Knockouts

The greatest number of knockouts in a career is 145 (129 in professional bouts) by Archie Moore (1936 to 1963). The record for consecutive KO's is 44, set by Lamar Clark of Utah at Las Vegas, Nev, Jan 11, 1960. He knocked out 6 in one night (5 in the first round) in Bingham Canyon, Utah, on Dec 1, 1958.

Referee Counted Out

While Ruby Goldstein was refereeing a light-heavyweight title bout on June 25, 1952, he was overcome by the intense heat at the end of the 12th round and had to be replaced.

Fighter Endures Plane Crash

Featherweight Willie Pep (1942–50) was severely injured in a plane crash in 1947. Told he would never fight again, maybe not even walk without crutches, Pep defied everyone, came back in 5 months to win the first of 26 consecutive bouts, and retain his world title.

Double Knockouts

In 1887, an earlier Jack Dempsey (Ireland) retained his world middleweight title by knocking out Johnny Reagan (US) in two rings! The fight began in Huntington, Long Island, NY, but in the 8th round, the tide flooded the ring, so the fighters and spectators boarded a tug and continued the bout some 25 miles away.

Danny Lopez (US) had to knock out Mike Ayala twice on June 17, 1979, in San Antonio to make his victory stick. In the 11th round Ayala was counted out but his followers complained to the referee that their man was up at the count of 9, so Lopez did it a second time in the 15th round.

Closest Call

With just one second to go in the 15th and final round of their light-heavyweight title bout, Victor Galindez (Arg) knocked out Richie Kates (US).

The Real McCoy

A boxer named Charles ''Kid'' McCoy in the 1890's is responsible for an expression that got into the language. With 10 marriages to his credit, incidentally, McCoy had a trick of making believe he was ill or in difficulty, so his opponent would be fooled into letting up on him, then suddenly regaining his strength, which led his opponents into asking: ''Which is the real McCoy?''

Greatest ''Tonnage''

The greatest ''tonnage'' in a world title fight was 488¾ lb when Primo Carnera (259½ lb) fought Paolino Uzcudun (229¼ lb) of Spain, in Rome, Italy, Oct 22, 1933.

The greatest ''tonnage'' recorded in any fight is 700 lb, when Claude ''Humphrey'' McBride of Okla at 340 lb knocked out Jimmy Black of Houston at 360 lb in the 3rd round at Oklahoma City, June 1, 1971.

Smallest Champions

The smallest man to win any world title has been Netranoi Vorsingh (b Apr 22, 1959) (Thailand), WBC light-flyweight champion from May to Sept 1978, at 4 ft 11 in tall. Jimmy Wilde (b Merthyr Tydfil, 1892, d 1969, UK), who held the flyweight title from 1916 to 1923, was reputed never to have fought above 108 lb.

Most Fights

The greatest recorded number of fights in a career is 1,024 by Bobby Dobbs (US) (1858–1930), who is reported to have fought from 1875 to 1914, a period of 39 years. Abraham Hollandersky, *alias* Abe the Newsboy (US), is reputed to have had 1,309 fights in the 14 years from 1905 to 1918, but many of them were one-round exhibition bouts. Len Wickwar, an English lightweight who fought between 1928–47, had 463 documented fights.

CANOEING AND KAYAKING

Origins

Modern canoes and kayaks originated with the Indians and Eskimos of North America. French trappers were the first to compete in canoe races (1790).

The acknowledged pioneer of canoeing as a modern sport was John Macgregor (1825–92), a British barrister, in 1865. The Canoe Club was formed on July 26, 1866.

Olympic and World Titles

Gert Fredrikson (b Nov 21, 1919) of Sweden has won the most Olympic gold medals with 6 (1948, 52, 56, 60), and a silver and a bronze for record total of 8. The most by a woman is 3 by Ludmila Pinayeva (*née* Khvedosyuk, b Jan 14, 1936) (USSR) in the 500-m K.1 in 1964 and 1968, and the 500-m K.2 in 1972. The most gold medals at one Games is 3 by Vladimir Parfenovich (b Dec 2, 1958) (USSR) in 1980 and by Ian Ferguson (NZ) (b July 20, 1952) in the 1984 Olympics (one individually at 500 m and 2 on New Zealand boat at 500 m and 1,000 m). Ferguson was a winner in 1988 at 500m with Paul MacDonald in the pairs event. Other gold medal winners in the 1988 Games were:

CANOEING
500 m Singles: Olaf Heukrodt (E Ger) 1:56.42
1000 m Singles: Ivan Klementyev (USSR) 4:12.78
500 m Pairs: Victor Reneiski and Nikolai Jouravski (USSR) 1:41.77
1000 m Pairs: Victor Reneiski and Nikolai Jouravski (USSR) 3:48.28

KAYAKING
500 m Singles: Zsolt Gyulay (Hungary) 1:44.82
1000 m Singles: Greg Barton (US) 3:55.27
500 m Pairs: Ian Ferguson and Paul MacDonald (NZ) 1:33.98
1000 m Pairs: Greg Barton and Norm Bellingham (US) 3:32.42
1000 m Fours: Hungary (Zsolt Gyulay, Ferenc Csipes, Sandor Hodosi, Attila Abraham) 3:00.20

WOMEN—KAYAKING
500 m Singles: Vania Guecheva (Bulgaria) 1:55.19
500 m Pairs: Birgit Schmidt and Anke Nothnagel (E Ger) 1:43.46
500 m Fours: E Ger (Birgit Schmidt, Anke Nothnagel, Ramona Portwich, Heike Singer) 1:40.78

Thirteen titles (including Olympic titles) have been won by Fredrikson (see above) and by Rüdiger Helm (E Ger) (b Oct 6, 1956), ten world and three Olympic between 1976 and 1983, and by Ivan Patzaichin (Rumania) (b Nov 26, 1949) 1968–84. Birgit Fischer (now Schmidt) (E Ger) (b Feb 25, 1962) won two more Olympic gold medals in 1988, for a total of 22 world titles, 1978–88, including 3 Olympic golds.

Longest Journey

The longest journey ever made by canoe is 12,181 miles by father and son Dana and Donald Starkell from Winnipeg, Manitoba, Canada by ocean and river to Belem, Brazil from June 1, 1980 to May 1, 1982. All portages were human powered.

The longest journey without portage or aid of any kind is one of 6,102 miles by Richard H. Grant and Ernest "Moose" Lassy circumnavigating the eastern US from Chicago to New Orleans to Miami to NYC, returning back to Chicago *via* the Great Lakes, from Sept 22, 1930, to Aug 15, 1931.

Longest Open Sea Voyage

Beatrice and John Dowd, Ken Beard and Steve Benson (Richard Gillett replaced him mid-journey) paddled 2,170 miles out of a total journey of 2,192 miles from Venezuela to Miami, Fla, via the West Indies from Aug 11, 1977, to Apr 29, 1978, in two Klepper Aerius 20 kayaks.

Eskimo Rolls

Ray Hudspith (b Apr 18, 1960) achieved 1,000 Eskimo rolls in 34 min 43 sec at the Elswick Pool, Newcastle-upon-Tyne, Eng, on Mar 20, 1987. Julian Dean achieved 1,555 continuous rolls at Casterton Swimming Pool, Cumbria, Eng, taking 1 hour 49 min 45 sec on Dec 6, 1983. Colin Brian Hill (b Aug 16, 1970) set a "hand-rolling" record of 1,000 rolls in 31 min 55.62 sec at Consett, Durham on Mar 12, 1987. He achieved 100 rolls in 2 min 39.2 sec at Crystal Palace, London on Feb 22, 1987.

DOWNSTREAM CANOEING

River	Miles	Name and Country	Route	Date	Duration
Murray–Darling	1980	Six students of St Albert's College, UNE (Australia)	Gunnedah, NSW to Lake Alexandria, SA	Dec 1975	——
Mississippi	2552	Valerie Fons and Verlen Kruger (US)	Lake Itasca, Minnesota to Gulf of Mexico	Apr 27–May 20, 1984	23 days 10 hr 20 min
Zaire (Congo)	2600	John and Julie Batchelder (GB)	Mossampanga to Banana	May 8–Sept 12, 1974	128 days
Amazon	3800	Alan Trevor Holman (GB/Aus) (b. 21 Feb 1944)	Quitani, Peru to Cabo Maguavi, Brazil	Aug 9–Dec 3, 1982	116 days
Mississippi–Missouri	3810	Nicholas Francis (GB)	Three Forks, Montana to New Orleans, La.	July 13–Nov 25, 1977	135 days
		Mary Schmidt and Bev Gordon (US)	Three Forks to New Orleans	July 4–Oct 13, 1984	98 days (unratified)
Nile	4000	John Goddard (US), Jean Laporte and André Davy (France)	Kagera to the Delta	Nov 1953–July 1954	9 months

Highest Speed

The Olympic 1,000-m best performance of 3 min 02.70 sec by the 1980 USSR K4 on July 31, 1980, represents a speed of 12.24 mph. They achieved 13.14 mph over the first quarter of the course.

Fastest 24 Hours

The solo 24-hour canoe record is 143.32 mi by Dr Chris Greiff (S Africa) in a Jaguar K1 canoe on the Breede River, Robertson to Cape Infanta, Cape Province, S Africa, Aug 11–12, 1985. The women's record is 97.2 mi set by Lydia Formentin on the Swan River, W Australia in 1979.

The record in flat water, without benefit of current, is 123.98 miles by Lt Col Thomas J. Mazuzan (USAF) on the Barge Canal, NY State, Sept 24–5, 1986. Mazuzan, a 57-year-old grandfather, in July 1988 crossed Lake Ontario solo at its widest in a record 16 hours 12 min 47 sec, made a solo crossing of Lake Erie at its widest in 17 hours 55 min 38 sec Aug 27–28, 1988, and is aiming to canoe across all the Great Lakes solo in record time.

The record in open sea is 120.6 miles by Randy Fine (US) along the Florida coast June 26–7, 1986.

Downstream Canoeing

The record for canoeing down the Mississippi from Lake Itasca, Minn to the Gulf of Mexico is 23 days 10 hours 20 min by Valerie Fons and Verlen Kruger, Apr 27–May 20, 1984.

Greatest Lifetime Distance

Fritz Lindner of Berlin, W Germany, totaled 56,847 mi from 1928 to 1983, for the greatest lifetime distance.

Longest Race

The longest race ever staged was 3,283 mi from Rocky Mountain House, Alberta, to the Expo 67 site at Montreal, Quebec as the Canadian Government Centennial Voyageur Canoe Pageant and Race. Ten canoes represented Canadian provinces and territories. The winner of the race, which took from May 24 to Sept 4, 1967, was the Province of Manitoba canoe *Radisson*.

The longest regularly held canoe race in the US is the Texas Water Safari (instituted 1963) which covers 265 twisting mi from San Marcos to Seadrift, Tex, on the San Marcos and Guadalupe Rivers. Mike Wooley and Howard Gore set the record of 36 hours, 40 min, June 2–3, 1979.

CANOEING TOGETHER: Ken Beard and Steve Benson paddle in the Gulf Stream. Along with Beatrice and John Dowd, they completed the longest open sea voyage ever made by canoe.

CROQUET

Origins

Some say croquet began in the 12th to 14th century in France when peasants used crude mallets to knock balls through hoops made of bent willow branches. Americans contend that, since one needed a large lawn, or at least a large backyard, peasants could not have invented the game.

It was probably first popular in England as a country-house game in the mid-1600's, when it was called "crokey." Professional groundskeepers were hired and lawns became "greenswards." Oddly enough (according to a recent book by Jack Osborn and Jesse Kornbluth), "one court was made of powdered cockleshell and its wickets were festooned with flowers."

The game has gone through several lapses into obscurity over the years, and in the last century was introduced from England into Australia and the US. The literary group that gathered around Herbert Bayard Swope and Alexander Woollcott in the 1920's (the Algonquin Round Table set which included George S. Kaufman and Dorothy Parker) brought croquet into the limelight. Croquet spread to Hollywood soon after, under the guidance of Darryl Zanuck and Samuel Goldwyn.

Today the U.S. Croquet Association has 300 clubs as members with 70 of them new in 1988. The Palm Beach, Fla, area with 20 championship courts

CROQUET CHAMPION attempts a pass roll: Dana Dribben, a pro at golf as well as croquet, is shown winning a match in Central Park, NYC. (US Croquet Assn)

is the largest croquet complex in the western hemisphere.

Marathon

A foursome at Birmingham Univ, Eng, played for 120 hours 25 min, June 14–19, 1986.

BETTER KNOWN as a marathon and road runner, Grete Waitz (Norway) (right) has won 5 victories in the international cross-country championships, 1978–81 and 1983. In the NYC Marathon she won 9 times, 1976–8, 1982–6 and 1988.

ROUGH RUNNING: French runner Alain Mimoun (#1) (below) streaks to one of his four world titles, a record he shares with Jack Holden and Gaston Roelants.

CROSS-COUNTRY RUNNING

International Championships

The earliest international cross-country race was run between England and France on a course 9 miles 18 yd long from Ville d'Avray, outside Paris, on March 20, 1898 (England won by 21 points to 69). The inaugural International Cross-Country Championships took place at the Hamilton Park Racecourse, Scotland, on March 28, 1903. Since 1973 the race has been run under the auspices of the International Amateur Athletic Federation.

The greatest margin of victory in the International Cross-Country Championships has been 56 sec, or 390 yd, by Jack T. Holden (England) (b Mar 13, 1907) at Ayr Racecourse, Scotland, March 24, 1934. The narrowest win was that of Jean-Claude Fayolle (France) at Ostend, Belgium, on March 20, 1965, when the timekeepers were unable to separate his time from that of Melvyn Richard Batty (England).

The greatest men's team wins have been those of England, with a minimum of 21 points (the first six runners to finish) on two occasions, 1924 and 1932 at Newcastle, Eng, and at the Hippodrome, Brussels, Belgium.

KENYANS WINNERS: At the 1988 World Cross-Country Championships in Auckland, New Zealand, 6 Kenyans were among the first 7 finishers. (All Sport/Simon Bruty)

Most Appearances

The runner with the largest number of international championship appearances is Marcel Van de Wattyne of Belgium, who participated in 20 competitions in the years 1946–65.

Most Wins

The most victories is 5 in the women's race by Doris Brown-Heritage (US) (b Sept 17, 1942), 1967–71; and by Grete Waitz (*née* Anderson) (Norway) (b Oct 1, 1953), 1978–81, 83.

The greatest number of men's individual victories is 4 by Jack Holden (England) in 1933–35, and 39; by Alain Mimoun-o-Kacha (b Jan 1, 1921) (France) in 1949, 52, 54 and 56; and by Gaston Roelants (b Feb 5, 1937) (Belgium) in 1962, 67, 69 and 72.

Largest Field

The largest recorded field in any cross-country race was 11,763 starters (10,810 finishers) in the 18.6-mi Lidingoloppet near Stockholm, Sweden, Oct 3, 1982.

CURLING

Origins

Although a 15th-century bronze figure in the Florence Museum appears to be holding a curling stone, the earliest illustration of the sport was in one of the winter scenes by the Flemish painter Pieter Brueghel,

c. 1560. The game was introduced into Canada in 1759. Organized administration began in 1838 with the formation of the Grand (later Royal) Caledonian Curling Club, the international legislative body until the foundation of the International Curling Federation in 1966. The first indoor ice rink to introduce curling was in Montreal, Canada in 1807.

Curling clubs were well established in the US by the mid-1800's. The first known was the Orchard Lake Club (Lake St Claire, Mich) founded in 1832. The first game on artificially cooled ice in N Amer was Milwaukee vs Chicago in 1892. The US Curling Assoc was founded in 1958.

About 2 million curlers can be found in 22 countries today, according to the US Curling Assoc.

The US won the first Gordon International Medal series of matches, between Canada and the US, at Montreal in 1884. The first Strathcona Cup match between Canada and Scotland was won by Canada in 1903. Although demonstrated at the Winter Olympics of 1924, 1932, and 1988, curling has never been included in the official Olympic program.

Most Titles

The record for the men's World Championship (inst 1959) (now the "International Curling Federation World Championship") is 19 wins by Canada (7 Scotch Cups, 9 Silver Brooms, and 3 ICF's). The most Strathcona Cup (inst 1903) wins is 7 by Canada (1903, 09, 12, 23, 38, 57, 65). The US is second. The most women's World Championships (inst 1979) is 5 for Canada (1980, 84, 85, 86, 87)

CURLING ACTION: This is the scene at the 1986 contest between Madison (Wis), the US champs, and Sweden for the men's World Curling Championship. (US Curling Assn)

Largest Rink

The world's largest curling rink is the Big Four Curling Rink, Calgary, Alberta, Canada, opened in 1959 at a cost of Can. $2,250,000. Each of the two floors has 24 sheets of ice, the total accommodating 96 teams and 384 players. (Only one floor is currently used for curling.) The largest in use in the US are 8-sheet rinks at St Paul and Duluth, Minn.

Largest Bonspiels

The largest indoor bonspiel is the Manitoba Bonspiel held in Winnipeg, Canada. At the 100th anniversary in 1988, 1,280 teams competed using 187 sheets of curling ice. The largest outdoor bonspiel is the "Grand Match" held on a loch in Scotland when weather is cold enough. It often attracts over 4,000 curlers.

Largest Prizes

Canada's "Gold Trail" men's tour offered the record purse—$1,178,900 in the 1988–89 season.

The largest single purse offered was the Canadian Airlines Double Carspiel, with the winning team getting $94,800, according to the Canadian Curling News.

"Perfect" Games

Stu Beagle, of Calgary, Canada, played a perfect game (48 points) against Nova Scotia in the Canadian championships (Brier) at Ft. William (now Thunder Bay), Ontario, on March 8, 1960. Bernice Fekete, of Edmonton, Canada, skipped her rink (team) to two consecutive eight-enders on the same sheet of ice at the Derrick Club, Edmonton, on January 10 and February 6, 1973. Andrew McQuistin, of Stranraer, Scotland, skipped a Scotland rink to a 1–0 victory over Switzerland, scoring in the tenth end after nine consecutive blank ends, in the Uniroyal World Junior Championships at Kitchener-Waterloo, Ontario, Canada, on March 16, 1980.

Marathon

The longest recorded curling match is one of 67 hours 55 min by the Capital Winter Club of New Brunswick, Canada, Apr 9–12, 1982. The duration record for 2 curlers is 43 hours 2 min by Brian Rankin and David Sencor at Bradford, W Yorkshire, Canada, July 5–7, 1988.

World Championships

The US curler who participated most on world championship teams is Bill Strum of the Superior (Wis) Curling Club, who was on 3 teams (1965, 74, 78) and on 5 USA championship teams (1965, 67, 69, 74, 78). Two others who were on 5 USA championship teams are Bud Somerville of Superior (1965, 68, 69, 74, 78) and Bruce Roberts of Hibbing, Minn (1966, 67, 76, 77, 84).

CYCLING

Earliest Race

The earliest recorded bicycle race was a velocipede race over 2 km (1.24 miles) at the Parc de St Cloud, Paris, on May 31, 1868, won by Dr James Moore (GB) (1847–1935).

The first American bicycle race was held May 24, 1878 in Boston's Beacon Park. Winner C. A. Parker of Harvard University covered the 3-mi course in 12 min, 27 sec.

SPEEDIEST BIKER: John Howard, riding in the vacuum created behind a large-tail racing car on a specially designed 46-lb bicycle, sped more than 152 mph on Bonneville Salt Flats in July 1985. (Al Gross)

The time-trial was devised in 1889–90 by F. T. Bidlake to avoid the congestion caused by ordinary mass road racing.

1988 Olympic Gold Medalists

MEN
Sprint: Lutz Hesslich (E Ger)
50 km Individual Points Race: Dan Frost (Den)
Road Race: Olaf Ludwig (E Ger)
1000 m Time Trial: Alexandre Kirichenko (USSR) 1:04.49
4000 m Individual Pursuit: Gintautas Umaras (USSR)
4000 m Team Pursuit: USSR 4:13.31
100 km Road Team Trial: E Ger

WOMEN
Sprint: Erika Salumae (USSR)
Road Race: Monique Knol (Neth)

Most World Titles

World championships, contested annually, were first staged for amateurs in 1893 and for professionals in 1895. The most wins at a particular event is 10 consecutively by Koichi Nakano (Japan) (b Nov 14, 1955), professional sprint champion 1977–86. The most wins at a men's amateur event is 7 by Daniel Morelon (France) (b July 28, 1944), sprint 1966–7, 69–71, 73, 75; and Leon Meredith (UK) (1882–1930), 100-km motor-paced 1904–5, 1907–9, 11, 13.

The most women's titles is 7 by Beryl Burton (UK) (b May 12, 1937), pursuit 1959–60, 62–63, 66 and road 1960, 67; and by Yvonne Reynders (Belgium) pursuit 1961, 64–65 and road 1959, 61, 63, 66.

Greg LeMond is the only American ever to win the World Professional Road Championship, taking the title Sept 4, 1983, at Altenrhein, Switzerland.

Highest Speed

John Howard (b Aug 16, 1947) of Encinitas, Calif, achieved 152.284 mph on July 20, 1985, riding a specially designed 46-lb bike with hydraulic forks and motorcycle wheels, at Bonneville Salt Flats, Utah. A former Olympic cyclist, he rode behind a car that gave him considerable help with a large tail section designed to cut down on air resistance and give a slipstreaming effect.

24-HOUR DISTANCE CHAMP: Jim Elliott raced 548.9 mi for a paced track record at the San Diego Velodrome Oct 29–30, 1988.

The greatest distance ever covered in one hour is 76 miles 604 yd by Leon Vanderstuyft (Belgium) on the Montlhéry Motor Circuit, France, Sept 30, 1928. This was achieved from a standing start paced by a motorcycle ahead. (Cycling rules permit a motorcycle to precede a bicycle in an event of over 10 km.) The 24-hour record behind pace is 860 miles 367 yd by Sir Hubert Ferdinand Opperman (b May 29, 1904) in Melbourne, Australia on May 23, 1932.

24-Hour Distance Record

The 24-hour human-paced outdoor record is 548.9 mi by Jim Elliott of San Diego, set Oct 29–30, 1988.

Indoors, unpaced, the 24-hour record is 516 mi 427 yd by Michael Secrest (b Jan 20, 1953) of Flint, Mich, who cycled this distance at the Montreal (Canada) Olympic Velodrome Mar 13–14, 1985.

One-Hour Distance Records

The greatest distance covered in 60 min unpaced is 31 mi 1,381 yd by Francesco Moser (Italy) at Mexico City on Jan 23, 1984. The International Cycling Union (UCI), which recognizes both sea-level and high-altitude hour records, classifies Moser's Mexico City distance in the high altitude category because it was achieved on a track located at an elevation greater than 600 m (above mean sea level). Moser also holds the sea-level 60 min distance record of 30 mi 1,665.6 yd in Milan, Italy on Oct 3, 1986.

The indoor 60 min distance record is 30 mi 1,742 yd by Viatcheslav Ekimov (USSR), ridden on the Olympic Velodrome in Moscow in Nov 1986.

Jeannie Longo of France holds the sea-level, indoor and high-altitude 60 min unpaced women's records. She cycled 27 mi 147 yds in Oct 1986 in Milan, Italy, for the sea-level mark and 27 miles 1,441 yds, Sept 20, 1986, in Colorado Springs, Colo for the altitude mark and then 27 mi 1,338 yds on Nov 7, 1986 in Paris for the indoor record.

Human-Powered Speed Record

Fred Markham (b May 9, 1957) of Aptos, Calif, became the first person to pedal a bicycle 65 mph on a level course, unpaced and unaided by wind. Riding on Big Sand Flat, Calif, on May 12, 1986, Markham pedaled a 31-lb covered recumbent to a record 65.484 mph. (His speed was calculated over a distance of 200 m.) He took approximately 2 mi to build up to top speed. The bike was covered with DuPont Kevlar to reduce wind resistance. Nearly all steel parts were replaced with lighter titanium or aluminum substitutes. Markham and bike designer Gardner Martin shared an $18,000 prize that was awarded by DuPont to the first cyclist to break 65 miles per hour under the above-specified conditions.

US Transcontinental

Date	Name	Mileage	Start-Finish	Days:Hours:Min
Men				
6/29/61	Jerry Hornig		San Francisco to NYC	17:05:15
4/22/72	Peter Duker		Santa Monica to NYC	18:02:38
3/17/73	Paul Cornish		Santa Monica to NYC	13:05:20
8/26/78	John Marino		Santa Monica to NYC	13:01:20
6/28/80	John Marino		Santa Monica to NYC	12:03:41
7/14/81	Lon Haldeman		Santa Monica to NYC	10:23:27
8/14/82	Lon Haldeman	2,986	Santa Monica to NYC	9:20:02
				Great American Bike Race '82
8/29/84	Pete Penseyres	3,047.4	Huntington Beach to Atlantic City, NJ	9:13:13 Race Across America '84
7/31/85	Jonathan Boyer	3,120.2	Huntington Beach to Atlantic City, NJ	9:02:06 Race Across America '85
7/14/86	Pete Penseyres	3,107.3	Huntington Beach to Atlantic City, NJ	8:09:47 McDonald's Race Across America '86
Women				
6/15/82	Ann Kovich		Santa Monica to NYC	14:14:54
7/13/82	Susan Notorangelo		Santa Monica to NYC	11:16:15
8/1/85	Susan Notorangelo-Haldeman	3,120.2	Huntington Beach to Atlantic City, NJ	10:14:25 Race Across America '85
7/16/86	Elaine Mariolle	3,107.3	Huntington Beach to Atlantic City, NJ	10:02:04 McDonald's Race Across America '86
Trans-Canada				
6/28/82	Wayne Phillips	3,800	Vancouver, B.C. to Halifax, Nova Scotia	14:22:47
U.S. Transcontinental Tandem West-East				
5/17/87	Pete Penseyres-Lon Haldeman	2,920	Huntington Beach, Calif to Atlantic City, NJ	7:14:55
US Transcontinental East-West				
7/2/81	Lon Haldeman (solo/unpaced)		NY to Santa Monica	12:18:49
7/7/81	Len Vreeland (solo/recumbent)		NY to Santa Monica	14:21:13
US Double Transcontinental				
10/84	Victor Vincente		Santa Monica to NY to Santa Monica	36:08:00
7/14/81	Lon Haldeman		NY to Santa Monica to NY	24:02:34
US 24-Hour Outdoor Track (San Diego Velodrome)				
10/29–30/88	Jim Elliott	548.9 mi		
US 24-Hour Indoor Track (Olympic Velodrome, Montreal, Canada)				
3/14/85	Michael Secrest	516 mi, 427 yd		
US 24-Hour Roller Record				
1/21/77	Bruce Hall	792.209 mi		
5/14/83	Richard Gunther	838.7 mi		
US Transcontinental West-East				
9/10/84	Sean O'Keefe 11 years (born 6/6/73), youngest to cross US on a bicycle		Santa Monica to NY	24 days
US West Coast				
6/27/84	Michael Shermer		Seattle to San Diego 3:23:49	

*US records from the Ultra Marathon Cycling Association, as of September 1986, courtesy of John Marino.

Tour de France

For the first time in 83 years the Tour de France was won by a non-European, Greg LeMond (b June 26, 1961) of Reno, Nevada. He beat the field in 1986, including his teammate Bernard Hinault (b Nov 14, 1954) (France) who won in 1978, 79, 81, 82 and 85. This race takes about 23 days to stage annually. The longest ever was in 1926 when it lasted for 29 days. It is estimated that as many as 10 million people watch some part of it. There were 198 cyclists racing in 1988.

The greatest number of wins in the Tour de France (inaugurated 1903) is 5 by Jacques Anquetil (b Jan 8, 1934) (France), who won in 1957, 1961–64; Eddy

FIRST AMERICAN WINNER of Tour de France: Greg LeMond of Reno, Nev, became the only non-European in 83 years to win the 23-day race in 1986. He was also the only American to win the World Professional Road Championship in Switzerland in 1983. (All-Sport)

Merckx (b June 17, 1945) (Belgium) who won five titles (1969–72, 1974); and Bernard Hinault (see above) who also won 5 times.

The closest race ever was in 1968 when after 2,898.7 mi over 25 days (June 27–July 21) Jan Jannssen (Netherlands) (b May 19, 1940) beat Herman van Springel (Belgium) in Paris by 38 sec. The longest course was 3,569 miles on June 20 to July 18, 1926. The length of the course is usually about 3,000 miles, but varies from year to year.

The fastest average speed was 24.18 mph by Pedro Delgado (Spain) in 1988. The greatest number of participants were 209 starters in 1987.

Cycling's Triple Crown

In 1987, Stephen Roche (b Nov 28, 1959) of Dublin, Ireland became only the second cyclist in history to win the Tour of Italy, the Tour de France and the World Road Championship all in the same year. Eddy Merckx of Belgium did it in 1974.

Coast-to-Coast Cycling

The US transcontinental men's unpaced record (West Coast to East Coast) has been cut in half since 1972. Pete Penseyres, 43, of Fallbrook, Calif, set the current mark of 8 days 9 hours 47 min in July 1986 during the Race Across America (3,107.3 mi, Huntington Beach, Calif to Atlantic City, NJ). The US transcontinental women's record of 10 days 2 hours 4 min, held by Elaine Mariolle of Berkeley, Calif, was also set during the '86 RAAM.

Pete Penseyres and Lon Haldeman of Harvard, Ill,

set a transcontinental tandem bicycle record of 7 days, 14 hours, 55 min (Huntington Beach, Calif to Atlantic City, NJ) in May 1987. It was the fastest-ever US crossing on a bicycle.

Wayne Phillips of Richmond, BC, rode across Canada from Vancouver, BC, to Halifax, Nova Scotia, covering the 3,800 miles in 14 days 22 hours 47 min June 13–28, 1982.

Longest One-Day Race

The longest single-day "massed start" road race is the Bordeaux-to-Paris, France, event of 342 to 385 miles. Usually paced over all or part of the route, the highest average speed in 1981 was 29.32 mph by Herman van Springel (Belgium) (b Aug 14, 1943) for 363.1 mi in 13 hours 35 min 18 sec.

Touring

The most participants in a bicycle tour were 27,220 in the 56-mile London-to-Brighton Bike Ride on June 15, 1986.

The longest cycle tour on record is the more than 402,000 miles amassed by Walter Stolle (b Sudetenland, 1926), an itinerant lecturer. From Jan 24, 1959 to Dec 12, 1976, he covered 159 countries, had 5 bicycles stolen and suffered 231 other robberies,

24-HOUR RECORDHOLDER: Michael Secrest cycled 516 + mi indoors unpaced in March 1985. He also won the 1987 Race Across America in 9 days 11 hours 35 min. (Red Roof Inns, Inc, Ohio)

FASTEST WOMAN CYCLIST: Jeanne Longo (France) (b Oct 31, 1958) dominates the field, having set women's records for 60-min runs, unpaced, at sea level, altitude and unpaced standing starts for 3 km, 5 km, 20 km and most km in 1 hour, Sept 13–19, 1987, all at Colorado Springs, Colo. However, she failed a drugs test on Sept 13, so these records have not been ratified. (Mike Powell/All Sport)

along with over 1,000 flat tires. From 1922 to Dec 25, 1973, Tommy Chambers (1903–84) of Glasgow, Scotland, rode a verified total of 799,405 miles.

John Hathaway of Vancouver, Canada, covered 50,600 miles, visiting every continent, from Nov 10, 1974 to Oct 6, 1976.

Veronica and Colin Scargill, of Bedford, England, traveled 18,020 miles around the world, on a tandem, Feb 25, 1974–Aug 27, 1975.

Endurance

Tommy Godwin (1912–75) (GB) in the 365 days of 1939 covered 75,065 miles or an average of 205.65 miles per day. He then completed 100,000 miles in 500 days to May 14, 1940. Jay Aldous and Matt DeWaal cycled 14,290 miles on a round trip from Place Monument, Salt Lake City, Utah, in 106 days, Apr 2–July 16, 1984.

Nicholas Mark Sanders (b Nov 26, 1957) of Glossop, Eng, circumnavigated the world (13,035 road miles) in 78 days, 3 hours 30 min between July 5 and Sept 21, 1985.

Carlos Vieira cycled for 191 hours "non-stop" at Leiria, Portugal June 8–16, 1983. The distance covered was 1,496.04 mi, and he was moving 98.7% of the time.

Daniel Buettner, Bret Anderson, Martin Engel and Anne Knabe cycled the length of the Americas, from Prudhoe Bay, Alaska to the Beagle Channel, Ushuaia, Argentina from Aug 8, 1986–June 13, 1987. They cycled a total distance of 15,266 mi.

Highest Altitude

Adrian Crane (UK) cycled from the lower summit of Mount Chimborazo, an altitude of 20,561 ft, to the town of Riobamba, Ecuador, at 9,022 ft on May 11, 1986. His brother Richard and cousin Nicholas Crane held the previous record, from Mount Kilimanjaro, Tanzania, at 19,340 ft.

Six-Day Races

The greatest number of wins in six-day races is 88 out of 233 events by Patrick Sercu (b June 27, 1944), of Belgium, 1964–83.

Bicycle Balancing

David Steed (b 1959) of Tucson, Ariz, balanced on his bicycle for 24 hours 6 min non-stop Mar 10–11, 1986 at the NYC Coliseum. Sitting astride his bike in a carpeted area of about 15 ft by 15 ft, Steed remained upright without a break, without touching a foot to the floor and without either of his bike wheels ever making a complete revolution forward or backwards.

Roller Cycling

The greatest distance achieved in 24 hours is 1,560.73 mi by Piet Vitten (Neth) at Midden, Beemster, The Netherlands on Mar 8–9, 1980. James Baker (US) achieved a record 129.1 mph on rollers at the Univ of Arizona in Tucson on Dec 6, 1986.

In a marathon try, Gilbert Bil rode 85 hours 24 min at De Weesper, Amsterdam, The Netherlands, Oct 10–14, 1986.

Unicycle Records

The tallest unicycle ever mastered is one 101 ft 9 in tall ridden by Steve McPeak (with a safety wire or mechanic suspended to an overhead crane) for a distance of 376 ft in Las Vegas in Oct 1980. The free-style riding of even taller unicycles must inevitably lead to serious injury or fatality.

Hanspeter Beck of Jindabyne, S Australia unicycled 3,876.08 mi in 51 days, 23 hours, 25 min, June 30–Aug 20, 1985, going from W Australia to Melbourne. Brian Davis of Tillicoultry, Scotland rode 901 mi from Land's End to John O'Groats May 16–June 4, 1980 in 19 days 1¾ hours. Floyd Beattie of Athens, O, set a record for 100 mi in 7 hours 18 min 55 sec on Oct 11, 1986. The sprint record from a standing start over 100 meters is 14.89 sec by Floyd Grandall of Pontiac, Mich, in Tokyo, Japan on Mar 24, 1980.

SIX DAYS ON THE TRACK: Patrick Sercu (Belgium) (leading) won 88 six-day races out of 233 events for a 39% record. The durable cyclist also holds 3 professional speed records for 1 kilometer.

EQUESTRIAN SPORTS

Origin

Men have ridden horses for 5,000 years. The Athenian general and historian Xenophon wrote a treatise on horsemanship 2,300 years ago, but it was not until the 16th century that schools of horsemanship, or equitation, became established, primarily in Italy and then in France. In Britain the first official competitions were held in 1865 under the auspices of the Royal Dublin Society, while the first jumping contest was at the Agricultural Hall, London in 1869. The dressage event was a direct outcome of the exercises taught in the early Italian and French academies. The Three-Day Event developed from cavalry endurance rides, one of the earliest being from Vienna to Berlin in 1892. There was a jumping event in the Olympic Games of 1900, but a full equestrian program was not instituted until 1912. The World Cup was instituted in 1979.

Most Olympic Medals

The greatest number of Olympic gold medals is 5 by Hans-Günter Winkler (b July 24, 1926) (W Germany), who won 4 team gold medals as captain in 1956, 60, 64 and 72, and won the individual Grand Prix in 1956. The most team wins in the Prix des Nations is 6 by Germany in 1936, 56, 60, 64, and as Federal Republic of Germany (W Ger) in 1972 and 1988.

The lowest score obtained by a winner for jumping was no faults, by Frantisek Ventura (Czechoslovakia) on "Eliot" in 1928, and by Alwin Schockemöhle (W Germany) on "Warwick Rex" in 1976. Pierre Jonqueres d'Oriola (France) is the only two-time winner of the individual gold medal, in 1952 and 1964.

In dressage, Henri St Cyr (Swe) has won four golds, including a unique two in the individual competition 1952–56. St Cyr was also a member of the winning Swedish team in 1948, but subsequently they were disqualified because one of them was not a military officer as the rules at that time decreed.

A record 7 Olympic team gold medals have been won in dressage by Germany in 1928, 36 and 64, and as W Germany in 1968, 76, 84 and 88.

Emphasizing the increasingly successful role of women in this sport, the most medals ever won is five by Liselott Linsenhoff (W Ger) between 1956 and 1972. In the Three-Day Event, Charles Pahud de Mortanges (Neth) won a record four gold medals, including two individual titles, from 1924 to 1932, as well as a team silver.

The 1988 gold medal winners were:

Individual Dressage: Nicole Uphoff (W Ger)
Individual Show Jumping: Pierre Durand (France)
Three-Day Event Individual: Mark Todd (NZ)
Team Dressage: W Ger
Team Jumping: W Ger
Three-Day Team Event: W Ger

World Team Championship

Instituted in 1965 as the President's Trophy and renamed the Prince Philip Trophy in 1985, it has been won a record 11 times by Great Britain, 1965, 67, 70, 72–74, 77–79, 83, 85.

Driving

The most wins at the biennial World Driving Championships (inst 1972) is 3, by Great Britain in 1972, 74 and 80; and by Hungary in 1976, 78 and 84.

World Cup

The only World Cup (inst 1969) double winner is Conrad Homfield (US) (b Dec 25, 1951) in 1980 and 1985.

Jumping Records

The official *Fédération Equestre Internationale* high jump record is 8 ft 1¼ in by "Huaso," ridden by Capt A. Larraguibel Morales (Chile) at Santiago, Chile, on Feb 5, 1949, but there are several reports of much higher jumps. The most extreme is a 9 ft 6 in clearance by "Ben Bolt" at the 1938 Royal Horse Show in Sydney, Australia.

The greatest height by a woman is 7 ft 8 in by Katrina Towns-Musgrove (Aust) on "Big John" in Cairns in 1978.

The greatest recorded height reached bareback is 7 ft by Michael Whitaker (b Mar 17, 1960) on "Red Flight" in Dublin, Eire, Nov 14, 1982.

The official long jump over water record is 27 ft 6¾ in by "Something" ridden by André Ferreira at Johannesburg, S Africa on April 26, 1975, but there have been many longer jumps recorded. The Australian record is 32 ft 10 in by "Monarch" at Brisbane in 1951, but "Solid Gold" jumped 36 ft 3 in at the Wagga Show, NSW, Australia, in 1936. In the US "Heatherbloom," ridden by Dick Donnelly, is reputed to have cleared 37 ft when high jumping 8 ft 3 in at Richmond, Va, in 1903. The most extreme claim made is for "Jerry M," the 1912 Grand National Steeplechase winner at Aintree, Eng, who is alleged to have jumped 40 ft over water there.

World Titles

The men's world championship in show jumping (instituted 1953) has been won twice by Hans-Günter Winkler of W Germany in 1954 and 1955, and Raimondo d'Inzeo of Italy in 1956 and 1960. The women's title (1965–74) was won twice by Jane "Janou" Tissot (*née* Lefebvre) of France on "Rocket" in 1970 and 1974. The three-day event was won 3 times by Bruce Davidson (US) (b Dec 13, 1949) in 1974, 1978 and 1986.

Gail Greenough of Canada is the first woman to win the individual gold at the World Championships in Aachen, W Germany in 1986.

Longest Ride

Henry G. Perry, a stockman, rode 14,021 mi around Australia in 157 days, May 1–Oct 4, 1985, using 6 horses. This topped the record of Thomas L. Gaddie (US) who rode 11,217.2 miles from Dallas, Tex, to Fairbanks, Alaska, and back in 295 days, Feb 12–Dec 2, 1980, with 7 horses.

The Bicentennial "Great American Horse Race," begun on May 31, 1976, from Saratoga Springs, NY, to Sacramento, Calif (3,500 miles) was won by Virl Norton on "Lord Fauntleroy"—a mule—in 98 days. His actual riding time was 315.47 hours.

First Solo Transcontinental Journey

Nan Jane Aspinwall left San Francisco on horseback on Sept 1, 1910. She arrived in NYC on July 8, 1911, having covered 4,500 miles in 301 days, 108 of which she spent traveling.

Marathon

Michael Jones rode for 101 hours at Redruth Plains, Queensland, Australia, June 19–23, 1984.

Ken Northdruft rode for 112½ hours at Kingsthorpe, Queensland, Australia, Aug 31–Sept 4, 1985.

"HEATHERBLOOM": Flying like a bird, this horse is said to have covered 37 feet in clearing an 8-foot-3-inch jump in 1903. She is here making a demonstration jump of 8 feet 2 inches in 1905.

THREE WORLD FOIL TITLES are held by Cornelia Hanisch (W Germany)—1979, 81, and 85—who shows great poise here in defending against an advance. (All-Sport)

FENCING

Origins

Fencing (fighting with single sticks) was practiced as a sport, or as part of a religious ceremony, in Egypt as early as *c.* 1360 BC.

Swords have been in use as combat weapons since ancient times. The first indication of sword fencing as a sport is on a relief in the temple of Medinet Habu, Luxor, Egypt built by Rameses III about 1190 BC.

The modern sport developed directly from the dueling, often to the death, of the Middle Ages. In the early 14th century the Marxbrüder Fencing Guild was flourishing in Frankfurt, Germany. In Britain, Edward I had specifically banned fencing tournaments in the City of London in 1285. Henry VIII, some 250 years later, founded the Corporation of Masters of Defence which was probably the first governing body of any sport in Britain. The mask was introduced by a Frenchman, La Boessière, in about 1780.

There are three swords used today. With the foil, first used as the practical sword in the 17th century, only the trunk of the body is acceptable as a target. The épée, established in the mid-19th century, is rather heavier and more rigid than the foil and has the whole body as a valid target. The saber, introduced by the Italians in the late-19th century, has cutting edges on the front and back of the blade, and can only score on the whole body from the waist upwards. In foil and épée, hits are scored with the point of the weapon, but with the saber, scoring is allowed using all of the front edge and part of the back edge of the blade.

US Championships

Peter Westbrook (b Apr 1952) of the NY Fencers Club won the saber title in the Div I National Championships for the 10th time in 1986, tying Norman Armitage's record in number of titles and setting a record in number of consecutive titles, 8, for any event in the Fencing Championships. Steve Mormondo (b Aug 1955) of the NY Fencers Club won the 1987 saber championship for his first title.

Michael Marx of Salle Auriol in Portland, Ore (b July 1958) won the 1987 Div I Foil Championships for the 6th time, tying the record set by Joseph Levis in 1954, and Lt George Calman in 1931.

Lee Shelley of Hackensack, NJ (b May 1956), representing Salle Santelli of NJ, won his 3rd épée title, closing on Paul Pesthy's 5 titles in men's épée. Tim Glass of Houston, Tex (b Dec 1955) representing Bayou City Blades won his 2nd épée title, 8 years after his first title.

Caitlin Bilodeaux of Concord, Mass (b Mar 1965) representing the NY Fencers Club won the women's foil title for the second time, having captured her second NCAA title in 1987. She also won two gold medals in the 1987 Pan Amer Games, one individual and one team.

In women's épée, now in its 5th year, Donna Stone (NJ) won her first title in 1987, and is one of the few women fencers to be nationally ranked in both foil and épée.

Most Olympic Titles

Fencing was included in the first modern Olympics in 1896.

The greatest number of individual Olympic gold medals won is 3 by Ramon Fonst (Cuba) (1883–1959) in 1900 and 1904 (2) and Nedo Nadi (Italy) (1894–1952) in 1912 and 1920 (2). Nadi also won 3 team gold medals in 1920 making a then unprecedented total of 5 gold medals at one Olympic meet.

Edoardo Mangiarotti (Italy) (b Apr 7, 1919) holds the record of 13 Olympic medals (6 gold, 5 silver, 2 bronze), won in the foil and épée competitions from 1936 to 1960.

The most gold medals won by a woman is four (one individual, three team) by Elena Novikova *née* Belova (USSR) (b July 28, 1947) from 1968 to 1976, and the record for all medals is 7 (2 gold, 3 silver, 2 bronze), by Ildikó Sagi-Retjö (formerly Ujlaki- Retjö) (Hungary) (b May 11, 1937) from 1960 to 1976.

The 1988 Olympics gold medalists were:

MEN
Individual Epee: Arnd Schmitt (W Ger)
Individual Foil: Stefano Cerioni (Italy)
Individual Saber: Jean Francois Lamour (France), the only repeat winner from 1984
Team Epee: France (Olivier Lenglet, Eric Srecki, Philippe Riboud, Jean Michel Henry, Frederic Delpla)
Team Foil: USSR (Aleksandr Romankov, Ilgar Mamedov, Vladimir Aptsiaouri, Anvar Ibraguimov, Boris Koretskii)
Team Saber: Hungary (Gyorgy Nebald, Bence Szabo, Imre Bujdoso, Imre Gedoevari, Laszlo Csongradi)

WOMEN
Individual Foil: Anja Fichtel (W Ger)
Team Foil: W Ger (Anja Fichtel, Zita Funkenhauser, Christiane Weber, Sabine Bau, Annette Klug)

World Championships

Other than at the Olympic Games, genuine world championships were not introduced until 1937, although the European titles, inaugurated in 1921 for men, were styled ''world championships.''

The greatest number of individual world titles won is 5 by Aleksandr Romankov (USSR) (b Nov 7, 1953) at foil 1974, 77, 79, 82 and 83, but note that Christian d'Oriola (France) won 4 world titles (1947, 49, 53–54) and also won 2 individual Olympic titles. Four women foilists have won 3 world titles: Helene Mayer (Germany), Ellen Müller-Preiss (Austria), Ilona Schacherer-Elek (Hungary), and Cornelia Hanisch (W Germ) (b June 12, 1952) 1979, 81, 85. Of these only Ilona Schacherer-Elek also won 2 individual Olympic titles (1936 and 48).

Amateur Fencing Association

The most titles won at one weapon is 10 at women's foil by Gillian Sheen (now Donaldson), 1949, 51–58, 60.

BALLET WITH SWORDS: Michael Marx (left) bends precariously as he duels with foils to win the silver medal in the 1985 US men's championship. (US Fencing Federation)

FORWARD LEADS IOWA to the university's first female field hockey NCAA championship. In 1986, Liz Tchon (#3), junior from Medford Lakes, NJ, helped Iowa defeat NH in overtime, 2–1. (Univ. of Iowa)

FIELD HOCKEY

Origins

A representation of two players with curved snagging sticks apparently in an orthodox "bully" position was found in Tomb No. 17 at Beni Hasan, Egypt, and has been dated to *c*. 2050 BC. There is a reference to the game in Lincolnshire, England, in 1277. The Fédération Internationale de Hockey was formed on Jan 7, 1924.

Highest Attendance

There were 65,165 at the women's hockey match between Eng and the US at Wembley, London, on Mar 11, 1978.

1988 Olympic Gold Medalists

Men: Great Britain (also winner in 1908 and 1920) Women: Australia

Highest International Score

The highest score in international field hockey was when India defeated the US 24–1 at Los Angeles, in the 1932 Olympic Games. The Indians were Olympic Champions from the re-inception of Olympic hockey in 1928 until 1960, when Pakistan beat them 1–0 at Rome. They had their eighth win in 1980. Of the 6 Indians who have won 3 Olympic gold medals, two have also won a silver medal—Leslie Claudius in 1948, 1952, 1956 and 1960 (silver), and Udham Singh in 1952, 1956, 1964 and 1960 (silver).

The highest score in a women's international match occurred when England defeated France 23–0 at Merton, Surrey, on Feb 3, 1923. A women's tournament was added to the Olympic Games in 1980, and the winners have been Zimbabwe in 1980, The Netherlands in 1984, and Australia in 1988.

Greatest Goalkeeping

Richard James Allen (b June 4, 1902) (India) did not concede a goal during the 1928 Olympic Tournament and only a total of 3 in the following two Olympics of 1932 and 1936. In these three Games India scored a total of 102 goals.

Longest Game

The longest international game on record was one of 145 min (into the sixth period of extra time), when Netherlands beat Spain 1–0 in the Olympic tournament at Mexico City on Oct 25, 1968.

Most Goals Scored

The greatest number of goals scored in international hockey is 150 by Paul Litjens (Neth) (b Nov 9, 1947) in 112 games.

Marathon

Two teams of 11 from KMHC Waalwijk at Waalwijk, The Netherlands, played for 48 hours, June 24–26, 1988.

FISHING

Origins

From time immemorial men have fished the seas and rivers of the world for food, but fishing for pleasure and leisure seems to have been practiced in Egypt, according to wall paintings, from the 5th Dynasty, 2470–2320 BC. On tomb inscriptions, Amenemhat, a prince of Beni Hasan, is described as "overseer of the swamps of enjoyment," a reference interpreted as fishing grounds.

Freshwater Casting

The longest freshwater cast ratified under ICF (International Casting Federation) rules is 574 ft 2 in by Walter Kummerow (W Germany), for the Bait Distance Double-Handed 30-g event held at Lenzerheide, Switzerland, in the 1968 Championships.

The longest Fly Distance Double-Handed cast is 257 ft 2 in by Sverne Scheen (Norway) also set at Lenzerheide in Sept 1968.

Longest Fight

The longest recorded fight between a fisherman and a fish is 32 hours 5 min by Donal Heatley (NZ) (b 1938) with a black marlin (estimated length 20 ft and weight 1,500 lb) off Mayor Island off Tauranga, New Zealand, Jan 21–22, 1968. It towed the 12-ton launch 50 miles before breaking the line.

World Championships

The *Confédération Internationale de la Pêche Sportive* championships were inaugurated as European championships in 1953. They were recognized as World Championships in 1957. France won 12 times between 1956 and 1981 and Robert Tesse (France) took the individual title uniquely three times, 1959–60, 65. The record weight (team) is 76 lb 8 oz in 3 hours by W Germany in the Neckar at Mannheim, W Germany on Sept 21, 1980. The individual record is 37 lb 7 oz by Wolf-Rüdiger Kremkus (W Germany) at Mannheim on Sept 20, 1980. The most fish caught is 652 by Jacques Isenbaert (Belgium) at Dunajvaros, Yugoslavia on Aug 27, 1967.

Most Fish Caught in a Season

In 77 days of fishing from Apr 1 to Oct 31, 1984, David Romeo of East Meadow, NY, caught on rod and reel 3,001 largemouth bass in the fresh waters of NY State and Florida, the most ever caught in a

CAUGHT 3,001 BASS in one season: The champ David Romeo of East Meadow, NY holds up a 5 lb-5 oz, 21⅝-in-long catch he made in 1986. (Photo by Bruce Cooper)

season. Mr. Romeo, who doesn't like eating fish but enjoys catching them, threw back all but 24 of them for this and legal reasons. His log books helped the environment conservation people to make "informed bass management decisions."

Largemouth Bass

A record of 22 lb 4 oz for a fish caught in Montgomery Lake, Georgia, by George W. Perry was set on June 2, 1932, and although millions of fishermen have tried to break this record since then, it still stands.

Largest Catches

Yet to be ratified is the largest fish ever caught by rod and line: A great white shark, 18 ft 9 in long, weighing 3,450 lb was landed off Montauk Marine Basin, LI, NY in August 1986 by Donnie Braddick and Frank Mundus. The shark fought for two hours, but this could not be accepted as a record because the men used a 150-lb test nylon line, heavier than the 130-lb IGFA limit.

FISHING WORLD RECORDS

Selected Sea and Freshwater fish records taken by tackle as ratified by the International Game Fish Association to Nov 6, 1987.

Species	Weight in lb	oz	Name of Angler	Location	Date
Amberjack	155	10	Joseph Dawson	Challenger Bank, Bermuda	June 24, 1981
Barracuda††	83	0	K. J. W. Hackett§§	Lagos, Nigeria	Jan 13, 1952
Bass (Largemouth)	22	4	George W. Perry	Montgomery Lake, Ga	June 2, 1932
Bass (Smallmouth)	11	15	David L. Hayes	Dale Hollow Lake, Ky	July 9, 1955
Bass (Giant Sea)	563	8	James D. McAdam, Jr	Anacapa Island, Calif	Aug 20, 1968
Bass (Striped)	78	8	Albert R. McReynolds	Atlantic City, NJ	Sept 21, 1982
Bluefish	31	12	James M. Hussey	Hatteras, NC	Jan 30, 1972
Carp†	75	11	Leo van der Gugten	Lac de St. Cassien, France	May 21, 1987
Cod	98	12	Alphonse J. Bielevich	Isle of Shoals, NH	June 8, 1969
Flounder	22	7	Charles Nappi	Montauk, LI, NY	Sept 15, 1975
Grouper (Black)	83	8	Phillip B. Reid	Panama City, Fla	Apr 3, 1986
Grouper (Black)	83	8	Thomas J. Hardesty	Marco Is, Fla	June 8, 1986
Halibut (Atlantic)	250	0	Louis P. Sirard	Gloucester, Mass	July 3, 1981
Mackerel (King)	90	0	Norton I. Thomton	Key West, Fla	Feb 16, 1976
Mackerel, Spanish	13	0	Robert Cranton	Ocracoke Inlet, NC	Nov 4, 1987
Marlin (Black)	1,560	0	Alfred C. Glassell, Jr	Cabo Blanco, Peru	Aug 4, 1953
Marlin (Atlantic Blue)	1,282	0	Larry Martin	St Thomas, US VI	Aug 6, 1977
Marlin (Pacific Blue)	1,376	0	Jay Wm. deBeaubien	Kaaiwi Point, Kona, Hawaii	May 31, 1982
Marlin (Striped)	494	0	Bill Boniface	Tutukaka, NZ	Jan 16, 1986
Marlin (White)	181	14	Evandro Luiz Coser	Vitoria, Brazil	Dec 8, 1979
Perch (Yellow)	4	3	Dr C C Abbot	Bordentown, NJ	May 1865
Pike (Northern)	55	1	Lothar Louis	Lake of Grefeern, W Ger	Oct 16, 1986
Sailfish (Atlantic)	128	1	Harm Steyn	Luanda, Angola	Mar 27, 1974
Sailfish (Pacific)	221	0	C. W. Stewart	Santa Cruz I, Ecuador	Feb 12, 1947
Salmon (Chinook)§	97	4	Les Anderson	Kenai River, Alaska	May 17, 1985
Salmon (Coho)	31	0	Mrs. Lee Hallberg	Cowichan Bay, BC, Canada	Oct 11, 1947
Salmon, Sockeye	15	3	Stan Roach	Kenai River, Alaska	Aug 9, 1987
Shark (Blue)	437	0	Peter Hyde	Catherine Bay, NSW, Aust	Oct 2, 1976
Shark (Hammerhead)	991	0	Allen Ogle	Sarasota, Fla	May 30, 1982
Shark (Mako)**	1,080	0	James L. Melanson	Montauk, NY	Aug 26, 1979
Shark (White or Man-eating)	2,664	0***	Alfred Dean	Ceduna, S Aust	Apr 21, 1959
Shark (Porbeagle)	465	0	Jorge Potier	Cornwall, England	July 23, 1976
Shark (Thresher)‡	802	0	Dianne North	Tutukaka, NZ	Feb 8, 1981
Shark (Tiger)	1,780	0	Walter Maxwell	Cherry Grove, SC	June 14, 1964
Snapper (Red)	46	8	E. Lane Nichols III	Destin, Fla	Oct 1, 1985
Sturgeon‡‡	468	0	Joey Pallotta, III	Benicia, Calif	July 9, 1983
Swordfish	1,182	0	L. E. Marron	Iquique, Chile	May 7, 1953
Tarpon	283	0	M. Salazar	Lake Maracaibo, Venez	Mar 19, 1956
Trout (Brook)	14	8	Dr. W. J. Cook	Nipigon R. Ont, Can	July 1916
Trout (Lake)¶	65	0	Larry Daunis	Great Bear Lake, NWT, Can	Aug 8, 1970
Trout (Rainbow)	42	2	David Robert White	Bell Is, Alaska	June 22, 1970
Tuna (Allison or Yellowfin)	388	12	Curt Wiesenhutter	San Benedicto Is, Mex	Apr 1, 1977
Tuna (Atlantic Big-eyed)	375	8	Cecil Browne	Ocean City, Md	Aug 26, 1977
Tuna (Pacific Big-eyed)	435	0	Dr Russel V. A. Lee	Cabo Blanco, Peru	Apr 17, 1957
Tuna (Bluefin)	1,496	0	Ken Fraser	Aulds Cove, Nova Scotia	Oct 26, 1979
Wahoo	149	0	John Pirovano	Cat Cay, Bahamas	June 15, 1962
Walleye	25	0	Mabry Harper	Old Hickory Lake, Tenn	Apr 1, 1960
Weakfish	19	2	Dennis R. Rooney	Jones Beach, NY	Oct 11, 1984

††A barracuda weighing 103 lb 4 oz was caught on an untested line by Chester Benet at West End, Bahamas, on Aug 11, 1932. Another weighing 48 lb 6 oz was caught barehanded by Thomas B. Pace at Panama City Beach, Fla, on Apr 19, 1974. §§Hackett was only 11 years 137 days old at the time. †A carp weighing 83 lb 8 oz was taken (not by rod) near Pretoria, South Africa. A 60-lb specimen was taken by bow and arrow by Ben A. Topham in Wythe Co, Va, on July 5, 1970. §A salmon weighing 126 lb 8 oz was taken (not by rod) near Petersburg, Alaska. **A 1,295-lb specimen was taken by two anglers off Natal, South Africa on March 17, 1939, and a 1,500-lb specimen harpooned inside Durban Harbour, South Africa, in 1933. ‡W. W. Dowding caught a 922-lb thresher shark in 1937 on an untested line. ‡‡An 834-lb sturgeon was landed (not by a rod) by Garry Oling at Albion, BC, Canada, from the Fraser River on Aug 11, 1981. ¶A 102-lb trout was taken from Lake Athabasca, northern Saskatchewan, Canada, on Aug 8, 1961. ***Unofficial 3,450-lb specimen caught on overweight line, Aug 1986 off Montauk, NY.

The largest fish ever caught on a rod is an officially ratified man-eating great white shark (*Carcharodon carcharias*) weighing 2,664 lb, and measuring 16 ft 10 in long, caught by Alf Dean at Denial Bay, near Ceduna, South Australia, on Apr 21, 1959. In June 1978 a great white shark measuring 29 ft 6 in in length and weighing over 10,000 lb was harpooned and landed by fishermen in the harbor of San Miguel, Azores.

A white pointer shark weighing 3,388 lb was

RECORD CATCH: E. Lane Nichols III holds a prize 46 lb 8 oz red snapper that he caught Oct 1, 1985 in Destin, Fla. (IGFA photo)

offered a $250,000 reward for landing an all-tackle world record fish in one of four categories.

McReynolds, 36, and his friend Pat Erdman were fishing from a jetty in their hometown, Atlantic City, NJ, on the night of Sept 21, 1982, when McReynolds hooked and, after a 2-hour fight, landed a 78-lb-8-oz striped bass—a world record for rod and reel. As one ordeal had ended, another began. McReynolds had to wait for the IGFA and ABU-Garcia to determine that the record was legitimate—a process that took nearly 5 months. Testing even included having the fish x-rayed to determine no stones or weights had been added to make the fish heavier.

It all ended happily on Feb 11, 1983, at the Explorers Club in NYC when McReynolds received a check for $250,000—the most money ever paid for a fish.

A claim has been made that two fishermen won $500,000 each in a fishing contest in Puget Sound, Wash in 1983. The objective was to catch one of 8 tagged fish. The two reportedly succeeded and split the $1 million prize.

caught on a rod by Clive Green off Albany, W Australia, on Apr 26, 1976, but this will remain unratified as whale meat was used as bait.

The largest marine animal ever killed by *hand* harpoon was a blue whale 97 ft in length by Archer Davidson in Twofold Bay, NSW, Australia, in 1910. Its tail flukes measured 20 ft across and its jaw bone 23 ft 4 in.

The biggest single freshwater catch ever ratified was on the Snake River, Idaho, in 1956 when Willard Cravens caught a white sturgeon weighing 360 lb. However, that may not be the last word as two years previously, in the same river, Glenn Howard claims to have caught one which weighed 394 lb.

The heaviest game fish caught on rod and line is a 468-lb sturgeon by Joey Pallotta on July 9, 1983 off Benicia, Calif. An 834-lb freshwater sturgeon was *landed* by Garry Oling from the Fraser River, Albion, Brit Columbia, on Aug 11, 1981.

Most Valuable Fish

It was a modern version of an old fairy tale. When Al McReynolds went fishing one stormy night, the fish he caught brought fame and fortune. In this case, the magic was supplied by ABU-Garcia, a leading manufacturer of fishing tackle, through a contest that

DUEL WITH SWORDFISH: Don Mann caught each of the 9 IGFA-recognized species of billfish within one year.

Smallest Catch

The smallest fish ever to win a competition was a smelt weighing 1/16 of an oz, caught by Peter Christian at Buckenham Ferry, Norfolk, England, on Jan 9, 1977. This beat 107 other competitors who failed to catch anything.

Spear-Fishing

The largest fish ever taken underwater was an 804-lb giant black grouper by Don Pinder of the Miami Triton Club, Fla, in 1955.

FOOTBAG

The sport originated in Oregon in 1972 and was invented by John Stalberger (US).

"Footbag consecutive," intercepting a footbag (see photo) in flight and keeping it airborne by kicking or striking it with the feet and knees, is the activity that started it all. The concept of this game is simple: keep the footbag in the air for the longest possible time. The contests are singles or doubles and can involve passing (one pass of 12 ft) or around a continuous circle.

"Footbag net" is played like volleyball in scoring with tennis playing rules. In singles, 2 kicks are allowed per side, and in doubles 3 kicks. The playing court is 44 ft × 20 ft with 4 quadrants and the net is 5 ft high.

"Footbag freestyle" is rhythmic, performed to music, singles or groups.

The only recordable competition is in "footbag consecutive," and the recordholders are:

Men's Singles: Ted Martin (Park Ridge, Ill) 48,825 kicks in 8 hours 11 min 25 sec on June 4, 1988.

Women's Singles: Francine Beaudry (Montreal, Canada) 15,458 kicks in 2 hours 35 min 13 sec on July 28, 1987.

Men's Doubles: Jim Caveney (Los Gatos, Calif) and Gary Lautt (Chico, Calif) 33,333 kicks in 5 hours 40 min 30 sec on July 31, 1986.

Women's Doubles: Constance Reed (Berkeley, Calif) and Marie Elsner (Grafton, Wisc) with 21,025 kicks in 3 hours 39 min 43 sec on July 31, 1986.

Men's Doubles One-Pass: Bill Langbehn and Brent Welch (both Berkeley, Calif) 10,454 kicks in 2 hours 14 min 10 sec on July 28, 1987.

Women's Doubles One-Pass: Constance Reed (Berkeley, Calif) and Tricia George (Portland, Ore) 6,136 kicks in 1 hour 4 min 23 sec on July 28, 1987.

FOOTBAG CHAMPION: Tricia Sullivan, women's world record holder in several categories, shows how she keeps the footbag aloft.

Men's Singles Timed: Derrick Fogel (Kansas City, Mo) 757 kicks in 5 min on July 26, 1988.

Women's Singles Timed: Heather Cook (Tempe, Ariz) 631 kicks in 5 min on July 26, 1988.

The largest continuous circle playing footbag is 862 people at Colorado State Univ, Ft Collins, Colo on June 25, 1986. It was organized by Scott Cleere.

FOOTBALL

Origins

The origin of modern football stems from the "Boston Game" as played at Harvard. Harvard declined to participate in the inaugural meeting of the Intercollegiate Football Association in NYC in Oct 1873, on the grounds that the proposed rules were based on the non-handling "Association" code of English football. Instead, Harvard accepted a proposal from McGill University of Montreal, which played the more closely akin English Rugby Football. The first football match under the Harvard Rules was thus played against McGill at Cambridge, Mass, in May 1874. Most sports historians point to a contest

MODERN MAJOR-COLLEGE INDIVIDUAL RECORDS
(Through 1988 Season)

Points
Most in a Game	43	Jim Brown (Syracuse)	1956
Most in a Season	234	Barry Sanders (Okla State)	1988
Most in a Career	393	Derek Schmidt (Fla State)	1984–87

Touchdowns
Most in a Game	7	Arnold Boykin (Mississippi)	1951
Most in a Season	39	Barry Sanders (Okla State)	1988
Most in a Career	59	Glenn Davis (Army)	1943–46
	59	Tony Dorsett (Pittsburgh)	1973–76

Field Goals
Most in a Game	7	Mike Prindle (W Mich)	1984
		Dale Klein (Nebraska)	1985
Most in a Season	29	John Lee (UCLA)	1984
Most in a Career	80	Jeff Jaeger (Washington)	1983–86
Most Consecutively (Career)	30	Chuck Nelson (Washington)	1981–82

Other Season Records
Yards Gained Rushing	2,628 yd	Barry Sanders (Okla State)	1988
Highest Average Gain per Rush (min. 150 attempts)	9.35 yd	Greg Pruitt (Oklahoma)	1971
Most Passes Attempted	511	Robbie Bosco (Brigham Young)	1985
Most Passes Completed	338	Robbie Bosco (Brigham Young)	1985
Most Touchdown Passes	47	Jim McMahon (Brigham Young)	1980
Most Yards Gained Passing	4,571 yd	Jim McMahon (Brigham Young)	1980
Most Passes Caught	134	Howard Twilley (Tulsa)	1965
Most Yards Gained on Catches	1,779 yd	Howard Twilley (Tulsa)	1965
Most Touchdown Passes Caught	18	Tom Reynolds (San Diego St)	1969
Most Passes Intercepted by	14	Al Worley (Washington)	1968
Highest Punting Average (min. 30 punts)	49.8 yd	Reggie Roby (Iowa)	1981

between Rutgers and Princeton at New Brunswick, NJ, on Nov 6, 1869, as the first football game, but many American soccer historians regard this contest as the first intercollegiate *soccer* game. (Rutgers won the game, 6 goals to 4, and there were 25 players to a side.) In Nov 1876, a new Intercollegiate Football Association, with a pioneer membership of 5 colleges, was inaugurated at Springfield, Mass, to reconcile the conflicting versions of the sport. It was not until 1880 that the game, because of the organizational genius of Walter Camp of Yale, began to take its modern form. Among other things, he reduced the number of players on a side to 11, which is today (and defined their positions), and also replaced the scrum with the line of scrimmage.

Professional football dates from the Latrobe, Pa vs Jeannette, Pa match at Latrobe, in Aug 1895. The National Football League was founded in Canton, Ohio, in 1920, although it did not adopt its present name until 1922. The year 1969 was the final year in which professional football was divided into separate National and American Leagues, for record purposes.

College Series Records

The oldest collegiate series still contested is that between Yale and Princeton dating from 1873, or 3 years before the passing of the Springfield rules, with 111 games played through the 1988 season. The most regularly contested series is between Lafayette and Lehigh, who have met 124 times, 1884 to 1988.

Yale University became the only college to win more than 700 games when it finished the 1979 season with a total of 701 victories in 107 seasons. Yale has 746 wins in 116 seasons to the end of 1988.

Longest Streaks

The longest collegiate winning streak is 47 straight by Oklahoma. The longest unbeaten streak is 63 games (59 won, 4 tied) by Washington from 1907 to 1917. Macalaster University of St Paul, Minn, ended a record 50-game losing streak when, with 11 sec remaining in the game, a 23-yd field goal beat Mount Senario, 17–14, on Sept 6, 1980. It was Macalaster's first victory since Oct 11, 1974.

SERVICE

Most Seasons, Active Player
26 George Blanda, Chi Bears, 1949–58; Balt, 1950; AFL: Hou, 1960–66; Oak, 1967–75

Most Games Played, Lifetime
340 George Blanda, Chi Bears, 1949–58; Balt, 1950; AFL: Hou, 1960–66; Oak, 1967–75

Most Consecutive Games Played, Lifetime
282 Jim Marshall, Cleve, 1960; Minn, 1961–79

Most Seasons, Head Coach
40 George Halas, Chi Bears, 1920–29, 33–42, 46–55, 58–67

SCORING

Most Seasons Leading League
5 Don Hutson, GB, 1940–44
Gino Cappelletti, Bos, 1961, 63–66 (AFL)

Most Points, Lifetime
2,002 George Blanda, Chi Bears, 1949–58; Balt, 1950; AFL: Hou, 1960–66; Oak, 1967–75 (9-td, 943-pat, 335-fg)

Most Points, Season
176 Paul Hornung, GB, 1960 (15-td, 41-pat, 15-fg)

Most Points, Rookie Season
144 Kevin Butler, Chi Bears, 1985 (51-pat, 31-fg)

Most Points, Game
40 Ernie Nevers, Chi Cards vs Chi Bears, Nov 28, 1929 (6-td, 4-pat)

Most Consecutive Games, Scoring
151 Fred Cox, Minn 1963-73

Touchdowns

Most Seasons Leading League
8 Don Hutson, GB, 1935–38, 41–44

Most Touchdowns, Lifetime
126 Jim Brown, Cleve, 1957–65 (106-r, 20-p)

Most Touchdowns, Season
24 John Riggins, Wash (24-r), 1983

Most Touchdowns, Rookie Season
22 Gale Sayers, Chi Bears, 1965 (14-r,6-p, 1-prb, 1-krb)

Most Touchdowns, Game
6 Ernie Nevers, Chi Cards vs Chi Bears, Nov 28, 1929 (6-r)
William (Dub) Jones, Cleve vs Chi Bears, Nov 25, 1951 (4-r, 2-p)
Gale Sayers, Chi Bears vs SF, Dec 12, 1965 (4-r, 1-p, 1-prb)

Most Consecutive Games Scoring Touchdowns
18 Lenny Moore, Balt, 1963–65

Points After Touchdown

Most Seasons Leading League
8 George Blanda, Chi Bears, 1956; AFL: Hou, 1961–62; Oak, 1967–69, 72, 74

Most Points After Touchdown, Lifetime
943 (out of 959 attempts)
George Blanda, Chi Bears, 1949–58; Balt, 1950; AFL: Hou, 1960–66; Oak, 1967–69, 72, 74

Most Points After Touchdown, Season
66 Uwe von Schamann, Miami 1984

Most Points After Touchdown, Game
9 Marlin (Pat) Harder, Chi Cards vs NY, Oct 17, 1948
Bob Waterfield, LA vs Balt, Oct 22, 1950
Charlie Gogolak, Wash vs NY Giants, Nov 27, 1966

Most Consecutive Points After Touchdown
234 Tommy Davis, SF, 1959–65

Field Goals

Most Seasons Leading League
5 Lou Groza, Cleve, 1950, 52–54, 57

Most Field Goals, Lifetime
373 Jan Stenerud, KC 1967–69; GB 1980–83, Minn 1984–85

Most Field Goals, Season
35 Ali Haji-Sheikh, NY Giants, 1983

Most Field Goals, Game
7 Jim Bakken, St L vs Pitt, Sept 24, 1967

Most Consecutive Games, Field Goals
31 Fred Cox, Minn, 1968–70

Highest Percentage, Lifetime
78.24 Morten Andersen, NO, 1982–88 (151–193)

Highest Field Goal Percentage, Season
95.24 Mark Mosely, Wash, 1982 (20–21)
Eddie Murray, Det, 1988 (20–21)

Most Consecutive Field Goals
23 Mark Mosely, Wash, 1981–82

Longest Field Goal
63 yd Tom Dempsey, NO vs Det, Nov 8, 1970

RUSHING

Most Seasons Leading League
8 Jim Brown, Cleve, 1957–61, 63–65

Most Yards Gained, Lifetime
16,726 Walter Payton, Chi Bears, 1975–87

Most Yards Gained, Season
2,105 Eric Dickerson, LA Rams, 1984

Most Yards Gained, Game
275 Walter Payton, Chi Bears vs Minn, Nov 20, 1977

Most Carries, Game
45 Jamie Morris, Wash vs Cin, 1988

Longest Run from Scrimmage
99 Tony Dorsett, Dall vs Minn, Jan 3, 1983 (td)

Highest Average Gain, Lifetime (799 att)
5.2 Jim Brown, Cleve, 1957–65 (2,359–12,312)

Highest Average Gain, Game (10 att)
17.1 Marion Motley, Cleve vs Pitt, Oct 29, 1950 (11–188)

Most Touchdowns Rushing, Lifetime
110 Walter Payton, Chi Bears 1975–86

Most Touchdowns Rushing, Season
24 John Riggins, Wash, 1983

Most Touchdowns Rushing, Game
6 Ernie Nevers, Chi Cards vs Chi Bears, Nov 28, 1929

PASSING

Most Seasons Leading League
6 Sammy Baugh, Wash, 1937, 40, 43, 45, 47, 49

Most Passes Attempted, Lifetime
6,467 Fran Tarkenton, Minn, 1961–66, 72–78; NY Giants, 1967–71

Most Passes Attempted, Season
623 Dan Marino, Miami, 1986

Most Passes Attempted, Game
68 George Blanda, Hou vs Buff, Nov 1, 1964 (AFL) (37 completions)

Most Passes Completed, Lifetime
3,686 Fran Tarkenton, Minn, 1961–66, 72–78; NY Giants, 1967–71

Most Passes Completed, Season
378 Dan Marino, Miami, 1986

Most Passes Completed, Game
42 Richard Todd, NY Jets vs SF, Sept 21, 1980 (59 attempts)

Most Consecutive Passes Completed
22 Joe Montana, SF vs GB, Dec 6, 1987

Longest Pass Completion (all tds)
99 Frank Filchock (to Farkas), Wash vs Pitt, Oct 15, 1939
George Izo (to Mitchell), Wash vs Cleve, Sept 15, 1963
Karl Sweetan (to Studstill), Det vs Balt, Oct 16, 1966
C. A. Jurgensen (to Allen), Wash vs Chi Bears, Sept 15, 1968
Jim Plunkett (to Branch) LA Raiders vs Wash Oct 2, 1983
Ron Jaworski (to Quick) Phil vs Atl, Nov 10, 1985

Most Yards Gained Passing, Lifetime
47,003 Fran Tarkenton, Minn, 1961–66, 72–78; NY Giants, 1967–71

Most Yards Gained Passing, Game
554 Norm Van Brocklin, LA vs NY Yanks, Sept 28, 1951 (41–27)

Most Yards Gained Passing, Season
5,084 Dan Marino, Miami, 1984

HEISMAN TROPHY WINNER 1988: Although a junior, Barry Sanders of Oklahoma State was chosen. He set a new rushing record of 2,628 yd in a season, beating Marcus Allen's mark of 2,342 yd set in 1981.

Most Touchdown Passes, Lifetime
  342 Fran Tarkenton, Minn, 1961–66, 72–78; NY Giants, 1967–71

Most Touchdown Passes, Season
  48 Dan Marino, Miami, 1984

Most Touchdown Passes, Game
  7 Sid Luckman, Chi Bears vs NY Giants, Nov 14, 1943
     Adrian Burk, Phil vs Wash, Oct 17, 1954
     George Blanda, Hou vs NY Titans, Nov 19, 1961 (AFL)
     Y. A. Tittle, NY vs Wash, Oct 28, 1962
     Joe Kapp, Minn vs Balt, Sept 28, 1969

Most Touchdown Passes, Consecutive Games
  47 John Unitas, Balt, 1956–60

Passing Efficiency, Lifetime (1,500 att)
  63.22 Joe Montana, SF 1979–88; (2,322–3,673)

Passing Efficiency, Season (100 att)
  70.55 Ken Anderson, Cin, 1982 (309–218)

Passing Efficiency, Game (20 att)
  90.91 Ken Anderson, Cin vs Pitt, Nov 10, 1974 (22–20)

Passes Had Intercepted

Most Passes Intercepted, Game
  8 Jim Hardy, Chi Cards vs Phil, Sept 24, 1950 (39 attempts)

Most Consecutive Passes Attempted, None Intercepted
  294 Bryan (Bart) Starr, GB, 1964–65

Fewest Passes Intercepted, Season (Qualifiers)
  1 Joe Ferguson, Buff, 1976 (151 attempts)

Lowest Percentage Passes Intercepted, Lifetime (1,500 att)
  2.70 Joe Montana, SF 1979–88 (3,673–99)

Lowest Percentage Passes Intercepted, Season (Qualifiers)
  0.66 Joe Ferguson, Buff, 1976 (151–1)

PASS RECEPTIONS

Most Seasons Leading League
  8 Don Hutson, GB, 1936–37, 39, 41–45

Most Pass Receptions, Lifetime
  791 Steve Largent, Sea, 1976–88

Most Pass Receptions, Season
  106 Art Monk, Wash, 1984

Most Pass Receptions, Game
  18 Tom Fears, LA Rams vs GB, Dec 3, 1950 (189 yd)

Longest Pass Reception (all tds)
  99 Andy Farkas (Filchock), Wash vs Pitt, Oct 15, 1939
     Bobby Mitchell (Izo), Wash vs Cleve, Sept 15, 1963
     Pat Studstill (Sweetan), Det vs Balt, Oct 16, 1966
     Gerry Allen (Jurgensen), Wash vs Chi Bears, Sept 15, 1968
     Cliff Branch (Plunkett), LA Raiders vs Wash, Oct 2, 1983
     Mike Quick (Jaworski), Phil vs Atl, Nov 10, 1985

Most Consecutive Games, Pass Receptions
167   Steve Largent, Seattle, 1976–88

Most Pass Receptions by a Running Back, Game
17   Clark Gaines, NY Jets vs SF, Sept 21, 1980

Most Yards Gained Pass Receptions, Game
309   Stephone Paige, KC vs SD, Dec 22, 1985

Most Yards, Pass Receptions, Lifetime
12,686   Steve Largent, Sea, 1976–88

Touchdowns Receiving

Most Touchdown Passes, Lifetime
99   Don Hutson, GB, 1935–45

Most Touchdown Passes, Season
22   Jerry Rice, SF, 1987

Most Touchdown Passes, Game
5   Bob Shaw, Chi Cards vs Balt, Oct 2, 1950
    Kellen Winslow, SD vs Oak, Nov 22, 1981

Most Consecutive Games, Touchdown Passes
13   Jerry Rice, SF, 1987

PASS INTERCEPTIONS

Most Interceptions by, Lifetime
81   Paul Krause, Wash (28), 1964–67; Minn (53), 1968–79

Most Interceptions by, Season
14   Richard (Night Train) Lane, LA Rams, 1952

Most Interceptions by, Game
4   By 17 players, twice by Jerry Norton St L vs Wash, Nov 20, 1960; St L vs Pitt, Nov 26, 1961

Most Touchdowns Interception Returns, Lifetime
9   Ken Houston, Hou 1967–79; Wash 1973–80

Longest Return
103   Vencie Glenn, SD vs Den, Nov 29, 1987

PUNTING

Most Seasons Leading League
4   Sammy Baugh, Wash, 1940–43
    Jerrel Wilson, AFL: KC, 1965, 68; NFL: KC, 1972–73

Most Punts, Season
114   Bob Parsons, Chi, 1981

Most Punts, Lifetime
1,154   Dave Jennings, NY Giants 1974–84, NY Jets 1985—87

Longest Punt
98 yd   Steve O'Neal, NY Jets vs Den, Sept 21, 1969 (AFL)

Most Punts, Game
15   John Telchik, Phila vs NY Giants, Dec 6, 1987

Average Yardage Punting

Highest Punting Average, Lifetime (300 punts)
45.1 yd   Sammy Baugh, Wash, 1937–52 (338)

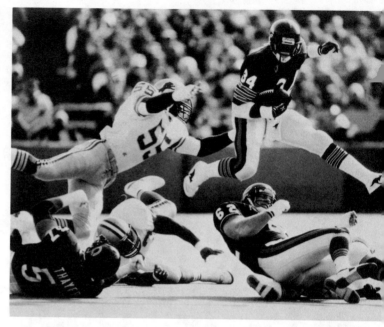

RUSHING RECORDHOLDER: Walter Payton of the 1986 Super-Bowl Champion Chicago Bears set a record of 77 games with 100 yds or more gained. In 1977 he broke the record for yds gained in one game (275). He rushed 16,726 yds in his career. (UPI—Bettmann Archive)

Highest Punting Average, Season (20 punts)
51.4 yd   Sammy Baugh, Wash, 1940 (35)

Highest Punting Average, Game (4 punts)
61.8 yd   Bob Cifers, Det vs Chi Bears, Nov 24, 1946

KICKOFF RETURNS
Yardage Returning Kickoffs

Most Yards Gained, Lifetime
6,922   Ron Smith, Chi Bears, 1965, 70–72; Atl, 1966–67; LA, 1968–69; SD, 1973; Oak, 1974

Most Yards Gained, Season
1,345   George (Buster) Rhymes, Minn 1985

Most Yards Gained, Game
294   Wally Triplett, Det vs LA, Oct 29, 1950 (4)

Longest Kickoff Return for Touchdown
106   Al Carmichael, GB vs Chi Bears, Oct 7, 1956
      Noland Smith, KC vs Den, Dec 17, 1967 (AFL)
      Roy Green, St L vs Dall, Oct 21, 1979

Average Yards Kickoff Returns

Highest Average, Lifetime (75 returns)
30.6   Gale Sayers, Chi Bears, 1965–71

Highest Average, Season (15 returns)
41.1   Travis Williams, GB, 1967 (18)

Highest Average, Game (3 returns)
73.5   Wally Triplett, Det vs LA Rams, Oct 29, 1950 (4–294)

Touchdowns Returning Kickoffs

Most Touchdowns, Lifetime
6   Ollie Matson, Chi Cards, 1952 (2), 54, 56, 58 (2)
    Gale Sayers, Chi Bears, 1965, 66 (2), 67 (3)
    Travis Williams, GB, 1967 (4), 69, 71

Most Touchdowns, Season
4   Travis Williams, GB, 1967
    Cecil Turner, Chi Bears, 1970

Most Touchdowns, Game
2   Thomas (Tim) Brown, Phil vs Dall, Nov 6, 1966
    Travis Williams, GB vs Cleve, Nov 12, 1967
    Ron Brown, LA Rams vs GB, Nov 24, 1985

PUNT RETURNS
Yardage Returning Punts

Most Yards Gained, Lifetime
3,317   Billy Johnson, Hou 1974–80, Atl 1982–87, Wash 1988

Most Yards Gained, Season
692   Fulton Walker, LA Raiders 1985

Most Yards Gained, Game
  207 LeRoy Irvin, LA Rams vs Atl,
        Oct 11, 1981

Longest Punt Return (all tds)
   98 Gil LeFebvre, Cin vs Brk, Dec
        3, 1933
        Charlie West, Minn vs Wash,
        Nov 3, 1968
        Dennis Morgan, Dall vs St L,
        Oct 13, 1974

Highest Average, Lifetime (75 or more returns)
12.78 George McAfee, Chi Bears,
        1940–41, 1945–50

Highest Average, Season (Qualifiers)
23.0 Herb Rich, Balt, 1950

Highest Average, Game (3 returns)
47.7 Chuck Latourette, St L vs NO,
        Sept 29, 1968

Most Touchdowns, Game
    2 Jack Christiansen, Det vs LA
        Rams, Oct 14, 1951; vs GB,
        Nov 22, 1951
        Dick Christy, NY Titans vs Den,
        Sept 24, 1961
        Rick Upchurch, Den vs Cleve,
        Sept 26, 1976
        LeRoy Irvin, LA Rams vs Atl,
        Oct 11, 1981
        Vai Sikahema, St L vs Tampa,
        Dec 21, 1986

Most Touchdowns, Lifetime
    8 Jack Christiansen, Det, 1951–58
        Rick Upchurch, Den, 1975–83

Most Touchdowns, Season
    4 Jack Christiansen, Det, 1951
        Rick Upchurch, Den, 1976

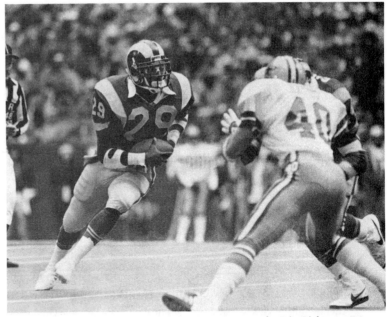

RUSHING RECORD of 2,105 yds in one season was set by Eric Dickerson (LA Rams) in his peak year 1984, eclipsing O.J. Simpson's record of 2,003 which had held for 11 years. (UPI—Bettmann Archive)

FUMBLES

Most Fumbles, Lifetime
  106 Dan Fouts, SD, 1973–87

Most Fumbles, Season
   17 Dan Pastorini, Hou, 1973
        Warren Moon, Hou 1984

Most Fumbles, Game
    7 Len Dawson, KC vs SD, Nov
        15, 1964 (AFL)

Longest Fumble Return
  104 Jack Tatum, Oak vs GB, Sept
        24, 1972

Most Opponents' Fumbles Recovered, Lifetime
   29 Jim Marshall, Cleve, 1960;
        Minn, 1961–79

Most Opponents' Fumbles Recovered, Season
    9 Don Hultz, Minn, 1963

Most Opponents' Fumbles Recovered, Game
    3 by 9 players 1949–85

SUPER BOWL RECORDS
(Through 1989 Game)

Most points, lifetime
   24 Franco Harris, Pitt, 4 games (4 td)

Most points, game
   18 Roger Craig, SF vs Miami, Jan
        20, 1985 (3 td)

Most field goals, lifetime
    5 Ray Wersching, SF, 2 games

Most field goals, game
    4 Don Chandler, GB vs. Oak, Jan
        14, 1968
        Ray Wersching, SF vs Cin, Jan
        24, 1982

LONGEST FIELD GOAL: Tom Dempsey (New Orleans Saints) kicked a record 63-yard field goal on the last play of an NFL game to beat the Detroit Lions 19–17 on Nov 8, 1970. Dempsey, who was born with only half a right foot and only part of his right arm, wore a special shoe for placekicking. He reportedly once kicked a 57-yarder without a shoe in a semipro game.

SUPER BOWL RECORDS
(continued)

Longest field goal
48 Jan Stenerud, KC vs Minn, Jan 11, 1970
Rick Karlis, Den vs NY Giants Jan 25, 1987

Most extra points, game
6 Ali Haj-Sheikh, Wash vs Den Jan 31, 1988

Most yards rushing, lifetime
354 Franco Harris, Pitt, 4 games

Most yards rushing, game
204 Tim Smith, Wash vs Den, Jan 31, 1988

Most yards passing, lifetime
932 Terry Bradshaw, Pitt, 4 games

Most yards, passing, game
357 Joe Montana, SF vs Cin, Jan 22, 1989

Most passes completed, lifetime
61 Roger Staubach, Dallas, 4 games

Joe Montana, SF, 3 games

Most passes completed, game
29 Dan Marino, Miami vs SF, Jan 20, 1985

Most touchdown passes, lifetime
9 Terry Bradshaw, Pitt, 4 games

Most touchdown passes, game
4 Terry Bradshaw, Pitt vs Dallas, Jan 21, 1979
Doug Williams, Wash vs Den, Jan 31, 1988

Longest completed pass
80 Jim Plunkett to Kenny King, Oak Raiders vs Phil, Jan 25, 1981
Doug Williams to Ricky Sanders, Wash vs Den, Jan 31, 1988

Best passing pct, game
.880 Phil Simms, NY Giants vs Den (22 of 25), Jan 25, 1987

Most yards receiving, lifetime
364 Lynn Swann, Pitt, 4 games

Most yards receiving, game
215 Jerry Rice, SF vs Cin, Jan 22, 1989

Most receptions, lifetime
16 Lynn Swann, Pitt, 4 games

Most receptions, game
11 Dan Ross, Cin vs SF, Jan 24, 1982
Jerry Rice, SF vs Cin, Jan 22, 1989

Most interceptions, game
3 Rod Martin, Oak Raiders vs Phil, Jan 25, 1981

Longest punt
63 Lee Johnson, Cin vs SF, Jan 22, 1989

Longest punt return
45 John Taylor, SF vs Cin, Jan 22, 1989

Longest kickoff return
98 Fulton Walker, Miami vs Wash, Jan 30, 1983

Most Prolific Recordbreaker

After he finished his 4-year career at Portland State U in 1980, Neil Lomax held 90 NCAA football records and was tied for two other records, mostly on the basis of his passing feats. No other football player, past or present, has been remotely close to holding that many records—in any college sport.

Highest Score

The most points ever scored (by one team and both teams) in a college football game was 222 by Georgia Tech, Atlanta, Ga, against Cumberland University of Lebanon, Tenn on Oct 7, 1916. Tech also set records for the most points scored in one quarter (63), most touchdowns (32) and points after touchdown (30) in a game, and the largest victory margin (Cumberland did not score).

First Televised Football Game

Fordham U, NYC, was the host to Waynesburg, a Pa school, in the first football game ever televised—in 1939. Fordham won, 34–7.

Statistical Leader

Oklahoma became the first team in major college football history to win 6 team championships in 1986 and then do it again in 1987 giving them 12 titles in 2 seasons. In the latest year, they led in rushing offense (428.2 yd per game), scoring offense (43.5), scoring defense (7.5), total defense (208.1 rushing-passing yd allowed per game), pass defense (102.4) and total offense (499.7).

Super Bowl Winners

1967 Green Bay Packers (NFL)
1968 Green Bay Packers (NFL)
1969 New York Jets (AFL)
1970 Kansas City Chiefs (AFL)
1971 Baltimore Colts (AFC)
1972 Dallas Cowboys (NFC)
1973 Miami Dolphins (AFC)
1974 Miami Dolphins (AFC)
1975 Pittsburgh Steelers (AFC)
1976 Pittsburgh Steelers (AFC)
1977 Oakland Raiders (AFC)
1978 Dallas Cowboys (NFC)
1979 Pittsburgh Steelers (AFC)
1980 Pittsburgh Steelers (AFC)
1981 Oakland Raiders (AFC)
1982 San Francisco 49ers (NFC)
1983 Washington Redskins (NFC)
1984 Los Angeles Raiders (AFC)
1985 San Francisco 49ers (NFC)
1986 Chicago Bears (NFC)
1987 New York Giants (NFC)
1988 Washington Redskins (NFC)
1989 San Francisco 49ers (NFC)

Coaching Records

The longest-serving head coach was Amos Alonzo Stagg (1862–1965), who served Springfield in 1890–91, Chicago from 1892 to 1932 and College of the Pacific from 1933 to 1946, making a total of 57 years. He later served as an assistant coach to his son.

The record for most victories by a coach of a professional team is 325, by George Halas (1895–1983), who coached the Chicago Bears, 1920–29, 33–42, 46–55, 58–67.

PUTTING THE FOOT IN FOOTBALL: Steve O'Neal (#20) of the NY Jets follows through on his punt from the end zone in Denver's Mile High Stadium. The line of scrimmage (from which punts are measured) had been the 1-yd line. The ball, which sailed well over the receiver's head, bounced and rolled to the Denver 1-yd line—a 98-yd punt! (Pro-Football Hall of Fame)

Through 1987, the 68-year-old Eddie Robinson compiled a 349–120–15 record at Grambling State University (Louisiana), the winningest coach in college football history. The previous record of 323 had been set by Paul "Bear" Bryant in 1982. Bryant had coached at Maryland (1945), Kentucky (1946–53), Texas A&M (1954–57) and Alabama (1958–82).

NFL Champions

The Green Bay Packers have won a record 11 NFL titles from 1929 through 1967. The Packers also won the first two Super Bowls (instituted Jan 1967), when the games were a competition between NFL and AFL champions. The Pittsburgh Steelers have the most Super Bowl victories with 4 (1975–76, 79–80). The 1972 Miami Dolphins had the best record for one season, including playoffs and Super Bowl (played Jan 1973), with 17 wins and no losses or ties.

Shortest Touchdown Pass

When the Dallas Cowboys had only 2 inches to go for a touchdown against the Washington Redskins on Oct 9, 1960, quarterback Eddie LeBaron did the unexpected. Knowing that everyone was looking to a powerful thrust at the line by the heaviest plunging back on his team, LeBaron took the ball from center and instead of handing it off to his fullback, slipped into the pocket and unleashed a short pass over the left side to his left end Bielski to set a world record for the shortest distance gained by a pass for a touchdown—2 inches.

Pro Playoff Heroes

On Jan 9, 1988, Anthony Carter, one of the smallest players in the National Football League at 166 lb, had one of the biggest days ever in playoff history. The Minnesota Vikings' wide receiver gained 227 yds, a record for postseason games, on 10 catches against the San Francisco 49ers.

Other outstanding playoff records include Bernie Kosar, the Cleveland Brown quarterback who passed for 489 yds against the NY Jets in 1986; Eric Dickerson, then of the Los Angeles Rams, who rushed for 248 yards against the Dallas Cowboys in 1985, and Daryle Lamonica, playing for the Oakland Raiders when he threw 6 touchdown passes against the Houston Oilers in 1969.

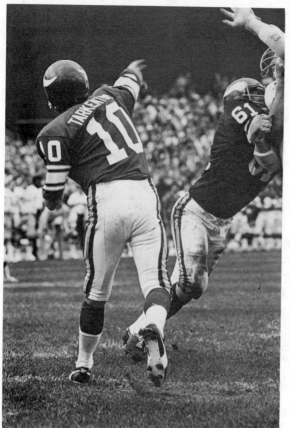

STRONG ARM: Fran Tarkenton set lifetime NFL records by attempting 6,467 passes and completing 3,686 of them during his 18-year career with the NY Giants and Minn Vikings. Tarkenton, who holds career passing records for touchdowns (342) and yards gained (47,003), was elected to the Hall of Fame in 1986.

SUPER PASSING: Phil Simms (NY Giants), most valuable player in the 1987 Super Bowl, set 2 major records, completing 10 passes in a row and finishing with 22 out of 25 attempts for a record .880 percentage.

FAMOUS FOOTBALLER: The man who played for Army and went on to become President is the third from the left in this photo—Dwight D. Eisenhower.

SUPER-BOWL RECORD: When the Chicago Bears beat the New Eng Patriots 46–10 in Jan 1986, it was the biggest margin of victory ever in the annual classic. This is how play looked at ground level. (All Sport)

HEADED FOR THE SUPER BOWL: Owner George Halas (standing center, in raincoat and baseball hat) coached the Chicago Bears for 40 seasons, piling up a record 325 victories. Here he watches Gale Sayers in 1965 take off around end. The Bears did not win their first Super Bowl until Jan 1986, long after Halas had passed away.

GAMES

BACKGAMMON

Forerunners of the game have been traced back to a dice and a board game found in excavations at Ur, dated to 3000 BC. Later the Romans played a game remarkably similar to the modern one. The name "Backgammon" is variously ascribed to Welsh ("little battle"), or Saxon ("back game"). Modern variations include the American Acey Deucey.

At present there are no world championships held, but a points rating system may soon be introduced internationally, thereby enabling players to be ranked.

Marathon

Dick Newcomb and Greg Peterson of Rockford, Ill, played backgammon for 151 hours 11 min, June 30–July 6, 1978.

Largest Board

The Bee Creek Wading Pool at College Station, Tex, had its 27 × 40 ft bottom painted like a backgammon board so that a giant game could be played there on June 16, 1979 by Noble Wagnon (winner) and Pat McConnell. The pool was filled to a depth of 3 ft and children were used as markers.

BLACKJACK

Marathon

Earl Arnall, a dealer at the King 8 Casino in Las Vegas, Nev, spent 190 hours at the blackjack table, June 22–30, 1977. Ardeth Hardy set the women's mark of 169 hours 47 min of continuous dealing during the same period. Both took 5-min rest breaks after each hour.

BRIDGE (CONTRACT)

Bridge (corruption of Biritch) is thought to be either of Levantine origin, similar games having been played there in the early 1870's, or to have come from the East—probably India.

Auction bridge (highest bidder names trump) was invented c. 1902. The contract principle, present in several games (notably the French game *Plafond, c.* 1917), was introduced to bridge by Harold S. Vanderbilt (US) on Nov 1, 1925, during a Caribbean voyage aboard the SS *Finland*. The new version became a worldwide craze after the US vs GB challenge match between Rumanian-born Ely Culbertson (1891–1955) and Lt-Col Walter Thomas More Buller (1887–1938) at Almack's Club, London, Sept 1930. The US won the 200-hand match by 4,845 points.

Most World Titles

The World Championship (Bermuda Bowl) has been won most often (13 times) by Italy's Blue Team between 1957 and 1975, and by the US team between 1950 and 1987. Italy also won the Olympiad in 1964, 68 and 72. Giorgio Belladonna (b 1923) was on all these Italian winning teams. The US won a record 4 times in the women's world championship for the Venice Trophy.

Possible Auctions

The number of possible auctions with North as dealer is 128,745,650,347,030,638,120,231,926, 111,609,371,363,122,697,557.

Perfect Deals

The mathematical odds against dealing 13 cards of one suit are 158,753,389,899 to 1, while the odds against a named player receiving a "perfect hand" consisting of all 13 spades, for example, are 635,013,559,599 to 1. The odds against each of the four players receiving a complete suit ("perfect deal") are 2,235,197,406,895,366,368,301,559,999 to 1.

Most Durable Player

Oswald Jacoby (b Dec 8, 1902), Dallas, Tex, d 1984) was a world-rank competitor for 52 years after winning his first world title in 1931. In Oct 1967, he became the first player to amass 10,000 master points. He retired in July 1983 but came back in Nov 1983 to be part of a team that won the North America team championship. (He also won the World Backgammon title.)

Most Players

The biggest tournament, called the Epson World Bridge Championship, held on June 3, 1988, was contested by 84,352 players playing the same hands at 2,500 centers.

In N Amer alone, there are 4,120 bridge clubs, according to the Amer Contract Bridge League (ACBL).

CHECKERS TOURNAMENT: (Right) In New Orleans in Nov 1988, Charles Walker, checkers luminary, drew a crowd of 201 opponents (including the youngster above) and beat them all simultaneously as he walked around the table. (Montgomery Stire)

Most Master Points

In the latest ranking list based on Master Points awarded by the World Bridge Federation, the leading male player in the world was Giorgio Belladonna, a member of Italy's Blue Team, with 1,821¼ points, followed by four more Italians. The world's leading woman player is Jacqui Mitchell (US) with 347 points.

As for master points awarded by the American Contract Bridge League, the leader was Barry Crane of Los Angeles (b 1927 Detroit, murdered July 5, 1985) who won a total of 35,137.6 points. Only 4 other players have even reached 25,000. The leader currently is Paul Soloway with 29,153 points to June 15, 1988. The most master points scored in a year is 3,270 by Grant Baze (US) in 1984.

Youngest Life Masters

Sam Hirschman of Southfield, Mich, became a Life Master in the ACBL on July 21, 1988, at the age of 11 years 9 months 5 days, beating the previous youngest master by 29 days.

Adair Gellman of Bethesda, Md, became the youngest-ever female Life Master at age 14 years 6 months 4 days on Oct 24, 1983, breaking a record that had stood for 6 years. Then on Nov 5, 1983, just 12 days later, she was toppled from her peak by a still younger lady, Patricia Thomas of Las Cruces, NM, who was 14 years and 28 days.

Oldest Active Players

Jay Feigus of Middletown, NJ at age 95 in Mar 1988 won a pairs title with Edwin Utan in a field of 90 pairs at the Univ of Scranton. His earliest was a 1929 Goldman Pair Championship.

Mrs Julia Chadwick of Torquay, Eng, at the age of 98 won two events in 1985.

Marathon

The longest recorded session was 186 hours 38 min by Jonathan Noad, Jeremy Cohen, Robert Pinder and Andrew Bale at Ariel Hotel, Hayes, Eng, Sept 20–28, 1986.

CHECKERS

Checkers, also known as draughts, has origins earlier than chess. It was played in Egypt in the second millennium BC. The earliest book on the game was by Antonio Torquemada of Valencia, Spain in 1547. There have been four US vs GB international matches (crossboard) in 1905, 27, 73, and 83, three won by the US and one by GB.

Asa Long (b 1904) of Toledo, Ohio, was the youngest player ever to win a US National checkers tournament (aged 18 years 2 months) in 1922, and also the oldest player to duplicate this (aged 79 years 11 months) in 1984 at Tupelo, Miss, a span of 62 years. He was also world champion 1934–48, and won 4 other US Nationals—1929, 37, 39, and 82.

Walter Hellman (US) (1916–75) won a record 8 world titles during his tenure as world champion 1948–75.

Dr Marion Tinsley (Tallahassee, Fla) has been undefeated in match play internationally from 1947 to 1988. Melvin Pomeroy (US) was internationally undefeated from 1914 until his death in 1933.

Most Opponents

Charles Walker played 201 opponents simultaneously on Nov 5, 1988 and beat them all in the Burger King World Championship Checkers Tournament in New Orleans. Walker is the vice-president of the Amer Checkers Federation and the founder of the International Checkers Hall of Fame.

Longest and Shortest Games

In competition the prescribed rate of play is not less than 30 moves per hour with the average game lasting about 90 min. In 1958 a match between Dr Marion Tinsley (US) and Derek Oldbury (GB) lasted 7 hours 30 min. The shortest possible game is one of 20 moves, composed by Alan Malcolm Beckerson (GB).

The longest session is 138 hours 28 min by Greg Davis and Mark Schumacher at Denny's Restaurant, Nunawading, Australia, Aug 26–Sept 1, 1985.

CHESS

The game originated in ancient India under the name Chaturanga (literally "four-corps")—an army game. The name chess is derived from the Persian word *shah*. The earliest reference is from the Middle Persian Karnamak (c. 590–628), though there are grounds for believing its origins are from the 2nd century, owing to the discovery, announced in Dec 1972, of two ivory chessmen in the Uzbek Soviet Republic, datable to that century. The *Fédération Internationale des Echecs* was established in 1924. There were an estimated 7 million registered players in the USSR in 1973.

The game of chess has led to the publication of at least 20,000 books, more than for any other game.

Most Opponents

Vlastimil Hort (b Jan 12, 1944) (Czechoslovakia), in Seltjarnes, Iceland, Apr 23–24, 1977, played 550 opponents, including a record 201 simultaneously. He only lost ten games.

Eric G. J. Knoppert (Neth) (b Sept 20, 1959) played 500 games of 10-min chess against opponents

DEFEATED ADULT EXPERT: 7-year-old Ariel Avigad-Vernon of NYC won against a Manhattan Chess Club ranked player on Dec 5, 1987.

averaging 2,002 on the Elo scale in 67 hours 58 min, Sept 13–16, 1985. He scored 413 points (1 for win, ½ for draw), a success rate of 82.6%.

The record for most consecutive games played is 663 by Vlastimil Hort over 32½ hours at Porz, W Germany on Oct 5–6, 1984. He played 60–100 opponents at a time, scoring over 80% and averaging 30 moves per game.

George Koltanowski (Belgium, later of US) tackled 56 opponents "blindfold" and won 50, drew 6, lost 0 in 9¾ hours at the Fairmont Hotel, San Francisco, on Dec 13, 1960.

Longest Games

The master game with the most moves on record was when Yedael Stepak (b Aug 21, 1940) (Israel) beat Yaakov Mashian (b Dec 17, 1943) (Iran, later Israel) in 193 moves in Tel Aviv, Israel, March 23–Apr 16, 1980. The total playing time was 24½ hours.

The slowest reported move (before modern rules) in an official event is reputed to have been played by Louis Paulsen (1833–91) (Germany) against Paul Charles Morphy (1837–84) (US) on Oct 29, 1857. The game ended in a draw on move 56 after 15 hours of play, of which Paulsen used most of the allotted time. Grandmaster Friedrich Sämisch (1896–1975) (Germany) ran out of the allotted time (2½ hours for

45 moves) after only 12 moves, in Prague, Czechoslovakia, in 1938.

The slowest move played, since time clocks were introduced, was at Vigo, Spain in 1980 when Francisco Trois (b Sept 3, 1946) took 2 hours 20 min for his seventh move *v.* Luis Santos (b June 30, 1955).

World Champions

World champions have been generally recognized since 1886. The longest undisputed tenure was 26 years 337 days by Dr Emanuel Lasker (1868–1941) of Germany, from 1894 to 1921. Robert J. (Bobby) Fischer (b Chicago, March 9, 1943) is reckoned on the officially adopted Elo system to be the greatest Grandmaster of all time at 2,785.

Gary Kimovich Kasparov (USSR) (b Apr 13, 1963) at 2,740 is currently the highest ranked player. He successfully defended his world championship title in Spain against Karpov late in 1987, but almost lost it through making a blunder. Needing only two draws to win, Kasparov got careless and sacrificed a rook, only to find that he had lost a game. Now he had to win to salvage a tie. He did just that. In astonishing play he carefully backed Karpov into a hopeless position and won the game, retained his title and a pot of more than $2 million!

The most active world champion has been Anatoliy Yevgenyevitch Karpov (USSR) (b May 23, 1951) who in his tenure as champion, 1975–85, averaged 45.2 competitive games per year, played in 32 tournaments and finished first in 26.

The women's world championship was held by Vera Menchik-Stevenson (1906–44) (USSR, later GB) from 1927 till her death, and was successfully defended a record 7 times. Nona Gaprindashvili (USSR) (b May 3, 1941) held the title from 1962 to 1978, and defended successfully 4 times. The highest-rated woman player is also the youngest champion, Maya Chiburdanidze (b Jan 17, 1961) of Tbilisi (USSR) at 2,530. She won the women's title in 1978 in a women-only match at the age of 17 and has held the title ever since. In the 1988 world championship match she beat her fellow countrywoman Nana Joseliana, 8½–7½, and won $21,280.

The youngest male world champion is Gary Kasparov who, at 22 years 210 days on Nov 9, 1985, beat Anatoliy Karpov. The oldest was Wilhelm Steinitz (1836–1900) (Czech) who was 58 years 10 days old when he lost his title to Lasker on May 26, 1894.

Ariel Avigad-Vernon, at 7 years 237 days, defeated Nick Dumyk, an adult with an Expert rating by the US Chess Federation, on Dec 5, 1987 at the Manhattan Chess Club in NYC.

José Raúl Capablanca (1888–1942) (Cuba) lost only 34 games in his adult career, 1909–39, for the fewest games lost by a world champion. He was unbeaten from Feb 10, 1916, to Mar 21, 1924, and was world champion from 1921 to 1927.

Marathon

The longest recorded session is one of 200 hours by Roger Long and Graham Croft in Bristol, Eng, May 11–19, 1984.

CRIBBAGE

The invention of the game (once galled Cribbidge) is credited to the English dramatist Sir John Suckling (1609–42). It is estimated that some ten million people play in the US alone.

Rare Hands

Mrs. Mary Matheson of Springhill, Nova Scotia, Canada, 1974–85, and William E. Johnson of Waltham, Mass, 1974–81, had 4 maximum 29-point hands. Paul Nault of Athol, Mass, had two such hands within eight games in a tournament on March 19, 1977. Derek Hearne dealt two hands of six clubs with the turn-up card the remaining club on Feb 8, 1976, in Blackpool, Lancashire, England. Bill Rogers of Burnaby, BC, Canada scored 29 in the crib in 1975.

Marathon

Four students from St Anselm's College, Wirral, Eng, played for 124 hours 15 min, July 14–19, 1986.

DARTS

The origins of darts date from the use by archers of heavily weighted 10-in throwing arrows for self-defense in close quarters fighting. The "dartes" were used in Ireland in the 16th century and darts was played on the *Mayflower* by the Plymouth pilgrims in 1620. The modern game dates from at least 1896 when Brian Gamlin of Bury, Lancashire, England, is credited with inventing the present numbering system on the board. The first recorded score of 180 (three triple 20's) was by John Reader at the Highbury Tavern in Sussex, England, in 1902. Today there are an estimated 6 million darts players in the British Isles.

Most Titles

Eric Bristow (b Apr 25, 1957) (GB) has the most wins in the World Masters Championships (instituted

1974) with 5, in 1977, 79, 81, and 83–84. He has also won the World Professional Championship (instituted 1978) five times, 1980, 81, and 84–86. In 1983 and 85 he also won the World Cup Singles. John Lowe (b July 21, 1945) (GB) is the only other man to have won each of the four major world titles: World Masters (1976 and 80), World Professional (1979 and 87), World Cup Singles (1981), and *News of the World* (1981).

Fastest 301 Match

The fastest time taken for a match of three games of 301 is 1 min 47 sec by Keith Deller on BBC-TV's *Record Breakers* program on Oct 22, 1985.

Fastest "Round the Board"

The record time for going round the board clockwise in "doubles" at arm's length is 9.2 sec by Dennis Gower at the Millers Arms, Hastings, England on Oct 12, 1975 and 14.5 sec in numerical order by Jim Pike (1903–60) at the Craven Club, Newmarket, England in March 1944. The record for this feat at the 9-ft throwing distance, retrieving own darts, is 2 min 13 sec by Bill Duddy (b Sept 29, 1932) at The Plough, Harringey, London, England on Oct 29, 1972.

Least Darts

Scores of 201 in four darts, 301 in six darts, 401 in seven darts and 501 in nine darts, have been achieved on numerous occasions. The lowest number of darts thrown for a score of 1,001 is 19 by Cliff Inglis (b May 27, 1935) (160, 180, 140, 180, 121, 180, 40) at the Bromfield Men's Club, Devon, England on Nov 11, 1975.

A score of 2,001 in 52 darts was achieved by Alan

Evans (b June 14, 1949) at Ferndale, Glamorgan, Wales, on Sept 3, 1976.

A score of 3,001 in 73 darts was thrown by Tony Benson at the Plough Inn, Manchester, Eng, on July 12, 1986.

A score of 100,001 was achieved in 3,732 darts by Alan Downie of Stornoway, GB on Nov 21, 1986.

Linda Batten (b Nov 26, 1954) set a women's 3,001 record of 117 darts at Enfield, Eng, Apr 2, 1986.

Marathon

David Dingley and Michael Poole played for 168 hours 4 min at The Three Horseshoes, Malvern, Eng in Nov 1986.

MARBLES' POPULARITY has continued since the 1st century AD when Augustus played the game as a child, using nuts. (All Sport)

MARBLES

Origins

Marbles may have been a children's game in ancient Egypt. It was introduced into Britain by the Romans in the 1st century AD and became a competitive sport under the British Marbles Board of Control in 1926.

Most Championships

The British Championship (established 1926) has been won most often by the Toucan Terribles with 20 consecutive titles (1956–75). Three founder members, Len Smith, Jack and Charlie Dempsey, played in every title win. They were finally beaten in 1976 by the Pernod Rams, captained by Len Smith's son, Paul. Len Smith (b Oct 13, 1917) has won the individual title 15 times (1957–64, 1966, 1968–73) but lost in 1974 to his son Alan.

24-HOUR HIGHEST SCORE	
Individual	486,470 by Duncan Swift at Felixstowe, Eng, Apr 7–8, 1987 (averaging 26.6 per dart).
TEN-HOUR HIGHEST SCORES	
Most trebles	3,056 (from 7,992 darts) by Paul Taylor at the Woodhouse Tavern, Leytonstone, London on Oct 19, 1985.
Most doubles	3,085 (from 9,945 darts) by David Broad at Blantyre Sports Club, Malawi, Africa, on Mar 17, 1984.
Highest score (retrieving own darts)	394,165 by Alan Clacey and Allan Jopling at The Rifle Volunteer, Wokingham, Berkshire on Dec 27, 1986.
Bulls (individual)	855 by Fred Carter (GB) at Accrington, Eng Jan 11, 1987.
SIX-HOUR HIGHEST SCORES	
Men	189,153 by Daniel Tryner at St Joseph's Catholic Club, Nottingham, Eng on Feb 9, 1986.
Women	89,697 by Karen Heavey at the Rose Inn, Gillingham, Kent, Eng on Apr 25, 1986.

RUSSIAN MONOPOLY: The popularity of this capitalist game has now reached the Soviet Union.

Speed Record

The record for clearing the ring (between 5¾ and 6¼ ft in diameter) of 49 marbles is 2 min 56 sec by the Black Dog Boozers of Crawley, West Sussex, Eng at BBC Television Center, London for BBC Television's *Record Breakers* on Sept 14, 1987.

MONOPOLY®

Monopoly, a real-estate trading game, of which Parker Brothers has sold in excess of 100 million copies in 23 languages (the most recent in Russian), was devised by Charles Darrow (1889–1967) of Germantown, Pa, in 1933. While unemployed as a heating engineer during the Depression he used as places on the board game the street names of Atlantic City, NJ, where he spent his vacations.

In the 8th World Monopoly Championship (held every 3 years under the auspices of Parker Bros) Ikuo Hiyakuta of Japan won after 2 days of grueling play, replacing Jason Bunn (UK).

Marathon

The longest game by four players ratified by Parker Brothers is 660 hours by Caara Fritz, Randy Smith, Phil Bennett, and Terry Sweatt in Atlanta, Ga July 12–Aug 8, 1981.

POKER

Joe Marquis dealt for 109 hours in a 7-card stud game at the Nevada Club in Laughlin, Nev, July 5–9, 1985, for the longest poker game on record.

POOL AND BILLIARDS

The earliest recorded mention of billiards was in France in 1429, while Louis XI, king of France 1461–83, is reported to have had a billiard table.

Pool or championship pocket billiards with numbered balls began to become standardized *c.* 1890. The greatest exponents were Ralph Greenleaf (US) (1899–1950), who won the "world" professional title 19 times (1919–1937), and "Willie" Mosconi (US) (b June 27, 1913), who dominated the game from 1941 to 1957.

Most popular of the billiards games is snooker in Great Britain; and in the US, straight pool (15 balls), nine-ball (9 balls), eight-ball (15 balls) and 7-ball, the first new fully authenticated game in a century.

Leading money winners at pool in 1988 are Earl Strickland of Richmond, Ky for men and Loree-Jon Jones (NJ), youngest champion ever at 15 years old, the leading woman player in the world.

In 1965, Cicero Murphy became a world champion on the 4½-ft × 9-ft table in his first attempt—only the second man in history to do this—the previous one was in 1916.

The record time for pocketing all 15 balls in a speed competition is 40.06 sec by Ross McInnes (b Jan 19, 1955) at Clacton, Essex, Eng on Sept 11, 1983. He also set a record for a break of 132 in 1984.

The longest game was 345 hours 4 min played by Mark Nally and Kevin Grover at Tenby, Dyfed, Wales, Apr 17–May 1, 1987.

3-Cushion Billiards

This pocketless variation dates back to 1878. The world governing body, *Union Mondiale de Billiard*, was formed in 1928. The most successful exponent, 1906–52, was William F. Hoppe (1887–1959), who won 51 billiards championships in all forms between 1906 and 1952. The most UMB titles have been won by Raymond Ceulemans (Belgium) (b July 12, 1935) with 19 (1963–66, 1968–73, 1975–81, 83, 85).

ROULETTE

The longest run in an ungaffed (*i.e.* true) wheel reliably recorded is six successive coups (in No. 10) at El San Juan Hotel, Puerto Rico, July 9, 1959. The odds with a double zero were 1 in 38^6, or 3,010,936,383 to 1. The longest "marathon" on record is one of 31 days from Apr 10 to May 11, 1970, at The Casino de Macao, to test the validity or invalidity of certain contentions in 20,000 spins.

SCRABBLE® CROSSWORD GAME

The crossword game was invented by Alfred M. Butts in 1931 and was developed, refined and trade-marked as Scrabble® Crossword Game by James Brunot in 1948. Coleco Industries of W Hartford, Conn is the manufacturer.

The largest Scrabble tournament in history was held at the Sahara Hotel, Las Vegas, Nev, the July 4th weekend, 1987, with 326 contestants from the US and 6 foreign countries. Winner was Rita Norr of Brooklyn, NY, a mother of 3 and a computer science graduate. It was the first time in history a large international tournament was won by a woman. Ms. Norr received a $5,000 check.

The highest score in one turn in sanctioned play was made by Jack Eichenbaum of NYC, who played "antiques" for 293 points.

Chuck Armstrong, a hospital worker from Saline, Mich, age 40, has won the most tournaments—55 to the end of 1988.

The highest number of points for a single game was made by NJ resident Chris Reslock for 719 points.

The longest continuous run of Scrabble Crossword Games is 153 hours by Peter Finan and Neil Smith at St Anselm's College, Merseyside, Eng, Aug 18–24, 1984. Ken Cardozo (GB) played for 155 hours 48 min against various opponents Dec 5–11, 1984, at "Perfect Pizza," Fulham, Eng.

TABLE SOCCER

A marathon record of 91 hours 20 min was set by Shaun Unterslak and Jay Boccia at Dewaal Hotel, Cape Town, S Africa, Apr 5–9, 1987.

June 28–30, 1985, in a contest on Dynamo Soccer Tables in Salt Lake City, Utah, Twin Galaxies crowned 3 "Players of the Year" for 1985. Best goalie: Mike Bowers of Denver, Colo, who registered 77% on blocking and 69% on clearing. Best forward: Tony Bacon of Seattle, Wash, who registered 62% on passing and 43% on scoring. Fastest shot: John Morgan of Salt Lake City, who achieved a speed of 28.22 mph measured by electronic equipment.

THROWING

In boomerang throwing, the longest distance for throw-and-return was 396.98 ft achieved by Christian Jabet (France) on Apr 5, 1986 near Lyon, France. Dr. Larry Ruhf (US) set a record of 2 min 31 sec for keeping a boomerang aloft in a throw-and-catch contest in Catskill, NY, sponsored by the US Boomerang Assoc and Palenville Interarts, Inc.

The longest independently authenticated throw of any inert object heavier than air is 1,257 ft, for an Aerobie flying ring, by Scott Zimmerman on July 8, 1986 at Fort Funston, Calif.

In Frisbee (flying disc) throwing, Don Cain of East Brunswick, NJ set the record for maximum time aloft by keeping a flying disc in the air for 16.72 sec in Phila, Pa, on May 26, 1986. For women, the time-aloft record is 11.47 sec, set in Sonoma, Calif, by Denise Garfield on Oct 5, 1980.

The greatest distance achieved for throwing a flying disc, running, and catching it is 291 ft by Pekka Ranta (Finland) on June 6, 1986 at Tali, Finland. The women's record is 196.9 ft by Judy Horowitz of NYC on June 29, 1985 at LaMirada, Calif.

The world record for outdoor distance is 612 ft 11½ in by Michael Canci (Australia) on Apr 11, 1987, at Bunbury, W Australia. The indoor distance record is held by Van Miller of Tempe, Ariz, with a 399-ft toss at Flagstaff, Ariz, on Sept 18, 1982.

Bethany Porter (US) holds the women's outdoor distance record at 409 ft 2½ in, set on Aug 21, 1987 at Fort Collins, Colo, while the women's indoor distance record belongs to Suzanne Fields, of Boston, who threw 229.6 ft in Cedar Falls, Iowa, Apr 26, 1981.

The 24-hour group distance record is 428.02 miles set in Vernon, Conn, by the South Windsor Ultimate Frisbee Disc Team, July 8–9, 1977. The outdoor pair distance record for 24 hours has been set at 303.38 mi by Leonard Muise and Gabe Ontiveros at Torrance, Calif, Aug 3–4, 1986. Jamie Knerr and Keith Biery set the indoor 24-hour pair distance mark with 298.37 miles, Aug 14–15, 1982, at Allentown, Pa.

THROWING ACROSS NIAGARA FALLS: Scott Zimmerman, record holder with an Aerobie throw of 1,257 ft, shows how he threw a flying disc from the Canadian side to the American. (Denis Cahill/St. Catherine's Standard)

The Prince George's Community College Flying High Club set the group marathon mark with 1,198 hours, June 1–July 22, 1983. The two-person marathon record is held by Jeremy Tubb and John Fischer who played for 118 hours 36 min Apr 21–26, 1988 at New London, Conn.

Alan Bonopane threw a professional model Frisbee disc at a speed of 74.03 mph and his teammate Tim Selinske made a clean catch of the throw on Aug 25, 1980 in San Marino, Calif.

TWISTER®

Twister is played on a mat of 24 colored dots. Players place their hands and feet on the dots and move them to other dots according to the results of an arrow spun on a board. As hands and feet become twisted, players fall and are eliminated. The last one to remain on all fours is the winner.

Mass Twister games are played with contestants starting with three players per mat and consolidating as some are eliminated. The record for the greatest number of participants in one game was set on May 2, 1987 by 4,160 students at the Univ of Mass at Amherst. The winner was Alison Culler of Amherst.

VIDEO GAMES

Player of the Year tournaments have been held each year since 1983 sanctioned by the U S National Video Game Team.

GLIDING

Humans have sought to emulate the birds from early times, and the first successful "glider pilot" may well have been the mythical Daedalus, of Athens, who made wings for himself and his son Icarus to escape captivity. Icarus soared too near the sun and melted the wax with which the wings were fastened, but according to legend his father flew from Crete to Sicily. Evidence has been found by Isadore William Deiches that gliders were used in ancient Egypt, *c.* 2500–1500 BC. In Italy, about 1500 AD Leonardo da Vinci defined the difference between gliding and powered flight in some drawings, and at the same period Danti of Perugia, an Italian mathematician, is said to have actually flown.

Emanuel Swedenborg (1688–1772) of Sweden made sketches of gliders *c.* 1714. The earliest man-carrying glider was designed by Sir George Cayley (1773–1857) and carried his coachman (possibly John Appleby) about 500 yd across a valley in Brompton Dale, Yorkshire, England, in the summer of 1853. Gliders now attain speeds claimed at over 100 mph.

Most World Titles

The most world individual championships (instituted 1948) won is 3 by Helmut Reichmann (b 1942) (W Germany) in 1970, 74 and 78; and Douglas George Lee (b Nov 7, 1945) (GB) in 1976, 78 and 81.

The women's single-seater world record for absolute altitude is 41,460 ft by Sabrina Jackintell (US) in an Astir CS on Feb 14, 1979.

HANG GLIDING

In the 11th century, the monk Eilmer is reported to have flown from the 60-ft-tall tower of Malmesbury Abbey, Wiltshire, England. The earliest modern pioneer was Otto Lilienthal (1848–96) of Germany who made about 2,500 flights in gliders of his own construction between 1891 and 1896. Professor Francis Rogallo of NASA developed a flexible "wing" in the 1950's from his research into space capsule re-entries.

The official FAI record for the farthest distance covered is 186.80 mi by John Pendry (GB) in an Airwave Magic 3, Horseshoe Meadows, Owens Valley, Calif, to Summit Mt, Monitor Range, Nev in July 1983.

The official FAI height gain record in a flexible-wing glider is 14,250 ft by Larry Tudor (US) at Horseshoe Meadows, Calif, Aug 4, 1985. The height gain record for a flex-wing micro-light glider is 16,168 ft by Bob Calvert (GB).

For distance to declared goal Klaus Kohmstedt (W Ger) glided 140.5 mi to a record over Owens Valley, Calif on July 13, 1983. He also holds the out-and-return distance to a goal record of 107.25 mi over Owens Valley set on June 15, 1983.

The women record holders are Judy Leden (GB) for 145.34 mi distance in a straight line; Lori Judy (US) for 77.38 mi for out-and-return; Jean Little (US) for 27.99 mi for distance to declared goal over Cerro Gordo, Calif on June 15, 1983; and Page Pfieffer (US) for 10,800 ft gain of height over Owens on July 12, 1980.

John Bird piloted a hang glider from the greatest height (39,000 ft from the ground) when he was

SELECTED SOARING WORLD RECORDS (SINGLE-SEATERS)

DISTANCE
	907.7 miles	Hans-Werner Grosse (W Germany) in an AS-W-12 on Apr 25, 1972, from Lübeck to Biarritz.

DECLARED GOAL FLIGHT
	779.4 miles	Bruce Drake, David Speight, S. H. "Dick" Georgeson (all NZ) all in Nimbus 2s, from Te Anau to Te Araroa, Jan 14, 1978.

ABSOLUTE ALTITUDE
	49,009 ft	Robert R. Harris (US) in a Grob G-102 from California City, Calif on Feb 17, 1986.
(women)	41,460 ft	Sabrina Jackintell (US) in an Astir CS Feb 14, 1979.

GOAL AND RETURN
	1,023.4 miles	Tom Knauff (US) in a Nimbus 3 from Williamsport, Pa, to Knoxville, Tenn on April 25, 1983

SPEED OVER TRIANGULAR COURSE
100 km	121.36 mph	Ingo Renner (Australia) in a Nimbus 3 on Dec 14, 1982.
300 km	105.32 mph	Jean-Paul Castel (France) in an AS-W 22 11–15–86
500 km	101.98 mph	Jean-Paul Castel (France) in an AS-W 22 12–10–86
750 km	98.42 mph	Hans-Werner Grosse (W Germany) in an AS-W-22 01–08–85
1,000 km	90.32 mph	Hans-Werner Grosse (W Germany) in an AS-W-17 over Australia, on Jan 3, 1979.
1,250 km	82.79 mph	Hans-Werner Grosse (W Germany) in an AS-W-17 over Australia, on Dec 9, 1980.

released from a hot-air balloon. He landed in Edmonton, Canada, on Aug 29, 1982, touching down 50 mi from his point of departure.

James W. Will, 37, of Honolulu stayed aloft for 34 hours over Makapuu and Waimanolo, Oahu, Hawaii, for an unofficial endurance record.

GOLF

Origins

It has been suggested that golf originated with Scottish shepherds using their crooks to knock pebbles into rabbit holes. This may be apocryphal, but somewhat firmer evidence exists. A stained glass window in Gloucester Cathedral, dating from 1350, portrays a golfer-like figure, but the earliest mention of golf occurs in a prohibiting law passed by the Scottish Parliament in March 1457, under which ''golff be utterly cryit doune and not usit.''

The Romans had a cognate game called *paganica*, which may have been carried to Britain before 400 AD. The Chinese National Golf Association claims the game is of Chinese origin (''*Ch'ui Wan*—the ball-hitting game'') from the 3rd or 2nd century BC. There were official ordinances prohibiting a ball game with clubs in Belgium and Holland from 1360. Gutta-percha balls succeeded feather balls in 1848, and were in turn succeeded in 1902 by rubber-cored balls, invented in 1899 by Coburn Haskell (US). Steel shafts were authorized in the US in 1925.

Golf was first played on the moon in Feb 1971 by Capt Alan Shepard (US), commander of the Apollo XIV spacecraft.

Oldest Clubs

The oldest club of which there is written evidence is the Gentleman Golfers (now the Honourable Company of Edinburgh Golfers) formed in March 1744— 10 years prior to the institution of the Royal and Ancient Club of St Andrews, Fife, Scotland. However, the Royal Burgess Golfing Society of Edinburgh claims to have been founded in 1735. The oldest existing club in North America is the Royal Montreal Club (Nov 1873) and the oldest in the US is St Andrews, Westchester County, NY (1888). An older claim is by the Foxbury Country Club, Clarion County, Pa (1887).

Longest Courses and Holes

The world's longest course is the par-77, 8,325-yd International GC, Bolton, Mass, from the "Tiger" tees, remodeled in 1969 by Robert Trent Jones. Its 16th hole of 270 yd is the longest par 3 in the world.

The longest par 4 is the 6th hole of the Dwight D. Eisenhower Golf Club at City of Industry, Calif, at 500 yd. The longest par 5 is the 17th hole of the Palmira Golf Club in St Johns, Ind, at 710 yd. The longest par 6 is the 17th hole of Black Mt GC, NC, at 747 yd, and the longest hole (par 7) is the 948-yd 7th at Koolan Is, W Australia.

Floyd Satterlee Rood used the entire United States as a course, when he played from the Pacific surf to the Atlantic surf from Sept 1963 to Oct 1964 in 114,737 strokes. He lost 3,511 balls on the 3,397.7 mi trail.

Highest and Lowest Courses

The highest golf course in the world is the Tuctu Golf Club in Morococha, Peru, which is 14,335 ft above sea level at its lowest point. Golf has, however, been played in Tibet at an altitude of over 16,000 ft.

The lowest golf course in the world is the par-70 Furnace Creek Golf Course, Death Valley, Calif, at a disputed average of 178–272 ft below sea level.

Biggest Bunkers

The world's biggest trap is Hell's Half Acre which stretches 200 yd across the fairway at the 585-yd 7th hole of the Pine Valley course, Clementon, NJ. Highest bunker is the 19-ft deep 115-yd-long trap along the 16th hole at the new PGA West course in Palm Springs, Calif.

Largest Green

Probably the largest green in the world is that of the par-6, 695-yd 5th hole at International GC, Bolton, Mass, with an area greater than 28,000 sq ft.

Lowest Scores for 9 and 18 Holes

Three professional players are recorded to have played a long course (over 6,000 yd) for a score of 57: Bill Burke at the Normandie Golf Club, St Louis (6,389 yds, par 71) on May 20, 1970; Tom Ward at the Searcy (Ark) Country Club (6,098 yds, par 70) in 1981; Augie Navarro at the Sim Park Golf Course (Wichita, Kans) in 1982.

Alfred Edward Smith (1903–85), the English professional at Woolacombe, achieved an 18-hole score of 55 (15 under bogey 70) on his home course on Jan 1, 1936.

Nine holes in 25 (4, 3, 3, 2, 3, 3, 1, 4, 2) was recorded by A. J. "Bill" Burke in his round of 57 (32 + 25) (see above), and by teenager Douglas Beecher at the Pitman (NJ) Country Club (3,150 yd, par 35) 1976. The tournament record is 27 by Mike Souchak (US) (b May 1927) for the second nine (par 35) first round of the 1955 Texas Open; Andy North (US) (b Mar 9, 1950) second nine (par 34), first round, 1975

BIGGEST BUNKER: The largest trap in the world, Hell's Half Acre, looks like a rough sea to the golfers at the 585-yd 7th hole of the Pine Valley course in Clementon, NJ. Built in 1912, it is 115 yd wide. (All Sport/David Cannon)

BC Open at En-Joie GC, Endicott, NY; and Jose Maria Canizares (Spain) (b Feb 18, 1947), first nine, third round, in the 1978 Swiss Open on the 6,811-yd Crans-Sur course, and by Robert Lee (GB) (b Oct 12, 1961) first nine, first round, in the Monte Carlo Open on the 6,249 yd Mont Agel course on June 28, 1985.

The US PGA tournament record for 18 holes is 59 (30 + 29) by Al Geiberger (b Sept 1, 1937) in the second round of the Danny Thomas Classic, on the 72-par, 7,249-yd Colonial CC course, Memphis, Tenn, June 10, 1977.

In non-PGA tournaments, Samuel Jackson Snead (b May 27, 1912) had 59 in the Greenbrier Open (now called the Sam Snead Festival), at White Sulphur Springs, W Va, on May 16, 1959; Gary Player (South Africa) (b Nov 1, 1935) carded 59 in the second round of the Brazilian Open in Rio de Janeiro on Nov 29, 1974; and David Jagger (GB) also had 59 in a Pro-Am tournament prior to the 1973 Nigerian Open at Ikoyi Golf Club, Lagos, and Miguel Martin (Spain) in the Argentine Southern Championship at Mar de Plata on Feb 27, 1987.

Women's Lowest Scores

The lowest recorded score on an 18-hole course (over 6,000 yd) for a woman is 62 (30 + 32) (9 under par) by Mary (Mickey) Kathryn Wright (b Feb 14, 1935), of Dallas, on the Hogan Park Course (6,286 yd) at Midland, Tex, in Nov 1964, and 62 (11 under par) by Vicki Fergon in the 2nd round of the 1984 San Jose Classic.

Wanda Morgan (b March 22, 1910) recorded a score of 60 (31 + 29) on the Westgate and Birchington Golf Club course, Kent, England, over 18 holes (5,002 yd) on July 11, 1929.

The LPGA record for 9 holes is held by Pat Bradley who scored 28 (7 under par) in Denver, Colo, Aug 24, 1984, and 28 (8 under par) by Mary Beth Zimmerman in the 1984 Rail Charity tournament.

Lowest Scores for 36 Holes

The record for 36 holes is 122 (59 + 63) by Sam Snead in the 1959 Greenbrier Open (now called the Sam Snead Festival) (non-PGA), May 16–17, 1959. Horton Smith (1908–63), twice Masters champion, scored 121 (63 + 58) on a short course (4,700 yd) on Dec 21, 1928.

Lowest for a woman is 129 (64–65) by Judy Dickinson in 1985 in the S&H Golf Classic.

Lowest Scores for 72 Holes

The lowest recorded score on a first-class course is 255 (29 under par) by Leonard Peter Tupling (b Apr 6, 1950) (GB) in the Nigerian Open at Ikoyi Golf Club, Lagos, in Feb 1981, made up of 63, 66, 62 and 64 (average 63.75 per round).

The lowest 72 holes in a US professional event is 257 (60, 68, 64 and 65) by Mike Souchak in the 1955 Texas Open at San Antonio.

The lowest for a woman is 242 (21 under par) by Trish Johnson in the Eastleigh Classic in Eng July 25–27, 1987. Nancy Lopez shot 268 (66–67–69–66) in the 1985 Hernedon Classic for the lowest finish in a US tournament.

Lowest Score with One Club

Playing only with a 6-iron, Thad Daber of Durham, NC, won the 1987 World One Club Championship with a record score of 70 (2 under par) on the 6,037-yd Lochmere Golf Club course in Cary, NC.

Longest Drive

In an official PGA long-driving contest at 5,200-ft altitude in Denver, Colo, at the John F. Kennedy Golf Course, on a clear day with a slight wind against him, Jack L. Hamm of Denver drove a ball 406 yd on July 12, 1986. The contest required the drive to land on a 40-yd wide fairway.

A drive of 2,640 yd (1½ miles) across ice was achieved by an Australian meteorologist named Nils Lied at Mawson Base, Antarctica, in 1962. On the moon, the energy expended on a mundane 300-yd drive would achieve, craters permitting, a distance of a mile.

Biggest Winning Margin

The greatest margin of victory in a major tournament is 21 strokes by Jerry Pate (b Sept 15, 1953) (US) in the Colombian Open with 262 on Dec 10–13, 1981.

Cecilia Leitch won the Canadian Ladies Open Championship in 1921 by the highest margin for a major title, 17 up and 15 to play.

Most Tournament Wins

The record for winning tournaments in a single season is 18 (plus one unofficial), including a record 11 consecutively, by Byron Nelson (b Feb 4, 1912) (US), March 8–Aug 4, 1945.

Sam Snead has won 84 official US PGA tour events to Dec 1979, and has been credited with a total 134 tournament victories since 1934.

Kathy Whitworth (b Sept 27, 1939) (US) topped this with her 88th LPGA victory through 1985, her 23rd year on the tour. Mickey Wright (US) won a record 13 tournaments in one year, 1963.

Jack Nicklaus (US) is the only golfer who has won all five major titles (British Open, US Open, Masters, PGA and US Amateur) twice, while setting a record total of 20 major tournament victories (1959–86). His remarkable record in the US Open is 4 firsts, 8 seconds and 2 thirds. Nicklaus has accumulated 71 PGA tournament wins in all.

In 1930 Bobby Jones achieved a unique "Grand Slam" of the US and British Open and British and US Amateur titles.

Longest Putt

The longest recorded holed putt in a major tournament was one of 86 ft on the vast 13th green at the Augusta National, Ga, by Cary Middlecoff (b Jan 1921) in the 1955 Masters Tournament.

Bobby Jones was reputed to have holed a putt in excess of 100 ft on the 5th green in the first round of the 1927 British Open at St Andrews, Scotland.

Bob Cook (US) sank a putt measured at 140 ft 2¾ in on the 18th at St Andrews, Scotland, in the International Fourball Pro-Am Tournament on Oct. 1, 1976.

LONGEST DRIVE: With a 406-yd drive in an official PGA driving contest, Jack L. Hamm of Denver, Colo, set a new world record on July 12, 1986. He had a slight wind against him on a clear day at 5,200-ft altitude; the contest was on a 40-yd wide fairway.

Liam Higgins (Ireland) drove an American-type ball 634.1 yd on an airport runway at Baldonnel Military Airport, Dublin, Ireland, Sept 25, 1984. Higgins also participated in a long-driving contest in Sept 1988 on the shore of the East River in NYC, when he was outdriven by Scott DeCandia, a pro with a studio in Westchester. They drove balls from the roof of the Water Club restaurant. DeCandia won with a 350-yd on-the-fly drive, measured by Coast Guard boats stationed at fixed points in the river.

The longest with wind assist is 515 yd by Michael Hoke Austin (b Feb 17, 1910) of Los Angeles, in the US National Seniors Open Championship at Las Vegas, Nev, Sept 25, 1974. Aided by an estimated 35-mph tailwind, the 6-ft-2-in 210-lb golfer drove the ball on the fly to within a yard of the green on the par-4, 450-yd 5th hole of the Winterwood Course. The ball rolled 65 yd past the flagstick.

The longest drive by a woman was 531 yd by Helen Dobson at RAF Honington, Eng, Oct 31, 1987.

MOST WINS IN MAJOR TOURNAMENTS

US Open	Willie Anderson (1880–1910)	4	1901–03–04–05
	Robert Tyre Jones, Jr (1902–71)	4	1923–26–29–30
	W. Ben Hogan (b Aug 13, 1912)	4	1948–50–51–53
	Jack William Nicklaus (b Jan 21, 1940)	4	1962–67–72–80
US Amateur	Robert Tyre Jones, Jr	5	1924–25–27–28–30
British Open	Harry Vardon (1870–1937)	6	1896–98–99, 1903–11–14
British Amateur	John Ball (1861–1940)	8	1888–90–92–94–99, 1907–10–12
PGA Championship (US)	Walter C. Hagen (1892–1969)	5	1921–24–25–26–27
	Jack W. Nicklaus	5	1963–71–73–75–80
Masters Championship (US)	Jack W. Nicklaus	6	1963–65–66–72–75–86
US Women's Open	Elizabeth (Betsy) Earle-Rawls (b May 4, 1928)	4	1951–53–57–60
	''Mickey'' Wright (b Feb 14, 1935)	4	1958–59–61–64
US Women's Amateur	Mrs Glenna Vare (*née* Collett) (b June 20, 1903)	6	1922–25–28–29–30–35

Highest Earnings

The greatest amount ever won in official US PGA golf prizes is $5,005,825 by Jack Nicklaus through 1988.

The record for a year in US PGA events is $1,147,644 by Curtis Strange (b Jan 20, 1955) in 1988. Worldwide earnings of over $1 million in 1 year were reported by Greg Norman (Aust) in 1986.

The highest LPGA career earnings by a woman is $2,442,315 by Pat Bradley (b Mar 24, 1951) through 1988. In 1986 she set a season record of $492,021, beating Nancy Lopez' 1985 winnings of $416,472.

Marathon Golf

The most holes played on foot in a week (168 hours) is 1,128 by Steve Hylton at the Mason

HIGHEST EARNINGS: Besides winning 20 major tournaments (71 in all) for a record, Jack Nicklaus (right) has earned $5,005,825 through 1988 in prize money. Nicklaus is the only golfer who has won all 5 major titles twice. (E. D. Lacey) **Arnold Palmer (below) prepares to putt as his many followers, known as Arnie's Army, look on. Palmer won the Masters 4 times and played on 6 winning teams in World Cup play. He was the first golfer to reach $1 million in career earnings.**

GOLFING LEGEND: Bobby Jones never turned pro. He won his first tournament, the US Open, in 1923 at the age of 21, and won it a total of 4 times, the British Open 3 times, the US Amateur 5 times, and the British Amateur once.

Rudolph Golf Club (6,060 yd), Clarksville, Tenn, Aug 25–31, 1980. The most holes in 24 hours is 401 by Ian Colston, 35, at Bendigo Golf Club, Victoria, Aust, par 73 (6,061 yd) on Nov 27–28, 1971.

Using golf carts for transport, Charles Stock played 783 holes in 24 hours at Arcadia Country Club in Lyndhurst, Ohio, July 20, 1987. Terry Zachary played 391 holes in 12 hours on the 6,706-yd course at Connaught Golf Club, Alberta, Canada on June 16, 1986. Dr. R. C. "Dick" Hardison, aged 61, played 236 holes under USGA rules in 12 hours at Sea Mountain GC, Punaluu, Hawaii July 31, 1984, maintaining an average score of 76 per round, with an average time per hole of 3.05 min. His best round was a 68, achieved in 49 min 58 sec, including a second nine of 30 in 24 min 28 sec. He used seven fore caddies and 26 electric golf carts, which he drove himself.

The most holes played in a week using a golf cart is 1,260 by Colin Young at Patshull Park Golf Club (6,412 yd), Pattingham, Eng, July 2–9, 1988.

Largest Tournament

The Volkswagen Grand Prix Open Amateur Championship (UK) attracted a record 321,778 (206,820 men and 114,958 women) competitors in 1984.

Youngest and Oldest Champions

The youngest winner of the British Open was Tom Morris, Jr (1851–75) at Prestwick, Ayrshire, Scotland, in 1868, aged 17 years 249 days. The oldest British Open champion was "Old Tom" Morris (1821–1908) who was aged 46 years 99 days when he won in 1867. In modern times, the oldest was 1967 champion Roberto de Vicenzo (Argentina), when aged 44 years 93 days.

The oldest US Amateur Champion was Jack Westland (b Dec 14, 1904) at Seattle, Wash, on Aug 23, 1952, aged 47 years 253 days. The oldest US Open champion was Raymond Floyd at 43 years 284 days on June 15, 1986. Isabella "Belle" Robertson (b Apr 11, 1936) won the 1986 Scottish Women's Championship aged 50 years 43 days.

HIGH DRIVE: Saul Ballesteros, 22, of Chicago, on a climb of Mt McKinley, Alaska, took time out to tee up and with a 1-iron drive a ball from 20,320 ft up off the south face.

US Open

This championship was inaugurated in 1895. The lowest 72-hole aggregate is 272 (63, 71, 70, 68) by Jack Nicklaus (b Jan 21, 1940) on the Lower Course (7,015 yd) at Baltusrol Golf Club, Springfield, NJ, June 12–15, 1980. The lowest score for 18 holes is 63 by Johnny Miller (b Apr 29, 1947) of Calif on the 6,921-yd, par-71 Oakmont, Pa, course on June 17, 1973, and Jack Nicklaus and Tom Weiskopf (b Nov 9, 1942), both on June 12, 1980.

The longest delayed result in any national open championship occurred in the 1931 US Open at Toledo, Ohio. George von Elm (1901–61) and Bill Burke (1902–72) tied at 292, then tied the first replay at 149. Burke won the second replay by a single stroke after 72 extra holes.

The winners:

Year	Winner	Score
1895	Horace Rawlins	173
1896	James Foulis	152
1897	Joe Lloyd	162
1898	Fred Herd	328
1899	Willie Smith	315
1900	Harry Vardon (GB)	313
1901	Willie Anderson	331
1902	Laurie Auchterlonie	307
1903	Willie Anderson	307
1904	Willie Anderson	303
1905	Willie Anderson	314
1906	Alex Smith	295
1907	Alex Ross	302
1908	Fred McLeod	322
1909	George Sargent	290
1910	Alex Smith	298
1911	John McDermott	307
1912	John McDermott	294
1913	Francis Ouimet	304
1914	Walter Hagen	290
1915	Jerome Travers	297
1916	Charles Evans, Jr	286
1919	Walter Hagen	301
1920	Edward Ray (GB)	295
1921	Jim Barnes	289
1922	Gene Sarazen	288
1923	Robert T. Jones, Jr	296
1924	Cyril Walker	297
1925	Willie Macfarlane	291
1926	Robert T. Jones, Jr	293
1927	Tommy Armour	301
1928	Johnny Farrell	294
1929	Robert T. Jones, Jr	294
1930	Robert T. Jones, Jr	287
1931	Billy Burke	292
1932	Gene Sarazen	286
1933	John Goodman	287
1934	Olin Dutra	293
1935	Sam Parks, Jr	299
1936	Tony Manero	282
1937	Ralph Guldahl	281
1938	Ralph Guldahl	284
1939	Byron Nelson	284
1940	Lawson Little	287
1941	Craig Wood	284
1946	Lloyd Mangrum	284
1947	Lew Worsham	282
1948	Ben Hogan	276
1949	Cary Middlecoff	286
1950	Ben Hogan	287
1951	Ben Hogan	287
1952	Julius Boros	281
1953	Ben Hogan	283
1954	Ed Furgol	284
1955	Jack Fleck	287
1956	Cary Middlecoff	281
1957	Dick Mayer	282
1958	Tommy Bolt	283
1959	Billy Casper	282
1960	Arnold Palmer	280
1961	Gene Littler	281
1962	Jack Nicklaus	283
1963	Julius Boros	293
1964	Ken Venturi	278
1965	Gary Player (S Afr)	282
1966	Billy Casper	278
1967	Jack Nicklaus	275
1968	Lee Trevino	275
1969	Orville Moody	281
1970	Tony Jacklin (GB)	281
1971	Lee Trevino	280
1972	Jack Nicklaus	290
1973	Johnny Miller	279
1974	Hale Irwin	287
1975	Lou Graham	287
1976	Jerry Pate	277
1977	Hubert Green	278
1978	Andy North	285
1979	Hale Irwin	284
1980	Jack Nicklaus	272
1981	David Graham (Aust)	273
1982	Tom Watson	282
1983	Larry Nelson	280
1984	Fuzzy Zoeller	276
1985	Andy North	279
1986	Ray Floyd	279
1987	Scott Simpson	277
1988	Curtis Strange	278

Richest Prize

The largest prize for a US PGA tournament is $2 million for the Nabisco Championship of Golf, held at Pebble Beach, Calif in Nov 1988. The winner of the first prize of $360,000 was Curtis Strange who won in a playoff with Tom Kite.

The greatest first-place money was $1,000,000 won by Ian Woosman (Wales) on Dec 6, 1987 at Sun City, Bophuthatswana, S Africa.

Highest Altitude

Saul Ballesteros of Chicago drove 3 golf balls off a tee on the south face near the summit of Mt McKinley, Alaska, 20,320 ft above sea level on May 31, 1987, using a 1-iron. It matched a feat by Timothy J. Ayers (US) on May 23, 1984.

Longest Span

Jacqueline Ann Mercer (*née* Smith) (b Apr 5, 1929) won her first South African title at Humewood GC, Port Elizabeth, in 1948, and her fourth title at Port Elizabeth GC on May 4, 1979, 31 years later.

Biggest Prize Putt

Jack Nicklaus' total earnings went up by $240,000 when he sank an 8-foot putt on the 18th green of the Desert Highlands course in Scottsdale, Ariz, on Nov 25, 1984 in a ''Skins'' match against Arnold Palmer, Gary Player and Tom Watson. All three of his opponents missed their birdie putts from farther distances and Nicklaus won the accumulated prize money.

British Open

The Open Championship was inaugurated in 1860 at Prestwick, Strathclyde, Scotland. The lowest score for 9 holes is 28 by Denis Durnian (b June 30, 1950) at Royal Birdale, Southport, Eng, in the second round on July 15, 1983.

The lowest scoring round in the Open itself is 63 by Mark Hayes (US, b July 12, 1949) at Turnberry, Strathclyde, Scotland, in the second round on July 7, 1977, and by Isao Aoki (Japan) (b Aug 31, 1942) in the third round at Muirfield, July 19, 1980. Greg Norman (b Feb 10, 1955) (Aust) equaled the record of 63 at Turnberry, July 18, 1986. Henry Cotton (b Jan 26, 1907) (GB) at Royal St George's, Sandwich, Kent, England, completed the first 36 holes in 132 (67 + 65) on June 27, 1934.

The lowest 72-hole aggregate is 268 (68, 70, 65, 65) by Tom Watson (US) (b Sept 4, 1949) at Turnberry, Scotland, ending on July 9, 1977.

The winners:

Year	Winner	Score
1860	Willie Park, Sr	174
1861	Tom Morris, Sr	163
1862	Tom Morris, Sr	163
1863	Willie Park, Sr	168
1864	Tom Morris, Sr	167
1865	Andrew Strath	162
1866	Willie Park, Sr	167
1867	Tom Morris, Sr	170
1868	Tom Morris, Jr	170
1869	Tom Morris, Jr	154
1870	Tom Morris, Jr	149
1871	Not held	
1872	Tom Morris, Jr	166
1873	Tom Kidd	179
1874	Mungo Park	159
1875	Willie Park, Sr	166
1876	Robert Martin	176
1877	Jamie Anderson	160
1878	Jamie Anderson	157
1879	Jamie Anderson	170
1880	Robert Ferguson	162
1881	Robert Ferguson	170
1882	Robert Ferguson	171
1883	Willie Fernie	159
1884	Jack Simpson	160
1885	Bob Martin	171
1886	David Brown	157
1887	Willie Park, Jr	161
1888	Jack Burns	171
1889	Willie Park, Jr	155
1890	John Ball	164
1891	Hugh Kirkaldy	169
1892	Harold Hilton	305
1893	William Auchterlonie	322
1894	John Taylor	326
1895	John Taylor	322
1896	Harry Vardon	316
1897	Harry Hilton	314
1898	Harry Vardon	307
1899	Harry Vardon	310
1900	John Taylor	309
1901	James Braid	309
1902	Alexander Herd	307
1903	Harry Vardon	300
1904	Jack White	296
1905	James Braid	318
1906	James Braid	300
1907	Arnaud Massy (France)	312
1908	James Braid	291
1909	John Taylor	295
1910	James Braid	299
1911	Harry Vardon	303
1912	Edward (Ted) Ray	295
1913	John Taylor	304
1914	Harry Vardon	306
1920	George Duncan	303
1921	Jock Hutchinson (US)	296
1922	Walter Hagen (US)	300
1923	Arthur Havers	295
1924	Walter Hagen (US)	301
1925	James Barnes (US)	300
1926	Robert T. Jones, Jr (US)	291
1927	Robert T. Jones, Jr (US)	285
1928	Walter Hagen (US)	292
1929	Walter Hagen (US)	292
1930	Robert T. Jones, Jr (US)	291
1931	Tommy Armour (US)	296
1932	Gene Sarazen (US)	283
1933	Denny Shute (US)	292
1934	Henry Cotton	283
1935	Alfred Perry	283
1936	Alfred Padgham	287
1937	Henry Cotton	283
1938	Reg Whitcombe	295
1939	Richard Burton	290
1946	Sam Snead (US)	290
1947	Fred Daly	293
1948	Henry Cotton	284
1949	Bobby Locke (S Afr)	283
1950	Bobby Locke (S Afr)	279
1951	Max Faulkner	285
1952	Bobby Locke (S Afr)	287
1953	Ben Hogan (US)	282
1954	Peter Thomson (Aus)	283
1955	Peter Thomson (Aus)	281
1956	Peter Thomson (Aus)	286
1957	Bobby Locke (S Afr)	279
1958	Peter Thomson (Aus)	278
1959	Gary Player (S Afr)	284
1960	Kel Nagle (Aus)	278
1961	Arnold Palmer (US)	284
1962	Arnold Palmer (US)	276
1963	Bob Charles (NZ)	277
1964	Tony Lema (US)	279
1965	Peter Thomson (Aus)	285
1966	Jack Nicklaus (US)	282
1967	Robert de Vicenzo (Arg)	278
1968	Gary Player (S Afr)	299
1969	Tony Jacklin	280
1970	Jack Nicklaus (US)	283
1971	Lee Trevino (US)	278
1972	Lee Trevino (US)	278
1973	Tom Weiskopf (US)	276
1974	Gary Player (S Afr)	282
1975	Tom Watson (US)	279
1976	Johnny Miller (US)	279
1977	Tom Watson (US)	268
1978	Jack Nicklaus (US)	281
1979	Severiano Ballesteros (Spain)	283
1980	Tom Watson (US)	271
1981	Bill Rogers (US)	276
1982	Tom Watson (US)	284
1983	Tom Watson (US)	275
1984	Severiano Ballesteros (Spain)	276
1985	Sandy Lyle (UK)	282
1986	Greg Norman (Australia)	280
1987	Nick Faldo (UK)	279
1988	Severiano Ballesteros (Spain)	273

Fastest Rounds

With such variations in lengths of courses, speed records, even for rounds under par, are of little comparative value. Rick Baker completed 18 holes (6,142 yd) in 25 min 48.47 sec at Surfer's Paradise, Queensland, Australia, Sept 4, 1982, but this test permitted striking the ball while it was still moving.

The record for a still ball is: James Carvill (Ireland) (b Oct 13, 1965) played a round at Warrenpoint Golf Club, Co Down, Ire, in 27 min 9 sec on Jun 18, 1987.

Forty-eight players completed a round of 18 holes in 9 min 51 sec on the 7,108-yd Kyalami course near Johannesburg, S Africa, on Feb 23, 1988, using only one ball. They scored 73.

GOLFING FIRSTS: The young Mary, Queen of Scots, playing golf at St Andrews in 1563, following in the footsteps of her grandfather, James IV, who was the first golfer in history that we know by name. She was accused of playing golf only a few days after her husband's death.

ON COURSE: "SLAMMIN' " Sam Snead (left) carded a 59 for 18 holes and 122 for 36 in the 1959 Greenbrier Open. Snead has been credited with 134 tournament victories since 1934. Mickey Wright (below) celebrates her record-tying 4th US Women's Open title. Her 62 is the all-time women's best for a full-size 18-hole course.

US Masters

The lowest score in the US Masters (instituted at the 6,980-yd Augusta National Golf Course, Ga, in 1934) was 271 by Jack Nicklaus in 1965 and Raymond Floyd (b Sept 4, 1942) in 1976. Jack Nicklaus has won most often—6 times. The lowest round is 63 by Nick Price (b Jan 28, 1957) (Zimbabwe) in 1986. The oldest champion was Jack Nicklaus at 46 years 114 days in 1986, and the youngest was Severiano Ballesteros (Spain) aged 23 years 4 days in 1980.

The winners:

	Score				Score
1934 Horton Smith	284	1955 Cary Middlecoff	279	1974 Gary Player (S Afr)	278
1935 Gene Sarazen	282	1956 Jack Burke	289	1975 Jack Nicklaus	276
1936 Horton Smith	285	1957 Doug Ford	283	1976 Ray Floyd	271
1937 Byron Nelson	283	1958 Arnold Palmer	284	1977 Tom Watson	276
1938 Henry Picard	285	1959 Art Wall	284	1978 Gary Player (S Afr)	277
1939 Ralph Guldahl	279	1960 Arnold Palmer	282	1979 Fuzzy Zoeller	280
1940 Jimmy Demaret	280	1961 Gary Player (S Afr)	280	1980 Severiano Ballesteros (Spain)	275
1941 Craig Wood	280	1962 Arnold Palmer	280	1981 Tom Watson	280
1942 Byron Nelson	280	1963 Jack Nicklaus	286	1982 Craig Stadler	284
1946 Herman Keiser	282	1964 Arnold Palmer	276	1983 Severiano Ballesteros (Spain)	280
1947 Jimmy Demaret	281	1965 Jack Nicklaus	271	1984 Ben Crenshaw	277
1948 Claude Harmon	279	1966 Jack Nicklaus	288	1985 Bernhard Langer (W Ger)	282
1949 Sam Snead	282	1967 Gay Brewer	280	1986 Jack Nicklaus	279
1950 Jimmy Demaret	283	1968 Bob Goalby	277	1987 Larry Mize	285
1951 Ben Hogan	280	1969 George Archer	281	1988 Sandy Lyle (Scotland)	281
1952 Sam Snead	286	1970 Billy Casper	279		
1953 Ben Hogan	274	1971 Charles Coody	279		
1954 Sam Snead	289	1972 Jack Nicklaus	286		
		1973 Tommy Aaron	283		

US PGA Championship

The Professional Golfers' Association championship was first held in 1916 as a match play tournament but since 1958 it has been contested over 72 holes of stroke play. It has been won a record five times by Walter Hagen between 1921 and 1927, and Jack Nicklaus between 1963 and 1980. The oldest champion was Julius Boros at 48 years 18 days in 1968 and the youngest was Gene Sarazen aged 20 years 5 months 20 days in 1922. Since 1958 the greatest margin of victory has been the seven-stroke lead by Nicklaus in 1980. The lowest aggregate was 271 by Bobby Nichols at Columbus, Ohio in 1964, and the lowest round was 63 by Bruce Crampton in 1975, Ray Floyd in 1982, and Gary Player in 1984. The lowest score for 36 holes has been 131 by Hal Sutton (65, 66) in 1983. The 54-hole mark is 202 (69, 66, 67) by Raymond Floyd in 1969.

The winners:

			Score		
1916 James Barnes	1937 Denny Shute	1957 Lionel Hebert		1977 Lanny Wadkins	282
1919 James Barnes	1938 Paul Runyan	1958 Dow Finsterwald	276	1978 John Mahaffey	276
1920 Jock Hutchison	1939 Henry Picard	1959 Bob Rosburg	277	1979 David Graham (Aus)	272
1921 Walter Hagen	1940 Byron Nelson	1960 Jay Hebert	281	1980 Jack Nicklaus	274
1922 Gene Sarazen	1941 Vic Ghezzi	1961 Jerry Barber	277	1981 Larry Nelson	273
1923 Gene Sarazen	1942 Sam Snead	1962 Gary Player (S Afr)	278	1982 Ray Floyd	272
1924 Walter Hagen	1943 Not held	1963 Jack Nicklaus	279	1983 Hal Sutton	274
1925 Walter Hagen	1944 Bob Hamilton	1964 Bob Nichols	271	1984 Lee Trevino	273
1926 Walter Hagen	1945 Byron Nelson	1965 Dave Marr	280	1985 Hubert Green	278
1927 Walter Hagen	1946 Ben Hogan	1966 Al Geiberger	280	1986 Bob Tway	276
1928 Leo Diegel	1947 Jim Ferrier	1967 Don January	281	1987 Larry Nelson	287
1929 Leo Diegel	1948 Ben Hogan	1968 Julius Boros	281	1988 Jeff Sluman	272
1930 Tommy Armour	1949 Sam Snead	1969 Ray Floyd	276		
1931 Tom Creavy	1950 Chandler Harper	1970 Dave Stockton	279		
1932 Olin Dutra	1951 Sam Snead	1971 Jack Nicklaus	281		
1933 Gene Sarazen	1952 Jim Turnesa	1972 Gary Player (S Afr)	281		
1934 Paul Runyan	1953 Walter Burkemo	1973 Jack Nicklaus	277		
1935 Johnny Revolta	1954 Chick Harbert	1974 Lee Trevino	276		
1936 Denny Shute	1955 Doug Ford	1975 Jack Nicklaus	276		
	1956 Jack Burke	1976 Dave Stockton	281		

MOST TOURNAMENT VICTORIES: Byron Nelson (left) in 1945 won 18 tournaments (plus one unofficial), including 11 in a row. He might have won more, but the Masters and the British and US Opens were not contested during the war years. Kathy Whitworth (center) has won 88 LPGA contests in 23 touring years through 1985. BIGGEST PRIZE WINNER: Johnny Miller (right) captured the $500,000 prize offered by Sun City, a course in an enclave in S Africa, in 1982 after a playoff against Severiano Ballesteros of Spain.

LONGEST PUTT: Cary Middlecoff holed an 86-foot putt on the 13th green at the Augusta National, Georgia, in 1955. The record putt helped him to win the Masters.

RECORDS IN THE 20's: Walter Hagen (US) blasting from a bunker at the 17th green at Holylake in the 1923 British Open. He did not win that year but he did win that event 4 times, the US Open twice and the PGA 5 times. (Radio Times—Hulton)

US Women's Open

This tournament was first held in 1946, and currently is played over 72 holes of stroke play. Betsy Rawls won a record four times between 1951 and 1960, and this was equalled by Mickey Wright between 1958 and 1964. The oldest champion was Fay Crocker (Uru) at 40 years 11 months in 1955, while the youngest was Catherine Lacoste (France) at 22 years 5 days in 1967, when she became the only amateur player to win the title. The greatest margin of victory was by Babe Didrikson Zaharias who beat Betty Hicks by 12 strokes in 1954. The lowest aggregate score has been 280 (70, 70, 68, 72) by Amy Alcott in 1980, and the lowest round was 65 by Sally Little in 1978. The record for 36 holes is 139 by Carol Mann and Donna Caponi in 1970, the latter going on to a 54-hole score of 210.

The winners:

	Score
1946 Patty Berg beat Betty Jameson 5 and 4	
1947 Betty Jameson	295
1948 Mildred Zaharias	300
1949 Louise Suggs	291
1950 Mildred Zaharias	291
1951 Betsy Rawls	293
1952 Louise Suggs	284
1953 Betsy Rawls	302
1954 Mildred Zaharias	291
1955 Fay Crocker (Uru)	299
1956 Kathy Cornelius	302
1957 Betsy Rawls	299
1958 Mickey Wright	290
1959 Mickey Wright	287
1960 Betsy Rawls	292
1961 Mickey Wright	293
1962 Murle Lindstrom	301
1963 Mary Mills	289
1964 Mickey Wright	290
1965 Carol Mann	290
1966 Sandra Spuzich	297
1967 Catherine Lacoste (France)	294
1968 Sue Berning	289
1969 Donna Caponi	294
1970 Donna Caponi	287
1971 JoAnne Carner	288
1972 Sue Maxwell Berning	290
1973 Sue Maxwell Berning	290
1974 Sandra Haynie	295
1975 Sandra Palmer	295
1976 JoAnne Carner	292
1977 Hollis Stacy	298
1978 Hollis Stacy	289
1979 Jerilyn Britz	284
1980 Amy Alcott	280
1981 Pat Bradley	279
1982 Janet Alex	283
1983 Jan Stephenson	290
1984 Hollis Stacy	290
1985 Kathy Baker	280
1986 Jane Geddes	287
1987 Laura Davies	285
1988 Liselotte Neumann (Sweden) (record low)	277

LEADING PROS: Severiano Ballesteros (Spain) (left) began winning major tournaments in 1979 when he was victorious in the British Open. Then he won the Masters in 1980 and 1983, and the British Open again in 1984. Here he is preparing to enter the water to retrieve an errant shot. (Phil Sheldon) Nancy Lopez (center) in 1985 set a season record by winning $416,472, only to be beaten by Pat Bradley (right) who earned $492,021 in tournament play. Bradley's career earnings reached $2,442,315 by the end of 1988. (Lopez photo by All-Sport; Bradley photo LPGA by SPORTSELL)

US Amateur

Initially held in the same week and at the same venue as the first US Open in 1895. Bobby Jones won a record five times between 1924 and 1930, having first qualified for the tournament in 1916, aged 14 yr 5½ months, the youngest ever to do so. The oldest player to win the title was Jack Westland, aged 47 years 8 months 9 days in 1952, while the youngest was Robert Gardner at 19 years 5 months in 1909. (Three years later, in 1912, Gardner broke the world pole vault record becoming the first to clear 13 ft.)

The winners:

1895 Charles Macdonald	1926 George Von Elm	1960 Deane Beman
1896 H. J. Whigham	1927 Robert T. Jones, Jr	1961 Jack Nicklaus
1897 H. J. Whigham	1928 Robert T. Jones, Jr	1962 Labron Harris
1898 Findlay Douglas	1929 Harrison Johnston	1963 Deane Beman
1899 H. M. Harriman	1930 Robert T. Jones, Jr	1964 Bill Campbell
1900 Walter Travis	1931 Francis Ouimet	1965 Bob Murphy
1901 Walter Travis	1932 Ross Somerville (Can)	1966 Gary Cowan (Can)
1902 Louis James	1933 George Dunlap, Jr	1967 Bob Dickson
1903 Walter Travis	1934 Lawson Little	1968 Bruce Fleisher
1904 Chandler Egan	1935 Lawson Little	1969 Steve Melnyk
1905 Chandler Egan	1936 John Fisher	1970 Lanny Wadkins
1906 Eben Byers	1937 John Goodman	1971 Gary Cowan (Can)
1907 Jerome Travers	1938 William Turnesa	1972 Marvin Giles
1908 Jerome Travers	1939 Marvin Ward	1973 Craig Stadler
1909 Robert Gardner	1940 Richard Chapman	1974 Jerry Pate
1910 William Fownes, Jr	1941 Marvin Ward	1975 Fred Ridley
1911 Harold Hilton (GB)	1946 Stanley Bishop	1976 Bill Sander
1912 Jerome Travers	1947 Robert Riegel	1977 John Fought
1913 Jerome Travers	1948 William Turnesa	1978 John Cook
1914 Francis Ouimet	1949 Charles Coe	1979 Mark O'Meara
1915 Robert Gardner	1950 Sam Urzetta	1980 Hal Sutton
1916 Charles Evans, Jr	1951 Billy Maxwell	1981 Nathaniel Crosby
1919 Davidson Herron	1952 Jack Westland	1982 Jay Sigel
1920 Charles Evans, Jr	1953 Gene Littler	1983 Jay Sigel
1921 Jesse Gullford	1954 Arnold Palmer	1984 Scott Vertplank
1922 Jesse Sweetser	1955 Harvie Ward	1985 Sam Randolph
1923 Max Marston	1956 Harvie Ward	1986 Stewart Alexander
1924 Robert T. Jones, Jr	1957 Hillman Robbins	1987 Billy Mayfair
1925 Robert T. Jones, Jr	1958 Charles Coe	1988 Eric Meeks
	1959 Jack Nicklaus	

US Women's Amateur Championship

Instituted in Nov 1895, and currently 36 final holes of match play after 36 qualifying holes of stroke play. Glenna Collett Vare won a record 6 titles between 1922 and 1935. The oldest champion was Dorothy Campbell-Hurd (GB) aged 41 years 4 months when winning her third title in 1924, and the youngest was Laura Baugh at 16 years 2 months 21 days in 1971. Margaret Curtis beat her sister, Harriot, in the 1907 final—they later presented the Curtis Cup for competition between the US and GB.

Most Shots One Hole

The highest number of strokes taken at a single hole in a major tournament was achieved in the inaugural (British) Open Championship at Prestwick, Scotland, in 1860, when an unnamed player took 21. In the 1938 US Open, Ray Ainsley achieved instant fame when he took 19 strokes at the par-4 16th hole. Most of them were in an attempt to hit the ball out of a fast-moving brook. Hans Merrell of Mogadore, Ohio, took 19 strokes on the par-3, 222-yd 16th during the Bing Crosby tournament at Cypress Point Club, Del Monte, Calif, on Jan 17, 1959. At Biarritz, France in 1888 it was reported that Chevalier von Cittern took 316 for 18 holes, thus averaging 17.55 strokes per hole.

The story to top them all concerns a lady player in the qualifying round of a tournament in Shawnee-on-Delaware, Pa in the early part of the century. Her card showed she took 166 strokes for the short 130-yd 16th hole. Her tee shot landed and floated in a nearby river, and, with her meticulous husband, she set out in a boat and eventually beached the ball 1½ mi downstream. From there she had to play through a forest until finally she holed the ball. A. J. Lewis, playing at Peacehaven, Sussex, Eng, in 1890 had 156 putts on one green without holing the ball.

OUTSIDE CHOICE: Laura Davies was the first Briton to win the US Women's Open since the tournament began, when she took the 1987 title. (All-Sport)

Most Balls Hit in One Hour

The most balls driven in one hour, over 100 yds and into a target area, is 1,064 (from 1,290 attempts) by David Morris at Abergele Golf Club, Clwyd, Wales, May 21, 1988.

Ryder Cup

The biennial Ryder Cup (instituted 1927) professional match between the US and GB (Europe since 1979) has been won by the US 21½–5½. William Earl "Billy" Casper (b San Diego, Calif, June 24, 1931) has the record of winning most matches, with 20 won out of 37 (1961–75). Neil Cales (GB) played in a record 40 matches (1961–77).

In 1987, Ian Woosman (Wales) (b 1958) 5 ft 4½ in, played a starring role against the US at Muirfield Village, Ohio, as GB won.

HOLES-IN-ONE

Golf Digest was notified in 1987 of 41,406 holes-in-one.

Longest

The longest straight hole shot in one is the 10th hole (447 yd) at Miracle Hills GC, Omaha, Neb. Robert Mitera achieved a hole-in-one there on Oct 7, 1965. Mitera, aged 21 and 5 ft 6 in tall, weighed 165 lb. A two-handicap player, he normally drove 245 yd. A 50-mph gust carried his shot over a 290-yd

drop-off. The group in front testified to the remaining distance.

The women's record is 393 yd by Marie Robie of Wollaston, Mass, on the first hole of the Furnace Brook GC, Sept 4, 1949.

The longest dogleg achieved in one is the 480-yd 5th hole at Hope CC, Ark, by Larry Bruce on Nov 15, 1962.

Consecutive

There is no recorded instance of a golfer performing three consecutive holes-in-one, but there are at least 16 cases of "aces" being achieved in two consecutive holes, of which the greatest was Norman L. Manley's unique "double albatross" on two par-4 holes (330-yd 7th and 290-yd 8th) on the Del Valle CC course, Saugus, Calif, on Sept 2, 1964.

The first woman ever to card consecutive aces is Sue Prell, on the 13th and 14th holes at Chatswood GC, Sydney, Australia, on May 29, 1977.

The closest recorded instances of a golfer getting 3 consecutive holes-in-one were by the Rev Harold Snider (b July 4, 1900) who aced the 8th, 13th and 14th holes of the par-3 Ironwood course in Phoenix, Ariz, on June 9, 1976, and the late Dr Joseph Boydstone on the 3rd, 4th and 9th at Bakersfield GC, Calif on Oct 10, 1962.

Most Aces

The most aces in one year is 33 by Scott Palmer (b Nov 22, 1958) June 5, 1983–May 31, 1984, all on holes between 130 and 350 yd in length in San Diego County, Calif. He also made 4 aces in 4 consecutive rounds, Oct 9–12, 1983.

The greatest number of holes-in-one reported in a career is 98, also by Scott Palmer (see above) through 1988. Of these aces, 26 were shot on short courses, but none were on holes of less than 100 yd.

Douglas Porteous, 28, aced 4 holes over 39 consecutive holes—the 3rd and 6th on Sept 26, and the 5th on Sept 28 at Ruchill GC, Glasgow, Scotland, and the 6th at the Clydebank and District GC Course on Sept 30, 1974. Robert Taylor holed the 188-yd

---

Most Eagles in One Round

Keith Kollmeyer had four 3's on par-5 holes in one round at the Waialae Country Club, Honolulu, Hawaii, on June 11, 1988, tying the 1981 record set by Ken Harrington at the Silver Lake C.C. in Cuyahoga Falls, O.

YOUNGEST AND OLDEST TO SHOOT ACES: Scott Statler (left) at the age of 4 shot an ace on his father's par-3 golf course in Greensburg, Pa in 1962. Otto Bucher of Switzerland holed one at the age of 99 years 244 days in 1985 at the club owned by a brother of Seve Ballesteros.

16th hole at Hunstanton, Norfolk, England, on three successive days—May 31, June 1 and 2, 1974. On May 12, 1984, Joe Lucius of Tiffin, Ohio, aced for the 13th time the par-3, 141-yd 15th hole at the Mohawk Golf Club. Lucius has 10 aces for the 10th hole on the same course, and 31 aces in all.

Youngest and Oldest

The youngest golfer recorded to have shot a hole-in-one was Scott Statler of Greensburg, Pa, now of Los Alamitos, Calif. At the age of 4 years 172 days on July 30, 1962, he shot an ace on hole 7 of Statler's Par 3 Golf Course, Greensburg, Pa. *Golf Digest* credits Tommy Moore (6 yrs 1 month 7 days) of Hagerstown, Md with being the youngest for an ace he shot on a 145-yd hole in 1969.

The oldest golfer to have performed the feat is Otto Bucher (Switz) (b May 12, 1885) aged 99 years 244 days on Jan 13, 1985 when he aced the 130-yd 12th hole at La Manga GC, Spain.

The oldest woman to score an ace is Erna Ross, aged 95 years 257 days, who holed-in-one on the 112-yd 17th hole of the Everglades Club, Palm Beach, Fla, on May 25, 1986.

The oldest player to score his age is C. Arthur Thompson (1869–1975) of Victoria, BC, Canada, who scored 103 on the Uplands course of 6,215 yd when age 103 in 1973.

GREYHOUND RACING

The first greyhound meeting was staged at Hendon, North London, Eng, with a railed hare operated by a windlass, in Sept 1876. Modern greyhound racing originated with the perfecting of the mechanical hare by Owen Patrick Smith at Emeryville, Calif in 1919. St Petersburg Kennel Club, in St Petersburg, Fla, which opened on Jan 3, 1925, is the oldest greyhound track in the world still in operation on its original site.

Fastest Greyhound

The highest speed at which any greyhound has been timed is 41.72 mph (410 yd in 20.1 sec) by *The Shoe* on the then straightaway track at Richmond, NSW, Australia on Apr 25, 1968. It is estimated that he covered the last 100 yd in 4.5 sec or at 45.45 mph.

Fastest Speeds for 4-Bend Tracks

The fastest automatically timed speed recorded for a full 4-bend race is 38.89 mph at Brighton, Eng, by *Glen Miner* on May 4, 1982 with a time of 29.62 sec for 563 yd. The fastest over hurdles is 37.64 mph at Brighton, Eng, by *Wotchit Buster* on Aug 22, 1978.

Most Wins

The most career wins is 143 by the American greyhound *JR's Ripper* in 1982–6. The world record for consecutive victories is 32 by *Ballyregan Bob,* owned by Cliff Kevern and trained by George Curtis from 1985 to Dec 8, 1986, including 16 track record times. His race wins were by an average of more than nine lengths.

Highest Earnings

The career earnings record is held by *Homspun Rowy* with $297,000 in the US, 1984–7. The richest first prize for a greyhound race is $200,000 won by *Dacia* in the Great Greyhound Race at Seabrook, NH, in 1987.

Longest Odds

Apollo Prince won at odds of 250–1 at Springvale, Vic, Australia on Nov 14, 1968.

GYMNASTICS

Earliest References

Tumbling and similar exercises were performed *c.* 2600 BC as religious rituals in China, but it was the Greeks who coined the word gymnastics. A primitive form was practiced in the ancient Olympic Games, but it was not until Johann Friedrich Simon began to teach at Basedow's Gymnasium in Dessau, Germany, in 1776 that the foundations of the modern sport were laid. The first national federation was formed in Germany in 1860 and the International Gymnastics Federation was founded in Liège, Belgium in 1881. The sport was included at the first modern Olympic Games at Athens in 1896.

Current events for men are: floor exercises, horse vault, rings, pommel horse, parallel bars and horizontal bar, while for women they are: floor exercises, horse vault, asymmetrical bars, and balance beam.

American Cup Titles

Olympic gold medalist Mary Lou Retton (b 1968) of Fairmont, W Va won her first American Cup in 1983 in NYC and has not relinquished the title since that competition. She is the only female gymnast to hold the title for three straight years. US gymnast Kurt Thomas won the title three years in a row from 1978 to 1980.

World Cup Titles

Gymnasts to have won two World Cup (inst 1975) overall titles are three men, Nikolai Andrianov (USSR), Aleksandr Ditiatin (USSR) and Li Ning

WALL PRESS: Backing a human body with an arched spine against a wall and keeping it there for more than 1¼ hours is the record set by Kevin DeWitt of Kennewick, Wash, in July 1986. (Bob Brawdy/Trinity Herald)

(China) (b Sept 8, 1963) and one woman Maria Filatova (USSR) (b July 19, 1961).

Modern Rhythmic Gymnastics

This recent addition to the female side of the sport incorporates exercises with different hand-held apparatus, including ribbons, balls, ropes, hoops and Indian clubs. The most overall titles won in world championships is 3 by Maria Gigova (Bulgaria) 1969, 71, and 73 (shared), while the most individual apparatus titles is 9 by Gigova and Galina Shugurova (USSR). The latter has also won a record total of 14 medals. This category of the sport was included in the Olympic Games for the first time in 1984.

World and Olympic Championships

In Olympic years, the Olympic title is the World Championship title. Since 1952, the USSR has won 18 out of 21 titles, including 9 Olympic and 9 World titles.

In the 1988 Olympic Games, the USSR not only

won 9 gold medals outright but tied in 2 other categories, while Romania won 3 of the women's events.

The greatest number of individual titles won by a man in the World Championships (including 6 Olympics) is 10 by Boris Shakhlin (USSR) between 1954 and 1964. He was also on three winning teams. The women's record is 12 individual wins and 5 team titles by Larissa Semyonovna Latynina (b Dec 27, 1934, retired 1966) of the USSR, between 1956 and 1964, including Olympics. She has the most medals, 33, of which 18 are Olympic medals. Japan has won the men's team title a record 10 times (including 5 Olympics) between 1960 and 1978 and the USSR the women's team title on 17 occasions (including 8 Olympics) out of 20 since 1952.

MEN
Team: USSR (Vladimir Gogoladze, Vladimir Nouvikov, Sergey Kharkov, Dmitri Bilozertchev, Vladimir Artemov, Valeri Lyukhin)
All-Around: Vladimir Artemov (USSR)
Floor Exercise: Sergey Kharkov (USSR)
Pommel (tie): Lyubomir Geraskov (Bulgaria), Zsolt Borkai (Hungary), Dmitri Bilozertchev (USSR)
Rings (tie): Holger Behrendt (E Ger), Dmitri Bilozertchev (USSR)
Vault: Lou Yun (China)
Parallel Bars: Vladimir Artemov (USSR)
Horizontal Bar (tie): Vladimir Artemov (USSR), Valeri Lyukhin (USSR)

WOMEN
Team: USSR (Svetlana Baitova, Elena Chevtchenko, Olga Strajeva, Svetlana Boginskaya, Natalia Lachtchenova, Elena Shushunova)
All-Around: Elena Shushunova (USSR)
Vault: Svetlana Boginskaya (USSR)
Uneven Bar: Daniela Silivas (Romania)
Balance Beam: Daniela Silivas (Romania)
Floor Exercise: Daniela Silivas (Romania)
Rhythmic Gymnastics: Marina Lobatch (USSR)

Wall Press (Samson's Chair)

Sitting unsupported, back 90° flat against a wall, looks simple, but the longest anyone can stay in that position (see photo) is 1 hour, 16 min, 12 sec, a record set by Kevin DeWitt of Kennewick, Wash, Dec 1986.

Youngest International Competitors

Pasakevi "Voula" Kouna (b Dec 6, 1971) was aged 9 years 299 days at the start of the Balkan Games at Serres, Greece on Oct 1, 1981, when she represented Greece. Olga Bicherova (b Oct 26, 1966) won the women's world title at 15 years 33 days in Nov 1981. The youngest men's champion was Dmitri Relozerchev (USSR) at 16 years 315 days at Budapest, Hungary in 1983.

SKIP-RUNNING: Ashrita Furman set another world record when he ran 10 miles like this in 76 min 33 sec in May 1987, to add to his records. He now has 11 in all. (See full chart with photos on p. 6)

ROPE-JUMPING MARATHON: Randall R. Schneider skipped rope for 22 hours 5 min 2 sec at the Wisconsin State Fair, May 7, 1988.

A PERFECT "10": Nadia Comaneci (Romania) (left and right above) was 14 years old when she made Olympic history as the first gymnast ever to be awarded a perfect score. Her unprecedented feat came during the 1976 Olympics in Montreal. She went on to earn 6 more 10's for a remarkable total of 7 flawless routines (4 on uneven parallel bars and 3 on the balance beam).

RHYTHMIC GYMNASTS: Exercising with ribbons was included in the 1984 Olympics for the first time. Marina Kunyavsky of LA, 1987 National Champion (right), and Diane Simpson of Evanston, Ill (below) show how it is performed. (Konica, official sponsor of US Rhythmic Gymnastics Team)

BEST ALL-AROUND OLYMPIC GYMNAST: Mary Lou Retton (US) won the gold medal in this category, silver medal in the vault and bronze medal in the uneven parallel bars in the 1984 Games.

Rope Jumps in One Hour

Robert R. Commers (b May 15, 1950) of Connellsville, Pa, set a new record by rope jumping 13,160 revolutions with zero faults in one hour on Mar 19, 1988, beating the old record by 664 jumps.

Push-Ups

Paul Lynch (GB) did 32,573 push-ups in 24 hours at Bedford Hall, London, Sept 12–13, 1987, and also holds the record for 3,857 one-arm push-ups in 5 hours in London's Guinness World of Records, June 6, 1987.

John Decker did 5,010 finger-tip push-ups in 5 hours at a department store in Manchester, Eng, June 19, 1987.

Harry Lee Welch, Jr did 100 one-finger consecutive push-ups in Durham, NC on Mar 31, 1985.

Chung Kwun Ying (Hong Kong) did 2,750 hand-stand push-ups at Government City Hall, Hong Kong, on May 18, 1986. In one hour he did 1,985.

In one year (1985) Adam Parsons, a retired Lt Col in the USAF, did 1,293,850 documented push-ups in Akron, O.

Chinning the Bar

The greatest number of continuous chin-ups (from a dead hang position) is 370 by Lee Chin Yong (b Aug 15, 1925) at Backyon Gymnasium, Seoul, S Korea on May 14, 1988. Robert Chisnall (b Dec 9, 1952) performed 22 one-arm (his right) chin-ups, from a ring, 18 two-finger chins and 12 one-finger chins, from a nylon strap on Dec 3, 1982 at Queen's Univ, Kingston, Ont, Canada.

Jumping Jacks

The greatest number of side-straddle hops continuously is 104,538 by Louis Scripa, Jr, in Sacramento, Calif, Dec 2, 1986.

PFC Troy Shawn Harris, at Fort Bragg, NC, set a record of 50,482 jumping jacks in 12 hours 27 min on Aug 20, 1988. He went for the record after discovering he could do 1,000 jumping jacks in 15 min.

Parallel Bar Dips

Michael Williams performed 2,682 parallel bar dips in 1 hour on July 29, 1988 at Don Styler's Gym, Gosport, Eng.

Somersaults

Ashrita Furman (US) performed 8,341 forward rolls over 12 miles 390 yards in 10½ hours on Apr

PUSH-UP CHAMPION: Paul Lynch of London holds the record for one-arm push-ups with 3,857 in 5 hours, set on June 6, 1987. He also set a new record for 2-arm push-ups (correct position shown here) at 32,573 in 24 hours in Sept 1987. (Jon Arns)

HUMAN SUSPENSION BRIDGE: 300 gymnasts of NSA constructed this bridge in Worcester, Mass on July 10, 1988, and held the position for over 45 sec. The human ladder towers were 25 ft high and the bridge "cables" were 7 ft off the floor at the lowest point. (Nichiren Shoshu Soka Gakkai of America)

30, 1986, performing from Lexington to Charlestown (Boston), Mass.

Shigeru Iwasaki (b 1960) backwards somersaulted over 50 m (54.68 yd) in 10.8 sec in Tokyo, March 30, 1980.

Sit-Ups and Leg Raises

Lou Scripa, Jr of Sacramento, Calif did 100,003 sit-ups in 50 hours, Aug 5–7, 1985. During the first 24 hours he did 60,405. These were done with his legs straight, with no weights or anyone holding his legs.

Tim Kides of W New York, NJ, set a record for leg raises—25,000 in 11 hours 57 min 15 sec on Oct 14, 1986.

Pummel Horse

Lee Thomas (GB) did 75 consecutive double circles on BBC television on Dec 12, 1985.

HANDSTAND PUSH-UP CHAMPION (right): 8-year-old Chung Kwun Ying pushed-up 2,750 times consecutively like this in Hong Kong, May 18, 1986. In one hour he did 1,985. (AP)

ROPE JUMPING

The longest recorded rope-jumping marathon (with 5-min rest break after each hour) was one of 22 hours 5 min 2 sec by Randall R. Schneider (US) at W Allis, Wis, on May 7, 1988.

Other rope-jumping records made without a break and with no faults:

Most turns in 1 minute	418	Tyrone Krohn	Middletown (NY) HS	July 10, 1984
Most turns in 10 seconds	128	Albert Rayner	Birmingham, Eng	Nov 19, 1982
Most turns in 1 hour	13,160	Robert R. Commers	Connellsville, Pa	Mar 19, 1988
Most doubles (with cross)	2,411	Ken Solis	Glendale, Wis	Mar 22, 1988
Double turns	10,133	Katsumi Suzuki (Japan)	Saitama	Sept 29, 1979
Treble turns	381	Katsumi Suzuki (Japan)	Saitama	May 29, 1975
Quadruple turns	51	Katsumi Suzuki (Japan)	Saitama	May 29, 1975
Quintuple turns	6	Hideyuki Tateda (Japan)	Aomori	June 19, 1982
Duration	1,264 miles	Tom Morris (Aust)	Brisbane-Cairns	1963
Most on a single rope (minimum 12 turns obligatory)	181	(160-ft rope)	Greeley, Colo	June 28, 1988
Most turns on single rope (team of 90)	163	Students at Nishigoshi Higashi Elementary School	Kumamoto, Japan	Feb 27, 1987
On a tightrope (consecutive)	58	Bryan Andrew (*née* Dewhurst)	TROS TV, The Netherlands	Aug 6, 1981
Skip-running	10 mi in 71 min 54 sec	Ken Solis	Johnstown, Pa	Aug 6, 1988

ROPE-SKIPPERS GALORE: A record-breaking 181 rope-jumpers set a mark for most on a single rope. The 181 did the obligatory 12 turns on a 165-ft rope on June 28, 1988 at the International Rope Skipping Organization Championships at Greeley, Colo.

MOST SUCCESSFUL WOMAN GYMNAST in the Olympics has been Vera Caslavska-Odlozil (Czech) with 7 individual golds. (Tony Duffy-All Sport)

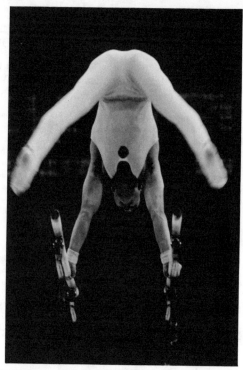

MOST MEDALS: Aleksandr Ditiatin (USSR) is the only person to win a medal in all 8 categories in one Games (1980, Moscow).

GYMNASTIC GOLDS: The only men to win 6 gold medals in the Olympics are these two Russians, Boris Shakhlin (left) and Nikolai Andrianov (right).

HANDBALL

U.S. Handball Association National Champions

PROFESSIONAL SINGLES

1951	Walter Plekan
1952	Vic Hershkowitz
1953	Bob Brady
1954	Vic Hershkowitz
1955–57	Jim Jacobs
1958–59	John Sloan
1960	Jim Jacobs
1961	John Sloan
1962–63	Oscar Obert
1964–65	Jim Jacobs
1966–67	Paul Haber
1968	Simon (Stuffy) Singer
1969–71	Paul Haber
1972	Fred Lewis
1973	Terry Mack
1974–76	Fred Lewis
1977	Naty Alvarado
1978	Fred Lewis
1979–80	Naty Alvarado
1981	Fred Lewis
1982–85	Naty Alvarado

FOUR-WALL DOUBLES

1951–52	Frank Coyle and Bill Baier
1953	Sam Haber and Harry Dreyfuss
1954–56	Sam Haber and Ken Schneider
1957–59	Phil Collins and John Sloan
1960	Jim Jacobs and Dick Weisman
1961	John Sloan and Vic Hershkowitz
1962–63	Jim Jacobs and Marty Decatur
1964	John Sloan and Phil Ebert
1965	Jim Jacobs and Marty Decatur
1966	Pete Tyson and Bob Lindsay
1967–68	Jim Jacobs and Marty Decatur
1969	Lou Kramberg and Lou Russo
1970	Carl Obert and Rudy Obert
1971	Ray Neveau and Simie Fein
1972	Kent Fusselman and Al Drews
1973–74	Ray Neveau and Simie Fein
1975	Steve Lott and Marty Decatur
1976	Dan O'Connor and Gary Rohrer
1977	Matt Kelley and Skip McDowell
1978–79	Marty Decatur and Simon (Stuffy) Singer
1980	Skip McDowell and Harry Robertson
1981	Jack Roberts and Tom Kopatich
1982–85	Vern Roberts and Naty Alvarado

Origin

Handball is a game of ancient Celtic origin. In the early 19th century only a front wall was used, but later side and back walls were added. The court is now standardized 60 feet by 30 feet in Ireland, Ghana and Australia, and 40 feet by 20 feet in Canada, Mexico and the US. The game is played with both a hard and soft ball in Ireland, and a soft ball only, elsewhere.

The earliest international contest was in New York

OFF THE WALL: Jim Jacobs (d 1988), better known as co-manager of Mike Tyson and other boxers, was the most successful player in the USHA National Four-Wall Championships with 6 singles and 6 doubles titles.

City in 1887, between the champions of the US and Ireland.

Handball was introduced into the Olympic Games at Berlin in 1936 as an 11-a-side outdoor game with Germany winning, but when re-introduced in 1972 it was an indoor game with seven-a-side, the standard size of team since 1952.

Most Titles

The most successful player in the U.S.H.A. National Four-Wall Championships has been James Jacobs (US), who won a record 6 singles titles (1955–56–57–60–64–65) and shared in 6 doubles titles (1960–62–63–65–67–68). Martin Decatur has won 8 doubles titles (1962–63–65–67–68–75–78–79), 5 of these with Jacobs as his partner. Fred Lewis has also won 6 singles titles (1972–74–75–76–78–81).

One-wall handball is played almost exclusively in NYC at almost 2,000 one-wall courts, in playgrounds and schools. Among the most successful players have been Steve Sandler, Oscar Obert and Vic Hershkowitz. The current singles champion is Eddie Golden.

HANDBALL (Team)

Handball was first played without a wall *c.* 1895 in Germany. It was introduced into the Olympic Games at Berlin in 1936 as an 11-a-side outdoor game, with Germany winning, but when re-introduced in 1972 it was an indoor game with 7-a-side, the standard size of teams since 1952.

The International Handball Federation was founded in 1946. The first international match was held at Halle/Saale on Sept 3, 1925 when Austria beat Germany 6–3.

Olympics and World Championships

Four Olympic titles have been won by the USSR (men 1976 and 1988, women 1976 and 1980). S Korean women won in 1988. World championships were inaugurated in New York in October, 1964, with competitors from Australia, Canada, Ireland, Mexico and the US. The US is the only nation to have won twice, with victories in 1964 and 1967 (shared). The Super Cup, contested by men's Olympic and World Champions, was first held in 1979. W Germany and the USSR have each won once.

Most Championships

The most victories in world championship (inst.

HANDBALL WITHOUT A WALL: This version of the game, an Olympic sport, played on a court with a soccer ball, goal posts, and a net similar to hockey is popular in Europe. In this picture, the USSR is trying for a goal. (All-Sport)

1938) competition are by Rumania with four men's and three women's titles from 1956 to 1974.

Highest Score

The highest score in an international match was recorded when the USSR beat Afghanistan 86–2 in the "Friendly Army Tournament" at Miskolc, Hungary in August 1981.

Marathon

At the Castlebridge Handball Club, County Wexford, Ireland, a game lasted 45 hours 50 min, Sept 26–28, 1986.

HARNESS RACING

Origins

Trotting races were held in Valkenburg, Netherlands, in 1554. In England the trotting gait (the simultaneous use of the diagonally opposite legs) was known in the 16th century. The sulky first appeared in harness racing in 1829. Pacers thrust out their fore and hind legs simultaneously on one side.

PACER "Matt's Scooter," driven by Michel Lachance, set a time trial record of 1:48.4 on a mile track at Lexington, Ky, Sept 22, 1988. (US Trotting Assn)

"CALL FOR RAIN," pacer driven by Clint Galbraith, tied the race record of 1:49.6 for a mile at Lexington, Ky, Oct 1, 1988. (US Trotting Assn)

Greatest Winnings

The greatest award won by any harness horse is the $3,225,653 won by the pacer "Nihilator," who was victorious in 35 of 38 races, 1984–85. He also holds the single season winnings record with $1,864,286 in 1985.

HARNESS RACING RECORDS AGAINST TIME

TROTTING

Time Trial (mile track)	1:53.4	"Prakas" (driver William O'Donnell) (Can) at Du Quoin, Ill	Aug 31, 1985
Race Record (mile)	1:52.2	"Mack Lobell" (driver John D. Campbell) (US) at Springfield, Ill	Aug 21, 1987

PACING

Time Trial (mile track)	1:48.4	"Matt's Scooter" (driver Michel Lachance) (US) at Lexington, Ky	Sept 22, 1988
Race Record (mile)	1:49.6	"Nihilator" (driver William O'Donnell) (Can) at East Rutherford, NJ	Aug 3, 1985
	(tied) 1:49.6	"Call for Rain" (driver Clint Galbraith) at Lexington, Ky	Oct 1, 1988

The greatest amount won by a trotting horse is $2,919,421 by "Ourasi" (France) through 1988.

The largest purse ever was $2,161,000 for the Woodrow Wilson 2-year-olds race over 1 mi at Meadowlands, NJ, on Aug 16, 1984, of which a record $1,080,500 went to the winner "Nihilator" driven by Billy O'Donnell (b May 4, 1948).

Highest Prices

The highest price ever paid for a pacer is for "Nihilator," who was syndicated for $19.2 million in 1984, topping the record of $10 million set by his father, "Niatross," in 1979.

The highest price paid for a trotter is $5.25 million for "Mystic Park" by Lana Lobell Farms from Allen, Gerald and Irving Wechter of NY and Robert Lester of Florida, announced on July 13, 1982. Upon syndication on May 28, 1988, "Mack Lobell" owned by Louis P. Guida of Lawrenceville, NJ and Blaedingeaas Stuteri, Inc, of Vislanda, Sweden, was valued at $6–8 million.

Most Successful Driver

The $70,123,356 won by John D. Campbell (b Apr 8, 1955) through 1988, set a record for earnings in a career. The most in a year are $11,148,565 in 1988 by Campbell also.

The most successful sulky driver in North America has been Herve Filion (Canada) (b Quebec, Feb 1, 1940) who achieved 11,193 wins and earnings of $61,430,404 from the start of his career through 1988. A fellow Canadian, Michel Lachance, broke Filion's 1974 season record of 637 victories by winning 770 races in 1986. Filion broke that record in 1988 with 798 victories.

HOCKEY

Origins

There is pictorial evidence of a hockey-like game (Kalv) being played on ice in The Netherlands in the early 16th century. The game probably was first played in North America on Dec 25, 1855, at Kingston, Ontario, Canada, but Halifax also lays claim to priority.

The International Ice Hockey Federation was founded in 1908. The National Hockey League was inaugurated in 1917. The World Hockey Association was formed in 1971 and disbanded in 1979 when 4 of its teams joined the NHL.

World Championships and Olympic Games

World Championships were first held for amateurs in 1920 in conjunction with the Olympic Games, which were also considered as World Championships up to 1968. From 1977 the World Championships have been open to professionals. The USSR has won 20 world titles since 1954, including the Olympic

NATIONAL HOCKEY LEAGUE ALL-TIME RECORDS

(Through 1987–88 season; the number of a year refers to the season that commenced in the year before.)

REGULAR SEASON

Service

Most Seasons
26 Gordie Howe, Det, 1947–71; Hart, 1980

Most Games, Lifetime
1,767 Gordie Howe, Det, 1947–71; Hart, 1980

Consecutive Games Played
962 Doug Jarvis, Mon-Wash-Hart, Oct 8, 1975–Apr 5, 1987

Scoring

Most Points, Lifetime
1,850 Gordie Howe, Det, 1947–71; Hart, 1980

Most Points, Season
215 Wayne Gretzky, Edm, 1986

Most Points, Game
10 Darryl Sittler, Tor vs Bos, Feb 7, 1976

Most Points, Period
6 Bryan Trottier, NY Isl vs NY Ran, Dec 23, 1978

Consecutive Games Scoring Points
51 Wayne Gretzky, Edm, Oct 5, 1983–Jan 27, 1984

Most Goals, Lifetime
801 Gordie Howe, Det, 1947–71; Hart, 1980

Most Goals, Season
92 Wayne Gretzky, Edm, 1982

Most Goals, Game
7 Joe Malone, Que Bulldogs vs Tor St Pat, Jan 31, 1920

Most Goals, One Period
4 Harvey Jackson, Tor vs St L, Nov 20, 1934
Max Bentley, Chi vs NY Ran, Jan 28, 1943
Clint Smith, Chi vs Mont, Mar 4, 1945
Red Berenson, St L vs Phil, Nov 7, 1968
Wayne Gretzky, Edm vs St L, Feb 18, 1981
Grant Mulvey, Chi vs St L, Feb 3, 1982
Bryan Trottier, NY Isl vs Phil, Feb 13, 1982
Al Secord, Chi vs Tor, Jan 7, 1987

Most Hat Tricks (3 or more goals in a game), Lifetime
43 Wayne Gretzky, Edm, 1980–88

Most Hat Tricks, Season
10 Wayne Gretzky, Edm, 1982, 1984

Consecutive Games Scoring Goals
16 Harry Broadbent, Ottawa, 1921–22

STAR OF HIS GENERATION: Since 1982, Wayne Gretzky has set records in points, goals, hat tricks and assists. It was a major news event when he left the Edmonton Oilers to join the LA Kings in Aug 1988. (All Sport/Mike Powell)

Most Assists, Lifetime
1,086 Wayne Gretzky, Edm 1980–88

Most Assists, Season
163 Wayne Gretzky, Edm, 1986

Most Assists, Game
7 Billy Taylor, Det vs Chi, Mar 16, 1947
Wayne Gretzky, Edm vs Wash, Feb 15, 1980; vs Chi Dec 11, 1985; vs Que Feb 14, 1986

Most Assists, Period
5 Dale Hawerchuk, Win vs LA, Mar 6, 1984

Goaltending

Games Played, Lifetime
971 Terry Sawchuk, Det-Bos-Tor-LA-NY Ran, 1950–70

Shutouts, Lifetime
103 Terry Sawchuk, Det-Bos-Tor-LA-NY Ran, 1950–70

Shutouts, Season
22 George Hainsworth, Mont, 1929

Consecutive Scoreless Streak
461 min 29 sec Alex Connell, Ottawa, 1927–28

Consecutive Games Without Defeat
32 Gerry Cheevers, Bos, Nov 14, 1971–Mar 27, 1972

Most Saves, One Game
70 Roy Worters, Pitt Pirates vs NY Americans, Dec 24, 1925

Most Victories, Season
47 Bernie Parent, Phil, 1974

Penalties

Most Minutes Penalized, Lifetime
3,966 David (Tiger) Williams, Tor-Van-Det-LA-Hart, 1975–87

Most Minutes Penalized, Season
472 Dave Schultz, Phil, 1975

Most Minutes Penalized, Game
67 Randy Holt, LA vs Phil, Mar 11, 1979

STANLEY CUP

Most Games, Lifetime
185 Denis Potvin, NY Isl, 1974–88

Most Points, Lifetime
252 Wayne Gretzky, Edm, 1980–88

Most Points, Season
47 Wayne Gretzky, Edm, 1985

Most Points, Game
8 Patrik Sundstrom, NJ vs Wash Capitals Apr 22, 1988

Most Goals, Lifetime
85 Mike Bossy, NY Isl, 1978–87

Most Goals, Season
19 Reggie Leach, Phil, 1976
Jarri Kurri, Edm, 1985

Most Goals, Game
5 Maurice Richard, Mont vs Tor, Mar 23, 1944
Darryl Sittler, Tor vs Phil, Apr 22, 1976
Reggie Leach, Phil vs Bos, May 6, 1976

Most Assists, Lifetime
171 Wayne Gretzky, Edm, 1980–88

Most Assists, Season
31 Wayne Gretzky, Edm, 1988

Most Assists, Game
6 Mikko Leinonen, NY Ran vs Phil, Apr 8, 1982
Wayne Gretzky, Edm vs LA, Apr 9, 1987

Most Shutouts by Goalie, Lifetime
14 Jacques Plante, Mont, 1953–63; St L, 1969–70

Most Victories by Goalie, Lifetime
88 Billy Smith, NY Isl, 1975–88

FASTEST SKATER: Bobby Hull was timed at 29.7 mph. His slap shot went screaming at goaltenders at 118.3 mph. Hull was the only player besides Gordie Howe to score 1,000 NHL and WHA goals.

Longest Career

Gordie Howe (b March 31, 1928, Floral, Saskatchewan, Canada) skated 25 years for the Detroit Red Wings from 1946–47 through the 1970–71 season, playing in a total of 1,687 NHL regular-season games.

After leaving the Red Wings, he ended a 2-year retirement to skate with his two sons as teammates and played for 6 more seasons with the Houston Aeros and the New England Whalers of the World Hockey Association, participating in 497 games.

With the incorporation of the (now Hartford) Whalers into the NHL for the 1979–80 season, Gordie Howe skated in all 80 regular season games (for a record total of 1,767) in his record 26th year in that league. The remarkable 52-year-old grandfather was again selected as an NHL all-star, more times than any other player. Including Howe's 157 NHL playoff appearances, he skated in 2,421 "major league" games in all.

Fastest Scoring

Toronto scored 8 goals against the NY Americans in 4 min 52 sec on March 19, 1938.

The St. Louis Blues were protecting a 6–4 lead in an NHL game against the Bruins in Boston on Dec 19, 1987 when Ken Linseman scored for the Bruins with

titles of 1956, 64, 68, 72, 76, 84 and 88. Canada won 19 titles between 1920 and 1961, including 6 Olympic titles (1920, 24, 28, 32, 48 and 52). The longest Olympic career is that of Richard Torriani (b Oct 1, 1911) (Switzerland) from 1928 to 1948. The most gold medals won by any player is 3; this was achieved by 4 USSR players in the 1964, 68 and 72 Games— Vitaliy Davidov, Aleksandr Ragulin, Anatoliy Firssov and Viktor Kuzkin. Goalie Vladislav Tretiak (USSR) won 3 golds (1972, 1976 and 1984) as well as a silver in 1980.

Longest Season

The only man ever to play 82 games in a 78-game season is Ross Lonsberry. He began the 1971–72 season with the Los Angeles Kings where he played 50 games. Then, in January, he was traded to the Philadelphia Flyers (who had played only 46 games at the time) where he finished out the season (32 more games).

Brad Marsh (b Mar 31, 1958) played 83 games (17 with Calgary and 66 with Philadelphia) during an 80-game season in 1981–82.

LONGEST CAREER: Gordie Howe played in the NHL for 26 seasons and collected career records for most games (1,767), goals (801), and points (1,850), was selected as an all-star a record 21 times, and also collected 500 stitches in his face.

10 sec left. As the Blues' Doug Gilmour took to the ensuing center-ice face-off circle, the Bruins kept their goalie on the bench, hoping for an added advantage. But Gilmour slapped the face-off toward the Bruin goal. It went in, giving the two teams goals just 2 sec apart, faster than any pair of goals in NHL history.

The fastest goal ever scored from the opening whistle came at 5 sec of the first period. This occurred twice, most recently by Bryan Trottier of the NY Islanders vs Boston Bruins on Mar 22, 1984. The previous time was by Doug Smail of the Winnipeg Jets against St Louis on Dec 20, 1981. Claude Provost of the Canadiens scored a goal against Boston after 4 sec of the opening of the second period on Nov 9, 1957.

The Boston Bruins set an NHL record with three goals in a span of 20 sec against the Vancouver Canucks on Feb 25, 1971. Left winger John Bucyk began the record-breaking feat with a goal at the 4 min 50 sec mark of the third period. Center Ed Westfall scored 12 sec later at 5 min 2 sec, while defenseman Ted Green rounded out the surge with a goal at the 5 min 10 sec mark.

The fastest scoring record is held by Bill Mosienko (Chicago) who scored 3 goals in 21 sec against the NY Rangers on March 23, 1952. In a playoff game Pat LaFontaine of the NY Islanders scored 2 goals in 22 sec vs Edmonton Oilers, May 19, 1984.

Gus Bodnar (Toronto Maple Leafs) scored a goal against the NY Rangers at 15 sec of the first period of *his first NHL game* on Oct 30, 1943. Later in his career, while with Chicago, Bodnar again entered the record book when he assisted on all 3 of Bill Mosienko's quick goals.

Several fast scoring feats have been reported from non-NHL competition: Kim D. Miles scored in 3 sec

MOST STANLEY CUP GOALS: Mike Bossy, right wing of the NY Islanders, when he retired in 1987, had the most goals (85) in Stanley Cup play.

for Univ of Guelph vs Univ of W Ontario on Feb 11, 1975; Steve D'Innocenzo scored 3 goals in 12 sec for Holliston vs Westwood in a high school game in Mass on Jan 9, 1982; Clifford "Fido" Purpur, 38, scored 4 goals in 25 sec for the Grand Forks Amerks vs Winnipeg All Stars in Grand Forks, ND, on Jan 29, 1950. In team play, the Skara Ishockeyclubb, Sweden, scored 3 goals in 11 sec against Orebro IK at Skara on Oct 18, 1981; the Vernon Cougars scored 5 goals in 56 sec against Salmon Arm Aces at Vernon, BC, Canada, on Aug 6, 1982; the Kamloops Knights of Columbus scored 7 goals in 2 min 22 sec vs Prince George Vikings on Jan 25, 1980.

Team Scoring

The greatest number of goals recorded in a World Championship match has been 58–0 when Australia beat New Zealand on Mar 15, 1987.

The Edmonton Oilers set an NHL record of 446 goals in the 1983–84 season.

The NHL record for both teams is 21 goals, scored when the Montreal Canadiens beat the Toronto St Patricks at Montreal 14-7 on Jan 10, 1920. The most

MVP Most Times

Wayne Gretzky (b Jan 26, 1961) of the Edmonton Oilers won the Hart Trophy, the most valuable player of the NHL, for the 8th consecutive year in 1987, at age 26. No player in any North American major league sport had been honored so often.

His latest feat is surpassing Gordie Howe's lifetime assist record of 1,049. Gretzky needed only 9 years to achieve what Howe did in 26.

Then in August 1988 Gretzky made his biggest news of all: He was traded to the Los Angeles Kings.

goals ever scored by one team in a single game was set by the Canadiens, when they defeated the Quebec Bulldogs on March 3, 1920 by a score of 16-3.

The most goals in a period is 9 by the Buffalo Sabres in the second period of their 14–4 victory over Toronto on March 19, 1981.

The Detroit Red Wings scored 15 consecutive goals without an answering tally when they defeated the NY Rangers 15-0 on Jan 23, 1944.

Longest Game

The longest game was 2 hours 56 min 30 sec (playing time) when the Detroit Red Wings eventually beat the Montreal Maroons 1-0 in the 17th minute of the sixth period of overtime at the Forum, Montreal, at 2:25 A.M. on March 25, 1936, 5 hours 51 min after the opening faceoff. Norm Smith, goaltender for the Red Wings, turned aside 92 shots in registering the NHL's longest single shutout.

Longest Streaks

In the 1981–82 season, the NY Islanders won 15 consecutive regular season games, Jan 21–Feb 20, 1982. The Detroit Red Wings also won 15 from Feb 27–Apr 5, 1955, but that streak included 6 playoff games. The longest a team has ever gone without a defeat is 35 games, set by the Philadelphia Flyers with 25 wins and 10 ties from Oct 14, 1979, to Jan 6, 1980.

Penalties

The most any team has been penalized in one season is the 2,621 min assessed against the Philadelphia Flyers in 1980–81. The most penalty-filled game was a contest between Boston and Minnesota in Boston on Feb 26, 1981, with a total of 84 penalties (42 by each team) for 406 min (211 min by Minnesota).

Stanley Cup

This cup, presented by the Governor-General Lord Stanley (original cost $48.67), became emblematic of world professional team supremacy 33 years after the first contest at Montreal in 1893. It has been won most often by the Montreal Canadiens, with 22 wins in 1924, 30–31, 44, 46, 53, 56–60 (a record 5 straight), 65–66, 68–69, 71, 73, 76–79, 86. Henri Richard of Montreal played in his eleventh finals in 1973.

Winners from 1970 are:

1970 Boston Bruins	1980 New York Islanders
1971 Montreal Canadiens	1981 New York Islanders
1972 Boston Bruins	1982 New York Islanders
1973 Montreal Canadiens	1983 New York Islanders
1974 Philadelphia Flyers	1984 Edmonton Oilers
1975 Philadelphia Flyers	1985 Edmonton Oilers
1976 Montreal Canadiens	1986 Montreal Canadiens
1977 Montreal Canadiens	1987 Edmonton Oilers
1978 Montreal Canadiens	1988 Edmonton Oilers
1979 Montreal Canadiens	

HORSE RACING

Origins

There is evidence that men were riding horses, as distinct from riding in chariots pulled by horses, in Assyria and Egypt c 1400 BC. However, early organized racing appears to have been confined to chariots, for which the Roman method used riders with a foot on each of two horses. The first racing on horseback was by the Greeks in the 33rd Olympic Games in 648 BC. The earliest recorded race in Britain was at Netherby, Cumbria in 210 AD between Arabian horses brought to Britain by the Roman Emperor, Lucius Septimius Severus. The first recognizable regular race meeting was that held at Smithfield, London at the weekly horse fairs on Fridays in 1174. The first known prize money was a purse of gold presented by Richard I (the Lion-heart) in 1195 for a race between knights over a distance of 3 mi.

Organized horse racing began in New York State at least as early as March 1668. The original Charleston (Va) Jockey Club, organized in 1734, was the world's first.

Racing colors (silks) became compulsory in 1889.

All thoroughbred horses in the world today are descended from at least one of three great stallions, which were imported into Britain in the 17th and 18th centuries. The "Darley Arabian" was brought from Aleppo, Syria by the British Consul Richard Darley of Yorkshire c 1704; the "Byerley Turk" was brought to England from Turkey c 1685 and used by Captain Byerley as a charger in Ireland; and the Godolphin Barb—the latter word derived from the Barbary Coast of North Africa—was originally brought from France by Edward Coke in about 1735 and then acquired by the Earl of Godolphin.

MOST SUCCESSFUL JOCKEY: Willie Shoemaker, who weighs 94 lb and stands 4 ft 11 in tall, atop "Ferdinand" riding to victory in the 1987 Breeders' Cup Classic, the world's richest race ($3 million one race, $10 million for the meet). Shoemaker (walking on the right) from Mar 19, 1949 to Nov 6, 1988 rode 8,784 winners out of 40,043 mounts and earned $121,596,661 for the owners. (All Sport)

Largest Prizes

The richest races ever held are the Breeders' Cup 7-race meetings, run most recently at Churchill Downs in Louisville, Ky, on Nov 5, 1988, which paid $10 million total in prize money again, as it had in 1986. This included a total purse of $3 million to the top winners of the 1¼-mi Breeders' Cup Classic.

Speed (see table)

"Big Racket" reached 43.26 mph in setting his ¼-mi record in 1945. "Fiddle Isle" sped 37.76 mph over 1½ mi on Mar 21, 1970, and "John Henry" duplicated this speed in his record run on Mar 16, 1980. Both times were recorded at Santa Anita Park, Arcadia, Calif.

Victories

The horse with the best win-loss record was "Kincsem," a Hungarian mare foaled in 1874, who was unbeaten in 54 races (1876–79), including the English Goodwood Cup of 1878.

The longest winning sequence is 56 races, in

HORSES' SPEED RECORDS

Distance	Time mph	Name	Course	Date
¼ mile	20.8s. 43.26	•*Big Racket* (Mex)	Mexico City, Mex	Feb 5, 1945
½ mile	44.4s. 40.54	*Sonido* (Ven)	‡Caracas, Ven	June 28, 1970
	44.4s. 40.54	*Western Romance* (Can)	Calgary, Can	Apr 19, 1980
	44.4s. 40.54	*Northern Spike* (Can)	Winnipeg, Can	Apr 23, 1982
⅝ mile	53.6s. 41.98†	*Indigenous* (GB)	‡*Epsom, Eng	June 2, 1960
	53.89s. 41.75††	*Raffingora* (GB)	‡*Epsom, Eng	June 5, 1970
	55.2s. 40.76	*Chinook Pass* (US)	Seattle, Wash	Sept 17, 1982
¾ mile	1m. 06.2s. 40.78	*Broken Tendril* (GB)	*Brighton, Eng	Aug 6, 1929
	1m. 07.2s. 40.18	*Grey Papa* (US)	Longacres, Wash	Sept 4, 1972
	1m. 07.2s. 40.18	*Petro D. Jay* (US)	Phoenix, Ariz	May 9, 1982
Mile	1m. 31.8s. 39.21	*Soueida* (GB)	*Brighton, Eng	Sept 19, 1963
	1m. 31.8s. 39.21	*Loose Cover* (GB)	*Brighton, Eng	June 9, 1966
		Traditional Miss (GB)	Chepstow, Wales	June 27, 1981
		Traditional Miss (GB)	Chepstow, Wales	Aug 31, 1981
1¼ miles	1m. 57.4s. 38.33	*Double Discount* (US)	Arcadia, Calif	Oct 9, 1977
1½ miles	2m. 23.0s. 37.76	•*Fiddle Isle* (US)	Arcadia, Calif	Mar 21, 1970
		•*John Henry* (US)	Arcadia, Calif	Mar 16, 1980
2 miles	3m. 16.75s.	*Il Tempo* (NZ)	Trentham, Wellington, NZ	Jan 17, 1970
2½ miles	4m. 14.6s. 35.35	*Miss Grillo* (US)	Pimlico, Md	Nov 12, 1948
3 miles	5m. 15.0s. 34.29	*Farragut* (Mex)	Aguascalientes, Mex	Mar 9, 1941

*Course downhill for ¼ of a mile.
†Hand-timed.   ††Electrically timed.   ‡Straight courses.   •World record speeds.

Puerto Rico 1953–5, by "Camarero," foaled in 1951. He had 73 wins in 77 starts altogether. The most wins in a career is 137 from 159 starts by "Galgo Jr" (foaled 1928) in Puerto Rico between 1930 and 1936; in 1931 he won a record 30 races in one year. The only horse to win the same race in 7 successive years was "Doctor Syntax" (foaled 1811) in the Preston Gold Cup, 1815–21.

Greatest Winnings

The most won in a single race is $2.6 million by "Spend a Buck" on May 27, 1985 at Garden State Park in Cherry Hill, NJ. This included a $2 million bonus for also winning the Kentucky Derby and 2 preparatory races at Garden State Park. His total for 1985 was $3,552,704, also a record.

The greatest amount ever won by a horse is $6,679,242 by Alysheba, who retired after winning the Breeder's Cup Classic at Churchill Downs on Nov 5, 1988. Trained by Jack Van Berg from 1986, the 4-year-old colt has now started a stud career in Kentucky. "All Along" set the one-year record with $2,138,963 in 1983.

"Lady's Secret," who raced 1984–87, is the leading money winner among fillies and mares with a total of $3,021,425.

Owners

The most lifetime wins by an owner is 4,775 by Marion Van Berg in N America in the 35 years up to his death in 1971.

The most winners by an owner in one year is 494 by Dan R. Lasater (US) in 1974. The greatest amount won in a year is $5,743,134 by Eugene Klein (US) in 1987. His total winnings 1983–87 were $18,309,316.

Trainers

The greatest number of wins by a trainer is 496 in one year by Jack Van Berg in 1976, and 4,750 in his career to 1988. The greatest amount won in a year is $17,842,358 by D. Wayne Lukas (US) in 1988. The only trainer to saddle the first 5 finishers in a championship race is Michael Dickinson in the 1983 Cheltenham Gold Cup. On Dec 27, 1982, he won a record 12 races in one day.

Topmost Tipster

The only recorded instance of a racing correspondent forecasting ten out of ten winners on a race card was at Delaware Park, Wilmington, Del, on July 28, 1974, by Charles Lamb of the *Baltimore News American*.

Kentucky Derby Winners

1¼ miles at Churchill Downs, Louisville, Kentucky; first held in 1875.

Year *Winner*, Jockey	
1875 *Aristides*, O. Lewis	1932 *Burgoo King*, E. James
1876 *Vagrant*, R. Swim	1933 *Brokers Tip*, D. Meade
1877 *Baden Baden*, W. Walker	1934 *Cavalcade*, M. Garner
1878 *Day Star*, J. Carter	1935 *Omaha*, W. Saunders
1879 *Lord Murphy*, C. Schauer	1936 *Bold Venture*, I. Hanford
1880 *Fonso*, G. Lewis	1937 *War Admiral*, C. Kurtsinger
1881 *Hindoo*, J. McLaughlin	1938 *Lawrin*, E. Arcaro
1882 *Apollo*, B. Hurd	1939 *Johnstown*, J. Stout
1883 *Leonatus*, W. Donohue	1940 *Gallahadion*, C. Bierman
1884 *Buchanan*, I. Murphy	1941 *Whirlaway*, E. Arcaro
1885 *Joe Cotton*, E. Henderson	1942 *Shut Out*, W. D. Wright
1886 *Ben Ali*, P. Duffy	1943 *Count Fleet*, J. Longden
1887 *Montrose*, I. Lewis	1944 *Pensive*, C. McCreary
1888 *Macbeth II*, G. Covington	1945 *Hoop, Jr.*, E. Arcaro
1889 *Spokane*, T. Kiley	1946 *Assault*, W. Mehrtens
1890 *Riley*, I. Murphy	1947 *Jet Pilot*, E. Guerin
1891 *Kingman*, I. Murphy	1948 *Citation*, E. Arcaro
1892 *Azra*, A. Clayton	1949 *Ponder*, S. Brooks
1893 *Lookout*, E. Kunze	1950 *Middleground*, W. Boland
1894 *Chant*, F. Goodale	1951 *Count Turf*, C. McCreary
1895 *Halma*, J. Perkins	1952 *Hill Gail*, E. Arcaro
1896 *Ben Brush*, W. Simms	1953 *Dark Star*, H. Moreno
1899 *Manuel*, F. Taral	1954 *Determine*, R. York
1900 *Lieutenant Gibson*, J. Boland	1955 *Swaps*, W. Shoemaker
1901 *His Eminence*, J. Winkfield	1956 *Needles*, D. Erb
1902 *Alan-a-Dale*, J. Winkfield	1957 *Iron Liege*, W. Hartack
1903 *Judge Himes*, H. Booker	1958 *Tim Tam*, I. Valenzuela
1904 *Elwood*, F. Prior	1959 *Tomy Lee*, W. Shoemaker
1905 *Agile*, J. Martin	1960 *Venetian Way*, W. Hartack
1906 *Sir Huon*, R. Troxler	1961 *Carry Back*, J. Sellers
1907 *Pink Star*, A. Minder	1962 *Decidedly*, W. Hartack
1908 *Stone Street*, A. Pickens	1963 *Chateaugay*, B. Baeza
1909 *Wintergreen*, V. Powers	1964 *Northern Dancer*, W. Hartack
1910 *Donau*, F. Herbert	1965 *Lucky Debonair*, W. Shoemaker
1911 *Meridian*, G. Archibald	1966 *Kauai King*, D. Brumfield
1912 *Worth*, C. H. Shilling	1967 *Proud Clarion*, R. Ussery
1913 *Donerail*, R. Goose	1968 *Forward Pass**, I. Valenzuela
1914 *Old Rosebud*, J. McCabe	1969 *Majestic Prince*, W. Hartack
1915 *Regret*, J. Nutter	1970 *Dust Commander*,
1916 *George Smith*, J. Loftus	M. Manganello
1917 *Omar Khayyam*, C. Borel	1971 *Canonero II*, G. Avila
1918 *Exterminator*, W. Knapp	1972 *Riva Ridge*, R. Turcotte
1919 *Sir Barton*, J. Loftus	1973 *Secretariat*, R. Turcotte
1920 *Paul Jones*, T. Rice	1974 *Cannonade*, A. Cordero
1921 *Behave Yourself*,	1975 *Foolish Pleasure*, J. Vasquez
C. Thompson	1976 *Bold Forbes*, A. Cordero
1922 *Morvich*, A. Johnson	1977 *Seattle Slew*, J. Cruguet
1923 *Zev*, E. Sande	1978 *Affirmed*, S. Cauthen
1924 *Black Gold*, J. D. Mahoney	1979 *Spectacular Bid*, R. Franklin
1925 *Flying Ebony*, E. Sande	1980 *Genuine Risk*, J. Vasquez
1926 *Bubbling Over*, A. Johnson	1981 *Pleasant Colony*, J. Velasquez
1927 *Whiskery*, L. McAtee	1982 *Gato del Sol*, E. Delahoussaye
1928 *Reigh Count*, C. Lang	1983 *Sunny's Halo*, E. Delahoussaye
1929 *Clyde Van Dusen*, L. McAtee	1984 *Swale*, L. Pincay
1930 *Gallant Fox*, E. Sande	1985 *Spend a Buck*, A. Cordero
1931 *Twenty Grand*, C. Kurtsinger	1986 *Ferdinand*, W. Shoemaker
	1987 *Alysheba*, C. McCarron
	1988 *Winning Colors*, G. Stevens

*Dancer's Image finished first but was disqualified after drug tests.

Largest Grandstand

The largest at a racecourse is at Belmont Park, Long Island, NY, which seats 30,000 and is 440 yd long.

BIGGEST MONEY WINNER: "Aly-sheba," late in 1988, beat all racing horses with total winnings of $6,679,242 in his career. Here he is with Chris McCarron up, winning the Breeder's Cup, after which he retired. (© Skip Dickstein 1988)

Longest Race

The longest recorded horse race was one of 1,200 miles in Portugal, won by "Emir," a horse bred from Egyptian-bred Blunt Arab stock. The holder of the world record for long distance racing and speed is "Champion Crabbet," who covered 300 miles in 52 hours 33 min, carrying 245 lb, in 1920.

Triple Crown

Eleven horses have won all three races in one season which constitute the American Triple Crown (Kentucky Derby, Preakness Stakes and the Belmont Stakes). This feat was first achieved by "Sir Barton" in 1919, and most recently by "Seattle Slew" in 1977 and "Affirmed" in 1978.

The only Triple Crown winner to sire another winner was "Gallant Fox," the 1930 winner, who sired "Omaha," who won in 1935. The only jockey to ride two Triple Crown winners is Eddie Arcaro (b Feb 19, 1916), on "Whirlaway" (1941) and "Citation" (1948).

Most Valuable Horses

The most expensive horse ever is the 1983 Irish Derby winner "Shareef Dancer." Reportedly 40 shares in the horse were sold at $1 million each in 1983 by his owner, Sheikh Mohammed bin Rashid al Maktoum.

The highest price for a yearling is $13.1 million for "Seattle Dancer" on July 23, 1985, in Keeneland, Ky, by Robert Sangster and partners.

Dead Heats

There is no recorded case in turf history of a quintuple dead heat. The nearest approach was in the Astley Stakes at Lewes, England, on Aug 6, 1880, when "Mazurka," "Wandering Nun" and "Scobell" triple dead-heated for first place, just ahead of "Cumberland" and "Thora" who dead-heated for fourth place. Each of the five jockeys thought he had won. The only three known examples of a quadruple dead heat were between "Honest Harry," "Miss Decoy," "Young Daffodil" and "Peteria" at Bogside, England, on June 7, 1808; between "Defaulter," "The Squire of Malton," "Reindeer" and "Pulcherrima" in the Omnibus Stakes at The Hoo, England, on Apr 26, 1851; and between "Overreach," "Lady Go-Lightly," "Gamester" and "The Unexpected" at Newmarket, England, on Oct 22, 1855.

Since the introduction of the photo-finish, the highest number of horses in a dead heat has been three, on several occasions.

Most Horses in a Race

In the Grand National (England) on Mar 22, 1929, there were 66 horses.

Jockeys

The most successful jockey of all time is William Lee (Bill or Willie) Shoemaker (b at 2½ lb on Aug 19, 1931) now weighing 94 lb and standing 4 ft 11 in. (His wife is nearly 1 ft taller than he is.) From Mar

1949 through 1988, he rode 8,788 winners in 40,063 mounts, earning $121,780,386.

The jockey with most earnings is Laffitt Pincay, Jr (b Dec 29, 1946, Panama City, Panama) who has earned a record $136,751,125 from 1966 through 1988.

The most won in one year is $14,877,298 by Jose Santos (b Chile, Apr 26, 1961) in 1988. Santos had been racing less than 5 years.

Chris McCarron (US), (b 1955), won a total of 546 races in 1974 out of 2,199 mounts.

The most winners ridden on one card is 8 by Hubert S. Jones, 17, out of 13 mounts at Caliente, Calif, on June 11, 1944 (of which 5 were photo-finishes); by Oscar Barattuci at Rosario, Argentina, on Dec 15, 1957; by Dave Gall from 10 mounts at Cahokia Downs, East St Louis, Ill, on Oct 18, 1978; by Chris Loseth, 29, out of 10 mounts at Exhibition Park in Vancouver, BC, Canada on Apr 9, 1984, and by Robert Williams from 10 rides at Lincoln, Neb, Sept 29, 1984.

The youngest jockey was Australian-born Frank Wootton (1893–1940) (Eng champion 1909–12), who rode his first winner in Africa, aged 9 years 10 months. The oldest jockey is Bill Shoemaker (see above) who won the Kentucky Derby in 1986 at the age of 55.

The lightest jockey recorded was Kitchener (Eng) (d 1872), who won the Chester Cup on ''Red Deer'' in 1844 at 49 lb. He is said to have weighed only 35 lb in 1840.

HORSESHOE PITCHING

Origins

This sport was derived from military blacksmiths and is of great antiquity. The first formal World Championships were staged at Bronson, Kansas, in 1909.

Most Titles

The record for men's titles is 10 by Ted Allen (Boulder, Colorado) in 1933–34–35–40–46–53–55–56–57–59. The women's record is also 10 by Vicki Chapelle Winston (LaMonte, Missouri) in 1956–58–59–61–63–66–67–69–75–81.

Most Ringers

The most ringers in a single game is 175 by Glen Henton of Maquoketa, Iowa, in 1965.

Marathon

The longest continuous session of a 4-man contest, two teams pitching continuously and without substitutions, is 96 hours by Gary Alexander, Ralph Lewis, Mylin Sorber and Patricia Reynolds in Idaho Springs, Colorado, August 6–10, 1980.

Highest Percentage

The record for consecutive ringers is 72 by Ted Allen in 1955 for men, and 42 by Ruth Hangen in 1974 for women. The highest percentage for a single game is 100 percent by two different players: Guy Zimmerman (Alamo, Calif) 44 ringers in 44 shoes in 1948, and Elmer Hohl (Wellesley, Ont, Canada) 30 in 30 in 1968.

The highest world tournament averages were: Elmer Hohl (Canada) 88.2% in 1968 in the men's division; Sandy McLachlin (Canada) 88.2% in 1987 in the women's division; and John Passmore (Indiana) 89.5% in 1975 in the junior division.

ICE and SAND YACHTING

Origins

The sport originated in The Netherlands and Belgium from the year 1600 (earliest patent granted) and along the Baltic coast. The earliest authentic record is Dutch, dating from 1768. Land or sand yachts of Dutch construction were first reported on beaches (now in Belgium) in 1595. The earliest international championship was staged in 1914.

Largest Yacht

The largest ice yacht was *Icicle,* built for Commodore John E. Roosevelt for racing on the Hudson River, NY, in 1869. It was 68 ft 11 in long and carried 1,070 sq ft of canvas.

Highest Ice Speeds

The highest speed officially recorded is 143 mph by John D. Buckstaff in a Class A stern-steerer on Lake Winnebago, Wis, in 1938. Such a speed is possible in a wind of 72 mph.

Highest Sand Speeds

The official world record for a sand yacht is 66.48 mph set by Christian-Yves Nau (b 1944) (France) in *Mobil* at Le Touquet, France on Mar 22, 1981, when the wind speed reached 75 mph. A speed of 88.4 mph was attained for a moment only by Nord Embroden (US) in *Midnight at the Oasis* at Superior Dry Lake, Calif, on Apr 15, 1976.

SAND YACHTING SPEEDS in excess of 66 mph with favorable winds are attainable. This is a race in the Speed-Sail World Cup at Oostvoorne, Holland, in 1987.

ICE SKATING

Origins

The earliest skates were made of animal bones, such as those found in France and thought to be 20,000 years old. The first reference to skating is in early Norse literature *c*. 200 AD but the earliest report of skating as a sport or pastime is in a British chronicle by William Fitzstephen of 1180. The first club was founded in Edinburgh in 1744, and the earliest artificial ice rink was opened in London in 1876.

Speed skating or racing must have taken place from the earliest times, although curved rinks, especially for racing, did not appear until the 1880s. Two Americans developed figure skating into an art. E. W. Bushnell invented steel blades in 1848 and thereby provided the precision skate needed for ever more intricate figures, and the first true innovator and teacher was Jackson Haines. He was a ballet master who transferred the artistry of the dance to the ice when he went to Vienna in 1864. Louis Rubinstein was a founder of the Amateur Skating Association of Canada in 1887, the first national governing body in the world. In 1892 the International Skating Union was set up at Scheveningen, Netherlands.

Longest Race

The longest race regularly held was the "Elfstedentocht" ("Tour of the Eleven Towns") in The Netherlands, covering 200 km (124 miles 483 yd). The fastest time was 6 hours 5 min 12 sec by Jan-Roelof Kruithof (Neth) on Feb 25, 1979 at Oulu, Finland. Kruithof won the race 8 times, 1974, 76–77, 79–83. The race was transferred to Finland in 1964 and subsequently to Canada, but it was returned to The Netherlands in 1985. An estimated 16,000 skaters took part in 1986.

Largest Rink

The world's largest indoor artificial ice rink is in the Moscow Olympic arena which has an ice area of 86,800 sq ft. The largest outdoors is the Fujikyu Highland Promenade Rink complex in Japan with 285,243 sq ft.

FIGURE SKATING

Most Difficult Jumps

Many of the most difficult jumps in skating are named after their originators, such as the Axel (after Axel Paulsen of Norway) and the Salchow (after Ulrich Salchow of Sweden).

The first woman to attempt a jump in major competition is said to have been Theresa Weld (US) who was reprimanded for her "unfeminine behavior" in the 1920 Olympic events. Cecilia Colledge (GB) was the first woman to achieve two turns in the air a few years later. In the 1962 World Championships Donald Jackson (Can) performed the first triple Lutz in a major competition and in the 1978 championships Vern Taylor, another Canadian, achieved the first triple Axel. Among women, the first triple Salchow was done by Sonja Morgenstern (E Ger) in 1972, and the first triple Lutz by Denise Beilmann

MOST DIFFICULT JUMP-LIFT: Marina Tcherkasova was only 12 years old when she and Sergei Shakrai first performed their unique quadruple twist lift in 1977. Shakrai was 18 years old at the time. (Popperfoto)

(Switz) in the 1978 European championships. Incidentally, the latter has a spin named after her.

The first quadruple twist was performed by Marina Tcherkasova and Sergei Shakrai (USSR) in a pairs competition in Helsinki in 1977. They were able to achieve this because of the unusual difference in size between the tiny 12-year-old girl and her tall male partner.

A backward somersault jump was successfully negotiated by Terry Kubicka (US) in the 1976 World Championships but it was immediately banned as being too dangerous.

Kurt Browning (Canada) was the first to achieve a quadruple jump in competition—a toe loop in the World Championships at Budapest, Hungary on Mar 25, 1988.

Highest Marks

The highest tally of maximum "six" marks awarded in an international championship was 29 to Jayne Torvill and Christopher Dean (GB) in the World Ice Dance Championships at Ottawa, Canada, Mar 22–24, 1984. This comprised 7 in the compul-

sory dances, a perfect set of 9 for presentation in the set pattern dance and 13 in the free dance, including another perfect set from all 9 judges for artistic presentation. They previously gained a perfect set of 9 "sixes" for artistic presentation in the free dance at the 1983 World Championships in Helsinki, Finland, and at the 1984 Olympic Games in Sarajevo, Yugoslavia. In their career Torvill and Dean received a record total of 136 "sixes."

Donald Jackson (Canada) was awarded 7 "sixes" (the most by a soloist) in the world men's championship at Prague, Czechoslovakia, in 1962.

World Titles

The greatest number of individual world men's figure skating titles (instituted 1896) is 10 by Ulrich Salchow (1877–1949), of Sweden, in 1901–05, 07–11. The women's record (instituted 1906) is also 10 individual titles, by Sonja Henie (Apr 8, 1912–Oct 12, 1969), of Norway, between 1927 and 1936. Irina Rodnina (b Sept 12, 1949), of the USSR, has won 10 pairs titles (instituted 1908)—four with Aleksiy Ulanov (1969–72) and six with her husband Aleksandr Zaitsev (1973–78). The most ice dance titles (instituted 1952) won is 6 by Aleksandr Gorshkov (b Oct

MOVIE STAR Sonja Henie (Norway) earned an estimated $47 million in ice shows and films after winning 3 Olympic golds in 1928–32–36 and 10 world titles.

8, 1946) and his wife, Ludmilla Pakhomova (1946–86), both of the USSR, in 1970–74 and 76. They also won the first ever Olympic ice dance title in 1976.

Olympic Titles in Figure Skating

The most Olympic gold medals won by a figure skater is 3 by Gillis Grafström (1893–1938), of Sweden, in 1920, 24 and 28 (also silver medal in 1932); by Sonja Henie in 1928, 32 and 36; and by Irina Rodnina in the pairs event in 1972, 76 and 80.

Distance

Robin Cousins (GB) (b Mar 17, 1957) achieved 19 ft 1 in in an Axel jump and 18 ft with a back flip at Richmond Ice Rink, Surrey, Eng on Nov 16, 1983.

SPEED SKATING

World Titles

The greatest number of world overall titles (instituted 1893) won by any skater is 5 by Oscar Mathisen (Norway) (1888–1954) in 1908–09, 12–14, and Clas Thunberg (1893–1973) of Finland, in 1923, 25, 28–29 and 31. The most titles won by a woman is 5 by Karin Kania *née* Enke (b June 20, 1961) (E Ger) 1982, 84 and 86–88. Enke also won a record 6 overall titles at the World Sprint Championships 1980–81, 1983–84, and 1986–87.

Olympic Titles

The most Olympic gold medals won in speed skating is 6 by Lidia Skoblikova (b March 8, 1939),

FASTEST WOMAN ON SKATES: Bonnie Blair (US) won the 500-meter race in the 1988 Olympics in record time. (Bob Martin/All-Sport)

WORLD SPEED SKATING RECORDS

(Ratified by the I.S.U.)

Distance	min:sec	Name and Nationality	Place	Date
MEN				
500 m	36.23*	Nick Thometz (USA)	Medeo, USSR	Mar 26, 1987
	36.45	Jens-Uwe May (E Ger)	Calgary, Canada	Feb 14, 1988
1000 m	1.12.05	Nick Thometz (USA)	Medeo, USSR	Mar 27, 1987
1500 m	1.52.06	Andre Hoffman (E Ger)	Calgary, Canada	Feb 20, 1988
3000 m	3.59.27	Leo Visser (Neth)	Heerenveen, Netherlands	Mar 19, 1987
5000 m	6.47.01	Leo Visser (Neth)	Heerenveen, Netherlands	Feb 14, 1987
10,000 m	13.48.20	Tomas Gustafson (Swe)	Calgary, Canada	Feb 21, 1988
WOMEN				
500 m	39.10	Bonnie Blair (USA)	Calgary, Canada	Feb 22, 1988
1000 m	1.18.11	Karin Kania (*née* Enke) (GDR)	Calgary, Canada	Dec 5, 1987
1500 m	1.59.30	Karin Kania (GDR)	Medeo, USSR	Mar 22, 1986
3000 m	4.11.94	Yvonne van Gennip (Neth)	Calgary, Canada	Feb 23, 1988
5000 m	6.43.59	Yvonne van Gennip (Neth)	Calgary, Canada	Feb 28, 1988
10,000 m	15.25.25	Yvonne van Gennip (Neth)	Heerenveen, Neth	March 19, 1988

*Unofficial (represents an average speed of 30.87 mph.)

AMERICAN SPEEDSTER: His unprecedented 5-event sweep of the 1980 Olympic speed skating competition made Eric Heiden the first Olympic athlete to earn 5 individual (that is, not relay or team) gold medals at one Games.

of Chelyabinsk, USSR, in 1960 (2) and 1964 (4). The male record is held by Clas Thunberg (see above) with 5 gold (including 1 tied gold) and also 1 silver in

---

1988 OLYMPIC ICE SKATING GOLD MEDALISTS

Figure Skating

Individual—Men—Brian Boitano (US)
Individual—Women—Katarina Witt (E Ger)*
Pairs—Ekaterina Gordeeva and Sergei Grinkov (USSR)
Ice Dance—Natalya Beetemianova
    and Andrie Bukin (USSR)

Speed Skating—Men

   500m—Jens-Uwe Mey (E Ger) 36.45†
   1000m—Nikolai Gouliaev (USSR) 1:13.03
   1500m—Andre Hoffman (E Ger) 1:52.06†
   5000m—Tomas Gustafson (Sweden) 6:44.63*
   10,000m—Tomas Gustafson (Sweden) 13:48.20†

Speed Skating—Women

   500m—Bonnie Blair (US) 39.10†
   1000m—Christa Rothenburger (E Ger) 1:17.65**
   1500m—Yvonne Van Gennip (Neth) 2:00.64
   3000m—Yvonne Van Gennip (Neth) 4:11.94†
   5000m—Yvonne Van Gennip (Neth) 7:14.13

* Repeat winner
† World record
** Winner at 500m in 1984

1924 and 1 tied bronze in 1928; and by Eric Heiden (US) (b June 14, 1958) who won 5 gold medals, all uniquely at one Games at Lake Placid, NY, in 1980.

Marathon

The longest recorded skating marathon is 109 hours 5 min by Austin McKinley of Christchurch, NZ, June 21–25, 1977.

24 Hours

Martinus Kuiper (Neth) skated 339.68 mi in 24 hours in Alkmaar, Neth on Dec 12–13, 1987.

Barrel Jumping (on ice skates)

The official distance record is 29 ft 5 in over 18 barrels by Yvon Jolin at Terrebonne, Quebec, Canada, in 1981. The women's record is 20 ft 4½ in over 11 barrels by Janet Hainstock in Mich on Mar 15, 1980.

JAI-ALAI (Pelota)

Origins

The game, which originated in Italy as *longue paume* and was introduced into France in the 13th century, is said to be the fastest of all ball games. The glove or *gant* was introduced *c.* 1840 and the *chistera* was invented by Jean "Gantchiki" Dithurbide of Ste Pée, France. The *grand chistera* was invented by Melchior Curuchague of Buenos Aires, Argentina in 1888.

The world's largest *frontón* (enclosed stadium) is the World Jaï Alaï at Miami, Fla, which had a record attendance of 15,052 on Dec 27, 1975.

Olympic Sport

In the 1992 Games in Barcelona, Spain, jai-alai will be introduced as a demonstration sport.

World Championships

The Federacion Internacional de Pelota Vasca stages world championships every four years (first in 1952). The most successful pair has been Roberto Elias and Juan Labat (Argentina), who won the *Trinquete Share* four times, 1952, 1958, 1962 and 1966. Labat won a record 7 world titles in all. The most wins in the long court game *Cesta Punta* is 3 by Hamuy of Mexico, with two different partners, 1958, 1962 and 1966.

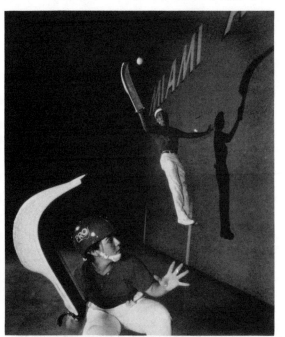

SPEEDIEST BALLGAME: In jai-alai, the ball travels as fast as 188 mph, rebounding high off the front, back and one side wall. The player catches the ball in the wicker basket (cesta) and throws it with the same motion. (All Sport/Bill Frakes)

Biggest Payout

The highest parimutuel payout in the US was for a group of bettors who won $988,326 (less $197,664 paid to the Internal Revenue) for a $2 ticket naming six consecutive winning jai-alai players at Palm Beach, Fla on Mar 1, 1983.

Highest Speed

An electronically measured ball velocity of 188 mph was recorded by José Ramon Arieto at the Newport Jai Alai, RI, on Aug 3, 1979.

Longest Domination

The longest domination as the world's No. 1 player was enjoyed by Chiquito de Cambo (né Joseph Apesteguy) (France), (1881–1955) from the beginning of the century until succeeded in 1938 by Jean Urruty (France) (b Oct 19, 1913).

JOGGLING (right) with 3 heavily-weighted sports balls in competition with unburdened runners in the LA marathon, Albert Lucas joggled the whole 26.2 mi in 4 hours 4 min 35 sec, beating the majority of the field. (Bill Giduz)

JOGGLING (Running While Juggling)

Joggling records are recognized only if set in official competitions:

5 objects (while joggling)	Bill Gillen (US) covered 1 mi in 8 min 28 sec, June 25, 1985
	Owen Morse (US) covered 100m in 13.8 sec on July 15, 1988
	Bill Gillen (US) covered 3/10ths of a mi without a drop
3 objects (while joggling)	Owen Morse (US) 100m in 11.9 sec on July 15, 1988
	Kirk Swenson (US) 1 mi in 4 min 43 sec, July 24, 1986
	Prof Helaman Pratt-Ferguson (US) 50 mi in 16 hours 12 min, May 8, 1987
	Kirk Swenson (US) 5 km in 16 min 55 sec in 1986
	A relay "Team Exerball" of 4 US men (Albert Lucas, Owen Morse, Jon Wee, Steve Wilson) ran 1 mile in 4 min 5.4 sec on July 15, 1988
3 heavily weighted sports balls	Albert Lucas (US) ran the full LA Marathon of 26.2 mi in 4 hours 4 min 35 sec.

JUDO

Origins

Judo is a modern combat sport which developed out of an amalgam of several old Japanese fighting arts, the most popular of which was *ju-jitsu* (*jiu-jitsu*), which is thought to be of Chinese origin. Judo has developed greatly since 1882, when it was first devised by Dr. Jigoro Kano (1860–1938). World Championships were inaugurated in Tokyo on May 5, 1956. The International Judo Federation was founded in 1951, and it no longer considers judo one of the martial arts, only a sport.

Grades

The efficiency grades in Judo are divided into pupil (*kyu*) and master (*dan*) grades. A white belt signifies a beginning student. The next 3 grades upwards are a brown belt, and the highest grade or black belt (*dan*) is divided into 10 degrees, with the 6th, 7th and 8th entitled to wear a red and white belt, and the 9th and 10th degrees a solid red belt. The solid red has been given to only 13 men, and the 11th *dan* never awarded.

A 12th *dan*, entitling the wearer to a white belt twice as wide as an ordinary belt, and the title *Shihan* (Doctor) was awarded to the founder of the sport, Jigoro Kano.

The only 2 Japanese have attained it, one being Ms Keiko Fukuda, living in San Francisco.

Olympics

Judo has been included since 1964, with the exception of 1968. Only 3 judoka, Wim Ruska (Neth), Hitoshi Saito (Japan) and Peter Seisenbacher (Austria) have won more than one title. One of the biggest upsets to national pride in any sport occurred in 1964 when the giant 6 ft 6 in Dutchman, Anton Geesink, won the Open category in Tokyo before some 15,000 partisan Japanese spectators. Yasuhiro Yamashita (Japan) (b June 1, 1957) added to his 7-year unbeaten record by winning the Open category in 1984.

The 1988 gold medalists were:

132 lb: Kim Jae-yup (S Korea)
143 lb: Lee Kyung-keun (S Korea)
156 lb: Marc Alexandre (France)
172 lb: Waldemar Legien (Poland)
189 lb: Peter Seisenbacher (Austria)
209 lb: Aurelio Miguel (Brazil)
Over 209 lb: Hitoshi Saito (Japan)

Beginning with the 1992 Games, women's judo will be included.

Throws

In a one-hour demonstration, 2 teams of 4 judo students switching every 3 min made 1,808 judo throws from a standing position, or one throw every 1.99 sec. The students were members of the Kano Ryu Club of the Fellowship of Christian Athletes of Kansas City, Mo, and the event took place on Oct 10, 1987.

World Champions

Judo World Championships were first held in Tokyo in 1956 and are now held biennially. New weight categories were applied to the 1979 competition and there are now 8 weight classes. Women's championships were first held in NYC in 1980.

Three men have won 4 world titles. Yasuhiro Yamashita won heavyweight in 1979, 1981, 1983 and Open 1981, and retired undefeated after 203 successive wins, 1977–85. Wilhelm Ruska (b Aug 29, 1940) of The Netherlands won the 1967 and the 1971 heavyweight and the 1972 Olympic heavyweight and Open titles, and Shozo Fujii (Japan) (b May 12, 1950) won the middleweight title in 1971, 1973, 1975, and 1979.

Ruska is one of only 3 men to have won 2 Olympic gold medals, the others being Peter Seisenbacher (Austria) (b Mar 25, 1960) who won in 1984 and 1988 at 86 kg, and Hitoshi Saito (Japan) (b Jan 2, 1961) who won in 1984 and 1988 at 95 kg.

Ingrid Berghmans (Belgium) (b Aug 24, 1961) with 10 has won most medals by a woman: at 72 kg she won 5 golds, 4 silver and one bronze, 1980–87. She also won a gold at 72kg in the 1988 Olympics when judo was a demonstration sport.

The first American to win a gold medal in a world championship was Michael Sevain of San Jose, Calif, in 1987 at 143 lb.

10 Hours and One Hour

The McManus brothers, Steven (b Dec 8, 1967) and Alan (b Aug 2, 1963), from the London East Side Judo Club completed 10,123 judo throwing techniques in a 10-hour period at Crystal Palace National Sports Centre, London, on Apr 11, 1987.

Marathon

The longest recorded Judo marathon with continuous play by pairs is 245½ hours by 5 of 6 people at the Smithfield RSL Youth Club, NSW, Australia, Jan 3–13, 1984.

YOUNGEST AND OLDEST BLACK BELTS: (Right) Bobby Woodard, who received his belt at age 5 years 10 months 10 days, with his coach, Grand Master S. T. Choe. (Left) Great-grandmother Lucille "Killer" Thompson, who was 90 when she received her belt in Tae Kwon Do.

KARATE

Origins

Originally *karate* (empty hand) is known to have been developed by the unarmed populace as a method of attack on, and defense against, armed Japanese aggressors in Okinawa, Ryukyu Islands, based on techniques devised from the 6th century Chinese art of Shaolin boxing (Kempo). Transmitted to Japan in the 1920's by Funakoshi Gichin, this method of combat was refined and organized into a sport with competitive rules.

The five major styles of *karate* in Japan are *Shotokan, Wado-ryu, Goju-ryu, Shito-ryu,* and *Kyokushinkai,* each of which places different emphasis on speed, power, etc. Other styles include *Sankukai, Shotokai* and *Shukokai.* The military form of *Taekwan-do* with 9 *dans* is a Korean equivalent of *karate.* Introduced into the 1988 Olympics as a demonstration sport, *Kung fu* is believed to have originated in Nepal or Tibet but was adopted within Chinese temples *via* India, and has in recent years been widely popularized through various martial arts films.

Wu shu is a comprehensive term embracing all Chinese martial arts.

Oldest and Youngest Black Belts

Great-grandmother Lucille "Killer" Thompson of Danville, Ill (b Mar 18, 1896) earned a black belt in Tae Kwon Do (Korean Karate) in 1986 when aged 90. The youngest at the same sport, Bobby Woodard of Lakeland, Fla, was 5 years 10 months 10 days old when he received his black belt.

Grades

The white belt in karate signifies beginner grade 9. As the student progresses he rises to grades 8 and 7 (yellow belt), 6 and 5 (green), 4 (purple), 3, 2, and 1 (brown) and finally black belt.

Most Titles

The only winner of 3 All-Japanese titles has been Takeshi Oishi, who won in 1969–70–71.

The leading exponents among karatekas are a number of 10th *dans* in Japan.

Great Britain has won a record 5 world titles, including 1988.

Olympic Winners

Koreans won 11 of the contests in the 16 men's and women's categories in 1988, when karate was a demonstration sport.

LACROSSE

Origin

The game is of American Indian origin, derived from the inter-tribal game *baggataway,* and was played by Iroquois Indians at lower Ontario, Canada, and upper NY State, before 1492. The French named it after their game of *Chouler à la crosse,* known in

1381. The game was included in the Olympic Games of 1904 and 1908, and featured as an exhibition sport in 1928, 1932, and 1948 Games. Women's lacrosse began in 1886 in Eng, and the game evolved from the men's game so that now the rules differ considerably.

World Championship

The US won 4 of the 5 modern World Championships, in 1967, 1974, 1982, and 1986 and also won the pre-Olympic tournament in 1984. Canada won in 1978, beating the US 17–16 in overtime. World Championships for women were instituted in 1969, and have been contested 4 times. Great Britain won the first title, the US won in 1974 and 1982 but was beaten 10–7 by Australia in the 1986 final.

Highest Score

The highest score in any international match was US over England, 32–8, at Toronto in 1986. The highest total goal output in the World Games competition was seen in Australia's win over Canada, 24–18, in the 1982 World Games in Baltimore. An international team representing Great Britain & Ireland defeated a Long Island team, 40–0, in their 1967 tour of the US.

Collegiate

Johns Hopkins University has won or shared 42 national championships since 1890.

John Cheek (Washington College) netted 200 career goals, while Doug Fry (Maryland–Baltimore County) holds the collegiate record (Division III) with 70 goals in one season.

Rick Gilbert (Hobart) holds the USILA record for single season assists (88) and points (122). He also holds career records with 287 assists and a remarkable 444 points.

Jeff Singer made a record 909 career saves as goaltender for MIT.

Women's Championship

The Association for Intercollegiate Athletics for Women (founded 1971) and the US Women's Lacrosse Association (founded 1932) jointly sponsored collegiate championships from 1978 to 1980. In 1981, the tournament was run solely by the A.I.A.W. Since then it has been sponsored by the National Collegiate Athletic Association. The rules differ considerably from the men's game.

MARATHONS (Running)

The inaugural marathon races were staged in Greece in 1896. There were two trial races before the first Olympic marathon at Athens. The race commemorated the legendary run of an unknown Greek courier, possibly Pheidippides, who in 490 BC ran some 24 miles from the Plain of Marathon to Athens with the news of a Greek victory over the numerically superior Persian army. Delivering his message—"Rejoice! We have won."—he collapsed and died. The Olympic races were run over varying distances until 1924 when the distance was standardized at 26 miles 385 yd, the distance first instituted in the 1908 Games in London.

There are no official records for the distance but the fastest times ever run are 2 hours 6 min 50 sec by Belaynah Dinsamo of Ethiopia among men (1988) and 2 hours 21 min 6 sec by Ingrid Kristiansen of Norway among women (1985).

In the NYC marathon in 1988, there were 22,912 starters, a record number.

Grete Waitz (Nor) won the women's title a record 9th time in 1988, following previous victories in 1976–8 and 1982–6.

The oldest man to complete a marathon was Dimitrion Yordanidis (Greece), aged 98, in Athens, Greece on Oct 10, 1976. He finished in 7 hours 33 min. Thelma Pitt-Turner (New Zealand) set the women's record in August 1985, completing the Hastings, New Zealand marathon in 7 hours 58 min at the age of 82.

Most Marathons Run

Jay F. Helgerson (b Feb 3, 1955) of Foster City, Calif, ran a certified marathon (26 miles 385 yd) or longer, each week for 52 weeks from Jan 28, 1979 to Jan 19, 1980, totalling 1,418 racing miles.

Sy Mah (b 1926), an instructor at Toledo University (Ohio), has entered 468 "marathons" of 26.2 mi or longer 1966–Aug 16, 1987 and claims to have run a total of 11,660 mi.

Marathon Progressive Record

Men

2:55:18.4	Johnny Hayes (US)	1908
2:52:45.4	Robert Fowler (US)	1909
2:46:52.6	James Clark (US)	1909
2:46:04.6	Albert Raines (US)	1909
2:42:31.0	Fred Barrett (GB)	1909
2:40:34.2	Thure Johansson (Swed)	1909
2:38:16.2	Harry Green (GB)	1913
2:36:06.6	Alexis Ahlgren (Swed)	1913
2:32:35.8	Hannes Kolehmainen (Fin)	1920
2:29:01.8	Albert Michelsen (US)	1925

THE BOSTON MARATHON (above), the oldest US race of its kind, was won 7 times by Clarence DeMar. The NYC MARATHON (left) with 22,000 or more runners, gets its start on the Verrazano Bridge.
BALANCING A BOTTLE on a tray is the way Roger Bourban (right) runs in every marathon.

2:27:49.0	Fusashige Suzuki (Japan)	1925
2:26:44.0	Yasao Ikenaka (Japan)	1935
2:26:42.0	Kitei Son (Japan)	1935
2:25:39.0	Yun Bok Suh (S Korea)	1947
2:20:42.2	Jim Peters (GB)	1952
2:18:40.2	Jim Peters (GB)	1953
2:18:34.8	Jim Peters (GB)	1953
2:17:39.4	Jim Peters (GB)	1954
2:15:17.0	Sergey Popov (USSR)	1958
2:15:16.2	Abebe Bikila (Ethiopia)	1960
2:15:15.8	Toru Terasawa (Japan)	1963
2:14:28.0*	Buddy Edelen (US)	1963
2:13:55.0	Basil Heatley (GB)	1964
2:12:11.2	Abebe Bikila (Ethiopia)	1964
2:12:00.0	Morio Shigematsu (Japan)	1965
2:09:36.4	Derek Clayton (Australia)	1967
2:08:33.6	Derek Clayton (Australia)	1969
2:08:05.2†	Alberto Salazar (US)	1981
2:08:05.0	Stephen Jones (GB)	1984
2:07:11.06	Carlos Lopes (Port)	1985
2:06:50.0	Belaynah Dinsamo (Ethiopia)	1988

Women

3:40:22.0	Violet Piercy (GB)	1926
3:27:45.0	Dale Greig (GB)	1964
3:19:33.0	Mildred Sampson (NZ)	1964
3:15:22.0	Maureen Wilton (Can)	1967
3:07:26.0	Anni Pede (W Ger)	1967
3:02:53.0	Caroline Walker (US)	1970
3:01:42.0	Elizabeth Bonner (US)	1971
2:46:30.0	Adrienne Beames (Australia)	1971
2:46:24.0	Chantal Langlace (France)	1974
2:43:54.5	Jackie Hansen (US)	1974
2:42:24.0	Liane Winter (W Ger)	1975
2:40:15.8	Christa Vahlensieck (W Ger)	1975
2:38:19.0	Jackie Hansen (US)	1975
2:35:15.4	Chantal Langlace (France)	1977
2:34:47.5	Christa Vahlensieck (W Ger)	1977
2:32:29.8	Grete Waitz (Nor)	1978
2:27:32.6	Grete Waitz (Nor)	1979
2:25:41.0	Grete Waitz (Nor)	1980
2:25:28.8†	Allison Roe (NZ)	1981
2:25:28.7†	Grete Waitz (Nor)	1983
2:22:43.0	Joan Benoit (US)	1984
2:21:06.0	Ingrid Kristiansen (Nor)	1985

* 36 yd (about 6 sec) under standard distance.
† NYC course used 1981–83 later found to be 170 yd or 30 sec short.

MODERN PENTATHLON

Origins

In the ancient Olympics the Pentathlon was the most prestigious event of the Games. Traditionally inspired by the city of Sparta, it consisted of the discus and javelin throws, running, jumping and wrestling, and the competitors were eulogized by Aristotle. The concept of the five-event all-round sporting contest was held dear by the founder of the modern Games, Baron de Coubertin, but it was not until 1912 that it was first held.

The events of the Modern Pentathlon are riding (on an unfamiliar horse over a 600-meter course with 15 fences), fencing (with electrically-wired épées against all others one at a time), shooting (with .22 caliber pistols at turning targets set at 25 meters), swimming (300 meter freestyle), and finally a 4000 meter cross-country run, each event held on a different day.

There is a story that the competitor is supposed to represent a King's messenger. First he rides like the wind to outdistance his pursuers, then when his horse is brought down, he fences his way out of trouble, following up with some good shooting to drive back the enemy's reserves. Then he crosses the final

RIDE, FENCE, SHOOT, SWIM AND RUN: András Balczó (left) of Hungary won a record 6 world titles and 2 Olympic gold medals (team) as well as the 1972 Olympic individual title, an extraordinary feat in this multifaceted event. Lars Hall (right) of Sweden has won 2 individual Olympic golds, 1952 and 1956.

obstacle, a river, and finally runs home to deliver his message. Certainly the qualities required of a Modern Pentathlete are not far removed from those of the messenger in the story.

Points are awarded for each activity with 1,000 being the standard for a good performance, excellence earning bonuses, and penalty points deducted for a sub-par performance. The winner is the one with the highest total after the five events. Initially only military personnel competed, but since the founding of the Union Internationale de Pentathlon Moderne et Biathlon (UIPMB) in 1948, non-military competitors have been allowed. The same Union administers the Biathlon. Women's competitions for 14-year-olds and over were first held internationally in 1977.

Olympic Titles

Hungary won the team title for the 4th time in the 1988 Games and Janos Martinek of Hungary won the individual gold medal. Hungary also has 9 World titles.

The greatest number of Olympic gold medals won is 3 by Balczó, a member of Hungary's winning team in 1960 and 68, and the 1972 individual champion. Lars Hall (Sweden) (b Apr 30, 1927) uniquely has won 2 individual championships (1952 and 56). Pavel Lednev (USSR) (b Mar 25, 1943) has won a record 7 medals (2 gold, 2 silver, 3 bronze), 1968–80.

The USSR has a record 12 World titles and 4 Olympic team titles.

Highest Scores

	Points	Name and Nationality	Date and Place
Shooting			
200/200	—[1]	Charles Leonard (US) (b Feb 23, 1913)	Aug 3, 1936 W Berlin, Germ
200/200	1,132	Daniele Masala (Italy) (b Feb 12, 1955)	Aug 21, 1978 Jönkoping, Swed
200/200	1,132	Geo Horvath (Swed) (b Mar 14, 1960)	July 22, 1980 Moscow, USSR
Swimming			
3 min 08.22 sec	1,368	John Scott (US) (b Apr 14, 1962)	Aug 27, 1982 London, Eng

[1] Points not awarded in 1936 Olympic Games.

Probably the greatest margin of victory was by William Oscar Guernsey Grut (b Sept 17, 1914) (Sweden) in the 1948 Games in London, when he won three events and placed fifth and eighth in the other two events.

Most World Championship Titles

World championships were first held in 1949 and annually since, except in Olympic years, when the Olympic and world titles are held simultaneously.

The record number of world titles won is 6 by András Balczó (Hungary) in 1963, 65–67 and 69, and the Olympic title in 1972. He also won 7 team titles (1960–70) with 5 world and 2 Olympic titles.

Point scores in riding, fencing, cross-country and hence overall scores have no comparative value between one competition and another. In shooting and swimming (300 m), where measurements are absolute, the point scores are of record significance.

MOTORCYCLING

Earliest Motorcycle

On Nov 10, 1885, a single-track vehicle, powered by an internal-combustion engine designed by Gottlieb Daimler, was ridden a little over 7 mi from Canstatt to Unterkheim, Germany. Daimler's vehicle, due to its engine location and basic design features which remain current today, is universally acknowledged as the world's first motorcycle, predating the first automobile—also by Daimler—by several months.

In the early days many races were for both motorcycles and cars, and often took the form of long-distance inter-city or inter-country events. These were heavily criticized following the aborted Paris to Madrid race of 1903 which resulted in a number of deaths of competitors and spectators. In 1904 the International Cup Race was held in France for motorcycles only, and on a closed road circuit. However, in 1905 the race was held again, and this is recognized as the first international motorcycling event. The venue was Dourdon near Paris, and it was organized by the newly formed Fédération Internationale des Clubs Motocyclistes (FIM). The race was a success and was won by an Austrian named Wondrick.

Earliest Races and Circuits

The first motorcycle race was held on an oval track of 1 mi at Sheen House, Richmond, Surrey, England, on Nov 29, 1897, won by Charles Jarrott (1877–1944) on a Fournier.

The Auto-Cycle Union Tourist Trophy (TT) series was first held on the 15.81-mile "Peel" ("St John's") course on the Isle of Man on May 28, 1907, and is still run on the island, on the "Mountain" circuit.

Longest Circuit

The 37.73-mile "Mountain" circuit on the Isle of Man, over which the two main TT races have been run since 1911, has 264 curves and corners and is the longest used for any motorcycle race.

Fastest Circuits

The highest average lap speed attained on any closed circuit is 160.288 mph by Yvon du Hamel (Canada) (b 1941) on a modified 903-cc four-cylinder Kawasaki Z1 on the 31-degree banked 2.5-mile Daytona International Speedway, Fla, in March 1973. His lap time was 56.149 sec.

The fastest road circuit is the Portstewart-Coleraine-Portrush circuit in Londonderry, N Ireland. The lap record (10.1 mile lap) is 4 min 53.2 sec (average speed 124.060 mph) by John Glyn Williams (1946–78) on a 747-cc four-cylinder Yamaha on lap five of the 750-cc event of the North-West 200, on May 21, 1977. Minor circuit changes prior to 1986 have resulted in slower times.

The TT circuit (Isle of Man) speed record is 118.54 mph for one lap by Joey Dunlop on a Honda on June 6, 1988.

Fastest Race

The fastest track race in the world was held at Grenzlandring, W Germany, in 1939. It was won by

QUICK AS A VINK: Henk Vink of The Netherlands set world records in 1977 for 1 kilometer and for 440 yds on his Kawasaki in 2-way runs from standing starts.

SMALLEST MOTORCYCLE: Paul Ashley of Baseldon, Essex, Eng, shows the vehicle he constructed—6.88-in wheelbase, 6.88-in seat height, with 1.96-in diameter wheels and powered by a 3.5-cc engine. He has ridden it at a speed of 5 mph.

Georg "Schorsh" Meier (b Germany Nov 9, 1910) at an average speed of 134 mph on a supercharged 495-cc flat-twin BMW.

The fastest road race is the 500-cc Belgian Grand Prix on the Francorchamps circuit. The record time for this 10-lap 87.74-mile race is 38 min 58.5 sec (average speed of 135.068 mph) by Barry Sheene (UK) on a 495-cc four-cylinder Suzuki on July 3, 1977.

Longest Race

The longest race is the Liège 24 Hours, run on the Francorchamps circuit. The greatest distance ever covered is 2,761.9 miles (average speed 115.08 mph) by Jean-Claude Chemarin and Christian Leon of

France on a 941-cc four-cylinder Honda on the Francorchamps circuit on Aug 14–15, 1976.

Speed Records

Official world speed records must be set with two runs over a measured distance within a time limit (one hour for FIM records, two hours for AMA records).

Donald Vesco (b Loma Linda, Calif, Apr 8, 1939) riding his 21-ft-long *Lightning Bolt* streamliner, powered by two 1,016-cc Kawasaki engines on Bonneville Salt Flats, Utah, on Aug 28, 1978, set AMA and FIM absolute records with an overall average of 318.598 mph and had a fastest run at an average of 318.66 mph.

The world record average speed for two runs over 1 km (1,093.6 yd) from a standing start is 16.68 sec by Henk Vink (b July 24, 1939) (Netherlands) on his supercharged 984-cc 4-cylinder Kawasaki, at Elvington Airfield, N Yorkshire, England on July 24, 1977. The faster run was made in 16.09 sec.

The world record for two runs over 440 yd from a standing start is 8.805 sec by Henk Vink on his supercharged 1,132-cc 4-cylinder Kawasaki, at Elvington Airfield, N Yorkshire, England, on July 23, 1977. The faster run was made in 8.55 sec.

The fastest time for a single run over 440 yd from a standing start is 7.08 sec by Bo O'Brechta (US) riding a supercharged 1,200-cc Kawasaki-based machine at Ontario, Calif, in 1980. The highest terminal velocity recorded at the end of a 440-yd run from a standing start is 201.34 mph by Elmer Trett at Indianapolis, on Sept 5, 1983.

FASTEST VELOCITY: Elmer Trett sped 201.34 mph at the end of a 440-yd run from a standing start to set the record for highest terminal velocity.

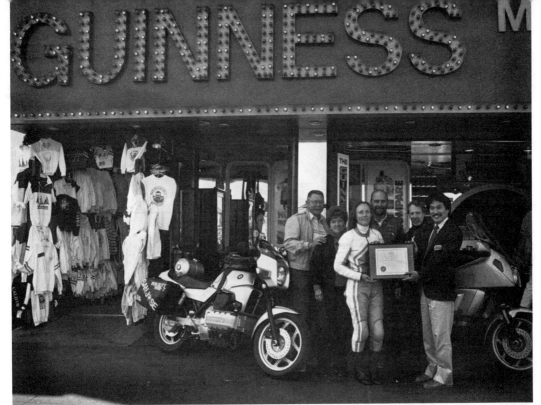

CROSS-US SPEED RECORD: Fran Crane receiving certificate from manager of Guinness Museum on Fisherman's Wharf, San Francisco, that commemorates her feat of motorcycling from NY 2,974 mi in 44 hours 20 min, June 9-11, 1988. Behind and on her left is Michael Kneebone who set a speed record for a 24-hour trip of 1,727 mi.

World Championships

Races are currently held for the following classes of motorcycles: 50 cc, 125 cc, 250 cc, 350 cc, 500 cc, and sidecars.

Most world championship titles (instituted by the *Fédération Internationale Motocycliste* in 1949) won are 15 by Giacomo Agostini (b Lovere, Italy, June 16, 1942) in the 350-cc class 1968–74 and in the 500-cc class 1966–72 and 75. Agostini is the only man to win two world championships in five consecutive years (350 and 500 cc titles 1968–72). Freddie Spencer (US) in 1985 became the first ever to win world titles at both 250 and 500 cc in the same year. Agostini won 122 races in the world championship series between Apr 24, 1965, and Sept 25, 1977, including a record 19 in 1970, also achieved by Stanley Michael ''Mike'' Hailwood, (b Oxford, England, 1940, d 1981) in 1966.

A record 3 world trials championships have been won by 3 men: Yrjö Vesterinen (Finland) 1976–8, Eddie Lejeune (Belgium), and by Thierry Michaud (France) 1985–6 and 1988.

Klaus Enders (Germany) (b 1937) won 6 world sidecar titles, 1967, 69–70, 72–74.

Angel Roldan Nieto (Spain) (b Jan 25, 1947) won a record seven 125-cc titles, 1971–72, 1979, and 1981–84.

Cross-US Trek

Fran Crane (b Nov 5, 1946) of Santa Cruz, Calif, traveled from NYC to San Francisco (2,974 mi) in a time of 44 hours 20 min June 9–11, 1988 for the best time by either a man or woman. She drove a BMW K100.

Matthew P. Guzzetta, 31, of Don Vesco Products, Spring Valley, Calif claims to have ridden a 260-lb, 125-cc revised Suzuki motorcycle whose shell he designed and built, from San Diego, Calif, to Daytona Beach, Fla, without refueling, Mar 3–17, 1984. With a writer friend, Gerald Foster, he covered the 2,443 mi on 11.83 gallons, for a record consumption of 214.37 mph. In a snowstorm, they had to put the motorcycle in a van for 36 mi.

24-Hour Distance Record

Michael Kneebone of Chicago beat his own record when he went 1,727 mi from San Francisco to Adair, Iowa July 9–10, 1988 as part of an attempt to cross the US in record time.

CROSS-US TREK: In this 260-lb 125-cc revised Suzuki, without refueling, Matt Guzzetta rode 2,443 mi from San Diego to Daytona Beach on 11.83 gallons in Mar 1984, for a record 214.37 mpg.

MOTO-CROSS RACE in progress. André Malherbe (Belgium) almost takes flight on his way to victory in the 500-cc contest in 1980.

Youngest and Oldest Champions

Alberto "Johnny" Cecotto (b Caracas, Venezuela, Jan 25, 1956) was the youngest person to win a world championship. He was aged 19 years 211 days when he won the 350-cc title on Aug 24, 1975. The oldest was Hermann-Peter Müller (1909–76) of W Germany, who won the 250-cc title in 1955, aged 46.

Moto-Cross (Scrambling)

This is a very specialized sport in which the competitors race over rough country including steep climbs and drops, sharp turns, sand, mud and water. The sport originated in England in 1924 when some riders competed in "a rare old scramble." Until the Second World War it remained a British interest but the Moto-Cross des Nations was inaugurated in 1947 and became an annual event, with the current rules formulated in 1963. In 1961 the Trophée des Nations, for 250 cc machines, was introduced by the FIM. World championships had been instituted in 1957.

Joël Robert (b Chatelet, Belgium, Nov 11, 1943) has won six 250-cc moto-cross (also known as "scrambles") world championships (1964, 68–72). Between Apr 25, 1964, and June 18, 1972, he won a record fifty 250-cc Grands Prix. He became the youngest moto-cross world champion on July 12, 1964, when he won the 250-cc championship aged 20 years 244 days.

PARTNERS IN CLIMB: Tenzing Norgay stood atop Mt Everest as Edmund Hillary took this historic photograph after the two men became the first to successfully climb the 29,028-ft mountain. Since then, so many climbers have made the attempt that the Nepalese Government is concerned about all the garbage left behind.

MOUNTAINEERING

Origins

Although Bronze-Age artifacts have been found on the summit (9,605 ft) of the Riffelhorn, Switzerland, mountaineering, as a sport, has a continuous history dating back only to 1854. Isolated instances of climbing for its own sake exist back to the 13th century. The Atacamenans built sacrificial platforms near the summit of Llullaillaco in South America (22,058 ft) in late pre-Columbian times, *c.* 1490.

Greatest Wall

The highest final stage in any wall climb is that on the south face of Annapurna I (26,545 ft). It was climbed by the British expedition led by Christian John Storey Bonington (UK) (b Aug 6, 1934) when from Apr 2–May 27, 1970, Donald Whillans, 36, and Dougal Haston, 27, scaled to the summit. They used 18,000 ft of rope.

The longest wall climb is on the Rupal-Flank from the base camp at 11,680 ft to the South Point (26,384

ft) of Nanga Parbat—a vertical ascent of 14,704 ft. This was scaled by the Austro-Germano-Italian expedition led by Dr Karl Maria Herrligkoffer in Apr 1970.

The most demanding free climbs are those rated at 5.13, the premier location for these being in the Yosemite Valley, Calif.

Yosemite Feats

Charles Cole, using standard equipment, on Aug 12, 1987 executed an 870-ft traverse from the top of Elephant Rock to the south rim of Yosemite Valley in 2 hours, 15 min for the record Tyrolean Traverse, exceeding the previous record by almost 300 feet. He was assisted by Russ Wallings, Dimitri Barton and John Long.

The first one-day ascent of El Capitan in Yosemite was made on June 15, 1975, by climbers John Long, Jim Bridwell and Billy Westbay. They began at 4 AM and completed the ascent at 6:45 PM.

The first one-day ascent of both El Capitan and Half Dome was made in Aug 1986, by John Bachar and Peter Croft. The ascents were accomplished in 18 hours, 2 min.

Mount Everest

Mount Everest (29,028 ft) was first climbed at 11:30 AM on May 29, 1953, when the summit was reached by Edmund Percival Hillary (b July 20, 1919), of New Zealand, and the Sherpa, Tenzing

LADY AT THE TOP: Junko Tabei was the first woman to reach the summit of Mt Everest on May 16, 1975. On the right is the south wall which she ascended. (Popperfoto)

YOSEMITE FEAT: Charles Cole executing the 870-ft Tyrolean Traverse, which beat the old record by almost 300 ft. He took 2 hours 15 min to go from Elephant Rock to the valley's south rim.

Norgay (b as Namgyal Wangdi, in Nepal in 1914, formerly called Tenzing Khumjung Bhutia). The successful expedition was led by Col (later Hon Brigadier) Henry Cecil John Hunt (b June 22, 1910).

Progressive Mountaineering Altitude Records

ft	Mountain	Climbers	Date
17,887	Popocatepetl, Mexico	Francisco Montano	1521
18,400	Mana Pass, Zasker Range, Kashmir	A. de Andrade, M. Morques	July 1624
18,893	On Chimborazo, Ecuador	Dr. Albert Von Humboldt, Aimé Bonpland, Carlos Montufar	June 23, 1802
19,411	On Leo Pargyal Range, Himalaya	Garrard and Lloyd	1818
22,260	On E. Abi Gamin, Garhwal Himalaya	A. & R. Schlagintweit	Aug 1855
22,606	Pioneer Peak on Baltoro Kangri, Kashmir	William M. Conway, Matthias Zurbiggen	Aug 23, 1892
22,834	On Pyramis Peak, Karakoram, Tibet	William H. Workman, J. Petigax Snr & Jnr, C. Savoie	Aug 12, 1903
23,787	On Gurla Mandhata, Tibet	Thomas G. Longstaff, Alexis & Henri Brocherel	July 23, 1905
c.23,900	On Kabru, Sikkim-Nepal	Carl W. Rubenson and Monrad Aas	Oct 20, 1907
24,607	On Chogolisa, Karakoram, Tibet	Duke of the Abruzzi, J. Petigax, H. & E. Brocherel	July 18, 1909
c.24,900	Camp V, Everest, Tibet-Nepal	G. L. Mallory, E. F. Norton, T. H. Somervell, H. T. Morshead	May 20, 1922
26,986	On Everest (North Face), Tibet	George L. Mallory, Edward F. Norton, T. Howard Somervell	May 21, 1922
c.27,300	On Everest (North Face), Tibet	George I. Finch, J. Granville Bruce	May 27, 1922
28,126	On Everest (North Face), Tibet	Edward Felix Norton	June 4, 1924
28,215	South Shoulder on Everest, Nepal	Raymond Lambert, Tenzing Norgay	May 28, 1952
28,721	South Shoulder on Everest, Nepal	Thomas D. Bourdillon, Robert C. Evans	May 26, 1953
29,028	Everest, Nepal-Tibet	Edmund P. Hillary, Tenzing Norgay	May 29, 1953

The first climber to succeed four times was the Sherpa, Sundare (or Sungdare) in 1979, 1981, 1982 and 1985. The first to succeed via three different routes was Yasuo Kato (Japan) (1949–82), who died shortly after his third ascent on Dec 27, 1982.

Franz Oppurg (1948–81) (Austria) was the first to make the final ascent solo, on May 14, 1978, while Reinhold Messner (Italy) was the first to make the entire climb solo on Aug 20, 1980. Messner and Peter Habeler (b July 22, 1942) (Austria) made the first entirely oxygen-less ascent on May 8, 1978. Ang Rita Sherpa was the first to scale Mt Everest three times without the use of bottled oxygen.

Five women have reached the summit, the first being Junko Tabei (b Sept 22, 1939) (Japan) on May 16, 1975. The oldest person was Richard Daniel Bass (b Dec 21, 1929) aged 55 years 130 days on Apr 30, 1985.

Reinhold Messner, with his ascent of Kangchenjunga in 1982, became the first person to climb the world's three highest mountains, having earlier reached the summits of Everest and K2. He is the only person to have successfully scaled all of the world's 14 main summits of over 8,000 m (26,250 ft), all without oxygen.

LEGATOR: Baron Pierre de Coubertin was the main force behind reviving the Olympic Games after a 1,503-year hiatus. Now, not even 100 years after the first modern Olympics, politics, nationalism, drug abuse and uncertain standards of amateurism threaten to end the Baron's dream of competition open to athletes of all nations.

Highest Bivouac

Two Japanese, Hironobu Kamuro (1951–83) and Hiroshi Yoshino (1950–83), bivouacked at 28,870 ft on Mt. Everest on the night of Oct 8/9, 1983. Yoshino died on Oct 9 while Kamuro died either during the bivouac night or next day.

Oldest Climber

Teiichi Igarashi (Japan) (b Sept 21, 1886) at age 99 years 302 days on July 20, 1986, climbed snow-topped Mt Fuji, Japan, 12,388 ft high.

OLYMPIC GAMES

Note: These records include the un-numbered Games held at Athens in 1906. World Records set at the 1988 Olympiad in Seoul, Korea will be found under the individual sports.

Origins

The earliest celebration of the ancient Olympic Games of which there is a certain record is that of July 776 BC (when Coroibos, a cook from Elis, won a foot race), though their origin probably dates from perhaps as early as *c.* 1370 BC. The ancient Games were terminated by an order issued in Milan in 393 AD

by Theodosius I, "the Great" (*c.* 346–95), Emperor of Rome. At the instigation of Pierre de Fredi, Baron de Coubertin (1863–1937), the Olympic Games of the modern era were inaugurated in Athens on Apr 6, 1896.

Most Medals

In the ancient Olympic Games, victors were given a chaplet (head garland) of olive leaves. Leonidas of Rhodos won 12 running titles from 164 to 152 BC.

The most individual gold medals won by a male competitor in the modern Games is 10 by Raymond Clarence Ewry (US) (b Oct 14, 1874, at Lafayette, Ind; d Sept 29, 1937), a jumper (see *Track and Field*). The female record is 7 by Vera Caslavska-Odlozil (b May 3, 1942) of Czechoslovakia, a gymnast.

Only 3 Olympians won 4 consecutive individual titles in the same event. They have been Alfred A. Oerter (b Sept 19,1936, NYC) who won the discus title in 1956, 60, 64 and 68; Ray Ewry (see above) who took both standing high jump and standing long jump 1900, 04, 06, 08, if you count the Intercalated Games of 1906; also Paul Elvstrom (Denmark) (b Feb 24, 1928) who won 4 gold medals at monotype yachting, 1948, 52, 56 and 60.

OLYMPICS OF 1900–04–08 and 1920 had contests in archery, and one medal winner was Queenie Newell (GB) who managed to be dressed fashionably as well as functionally.

The only man to win a gold medal in both the Summer and Winter Games is Edward F. Eagan (US) (1898–1967) who won the 1920 light-heavyweight boxing title and was a member of the winning four-man bob in 1932. The first woman to win Winter and Summer medals is Christa Luding (née Rothenburger) (E Ger) (b Dec 4, 1959) who took the silver at cycling sprints in Seoul in 1988, having won the speed skating 1000m gold and 500m silver at Calgary in 1988 and the 500m gold at Sarajevo in 1984.

Gymnast Larissa Latynina (b Dec 27, 1934) (USSR) won a record 18 medals (see *Gymnastics*). The record at one celebration is 8 medals by gymnast Alexandr Ditiatin (b Aug 7, 1957) (USSR) in 1980.

Most Participations

Five countries have never failed to be represented at the 22 celebrations of the Summer Games: Australia, France, Greece, Great Britain and Switzerland. Of these, only Great Britain has been present at all Winter celebrations as well.

Most and Fewest Competitors

The greatest number of competitors in any Summer Olympic Games has been more than 9,000 at Seoul in 1988. (Actually 9,677, but some dropped out and some were spurious.) A record 160 countries competed in 1988 with one more country sending just an official. The fewest was 311 competitors from 13 countries in 1896. In 1904 only 12 countries participated. The largest team was 880 men and 4 women from France at the 1900 Games in Paris.

Largest Crowds

The largest crowd at any Olympic site was 150,000 at the 1952 ski-jumping at the Holmenkollen, outside Oslo, Norway. Estimates of the number of spectators of the marathon race through Tokyo on Oct 21, 1964, have ranged from 500,000 to 1,500,000.

The total spectator attendance at Los Angeles in 1984 was given as 5,797,923.

Youngest and Oldest Medalists

The youngest woman to win a gold medal is Marjorie Gestring (US) (b Nov 18, 1922) aged 13 years 9 months, in the 1936 women's springboard event.

The oldest person was Oscar Swahn who won a silver medal for shooting running deer as a member of the Swedish team in 1920, aged 72 years 280 days. Swahn had won a gold medal in 1912 at the record age of 64 years 258 days.

The youngest to win an Olympic gold medal was a French boy who coxed the winning Dutch rowing pairs crew in the 1900 Games. His name is not known as he was a last-minute substitute but he was no more than 10 years old and may even have been as young as seven.

MOST MEDALS: It is unlikely that any Olympian will ever match the 10 gold medals won by Ray Ewry (US) in the standing jumps in four Games.

ATHENS STADIUM (Panathenean): Built for the 1896 Olympics, first in modern times, this arena was used again for the 1906 Games. The Greeks are making a strong bid to have their homeland, where the Olympics originated, named as the permanent site for all Games from the anniversary year of 1996 onwards.

Olympic Medals Restored

The star of the 1912 Olympic Games was an American Indian named Jim Thorpe. Held in Stockholm, the Games provided him with an opportunity to win two gold medals, one in the decathlon and one in the pentathlon. He also placed well in the high jump and long jump. He was greeted in New York with a ticker-tape parade, but in 1913 the International Olympic Committee demanded his medals back after it had come to light that prior to the Olympics he had played baseball for $25 a week and therefore was not strictly an amateur athlete. On Oct 13, 1982, 29 years after Thorpe's death, the I.O.C. presented his gold medals to his children and reinstated his name in the record books.

Longest Span

The longest competitive span of any Olympic competitor is 40 years by Dr Ivan Osiier (Denmark) (1888–1965), in fencing, 1908–32 and 48, and by Magnus Konow (Norway) (1887–1972) in yachting, 1908–20 and 36–48. The longest span for a woman is 24 years (1932–56) by the Austrian fencer Ellen Müller-Preiss. Raimondo d'Inzeo (b Feb 8, 1925) competed for Italy in equestrian events in a record 8 celebrations (1948–76), gaining one gold medal, 2 silver and 3 bronze medals. Janice Lee York Romary (b Aug 6, 1928), the US fencer, competed in all 6 Games from 1948 to 1968, and Lia Manoliu (Romania) (b Apr 25, 1932) competed 1952–72, winning the discus title in 1968.

Most Olympic Gold Medals at One Games

Mark Spitz (US), the swimmer, won a record 7 gold medals at one celebration (4 individual and 3 relay) at Munich in 1972.

The most gold medals won in individual events at one celebration is 5 by speed skater Eric Heiden (b June 14, 1958) (US) at Lake Placid, NY in 1980.

OLYMPIC CENTERPIECE: Americans never saw this Russian gymnastic display on TV as it happened in Moscow in 1980 when the Americans boycotted the Games.

The 1988 Summer Olympic Games

The site chosen, Seoul, capital of South Korea, has one of the largest populations of any city on earth—an estimated 9 million people. Nearly all the facilities for the Games were in place by the end of 1986 when the Asian Games were held there. These include a 100,000 capacity stadium as part of the sports complex on the bank of the Han River, where the water events were held. Swimming and diving were held in indoor pools.

The program was expanded to include tennis (reintroduced for the first time since 1924). Baseball, women's judo and tae-kwon-do were demonstration sports.

South Korea, despite threats of boycotts and insistence by North Korea on participation as co-host, was unmarred by political problems. The most disturbing event occurred when Ben Johnson, winner of the 100m dash, was disqualified for use of a banned substance, and other athletes were similarly deprived of their medals.

Overall, the USSR won 132 medals, including 53 golds, E Germany gained 102 (37 gold) and the US was third with 94 (36 gold).

At the 1988 Winter Olympics in Calgary, Canada, the weather was abnormally warm and snow didn't arrive at first. Bonnie Blair and Brian Boitano were American ice skating winners, but otherwise the US watched E Germany repeat its 1984 success in women's figure skating (Katarina Witt); Italy (Alberto Tomba) in 2 slaloms, Switzerland in downhill skiing, and Netherlands in speed skating.

The 1992 Summer Games will be held in Barcelona, Spain, and the Winter Games in Albertville, France.

ON THE BEAM: Larissa Latynina earned 18 Olympic medals—the record for either sex in any sport. Nine were gold. Latynina also won 10 individual and 5 team titles in the World Championships.

RUSSIA in the Olympics: 40 years elapsed between 1912 when Czarist Russia fielded a team (shown here), and 1952, when the first Soviet team participated.

MEDALS RESTORED: Jim Thorpe in decathlon, 1912.

IN DISCUS SUPREME: Al Oerter (US) won this event in 4 successive Olympics—1956, 60, 64, 68—a unique achievement in field events. (E. D. Lacey)

LARGEST OLYMPIC SKI CROWD: This record-breaking audience witnessed the ski jump at Holmenkollen, outside Oslo, Norway, at the 1952 Winter Games.

NATIONAL COSTUMES of the Mexicans were demonstrated at the 1968 opening ceremony of the Olympics in Mexico City. (Ed Lacey)

ORIENTEERING

Origins

Orienteering is basically a combination of cross-country running and map reading. Competitors in this little-known sport are given a map, marked with the locations of control points, and a compass. In the most common version of the sport, the control points must be achieved in specified order, and the fastest time wins. In other versions, a time limit is declared and point values are assigned to finding the control points, so competitors must decide which control points they can get to amass the highest score.

Orienteering as now known was invented by Major Ernst Killander in Sweden in 1918. It was based on military exercises of the 1890's. The term was first used for an event at Oslo, Norway, on October 7, 1900.

U.S. Champions

	Men	Women
1973	Jerry Rice, Quantico	Heidi Green, Trojan OC, NC
1974–75	Bob Turbyfill, Quantico	Cindy Prince (Fuller), Grazoo
1975–76	Bob Turbyfill, Quantico	Joanie Pezdir (Gunther), Quantico
1976–77	Peter Gagarin, New Eng	Jenny Tuthill, New Eng
1977	Peter Gagarin, New Eng	Sharon Crawford, New Eng
1978	Peter Gagarin, New Eng	Sharon Crawford, New Eng
1979	Peter Gagarin, New Eng	Sharon Crawford, New Eng
1980	Eric Weyman, Hudson Valley	Sharon Crawford, New Eng
1981	Eric Weyman, Hudson Valley	Sharon Crawford, New Eng
1982	Eric Weyman, Hudson Valley	Sharon Crawford, New Eng
1983	Peter Gagarin, New Eng	Virginia Lehman, New Eng
1984	Eric Weyman, Hudson Valley	Sharon Crawford, New Eng
1985	Dan Meenehan, St Louis	Sharon Crawford, New Eng
1986	Mikell Platt, Quantico	Sharon Crawford, New Eng
1987	Mike Eglinski, Kansas	Sharon Crawford, New Eng
1988	Mikell Platt, Blue Star Complex	Peggy Dickison, Quantico

At each US meet, there may be as many as 6 courses varying in degree of difficulty by how far off the main path the orienteer must go.

World championships were inaugurated in 1966 and are held biennially under the auspices of the International Orienteering Federation (founded 1961), located in Sweden. The US Orienteering Federation was founded in 1971 to serve as the governing body for the sport in America and to choose teams for world championship competition.

Most Competitors

The most competitors at an event in one day is 22,510 on the first day of the Swedish O-Ringen at Smaalaand on July 18, 1983.

TOP WOMAN ORIENTEER: Sharon Crawford of Concord, Mass, who has been US Champion 10 times in the last 11 years, is reading her map, planning her routes, as she runs from the start. (Photo from Orienteering/North America)

World Championships

Men's Individual	Women's Individual
1966 Aage Hadler (Nor)	Ulla Lindqvist (Swe)
1968 Karl Johansson (Swe)	Ulla Lindqvist (Swe)
1970 Stig Berge (Nor)	Ingred Hadler (Nor)
1972 Aage Hadler (Nor)	Sarolta Monspart (Fin)
1974 Bernt Frilen (Swe)	Mona Norgaard (Den)
1976 Egil Johansen (Nor)	Liisa Veijalainen (Fin)
1978 Egil Johansen (Nor)	Anne Berit Eid (Nor)
1979 Ogvin Thon (Nor)	Outi Bergonstrom (Fin)
1981 Ogvin Thon (Nor)	Annichen Kringstad (Swe)
1983 Morton Berglia (Nor)	Annichen Svensson (Swe)
1985 Kari Sallinen (Fin)	Annichen Svensson (Swe)
1987 Kent Olsson (Swe)	Arja Hannus (Swe)

Sweden has won the men's relay six times between 1966 and 1979 and the women's relay seven times, 1966, 1970, 1974, 1976, 1981, 1983, and 1985. Norway, by winning both men's and women's relays in 1987, has now equaled Sweden's men's record.

POLO

Origins

Polo is usually regarded as being of Persian origin, having been played as *Pulu c.* 525 BC. Other claims have come from Tibet and the Tang dynasty of China 250 AD.

The earliest club of modern times was the Kachar Club (founded in 1859) in Assam, India. The game was introduced into England from India in 1869 by the 10th Hussars at Aldershot, Hampshire, and the earliest match was one between the 9th Lancers and the 10th Hussars on Hounslow Heath, west of London, in July, 1871. The earliest international match between England and the US was in 1886.

Playing Field

The game is played (by two teams of four) on the largest field of any ball game in the world. The ground measures 300 yards long by 160 yards wide with side-boards or, as in India, 200 yards twice without boards.

Highest Handicap

The highest handicap based on eight 7½-minute "chukkas" is 10 goals, introduced in the US in 1891 and in the United Kingdom and in Argentina in 1910.

The latest of the 55 players to have received 10-goal handicaps are Carlos Gracida (Mex) and Ernesto Trotz (Argentina). A match of two 40-goal handicap teams was staged for the only time at Palermo, Buenos Aires, Argentina, in 1975.

Highest Score

The highest aggregate number of goals scored in an international match is 30, when Argentina beat the US 21–9 at Meadowbrook, Long Island, NY, in Sept, 1936.

Largest Crowd

Crowds of more than 50,000 have watched floodlit matches at the Sydney, Australia, Agricultural Shows.

Most Olympic Medals

Polo has been part of the Olympic program on five occasions: 1900, 1908, 1920, 1924 and 1936. Of the 21 gold medalists, a 1920 winner, John Wodehouse, the 3rd Earl of Kimberley, uniquely also won a silver medal (1908).

Most Internationals

Thomas Hitchcock, Jr. (1900–44) played five times for the US vs. England (1921–24–27–30–39) and twice vs. Argentina (1928–36).

ELEPHANT POLO: Polo was first played on elephant-back in Jaipur, India in 1976. The World Elephant Polo Association, formed in 1982, staged its first championships at Tiger Tops, Nepal in 1983, when the winners were the Tiger Tops Tuskers captained by Mark Payne. Other Polo Associations "take no cognisance" of elephant polo.

Polo on Elephant Back

A crowd of 40,000 watched a game played at Jaipur, India, in 1976, when elephants were used instead of ponies and longer than normal polo sticks were used.

POWERBOAT RACING

Origins

The first recorded race by powered boats was for steamboats at the Northern Yacht Club Regatta at Rothesay, Scotland in 1827. It was won by *Clarence,* a locally built vessel. Paddle steamers on the Mississippi were often pitted against each other in the 1840s for purely commercial reasons, such as getting to the markets first with their cargoes. In 1870 the *Robert E. Lee* had her famous race with the *Natchez* from New Orleans to St Louis, a distance of 1,027 miles, which the former won in 90 hours 30 min. This time was not beaten by any boat until 1929.

After 1903, racing developed mainly as a "circuit" or short, sheltered course type competition. Offshore or sea passage races also developed, initially for displacement (non-planing) cruisers. Offshore events for fast (planing) cruisers began in 1958 with a 170-mile passage race from Miami, Fla to Nassau, Bahamas. Outboard motor, *i.e.,* the combined motor/transmission detachable propulsion unit type racing began in the US in about 1920. Both inboard and outboard motor boat engines are mainly gasoline-fueled, but since 1950 diesel (compression ignition) engines have appeared and are widely used in offshore sport.

Highest Speeds

The highest speed ever achieved on water is an estimated 300 knots (345 mph) by Kenneth Peter Warby (GB) (b May 9, 1939) on the Blowering Dam Lake, NSW, Australia on Nov 20, 1977 in his unlimited hydroplane *Spirit of Australia.* The official world water speed record is 319.627 mph (277.57 knots) set on Oct 8, 1978 by Warby on Blowering Dam Lake.

The "official" water speed record is 229 mph by Eddie Hill in a propeller-driven boat, *The Texan,* in Chowchilla, Calif, Sept 5, 1982. He also set a 440-yd elapsed time record of 5.16 sec in this boat at Firebird Lake, Ariz on Nov 13, 1983.

The official record for a woman is 116.279 mph by Fiona Brothers (UK) in a Seebold marathon hull at Holme Pierrepont, Nottingham, Eng, on Sept 1, 1981. However, the fastest attained on water by a woman driver is 190 mph by Mary Rife (US) in a drag boat.

The official American Drag Boat Association record is 223.88 mph by *Final Effort,* a blown-fuel hydro boat driven by Bob Burns at Creve Coeur Lake, St Louis, Mo, on July 15, 1985 over a ¼ mile course.

Records are recognized by the Union Internationale Motonautique. The fastest speed recognized by the UIM is now for Class (e)GP: 177.61 mph by P. R. Knight on Lake Ruantaniwha, New Zealand, in a Chevrolet-engined Lauterbach hull powerboat.

Robert F. Hering (US) set the world Formula One record at 165.338 mph at Parker, Ariz on Apr 21, 1986.

FASTEST BOAT: Eddie Hill in this propeller-driven "The Texan" during his 229-mph run on Sept 5, 1982, in Chowchilla, Calif. (Left) "The Texan" also set a 440-yd record of 5.16 sec on Nov 13, 1983. (Jim Welch)

offshore boat is 154.438 mph for one way and 148.238 mph for two way runs by Tom Gentry (US) in his 49-ft catamaran powered by 4 Gentry Turbo Eagle V8 Chevrolet engines.

The fastest speed recorded for a diesel (compression ignition) boat is 135.62 mph by the hydroplane *Iveco World Leader,* powered by an Alfo-Fiat engine, driven by Carlo Bonomi at Venice, Italy in 1985.

The highest race speed is 103.29 mph set by Tony Garcia (US) in a Class I powerboat race at Key West, Fla, in Nov 1983.

Gold Cup

The Gold Cup (instituted 1903 by the American Power Boat Association) was won 8 times by Bill Muncey (1929–81) (US) (1956–57, 61–62, 72, 77–79). The highest lap speed reached in the competition is 128.338 mph by the hydroplane *Atlas Van Lines,* driven by Muncey in a qualifying round on the Columbia River, Wash in July 1977, and again in July 1978. *Atlas Van Lines* has won most, namely 7 times, 1972, 77–79, and 82–84. The race speed record is 120.054 mph by the same boat in 1982, driven by Chip Hanauer.

START OF A POWERBOAT RACE: This 1978 Cowes-Torquay contest in England was won by a woman for the first time at a then record average speed of 77.42 mph.

Longest Jump

The longest jump achieved by a jetboat has been 120 ft by Peter Horak (b May 7, 1943) (US) in a Glastron Carlson CVX 20 Jet Deluxe with a 460 Ford V8 engine (takeoff speed 55 mph) for a documentary TV film "The Man Who Fell from the Sky," at Salton Sea, Calif, on Apr 26, 1980.

The longest boat jump onto land is 172 ft by Norm Bagrie (NZ) from the Shotover River on July 1, 1982, in the 1½-ton jetboat *Valvolene.*

Fastest Transatlantic Crossing

A 65-ft powerboat, the *Virgin Atlantic Challenger II,* sailed by Richard Branson, a 35-year-old US businessman and his crew of 6, set a world record in June 1986 for all types of boats, by taking only 3 days 8 hours 31 min from NYC to Bishop's Rock off the coast of Eng. This beat the record held by the 51,988 gross ton transatlantic liner *United States* by 2 hours 11 min.

RIDING THE AIRWAVES: From a takeoff speed of 55 mph, Peter Horak jumped a powerboat 120 ft through the air for a television documentary. (Greg Meny)

Cowes International Offshore Powerboat Classic

Instituted in 1961, and originally held from Cowes to Torquay, Eng, in 1968 it was extended to include the return journey, a total distance of 246.13 miles. In 1982 the race became the Cowes International Powerboat Classic. The record for the race is 3 hours 4 min 35 sec by *Satisfaction* driven by Bill Elswick (US) averaging 79.64 mph in Aug 1980. The only 4-time winner is Renato Della Valle (Italy), 1982–85.

Longest Race

The longest offshore race has been the Port Richborough (London) to Monte Carlo Marathon Offshore International event. The race extended over 2,947 miles in 14 stages, June 10–25, 1972. It was won by

ITALIAN WINS POWERBOAT RACE: Renato della Valle drove this Ego Rothman to a record 4 consecutive victories (1982–85) in the 199-mile race off the English shore from Cowes to Torquay. (Steve Powell/All Sport)

H.T.S. (UK), driven by Mike Bellamy, Eddie Chater and Jim Brooks in 71 hours 35 min 56 sec (average speed 41.15 mph).

The longest circuit race has been the 24-hour race held annually since 1962 on the River Seine at Rouen, France. It was won in the fastest time in 1983 by a Johnson outboard-engined Piranha boat driven by Francois Greens, Jan van Brockels and Roger Robin (Belgium) at 46.63 mph.

RACQUETBALL

Racquetball, using a 40 ft by 20 ft court, was invented by Joe Sobek at the Greenwich YMCA, Conn. He originally named the game Paddle Rackets. The game grew in popular appeal in the 1960's and the International Racquetball Association was founded in 1968 by Bob Kendler (US). The major US event, the International Amateur Racquetball Association Championships, was initiated in 1969.

Winners in the singles in 1986 were Egan Inoue in the men's division and Cindy Baxter in the women's.

Marathon

The longest game was 72.3 hours by Bob Guerrero, 39, and Dennis Kaufman, 30, of Reno, Nev, Feb 10–12, 1988 at the Reno Athletic Club.

Playing against a series of opponents, Frank Araque (b Caracas, Venezuela 1957) of Edgewater Park, NJ, 5-ft-4-in tall, weighing 140 lb, played for 168 hours Apr 4–12, 1980. He won 225 of the 325 games he played.

Fastest Serve

In a club contest on Dec 2, 1979, Sol Abrevaya of Santa Monica, Calif, was officially clocked with a radar gun to have served before 100 witnesses at 179 mph, for the fastest serve in racket sports.

RODEO

Origins

While there is no known "first rodeo," as early as 1860 cowboys were competing at railheads and on trails for unofficial titles for bronc riding and other skills of their trade. After the great cattle drives were eliminated, due to the introduction of more and more railroads, large ranches began to "give a rodeo." As towns developed, they adopted the rodeo with Cheyenne, Wyo, claiming to have had the first in 1872.

A rodeo has been held each year in Prescott, Ariz, on the Fourth of July since 1888.

The sport was not organized until 1936 when a group of rodeo contestants founded the Cowboys Turtle Association (now the Professional Rodeo Cowboys Association) to standardize the sport. The official events now are saddle bronc riding, bareback riding, bull riding, calf roping, steer wrestling, and, in some states, team roping.

Largest Rodeos

The largest rodeo in the world is the National Finals Rodeo, held annually in Dec by the PRCA.

LONGEST GAME OF RACQUETBALL: In Reno, Nev, two players, Dennis Kaufman and Bob Guerrero, endured for 72.3 hours for a marathon record in Feb 1988.

RODEO: STAMPEDE! This chuckwagon race is the feature of the annual Calgary (Canada) Rodeo, and also was held in connection with the Winter Olympics in 1988. It has drawn crowds as big as 150,000.

The total prize money for the 1988 rodeo held in Las Vegas was a record $2,051,400.

In terms of attendance, the Calgary (Canada) Exhibition and Stampede, which had 156,280 spectators over a 10-day period in 1981, is the largest. The richest regular season rodeo, in terms of total added purse, is the one in Houston, Tex, with $125,000.

Most All-Around Titles and Highest Earnings

The record number of all-around cowboy titles in the Professional Rodeo Cowboys Association world championships is 6 by Larry Mahan (US) (b Nov 21, 1943) in 1966–70 and 1973 and, consecutively, 1974–9 by Tom Ferguson (b Dec 20, 1950). Tom Ferguson had record career earnings of $1,049,744 to 1986. Jim Shoulders (b 1928) of Henryetta, Okla has won a record 16 world championships between 1949 and 1959.

In the International Pro Rodeo Association, Dan Dailey has won 10 All Around World Championships (1976, 78–82, 84–87).

The record figure for prize money in a single season is $166,042 by Lewis Feild in 1986. He also set a record for earnings in one week of $75,218 at the 1987 National Finals Rodeo.

Charmayne James (b June 23, 1970), of Clayton, NM, won a record $151,969 in women's barrel (slalom) racing in 1986. She added $120,002 in earnings in 1987, the 4th year she dominated the event. In 1988, her winnings dropped to $85,768. She has earned more than the leading males in the PRCA.

Youngest Champion

The youngest winner of a world title is Metha Brorsen of Okla, who was only 11 years old when she won the International Rodeo Association Cowgirls barrel-racing event in 1975.

The youngest champion in the Women's Professional Rodeo Association competition is Jackie Jo Perrin of Antlers, Okla, who won the barrel-racing title in 1977 at age 13.

Time Records

Records for timed events, such as calf roping and steer wrestling, are not always comparable, because of the widely varying conditions due to the size of arenas and amount of start given the stock. The

ALL-AROUND WORLD CHAMPION COWBOY: Dan Dailey of Peaster, Tex, has been voted this title by the International Pro Rodeo Assoc 10 times 1976–87.

STEER WRESTLING CHAMPION: Steve Duhon holds numerous Pro Rodeo Cowboys Assoc records, including fastest time to throw a steer.

YOUNG BARREL-RACING CHAMP: Charmayne James, 16, is rounding a corner on her way to winning a record $151,969 in one year, 1986. (Springer)

BAREBACK CHAMPION
Lewis Feild on "Come Apart" scored 76 sec for this ride on the 5-time bareback horse of the year. Feild was the top money winner of the 1986 season ($166,042) and earned $75,218 in one week in the 1987 National Finals Rodeo
(PRCA)

fastest time recently recorded for roping a calf is 5.7 sec by Lee Phillips in Assiniboia, Saskatchewan, Canada, in 1978, and the fastest time for overcoming a steer is 2.4 sec by James Bynum at Marietta, Okla, in 1955; by Carl Deaton at Tulsa, Okla, in 1976; and by Gene Melton at Pecatonica, Ill, in 1976.

The standard required time to stay on in bareback, saddle bronc and bull riding events is 8 sec. In the now discontinued ride-to-a-finish events, rodeo riders have been recorded to have survived 15 min or more, until the mount had not a buck left in it.

The highest score in bull riding was 98 points out of a possible 100 by Denny Flynn on "Red Lightning" at Palestine, Ill, in 1979.

Champion Bull

The top bucking bull was probably "Red Rock" of Growney Bros Rodeo Co, who bucked out of the chute 307 times and was retired, unridden, after the 1987 National Finals Rodeo.

Champion Bronc

Traditionally a bronc called "Midnight" owned by Jim McNab of Alberta, Canada, was never ridden in 12 appearances at the Calgary Stampede.

ROLLER SKATING

Origins

The first roller skate was undoubtedly a pair of wooden spools, attached to a pair of ice skates minus the blades, sometime around 1700. The first recorded use of roller skates was in a play by Tom Hood, performed in 1743 at the Old Drury Lane Theatre, London, England. The first documented roller skate was invented by Jean Joseph Merlin of Huy, Belgium, in 1760, and demonstrated by him in London but with disastrous results. The forerunner of the modern four-wheel skate was invented by James L. Plimpton of Medfield, Mass, patented in 1863. The first indoor rink was opened in the Haymarket, London, in about 1824.

Largest Rink

The largest indoor rink ever to operate was located in the Grand Hall, Olympia, London, England. It had an actual skating area of 68,000 sq ft. It first opened in 1890 for one season, then again from 1909 to 1912.

The largest indoor rink now in operation is Guptill

STAYING POWER: Larry Mahan shares the record for most all-round world titles with 6.

Roll-Arena, Boght Corner, NY. The total rink measures 41,380 sq ft.

Free and Figure Skating

David DeMotte of Santa Ana, Calif, won the gold medal at the US Championships in Lincoln, Neb in 1988. In the World Championships in Paris he earned the silver medal, while Gregg Smith (US) took the gold; in pairs, DeMotte with Tammy Vaughn won the silver.

In the World Artistic competition in Pensacola, Fla in Oct 1988, Kevin Carroll defended his Figures title winning by a wide margin.

Marathon

The longest recorded continuous roller skating marathon was one of 344 hours 18 min by Isamu Furugen at Naha Roller Skate Land, Okinawa, Japan, Dec 11–27, 1983.

Endurance

Theodore J. Coombs (b 1954) of Hermosa Beach, Calif, skated 5,193 miles from Los Angeles to NYC

ROLLER HOCKEY will be a demonstration sport at the 1992 Olympic Games in Barcelona, Spain. Championships held annually in the US draw teams from both coasts. Here, Cliff Molette of the Olympia (Wash) Tornadoes chases the ball that Harry Cage of the Cumberland (Md) Raiders has under control. (Skate magazine)

and back to Yates Center, Kan, from May 30 to Sept 14, 1979. His longest 24-hour distance was 120 mi, June 27–28.

Roller Hockey

Roller hockey played 5-a-side (previously known as rink hockey and rink polo) began at the old Lava rink, Denmark Hill, London, Eng in the late 1870s. The Amateur Rink Hockey Association was formed in 1908, and in 1913 became the National Rink Hockey (now Roller Hockey) Association. England won the first four World Championships, 1936–9, since when Portugal has won most titles with 12 between 1947 and 1982. Portugal also won a record

FREE SKATING WINNER: David DeMotte, 20, was a double medalist in the 1988 World Championships. (Len Taylor)

ROLLER SKATE RACING (left) is not the only competition on roller skates. The US Amateur Federation of Roller Skating of Lincoln, Neb, also holds dance contests (right).

16 European (inst. 1926) titles between 1947 and 1987.

Roller hockey is scheduled as a demonstration sport for the 1992 Olympic Games in Barcelona, Spain.

Speed Records

The fastest speed (official world record) is 31.07.88 mph when L. Antoniel (Italy) recorded 24.99 sec for 300 m on a road in France in 1987. The women's record for 300 m is 26.794 sec by Marisa Canofoglia (Italy) on a road in Grenoble, France, on Aug 27, 1987.

The track record (indoor and outdoor) is 30.08.87 mph for 2,000 m by M. Bagnolini (Italy) in Grenoble, France in 1987. The women's speed on track record is also 30.08.87 by Canofoglia (see above) who traveled at that speed in the 3,000, 5,000 and 10,000 m races in Grenoble, France.

The greatest distance skated in one hour on a rink by a woman is 23.051 mi by Annie Lambrechts (Belgium) at Louvain, Belgium in July 1985, and 31.07 mi in one hour 21 min 25 sec as she went on.

ROWING

Oldest Race

The Sphinx stela of Amenhotep II (1450–1425 BC) records that he *stroked* a boat for some three miles. Warships were driven by human power in ancient times. The earliest literary reference to rowing is by the Roman poet Virgil in the *Aeneid,* published after his death in 19 BC. Rowing regattas were held in Venice *c.* 1300 AD. The world's oldest annual race was inaugurated on Aug 1, 1716 by Thomas Doggett, an Irish-born actor. He presented ''an Orange Colour Livery with a Badge'' for the winner of a competition for London watermen over a 4½-mi course from London Bridge to Chelsea. The world governing body, FISA, was founded in 1892, and the first major international meeting, the European championships, was held a year later.

Olympic and World Championships

In a 1986 revision of rowing rules, lightweight events were combined with the Open class at the World Championships, but were not included for the 1988 Olympics. Lightweight is defined as an average of 154.32 lb with a maximum of 159.84 lb for men, and an average of 125.66 lb with a maximum of 130.07 lb for women. Also, the distance for women

TRIPLE GOLD MEDALIST: John Kelly (US), winner in single and double sculls in 1920, and again in double in 1924, later saw his son win a bronze medal in rowing and his movie star daughter, Grace, marry a prince.

has been increased from 1,000m to 2,000m since 1985.

E German women won 5 of the 6 Olympic gold medals in 1988. The gold medalists were:

MEN

Single Sculls: Thomas Lange (E Ger) 6:49.86
Double Sculls: Netherlands (Ronald Florijn, Nicolaas Rienke) 6:21.13
Pairs with Coxswain: Italy (Carmine Abbagnale, Giuseppe Abbagnale) (Giuseppe Di Capua) 6:58.79
Pairs without Coxswain: GB (Andrew Holmes, Steven Redgrave) 6:36.84
Quadruple Sculls: Italy (Piero Poli, Gianluca Farina, Davide Tizzano, Agostino Abbagnale) 5:53.37
Fours with Coxswain: E Ger (Frank Klawonn, Bernd Eichwurzel, Bernd Niesecke, Karsten Schmeling) (Hendrik Reiher) 6:10.74
Fours without Coxswain: E Ger (Roland Schroeder, Thomas Greiner, Ralf Brudel, Olaf Foerster) 6:03.11
Eights: W Ger 5:46.05

WOMEN

Single Sculls: Jutta Behrendt (E Ger) 7:47.10
Double Sculls: E Ger (Birgit Peter, Martina Schroete) 7:00.48
Pairs without Coxswain: Romania (Rodica Arba, Olga Homeghi) 7:28.13
Quadruple Sculls: E Ger (Kerstin Foerster, Kristina Mundt, Beate Schramm, Jana Sorgers) 6:21.06
Fours with Coxswain: E Ger (Martina Walther; Gerlinde Doberschuetz, Carola Hornig, Birte Siech) (Sylvia Rose) 6:56.00
Eights: E Ger 6:15.17

Six oarsmen have won 3 Olympic gold medals: John B. Kelly (US) (1889–1960), father of the late Princess Grace of Monaco, in the sculls (1920) and double sculls (1920 and 24); his cousin Paul V. Costello (US) (b Dec 27, 1899) in the double sculls (1920, 24 and 28); Jack Beresford, Jr (GB) (1899–1977) in the sculls (1924), coxless fours (1932) and double sculls (1936); Vyacheslav Ivanov (USSR) (b July 30, 1938) in the sculls (1956, 60 and 64); Siegfried Brietzke in the coxless pairs (1972) and the coxless fours (1976 and 80); and Pertti Karppinen

BIG WINNERS IN THE OLYMPICS in rowing: The E German eight was victorious in the inaugural race in 1976 and again in 1980. In fact, in all but two inaugural rowing events in 1976, E Germans were winners, namely, single sculls, quadruple sculls, coxed fours and eights. Of course, in 1984, the E Germans did not compete, but in 1988, the E German men won both fours (with and without coxswain) and the E German women won all 5 finals for a shutout. (Tony Duffy—All Sport)

(Finland) in the single sculls (1976, 1980, 1984), who also won 2 world championships.

Karppinen, three-time Olympic gold medalist, set a world best at 2000 m as a single sculler at the World Championship, Sept 1, 1985, in Willebroek, Belgium. His time was 6:48.08.

Olympic Championships were first held in 1900. Separate world championships were first held for men

BY A NOSE: The US won a close finish in the Eights race for a gold medal in the 1932 Olympics at Los Angeles.

in 1962 and for women in 1974. The East German coxless pairs team of the twins Bernd and Jorg Landvoigt (b Mar 23, 1951) have won their event 4 times in world championships and twice in Olympic competition, setting a record for any rowing event. The female sculler Christine Scheiblich-Hann (E Ger) nearly matched this with one Olympic and four world titles.

DRAGON BOAT FESTIVAL GRAND FINAL: In Hong Kong Harbor, the top crews are battling it out in June 1986. A record number of 21 overseas teams took part that year. As many as 2,400 rowers are attracted to the annual races which the US Rowing Assoc (Phila) crew won in 1983.

SINGLE SCULLS RECORDHOLDER: Pertti Karppinen (Finland) (below) set a world mark in Sept 1985 after having earned 3 Olympic golds (1976, 80, 84). (Sporting Pictures)

Highest Speed

Speeds in tidal or flowing water are of no comparative value. The greatest speed attained on non-tidal water, over the standard men's rowing distance of 2000 m (2,187 yd), is 13.68 mph by the US eight on the Rotsee, Lucerne, Switzerland, in June 1984 when they clocked 5 min 27.14 sec. A crew from the Penn AC (US) was timed in 5 min 18.8 sec (14.03 mph) in the FISA Championships on the Meuse River, Liège, Belgium, on Aug 17, 1930, but with the help of the river current.

The fastest by a female eight is also by a US crew, who clocked 2 min 54.05 sec for the then standard women's distance of 1000 m (1,093.6 yd), achieving an average of 12.85 mph on the Rotsee, Lucerne in 1984. (The standard since 1985 has been 2000 m.) The best by a female sculler over 1000 m, 3 min 30.74 sec by Cornelia Linse (E Ger) in 1984, represents an average of 10.61 mph.

Heaviest Oarsmen

The heaviest man ever to row in a British Boat Race has been Stephen G. H. Plunkett, the No 5 in the 1976 Oxford boat at 229 lb. The 1983 Oxford crew averaged a record 204.3 lb.

The lightest coxes weighed 72 lb: Francis Archer (Cambridge) in 1862, and Hart Parker Vincent Massey (Oxford) in 1939.

Longest Race

The longest rowing race is the annual Tour du Lac Léman, Geneva, Switzerland for coxed fours (the five-man team taking turns as cox) over 99 miles. The record winning time is 12 hours 52 min by LAGA, Delft, The Netherlands, Oct 3, 1982.

John Kelly was thought to be a victim of class distinction when he was refused entry into the Diamond Sculls at Henley, Eng, in 1920, being unofficially informed that the muscles he had developed as a bricklayer gave him an unfair advantage over "gentlemen" competitors. Later, as a rich businessman, he saw his son John Kelly, Jr win the Diamond Sculls twice, in 1947 and 1949, and his filmstar daughter become Princess Grace of Monaco. Benjamin Spock, later author of a bestselling baby and child care book, was a member of the Yale crew which represented the US and won the 1924 Olympic Eights.

The longest distance rowed in 24 hours by a crew of 8 is 130 mi by members of the Renmark Rowing Club of S Australia Apr 1, 1984.

Longest in 24 Hours

The greatest distance rowed in 24 hours (upstream and downstream) by an eight is 130 miles by members of the Renmark Rowing Club, South Australia, on Apr 1, 1984.

Sculling

The record number of wins in the Wingfield Sculls on the Thames in London (Putney to Mortlake) (instituted 1830) is 7 by Jack Beresford, Jr 1920–26. The fastest time has been 21 min 11 sec by Leslie Frank (Dick) Southwood (b Jan 18, 1906) on Aug 12, 1933. The most world professional sculling titles (instituted 1831) won is 7 by William Beach (Australia) (1850–1935), 1884–87.

International Dragon Boat Races

Instituted in 1975 and held annually in Hong Kong, the fastest time achieved for the 640-meter (700-yd) course is 2 min 27.45 sec by the Chinese Shun De team on June 30, 1985. Teams have 28 members—26 rowers, one steersman and one drummer.

SHOOTING

Earliest Club

The Lucerne Shooting Guild (Switzerland) was formed c. 1466, and the first recorded shooting match was held at Zurich in 1472. Early contests had to be over very short range as it was not until rifling, to spin the bullet, was introduced to gun barrels in c. 1480 that accuracy over greater distances could be achieved.

Trap-shooting was introduced in the US in 1830, and skeet shooting in 1915, "skeet" being the old Norse world for "shoot."

Olympic Games

Shooting has been part of the Olympic program since the first Games in 1896, its inclusion possibly being because the Games' founder, Baron Pierre de Coubertin, was an excellent shot.

The record number of medals won is 11 by Carl Townsend Osburn (US) (1884–1966) in 1912, 1920 and 1924, consisting of 5 gold, 4 silver and 2 bronze.

Six other marksmen have won 5 gold medals. The only marksman to win 3 individual gold medals has been Gudbrand Gudbrandsönn, Skatteboe (Norway) (1875–1965) in 1906. Separate events for women were first held in 1984, although they had competed alongside their male counterparts since 1968.

The 1988 gold medal winners were:

MEN
Air Pistol: Taniou Kiriakov (Bulgaria)
Air Rifle: Goran Maksimovic (Yugo)
Free Pistol: Sorin Babii (Romania)
Rapid Fire Pistol: Afanasi Kouzmin (USSR)
Running Game Target: Tor Heiestad (Norway)
Small-Bore Rifle English Match:
  Miroslav Varga (Czech) 600 (world record)
Small-Bore Rifle 3 Positions: Malcolm Cooper (GB)

WOMEN
Air Pistol: Jasna Sekaric (Yugo)
Air Rifle: Irina Chilova (USSR)
Small-Bore Rifle 3 Positions: Silvia Sperber (W Ger)
Rapid-Fire Pistol: Nino Salukvadze (USSR)

OPEN CLASS
Clay Target-Trap: Dmitri Monakov (USSR)
Clay Target-Skeet: Axel Wegner (E Ger)

Bench Rest Shooting

The smallest group on record at 1,000 yd is 4.375 in with a score of 99 by Earl Chronister with a .30-378 Weatherby Mag at Williamsport, Pa on July 12, 1987.

SHARPSHOOTER Annie Oakley (1860–1926) joined the Buffalo Bill Circus while still in her teens and soon became famous for her remarkable shooting skills. She could hit a dime in mid-air at 30 paces and score 100 out of 100 consistently when trapshooting. (Amateur Trapshooting Assoc. Hall of Fame)

THREE WORLD RECORDS IN TWO DAYS: Malcolm Cooper (GB) (left) won free rifle and standard rifle contests in June 1985 to add to his winning gold medal at the 1984 Olympics in LA. He went on to better his own marks in 1986 and 1987, and won an Olympic gold in 1988. (Below) Cooper with his wife Sarah who competed together in the 1984 Olympics and again to win the Commonwealth Games gold medal at the small bore rifle 3 positions (pairs). (All-Sport, both photos)

Clay Pigeon Shooting

The record number of clay birds shot in an hour is 2,215 by Joseph Kreckman at the Paradise Shooting Center, Cresco, Pa, Aug 28, 1983. Graham Douglas Geater (b July 21, 1947) shot 2,264 targets in an hour on a trap-shooting range at the NILO Gun Club, Papamoa, NZ on Jan 17, 1981.

Most world titles have been won by Susan Nattrass (Canada) (b Nov 5, 1950) with 6, 1974–5, 77–9, 81.

A unique maximum 200/200 was achieved by Ricardo Ruiz Rumoroso at the Spanish clay pigeon championships at Zaragossa on June 12, 1983.

Highest Score in 24 Hours

The Easingwold (England) Rifle & Pistol Club team of John Smith, Edward Kendall, Paul Duffield and Philip Kendall scored 120,242 points (averaging 95.66 per card) on Aug 6–7, 1983.

INDIVIDUAL WORLD SHOOTING RECORDS

(as ratified by the International Shooting Union—UIT)

			Max-Score		
Free Rifle	300 m	3 x 40 shots	1200–1166	Malcolm Cooper (GB)	Zurich, Switz 1987
		60 shots prone	600–599	Malcolm Cooper (GB)	Skouder, Sweden, 1986
Standard Rifle	300 m	3 x 20 shots	600–583	Malcolm Cooper (GB)	Zurich, Switz, 1985
Small-Bore Rifle	50 m	3 x 40 shots	1200–1183	Peter Kurka (Czech)	Seoul, Korea, 1987
	50 m	60 shots prone	600–600	Alistair Allan (GB)	Titograd, Yugo, 1981
			600	Ernest Van de Zande (US)	Rio de Janeiro, 1981
			600	Kiril Ivanov (USSR)	Mexico City, 1987
				Plus 11 more men in 1988	
Free Pistol	50 m	60 shots	600–581	Aleksandr Melentyev (USSR)	Moscow, 1980
Rapid-Fire Pistol	25 m	60 shots	600–599	Igor Puzyrev (USSR)	Titograd, Yugo, 1981
Center-Fire Pistol	25 m	60 shots	600–597	Thomas D. Smith (US)	São Paulo, Brazil, 1963
Standard Pistol	25 m	60 shots	600–590	Eric Buljong (US)	Seoul, S Korea, 1988
Running Game Target	50 m	60 shots "normal runs"	600–595	Igor Sokolov (USSR)	Miskulc, Hungary, 1981
Olympic Trap	—	200 birds	200–200	Danny Carlisle (US)	Caracas, Venez, 1983
Olympic Skeet	—	200 birds	200–200	Matthew Dryke (US)	São Paulo, Brazil, 1981
			200	Jan Hula (Czech)	Zaragossa, Spain, 1984
Air Rifle	10 m	60 shots	600–596	Jean-Pierre Amat (France)	Zurich, Switz, 1987
Air Pistol	10 m	60 shots	600–591	Vladas Tourla (USSR)	Caracas, Venez, 1983
Air Pistol (women)			400–390	Nina Salaukvadzi (USSR)	Seoul, S Korea, 1988

The first woman to win a medal at shooting was Margaret Murdock (US) in the smallbore rifle (3 positions) event in 1976. It was originally announced that she had won by a single point, but an error was discovered and she was tied with her teammate Lonny Bassham. Then an examination of the targets indicated that one of the latter's shots was 1/25th of an inch closer to the center than previously determined, and so the gold medal was given to Bassham, who gallantly invited Murdock to share first place position on the award rostrum.

Small-Bore Rifle Shooting

Richard Hansen shot 5,000 bull's-eyes in 24 hours at Fresno, Calif, on June 13, 1929.

GAME SHOOTING

Record Heads

The world's finest head is the 23-point stag head in the Maritzburg collection, E Germany. The outside span is 75½ in, the length 47½ in and the weight 41½ lb. The greatest number of points is probably 33 (plus 29) on the stag shot in 1696 by Frederick III (1657–1713), the Elector of Brandenburg, later King Frederick I of Prussia.

Biggest Bag

The largest animal ever shot by any big game hunter was a bull African elephant (*Loxodonta africana africana*) shot by E. M. Nielsen of Columbus, Neb, 25 miles north-northeast of Mucusso, Angola, on Nov 7, 1974. The animal, brought down by a Westley Richards 0.425, stood 13 ft 8 in tall at the shoulder.

In Nov 1965, Simon Fletcher, 28, a Kenyan farmer, claims to have killed two elephants with one 0.458 bullet.

The greatest recorded lifetime bag is 556,813, including 241,234 pheasants, 124,193 partridges and 31,900 hares, by the 2nd Marquess of Ripon (1852–1923) of England. He himself dropped dead on a grouse moor after shooting his 52nd bird on the morning of Sept 22, 1923.

SKATEBOARDED 621 MILES like this: Mark Richardson rolled on his skates attached to skis from France to Eng, taking 15 days in May 1987. (Photostop)

SKATEBOARDING

Although no official association exists, "world" championships have been staged intermittently since 1966. David Frank, 25, covered 270.483 mi in 36 hours 43 min 40 sec in Toronto, Canada Aug 11–12, 1985.

The highest speed recorded on a skateboard is 71.79 mph on a course at Mt Baldy, Calif, in a prone position by Richard K. Brown, 33, on June 17, 1979.

The stand-up record is 53.45 mph by John Hutson, 23, at Signal Hill, Long Beach, Calif, June 11, 1978.

The record for high jump is 9½ ft above the ramp, set by Tony Magnuson on Sept 14, 1987, at Calif State U—Dominguez Hills, Carson, Calif. What is called a "high air" jump means the "greatest height in the air above the top of the ramp."

The high jump record of 9½ ft is actually held by two persons, Tony Magnuson (see above) and Christian Hosoi on May 30, 1988 at Raging Waters Amusement Park, San Jose, Calif.

At the same event, Steve Caballero in a "railslide" set an inaugural record with a 24-ft belly slide on the "Boomeramp" which is 132 ft long, 13 ft high at its highest wall and 47 ft wide. On the "long extended grind" on the lip of the ramp, Christian Hosoi set an inaugural record of 19 ft 8 in.

The longest jump from a skateboard over low barrels to land on a skateboard was the jump of 21 barrels by Paul Pearman (b Nov 10, 1960) in Augusta, Ga, at Regency Mall on May 28, 1987. In another attempt, Paul almost made it over 25 barrels 12 in wide but clipped the last barrel. The event was staged for United Cerebral Palsy who collected $500.

Christopher Von Guenthner, age 43, of Evergreen, Colo, claims an inaugural record of performing a handstand on a skateboard, traveling a distance of 803 ft on Nov 8, 1987.

SKIING

Origins

The most ancient ski in existence was found well preserved in a peat bog at Höting, Sweden, dating from c. 2500 BC. However, in 1934 a Russian archaeologist discovered a rock carving of a skier at Bessovysledki, USSR, which dates from c. 6000 BC. These early skiers used the bones of animals whereas wooden skis appear to have been introduced to Europe from Asia. The first reference in literature i⁻ in a work by Procopius c. 550 AD who referred t("Gliding Finns." Additionally in the Scandinaviaı sagas there occur gods of skiing. By 1199, the Danish historian Saxo was reporting the military use oi troops on skis by Sigurdsson Sverrir, the Norwegian King.

The modern sport did not develop until 1843 when the first known competition for civilians took place at Tromso, Norway. The first ski club, named the Trysil Shooting and Skiing Club, was founded in Norway in

SKATEBOARD RECORD HIGH JUMP: Tony Magnuson reaching 9½ ft above the top of the ramp.

SKATEBOARD RECORD LONG JUMP (below): Paul Pearman jumping over 21 barrels.

TRIPLE WINNER IN 1984 OLYMPICS: Marja-Liisa Hae-maelainen (Fin) dominated the women's cross-country skiing events, taking all three individual gold medals.

1861. Twenty years later ski bindings were invented by Sondre Nordheim, from Morgedal in the Telemark area, and the people of this region were the pioneers of the sport. The legendary "Snowshoe" Thompson, whose parents were Norwegian, was the earliest well-known skier in the US (1856) although skiing took place here in the 1840s. It was not until Olaf Kjeldsberg went to Switzerland in 1881 that the sport began to take hold in that country, and in 1889 one of the earliest of British exponents, Arthur Conan Doyle, began skiing at Davos, Switz. The first downhill race—as opposed to the Scandinavian races across country—was held at Kitzbuhel, Austria in 1908. The International Ski Federation (FIS) was founded on Feb 2, 1924. The Winter Olympics were inaugurated on Jan 25, 1924, and Alpine events have been included since 1936. The FIS recognizes both the Winter Olympics and the separate World Ski Championships as world championships.

Most Olympic Victories

Marja-Liisa Haemaelainen (Fin), after having twice won the women's World Cup title in Nordic, 1983–84, won all 3 individual gold medals in the 1984 Olympics.

The most Olympic gold medals won by a man for skiing is 4 by Sixten Jernberg (b Feb 6, 1929), of

Sweden, in 1956–64 (including one for a relay). In addition, Jernberg has won 3 silver and 2 bronze medals for a record 9 Olympic medals. Four were also won by Nikolai Zimjatov (b June 28, 1955) (USSR) in 1980 (30 km, 50 km and on the team for 4 × 10-km relay) and in 1984 (30 km).

The only woman to win 4 Olympic gold medals is Galina Koulakova (b Apr 29, 1942) of USSR who won the 5 km and 10 km (1972) and was a member of the winning 3 × 5-km relay team in 1972 and the 4 × 5-km team in 1976. Koulakova also has won 2 silver and 2 bronze medals, 1968, 76, 80.

The most Olympic gold medals won in men's Alpine skiing is 3, by Anton "Toni" Sailer in 1956 and Jean-Claude Killy in 1968.

1988 OLYMPIC SKIING GOLD MEDALISTS

Alpine Skiing—Men

Giant Slalom—Alberto Tomba (Italy)
Slalom—Alberto Tomba (Italy)
Downhill—Pirmin Zurbriggen (Switz)
Super Giant Slalom—Franck Piccard (France)
Combined—Hubert Strolz (Austria)

Alpine Skiing—Women

Giant Slalom—Vreni Schneider (Switz)
Slalom—Vreni Schneider (Switz)
Downhill—Marina Kiehl (W Ger)
Super Giant Slalom—Sigrid Wolf (Austria)
Combined—Anita Wachter (Austria)

Ski Jumping

70m Hill—Matti Nykaenen (Finland)†
90m Hill—Matti Nykaenen (Finland)*
90m Hill (team) Finland

Nordic Skiing—Men

15km—Mikhail Deviatiarov (USSR)
30km—Alexei Prokourorov (USSR)
50km—Gunde Svan (Sweden)*
Relay 4 x 10km—Sweden*
Combined—individual—Hippolyt Kempf (Switz)
Combined—team—W Germany

Nordic Skiing—Women

5km—Marjo Matikainen (Finland)
10km—Vida Ventsene (USSR)
20km—Tamara Tikhonova (USSR)
Relay 4 x 5km—USSR

Biathlon

10km—Frank-Peter Roetsch (E Ger)
20km—Frank-Peter Roetsch (E Ger)†
Relay 4 x 7.5km—USSR

* Repeat winner
† Silver medalist 1984

Most Alpine World Titles

The World Alpine Championships were inaugurated at Mürren, Switzerland, in 1931. The greatest number of titles won has been 13 by Christel Cranz (b

4 WORLD CUP TITLES in one year is the record. Jean-Claude Killy of France did it in 1967. Now Pirmin Zurbriggen (right) of Switzerland (b Feb 4, 1963) has done it, winning the 1987 downhill, giant slalom, super-giant slalom and overall titles. (Steve Powell/All Sport)

July 1, 1914), of Germany, with 7 individual—4 Slalom (1934, 37–39) and 3 Downhill (1935, 37, 39); and 5 Combined (1934–35, 37–39). She also won the gold medal for the Combined in the 1936 Olympics. The most titles won by a man is 7 by Anton "Toni" Sailer (b Nov 17, 1935), of Austria, who won all 4 in 1956 (Giant Slalom, Slalom, Downhill and the non-Olympic Alpine Combination) and the Downhill, Giant Slalom and Combined in 1958.

Most Nordic World Titles

The first world Nordic championships were those of the 1924 Winter Olympics at Chamonix, France. The greatest number of World titles won is 9 by Galina Koulakova (b Apr 29, 1942) (USSR), 1970–78. She also won 4 silver and 4 bronze medals for a record total of 17. The most won by a man is 8, including relays, by Sixten Jernberg (b Feb 6, 1929) (Sweden), 1956–64. Johan Grottumsbraaten (1899–1942), of Norway, won 6 individual titles (2 at 18 km cross-country and 4 Nordic Combined) in 1926–32. The record for a jumper is 5 by Birger Ruud

NORDIC SKIING: Sweden's Sixten Jernberg (right) earned 4 Olympic golds, and dominated the sport (1956–64) with a total of 9 Olympic medals.

(b Aug 23, 1911), of Norway, in 1931–32 and 1935–37. Ruud is the only person to win Olympic titles in each of the dissimilar Alpine and Nordic disciplines. In 1936 he won the ski-jumping and the Alpine downhill (which was not then a separate event, but only a segment of the Combined event).

Duration

The record distance covered in 48 hours of Nordic skiing is 319 mi 205 yd by Bjorn Lokken (Norway) (b Nov 27, 1937) Mar 11–13, 1982.

In 24 hours Teuvo Rantanen covered 249.35 miles at Jyväskylä, Finland Feb 1–2, 1986. The women's record is 205.05 miles by Sisko Kainulaisen of Finland at Jyväskylä on Mar 23–24, 1985.

The longest time spent in downhill skiing under regulated conditions is 87 hours 28 min by John Mordini at Kissing Bridge, NY, Jan 11–14, 1988. No time was wasted waiting for the lift.

Luc Labrie at Daie Comeau, Quebec, Canada, skied alone for 138 hours, Feb 20–25, 1984.

World Cup

The Alpine World Cup was instituted in 1967, and extended to include Nordic in 1981.

The most by a man is 85 by Ingemar Stenmark (b Mar 18, 1956) (Sweden), 1974–87, including a record 10 in one season in 1979. Franz Klammer (Austria) (b Dec 3, 1953) won a record 35 downhill races, 1974–85.

The women's cup has been won 6 times by the 5-ft-6-in 150-lb Annemarie Moser (*née* Proll) (Aus-

tria) in 1971–75 and 79. From Dec 1972 to Jan 1974 she completed a record sequence of 11 consecutive downhill victories. She holds the women's record of 62 individual event wins (1970–79).

Alexander Zavialov (USSR) (b June 2, 1955) has two wins, 1981 and 1983, in the cross-country or Nordic World Cup (inst 1979). Also with two wins are Marja-Liisa Haemaelainen (Finland) in 1983 and 1984, and Gunde Svan (Sweden) in 1984 and 1985. The jumping World Cup (inst 1980) has been twice won by Armin Kogler (Austria) (b Sept 4, 1959) 1981–2, and by Matti Nykanen (Finland) 1983 and 1985.

Highest Speed—Cross Country

Bill Koch (US) (b Apr 13, 1943) on Mar 26, 1981 skied ten times around a 5-km (3.11-mi) loop on

RECORDHOLDER: Gunde Svan (Sweden) won the 1984 Olympic gold for 15,000 m. In setting the 50-km Nordic uphill and downhill record, his average time was 14.25 mph. (All Sport)

4 CUPS, 4 TITLES AND A GOLD: Gustavo Thoeni (Italy) used his slalom expertise to win 4 Alpine World Cups, 4 world titles and an Olympic gold. (George Konig)

Marlborough Pond, near Putney, Vt. He completed the 50 km in 1 hour 59 min 47 sec, an average speed of 15.57 mph. A race includes uphill and downhill sections; the record time for a 50-km race is 2 hours 10 min 49.9 sec by Gunde Svan in the 1985 World

WINNER OF 35 DOWNHILL RACES: In World Cup competition Franz Klammer (above) (Austria) led all competition with victories, 1974–85.

MOST TITLES WON in Alpine World Championships was 7 earned by Anton "Toni" Sailer of Austria including 4 in 1956 alone. Here he is looking over the landscape at his home town of Kitzbuhel. (Photo by Bruno Engler)

BACKFLIP: The record for this popular stunt (sometimes called "hotdogging") has increased from 19 (as shown here) to 28 in just a few years. (Gary McMillin)

Championships, an average speed of 14.25 mph. The record for a 15-km Olympic or World Championship race is 38 min 52.5 sec by Oddvar Braa (Nor) (b Mar 16, 1951) at the 1982 World Championships, an average speed of 14.38 mph.

Closest Verdict

The narrowest winning margin in a championship ski race was one hundredth of a second by Thomas Wassberg (Sweden) (b March 23, 1956) over Juha Mieto (Finland) in the Olympic 15 km cross-country race at Lake Placid, NY on Feb 17, 1980. His winning time was 41 min 57.63 sec.

The narrowest margin of victory in an Olympic Alpine event was 2/100ths of a sec by Barbara Cochran (US) over Daniele De Bernard (France) in the 1972 slalom at Sapporo, Japan.

Longest Run

The longest all-downhill ski run in the world is the Weissfluhjoch–Küblis Parsenn course (7.6 miles long), near Davos, Switzerland. The run from the Aiguille du Midi top of the Chamonix lift (vertical lift 9,052 ft) across the Vallée Blanche is 13 miles.

Longest Jump

The longest ski jump ever recorded is one of 636 ft by Piotr Fijas (Poland) at Planica, Yugoslavia on Mar 14, 1987.

The women's record is 110 m (361 ft) by Tina Lehtola (Fin) (b Aug 3, 1962) at Ruka, Finland, on Mar 29, 1981.

Longest Lift

The longest gondola ski lift is 3.88 mi long at Grindelwald–Männlichen, Switzerland (in two sections, but one gondola). The longest chair lift was the Alpine Way to Kosciusko Châlet lift above Thredbo, near the Snowy Mountains, NSW, Australia. It took from 45 to 75 min to ascend the 3.5 mi, according to the weather. It has now collapsed. The highest is at Chacaltaya, Bolivia, rising to 16,500 ft.

Steepest Descent

Sylvain Saudan (b Lausanne, Switzerland, Sept 23, 1936) achieved a descent of Mt Blanc on the northeast side down the Couloir Gervasutti from 13,937 ft on Oct 17, 1967, skiing gradients of about 60 degrees.

Highest Altitude

Jean Atanassieff and Nicolas Jaeger (both France) skied down from 26,900 ft to 20,340 ft on Mt Everest in 1978.

Highest Speed—Downhill

The highest speed claimed for a skier is 139.030 mph by Michael Pruffer (France) and the fastest by a woman is 133.234 mph by Tara Mulari (Fin). Both times were achieved on Apr 16, 1988 at Les Arcs, France.

At the Les Arcs venue on Apr 18, 1987 Patrick Knauff (France) set a one-legged record of 115.012 mph.

The highest average race speed in the Olympic downhill was 64.95 mph by Bill Johnson (US) (b Mar 30, 1960) at Sarajevo, Yugoslavia, on Feb 16, 1984. The fastest in a World Cup downhill is 67.00 mph by

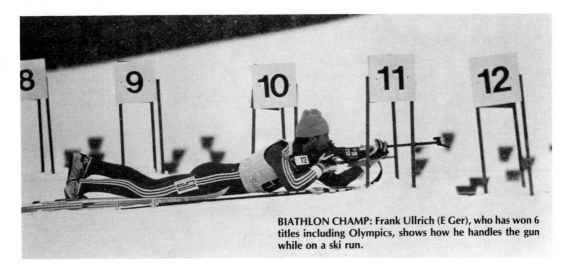

BIATHLON CHAMP: Frank Ullrich (E Ger), who has won 6 titles including Olympics, shows how he handles the gun while on a ski run.

Harti Weirather (Austria) (b Jan 25, 1958) at Kitzbuhel, Austria on Jan 15, 1982.

Most Competitors—Alpine

1,700 downhill skiers competed at Are, Jamtland, Sweden, on Apr 30, 1984.

Longest Races

The world's longest ski races are the Grenader, run just north of Oslo, Norway, and the König Ludwig Lauf in Oberammergau, W Germany. Both are 90 km (55.9 miles). The Canadian Ski Marathon at 160 km (99 miles) is longer, but is run in two parts on consecutive days.

The world's greatest Nordic ski race is the Vasaloppet, which commemorates an event in 1521 when Gustavus Vasa (1496–1560), later King of Sweden, fled 85.8 km (53.3 miles) from Mora to Sälen, Sweden. He was overtaken by loyal, speedy scouts on skis, who persuaded him to return eastwards to Mora to lead a rebellion and become the king of Sweden. The re-enactment of this return journey is now an annual event at 89 km (55.3 mi), contested by nearly 11,000 skiers. The fastest time is 3 hours 48 min 55 sec by Bengt Hassis (Swe) on Mar 2, 1986.

The Vasaloppet is now the longest of 10 long distance races, constituting the world loppet, staged in 10 countries.

The longest downhill race is the *Inferno* in Switzerland, 9.8 miles from the top of the Schilthorn to Lauterbrunnen. In 1981 there was a record entry of 1,401, with Heinz Fringen (Switz) winning in 15 min 44.57 sec. The record time of 15 min 26.44 sec was set in 1987 by Veli Grossniklaus (Switz).

Backflip on Skis

The greatest number of skiers to perform a back layout flip while holding hands is 28 at Bromont, Quebec, Canada, on Feb 10, 1982.

BIATHLON

The biathlon, which combines cross-country skiing and rifle shooting, was first included in the Olympic Games in 1960, and world championships were first held in 1958.

The biathlon is now competed over 10 km, 20 km and a 4 × 7.5 km relay.

Most Olympic Titles

Magnar Solberg (Norway) (b Feb 4, 1937), in 1968 and 1972, is the only man to have won two Olympic individual titles. The USSR has won all five 4 × 7.5 km relay titles, 1968–84. Aleksandr Tikhonov (b Jan 2, 1947) who was a member of the first 4 teams also won a silver in the 1968 20 km.

Most World Championships

Frank Ullrich (E Ger) (b Jan 24, 1958) has won a record six individual world titles, at 10 km, 1978–81, including the 1980 Olympics, and at 20 km 1982–83.

Aleksandr Tikhonov was in ten winning USSR relay teams, 1968–80, and won four individual titles. Ullrich has also won the world cup (inst 1979) three times, 1980–82.

SNOWSHOE RACING is a grueling sport. Most participants use specially designed snowshoes in the five officially sanctioned events: sprint, relay, hurdle, slalom, and biathlon. (David Verner/AMPS)

SNOWSHOE RACING

Records set in competition, recognized by the US Snowshoe Association are:

Men

100m	Walter Prow	16.81 sec
200m	Crispin McDonald	37.60 sec
400m	Michael Mieszczak	1 min 24.27 sec
1600m	Marc Lessard	7 min 56 sec

Women

100m	Laura Kleinke	21.95 sec
200m	Gwenne Church	49.87 sec
400m	Nancy Mieszczak	1 min 59.02 sec

SNOWMOBILING

The record speed for a snowmobile is 158.53 mph, set by Marv Jorgenson of Minneapolis at the St Paul Winter Carnival at Lake Phelan, Minn, on Feb 3, 1985.

RECORD SNOWMOBILE RUN: Marv Jorgenson of Minneapolis went more than 158 mph on this machine on Lake Phelan in Feb 1985.

SOCCER

Origins

Ball-kicking games were played very early in human history.

A game with some similarities termed *Tsu-chu* was played in China in the 3rd and 4th centuries BC. One of the earliest references to the game in England is a Royal Proclamation by Edward II in 1314 banning the game in the City of London. A soccer-type game called Calcio was played in Italy in 1410. The earliest clear representation of the game is in a print from Edinburgh, Scotland, dated 1672–73. The game became standardized with the formation of the Football Association in England on Oct 26, 1863. Eleven players on a side was standardized in 1870.

Highest Team Scores

The highest score recorded in any first-class match is 36. This occurred in the Scottish Cup match between Arbroath and Bon Accord on Sept 12, 1885, when Arbroath won 36–0 on their home ground. But for the lack of nets and the consequent waste of retrieval time, the score might have been even higher. Seven goals were disallowed for offside.

The highest margin recorded in an international match is 17, when England beat Australia 17–0 at Sydney June 30, 1951. This match is not listed as a *full* international.

World Cup

The World Cup Competition, which has been held 13 times through 1986, takes on new meaning for US citizens because the 15th tournament was awarded to the US to be played at several sites across the country in 1994. The *Fédération Internationale de Football Association* (FIFA), which was founded on May 21, 1904, instituted the first World Cup on July 13, 1930, in Montevideo, Uruguay. Thirteen nations took part then, playing for a trophy named after Jules Rimet, the late Honorary President of FIFA from 1921–1954. The first team to win the competition three times was to keep the trophy, a feat achieved by Brazil in 1970.

The only countries to win three times have been Brazil (1958, 62, 70) and Italy (1934, 38, 82). Brazil was also second in 1950, and third in 1938 and 1978, and uniquely has taken part in all 13 Finals.

Antonio Carbajal (b 1923) played for Mexico in goal in a record 5 competitions, in 1950, 54, 58, 62 and 66, playing in 11 games in all. Uwe Seeler (W Ger) (b Nov 5, 1936) shares with Wladyslaw Zmuda

ATHLETE OF THE CENTURY: Pelé celebrates one of his 1,285 goals, this one with the NY Cosmos of the NASL. In a seemingly premature poll of 20 international newspapers, the tremendously popular Brazilian soccer star was named "Athlete of the Century" by the French sports magazine "L'Equipe." Jesse Owens was runner-up.

(Poland) (b June 6, 1954) the record for the most appearances in final tournaments, playing in 21 games. Pelé is the only player to have been with 3 World Cup winning teams, all for Brazil. The youngest World Cup player ever was Norman Whiteside, who played for N Ireland vs Yugoslavia, aged 17 years 42 days on June 17, 1982.

The record goal scorer has been Just Fontaine (France) with 13 goals in 6 games in the final stages of the 1958 competition. Gerd Müller (W Ger) (b Nov 3, 1945) scored 10 goals in 1970 and 4 in 1974 for the highest aggregate of 14 goals. Fontaine and Jairzinho (Brazil) are the only two players to have scored in every game in a final series, as Jairzinho scored 7 in 6 games in 1970. The most goals scored in the final game is 3 by Geoffrey Hurst (b Dec 8, 1941) for England vs W Germany in 1966. Three

World Cup Winners

Winner	Locale
1930 Uruguay	Uruguay
1934 Italy	Italy
1938 Italy	France
1950 Uruguay	Brazil
1954 W Germany	Switzerland
1958 Brazil	Sweden
1962 Brazil	Chile
1966 England	England
1970 Brazil	Mexico
1974 W Germany	W Germany
1978 Argentina	Argentina
1982 Italy	Spain
1986 Argentina	Mexico

SOCCER BALL CONTROL CHAMPION: Mikael Palmquist (Sweden) improved on his own record in 1987 by heading a ball for more than 5 hours.

players have scored in 2 finals: Vava (real name, Edwaldo Izito Neto) (Brazil) in 1958 and 62, Pelé in 1958 and 70, and Paul Breitner (W Ger) in 1974 and 82.

The highest score in a World Cup match is New Zealand's 13–0 defeat of Fiji in a qualifying match at Auckland on Aug 16, 1981. The highest score in the Finals Tournament is Hungary's 10–1 win over El Salvador at Elche, Spain, on June 15, 1982. The highest match aggregate in the Finals Tournament is 12 when Austria beat Switzerland in 1954.

The highest-scoring team in a Finals Tournament has been W Germany, which scored 25 in 6 games in 1954 for the highest average of 4.17 goals per game. England has the best defensive record, conceding only 3 goals in 6 games in 1966. Curiously, no team has ever failed to score in a World Cup Final.

The fastest goal scored in World Cup competition was one in 27 sec by Bryan Robson for England vs France in Bilbao, Spain, on June 16, 1982.

Marathons

The longest outdoor game played was 75½ hours by two teams trying to establish a record at Roy High School, Roy, Utah by 22 students of the school, Aug 8–11, 1988. The indoor soccer record is 104 hours 10 min set by two teams from Rockhampton, Queensland, Australia, Nov 17–22, 1985.

Individual Scoring

The most goals scored by one player in a first-class match is 16 by Stephan Stanis (né Stanikowski, b Poland, July 15, 1913) for Racing Club de Lens vs Aubry-Asturies, in Lens, France, on Dec 13, 1942.

The record number of goals scored by one player in an international match is 10 by Sofus Nielsen (1888–1963) for Denmark vs France (17–1) in the 1908 Olympics and by Gottfried Fuchs for Germany, which beat Russia 16–0 in the 1912 Olympic tournament (consolation event) in Sweden.

An undocumented 1,329 goals were scored in a 43-year first-class career by Artur Friedenreich (1892–1969) of Brazil.

The most goals scored in a specified period is 1,216 by Edson Arantes do Nascimento (b Baurú, Brazil, Oct 23, 1940), known as Pelé, the Brazilian inside left, in the period Sept 7, 1956 to Oct 2, 1974 (1,254 games). His best year was 1959 with 126 goals. His *milesimo* (1,000th) came in a penalty for his club, Santos, in the Maracaña Stadium, Rio de Janeiro, on Nov 19, 1969, when he was playing in his 909th first-class match. He came out of retirement in 1975 to add to his total with the New York Cosmos of the North American Soccer League. By his retirement on Oct 1, 1977 his total had reached 1,281 in 1,363 games. He added 4 more goals later in special appearances.

HIGH SCORER in World Cup: Gerd Muller (W Germany) scored 14 goals in two World Cup finals (1970 and 1974).

NET WEIGHT: At 6 ft 3 in and 311 lb, Fatty Foulke was the most massive goalkeeper ever. One of his greatest exploits came off the field, however, when, appearing at the dinner table early one evening, Foulke ate the team's entire meal before any of his teammates arrived.

Franz (''Bimbo'') Binder (b Dec 1, 1911) scored 1,006 goals in 756 games in Austria and Germany between 1930 and 1950.

Longest Matches

The world duration record for a first-class match is 3 hours 30 min (with interruptions), in the Copa Libertadores championship in Santos, Brazil, Aug 2–3, 1962, when Santos drew 3–3 with Penarol FC of Montevideo, Uruguay.

At the college level, the longest game lasted 5½ hours (330 min) including 2 overtimes of 10 min followed by 10 sudden-death overtimes of 15 min. Then the teams (Forest Park and Meramac Community Colleges in Missouri) rested for 2 days, came back and played 70 min more, Oct 31–Nov 3, 1984, ending with a 15–11 score.

Goalkeeping

The longest that any goalkeeper has succeeded in preventing any goals being scored past him in international matches is 1,142 min for Dino Zoff (Italy) from Sept 1972 to June 1974.

The biggest goalie on record was Willie J. (''Fatty'') Foulke of England (1874–1916) who stood 6 ft 3 in and weighed 311 lb. By the time he died, he tipped the scales at 364 lb. He once stopped a game by snapping the cross bar.

Ball Control

Mikael Palmquist (Sweden) headed a regulation soccer ball non-stop for 5 hours 3 min 18 sec Oct 1, 1988 in Vasteras, Sweden, beating his 1984 record of 4½ hours and the record of 5 hours set in 1987 by Nyanjong (see below).

Allan Abuto Nyanjong (Kenya) juggled a regulation soccer ball for 16 hours 27 min 52 sec non-stop with feet, legs and head without the ball ever touching the ground at the Hyatt Regency Crystal City; Arlington, Va, Jan 16, 1988.

Janusz Chomontek of Gdanieck, Poland kept a ball up while he traveled a distance of 18.641 miles in 8 hours 25 min 20 sec on Sept 19, 1987.

Crowds

The greatest recorded crowd at any soccer match was 205,000 (199,854 paid) for the Brazil vs Uruguay World Cup final in Rio de Janeiro, Brazil, on July 16, 1950.

SOFTBALL

Origins

Softball, as an indoor derivative of baseball, now 100 years old, was invented by George Hancock at the Farragut Boat Club of Chicago, in 1887. Rules were first codified in Minneapolis in 1895 as Kitten Ball. The name Softball was introduced by Walter Hakanson at a meeting of the National Recreation Congress in 1926. The name was adopted throughout the US in 1930. Rules were formalized in 1933 by the International Joint Rules Committee for Softball and adopted by the Amateur Softball Association of America. The International Softball Federation was formed in 1950 as governing body for both fast pitch and slow pitch, and reorganized in 1965.

SOFTBALL STRIKEOUT ARTIST: Joan Joyce struck out 76 and pitched 2 perfect games in one season. Her fastball travels at 116 mph. She struck out Ted Williams in 1962 in a softball exhibition game. (ASA)

Pitchers

While softball pitchers, who stand 46 ft from the plate and hurl a 12-in spheroid, can't seriously be compared with major league hardball pitchers who stand 60½ ft from the plate, one pro pitcher, Eddie "The King" Feigner, set records that make major league stars look pale by comparison. In his 33-year span from 1946 through 1978, Feigner pitched in 6,177 games, won 5,144 (more than 10 times as many as Cy Young's 511 victories in the major leagues), lost 815, and struck out a total of 100,468 batters (more than 20 times Nolan Ryan's big league total of 4,577).

Along the way, Feigner once won 187 games in a row (more than 7 times as many as Carl Hubbell's 24 in a row), threw 1,581 shutouts (15 times as many as Walter Johnson's 110), and notched 216 perfect games (more than 40 times as many as Nolan Ryan's major league record of 5).

Big league hitters have on frequent occasions tried to hit fast pitch softball and they've generally failed. The latest was Reggie Jackson who couldn't hit the 96-mph pitching of Kathy Arendsen of Evanston, Ill and struck out 3 times in 1981 in an exhibition game. Babe Ruth, Hank Greenberg and Ted Williams have all been struck out by Joan Joyce and others. In the mid-1930s while facing a softball pitcher in an exhibition at Madison Square Garden (NYC) Babe Ruth missed a dozen straight pitches and finally, in sheer frustration, grabbed the ball and hit it with his

hang fungo style. After the ball hit the roof with enormous impact, Ruth growled, "I just wanted to see if it would go."

Slow Pitch vs Fast Pitch

Slow pitch softball, unlike hardball and fast pitch softball, gives the batter something to hit and statistics

DOMINATING SOFTBALL: Ty Stofflet (US) has struck out 33 in one world championship game and 98 in a series with his underhand fast-pitch.

become astronomical. For example, Mike Macenko, the 6-ft-3-inch 260-lb second baseman for the "Men of Steele" (Grafton, Ohio's entry in the Amateur Softball Association) slammed 844 homers and drove in almost 2,000 runs in the 1987 season. (Seasons generally run for 80 to 120 games.) Macenko has hit as many as 9 homers in a single game, and once he clubbed a shot that was tape-measured at 508 ft.

Marathons

The longest fast pitch marathon is 61 hours 36 min 33 sec by two teams of 9 (no substitutes) belonging to the Marines of the 2nd Radio Battalion at Camp Lejeune, NC, May 3–5, 1984. The game went 266 innings and the score was 343–296.

The longest slow pitch softball game was 111 hours 2 min by Brigade Service Support Group 1 vs Marine Aircraft Group 24 at Kareoke Marine Corps Air Station, Hawaii, Sept 3–8, 1986.

World Championships

The US has won the men's world championship (instituted in 1966) five times, 1966, 68, 76 (shared), 80, and 87. The US has also won the women's title (instituted in 1965) 4 times, in 1974, 78, 86 and 87.

In 1981, junior world championships for boys and girls were started, with Japan winning both divisions that year. In 1985, New Zealand won the boys' world championship and China the girls' division. In 1987, the US, behind the fast-pitching of teen-age star Michele Granger, 18, of Placentia, Calif, won the girls' world championship. Granger, 5 ft 10 in and 150 lb, has struck out as many as 103 in a major championship series (1986), third behind Joan Joyce, whose fastball traveled 116 mph when she was at her prime in 1962.

SQUASH

Earliest Champion

Although racquets with a soft ball (called "squashy") was played in 1817 at Harrow School (England), there was no recognized champion of any country until J. A. Miskey of Philadelphia won the American Amateur Singles Championship in 1907.

World Titles

Jahangir Khan (Pakistan) (b Dec 10, 1963) has won 5 times (1981–85), and was the youngest cham-

MOST SQUASH VICTORIES: Geoff Hunt (Aust) (nearer to camera) won 4 World Open tournaments and 3 World Amateur titles. Here he shows his 1969 form before becoming World champ. (AP)

FIRST TO BREAK KHAN'S 5-YEAR UNBEATEN STREAK: Ross Norman of New Zealand won the World Open title in Nov 1986, to end Jahangir Khan's (Pakistan) 1981–86 string of successes. (Colorsport)

pion in 1981 at age 17 years 354 days. He was beaten for the first time since 1981 when Ross Norman (NZ) beat him in 1986.

Geoffrey B. Hunt (b Mar 11, 1947) (Australia) won a record four World Open (inst 1976) titles, 1976–7 and 1979–80, and three World Amateur (inst 1967) titles. Australia has won a record four amateur team titles, 1967, 1969, 1971 and 1973.

Heather McKay (see below) won twice (1976 and 1979). Susan Devoy (New Zealand) also won twice (1985 and 1987).

British Open Championship

The most wins in the Open Championship (amateur or professional), held annually in Britain, is 8 by Geoffrey Hunt (Australia) in 1969, 74, and 76–81. Hashim Khan (b 1915) (Pakistan) won 7 times and has also won the Vintage title 6 times, 1978–83.

The most wins in the Women's Squash Rackets Championship is 16 by Heather Pamela McKay (*née* Blundell) (b July 31, 1941) of Australia, 1961 to 1977. She also won the World Open title (see above). In her career from 1959 to 1980 she lost only two games.

Longest and Shortest Championship Matches

The longest recorded championship match was one of 2 hours 45 min when Jahangir Khan (b Dec 10, 1963) (Pakistan) beat Gamal Awad (Egypt) (b Sept 8, 1955) 9–10, 9–5, 9–7, 9–2, the first game lasting a record 1 hour 11 min, in the final of the Patrick

HOLDING COURT: The winner of 16 British and 2 World Open championships, Heather McKay has not lost a match since 1961. She won all but 2 of the games she played. (George Herringshaw/Provincial Sports Photography)

LONGEST SURF PADDLE: Alan Coates (Queensland, Australia) (b Feb 14, 1944) paddled on a "surf ski" for 683 mi from Sydney to Noosa Heads along the Australia coast in 112 hours 30 min June 14–30, 1986.

International Festival at Chichester, W Sussex, England, Mar 30, 1983.

Suzanne Burgess beat Carolyn Mett in just 8 min, in the British Under-23 Open Championship at The Oasis Club, Marlow, Buckinghamshire, Eng, on Jan 20, 1986.

Marathon Record

The longest squash marathon is 126 hours 1 min by P. Etherton and L. Davies at Tannum Sands, Queensland, Australia, July 7–12, 1987. (*This category is now confined to two players only.*)

SURFING

Origins

The traditional Polynesian sport of surfing in a canoe was first recorded by Captain James Cook (GB) (1728–79) on his first voyage at Tahiti in Dec 1771. Surfing on a board was first described "most perilous and extraordinary . . . altogether astonishing and is scarcely to be credited" by Lt (later Capt) James King (GB) in Mar 1779 at Kealakekua Bay, Hawaii Island. A surfer was first depicted by this voyage's official artist John Webber. Stand-up surfing was revived at Waikiki by 1900. Hollow boards were introduced in 1929 and the light plastic foam type in 1956.

Sailsurfing is the more correct name for this branch of the sport that was previously called boardsailing or windsurfing.

Most Titles

World Amateur Championships were inaugurated in May 1964 at Sydney, Australia; the only surfer to win two titles has been Joyce Hoffman (US) in 1965 and 1966. A World Professional circuit was started in 1975 and Mark Richards (Australia) has won the men's title four times, 1979–82. Tommy Curren (US) won the World Pro title in 1986. The first surfer with a perfect score (1,220 points) in competition was Christopher Campen of Huntington Beach HS, Calif, in the 1976 amateur All American Surfing Contest held by the American Surfing Assoc.

Highest Waves Ridden

Makaha Beach, Hawaii provides the reputedly highest consistently tall waves, often reaching the ridable limit of 30–35 ft. The highest wave ever ridden was 51 ft high, ridden by Duke Paoa Kahanamoku in 1927 off the north shore of Oahu, Hawaii.

Longest Ride

About four to six times each year ridable surfing waves break in Matanchen Bay near San Blas, Nayarit, Mexico which makes a ride of *c.* 5,700 ft possible.

The longest measured ride on a surfboard standing or lying down was 2.94 mi by Colin Kerr Wilson (b June 23, 1954) (UK) on May 23, 1982 on the bore of the Severn River, Eng. A 3-mi wave ride, according

FIRST ENGLISH CHANNEL SWIMMER: British navy captain Matthew Webb swam breaststroke the whole way in 1875. It took him 21¾ hours, compared to the current record of 7 hours 40 min. (Mary Evans)

to Dr. Robert Clark of the International Surfing League, was made from the southernmost Atlantic shore tip of France to the northernmost Atlantic tip of Spain in 1952 by the 8-time All-American surfer, Gary Fairmont Filosa II of Palm Beach, Fla.

SWIMMING

Earliest References

Egyptian hieroglyphics, *c.* 3000 BC, indicate swimming figures, and a bronze of a diver dating from *c.* 510 BC was found near Perugia, Italy. Both Julius Caesar and Charlemagne were known to be good swimmers. Competitions took place in Japan in 36 BC, and that country was the first to take to the sport in a major way with an Imperial edict by the Emperor Go-Yozei decreeing its introduction in schools. In Britain, sea bathing was practiced as early as 1660 at Scarborough, but competitive swimming was not introduced until 1837, when competitions were held in London's artificial pools organized by the National Swimming Society, founded in that year. Australia was in the forefront of modern developments and an unofficial world 100-yd championship was held in Melbourne in 1858. With the foundation of the Amateur Swimming Association (though not known

by this name till later) in Britain in 1869 came the distinction between amateurs and professionals.

The first recognizable stroke style seems to have been the breaststroke, although the "dog-paddle" technique may well have preceded it. From this developed the sidestroke, which is the breaststroke performed sideways, a style which was last used by an Olympic champion in 1904, when Emil Rausch (Ger) won the 1-mi event. About the middle of the 19th century, some American Indians had swum in London exhibiting a style resembling the crawl. An Englishman, John Trudgen, noted a variation of this style while on a trip to South America in the 1870s. His forerunner to the modern crawl used the legs in basically a breaststroke way. However, from ancient carvings and wall paintings it would seem that the trudgen stroke was in use in early times.

Another "throwback" was the front or Australian crawl which is credited to a British emigrant to Australia, Frederick Cavill, and his sons, who noticed the unusual style of South Sea Island natives, and modified it to their own use. American swimmers developed this even further by variations of the kicking action of the legs. At the beginning of the 20th century some had shown their prowess by attempting the breaststroke on their backs, and later the crawl action was tried in the same position. Thus the backstroke was born. In the 1930s the idea of

SPRINT CHAMPION: Matt Biondi (US) won 2 individual gold medals and 3 team golds in the 1988 Olympics. On the right, he is shown accepting one of them. Besides, Biondi holds world records at 50m and 100m, and as part of the US 4-man team in 3 more relay records. (All Sport)

recovering the arms over the water in the breaststroke was developed, and led to a drastic revision of the record book, until the new style was recognized as a separate stroke, the butterfly, in 1952. Also in the 1930s came the introduction, mainly in the US, of medley events in which swimmers use all four major strokes during one event, a real test of all-around ability.

MOST WORLD RECORDS for a woman (23): Kornelia Ender (E Ger) holds the most records in swimming in metric-measured pools. Here she is getting started with her mouth open. (Tony Duffy—All-Sport)

World Titles

In the world swimming championships (instituted in 1973), the greatest number of medals won is 10 by Kornelia Ender of E Germany (8 gold, 2 silver) in 1973 and 75. The most by a man is 8 (5 gold, 3 silver) by Ambrose "Rowdy" Gaines (US, b Feb 17, 1959) in 1978 and 1982. The most gold medals by a man is 6 by James Montgomery (b Jan 24, 1955) in 1973 and 1975.

The most medals in a single championship is 7 by Matt Biondi (US) in 1986 with 3 gold, 1 silver and 3 bronze. The women's record is 6, shared by Tracy Caulkins (US) (b Jan 11, 1963) in 1978 with 5 gold and a silver; by Kristin Otto (E Ger) with 4 gold and 2 silver in 1986; and by Mary Meagher (US) with 1 gold, 3 silver, and 2 bronze in 1986. She won a record 48 US titles before she retired in 1984.

The most successful country in the championships has been the US with a total of 57 swimming, 11 diving and 8 synchronized swimming titles. However, in women's swimming events alone E Germany has a record total of 44 victories.

Other than relays, the only gold medalist in the same event at three championships is Phil Boggs (US) in springboard diving.

Most Individual Gold Medals

The record number of individual gold medals won is 4 shared by four swimmers: Charles M. Daniels (US) (1884–1973) (100 m freestyle 1906 and 1908, 220 yd freestyle 1904, 440 yd freestyle 1904); Roland Matthes (E Germany) (b Nov 17, 1950) with

MOST RECORDS: A young Mark Spitz (17 years old in this photo) is congratulated after setting a world record early in his career. Spitz might be considered (along with Matt Biondi) the most successful swimmer ever. Of his 9 Olympic gold medals (including the unequaled haul of 7 in 1972), 8 were won in world record time. In his 6-year career, Spitz set a total of 26 world records. (UPI)

HOLDER OF 3 RECORDS: Janet Evans of the US is the new queen of women freestylers, with world and Olympic records in distances of 400, 800 and 1,500 meters. (All-Sport)

100 m and 200 m backstroke 1968 and 1972; and Mark Spitz and Mrs Patricia McCormick.

Most World Records

Men: 32, Arne Borg (Sweden) (b 1901), 1921–29. Women: 42, Ragnhild Hveger (Denmark) (b Dec 10, 1920), 1936–42. Under modern conditions (only metric distances in 50-meter pools) the most is 26 by Mark Spitz (US, b Feb 10, 1950), 1967–72, and 23 by Kornelia Ender (now Matthes) (E Germany, b Oct 25, 1958), 1973–76.

Hveger's record of 42 gained for her the name "Golden Torpedo." Her records came in 18 different events. She was a virtual certainty to win at the 1940 Olympic Games, but, of course, war intervened. Retiring in 1945, she made a comeback for the 1952 Games and placed fifth in the 400 m freestyle.

Long Distance Swimming

A unique achievement in long distance swimming was established in 1966 by Mihir Sen of Calcutta, India. He swam the Palk Strait from Sri Lanka to India (in 25 hours 36 min, Apr 5–6); the Straits of Gibraltar (Europe to Africa in 8 hours 1 min on Aug 24); the Dardanelles (Gallipoli, Europe, to Sedulbahir, Asia Minor, in 13 hours 55 min on Sept 12); the Bosphorus (in 4 hours on Sept 21) and the entire length of the Panama Canal (in 34 hours 15 min, Oct

29–31). He had earlier swum the English Channel in 14 hours 45 min on Sept 27, 1958.

The longest ocean swim was one of 128.8 miles by Walter Poenisch (US) (b 1914), who started from Havana, Cuba, and arrived at Little Duck Key, Fla (in a shark cage and wearing flippers) 34 hours 15 min later, July 11–13, 1978.

The greatest recorded distance ever swum is 1,826 miles down the Mississippi from Ford Dam, near Minneapolis, to Carrollton Avenue, New Orleans, July 6 to Dec 29, 1930, by Fred P. Newton, then 27, of Clinton, Okla. He was in the water a total of 742 hours, and the water temperature fell as low as 47° F. He protected himself with petroleum jelly.

The longest swim using the highly exhausting butterfly stroke exclusively was 43.46 mi in 12 hours 20 min by Hugo Rodriguez Barroso (Mex) (b Apr 10, 1961) from Cozumel Island's dock to a point between Punta Cancun and Punta Nizuc, Mexico, on Aug 17, 1988.

The longest duration swim ever achieved was one of 168 continuous hours, ending on Feb 24, 1941, by the legless Charles Zibbelman, *alias* Zimmy (b 1894), of the US, in a pool in Honolulu, Hawaii.

The longest duration swim by a woman was 129 hours 45 min by Vicki Keith (b 1961) of Kingston, Ont, Canada, June 5–10, 1986. She covered about 78 mi in a pool. The first person to swim across all 5 Great Lakes, Vicki Keith conquered the fifth, Lake Ontario, 31 mi across in 24 hours, on Oct 14, 1988. Her Lake swims began in July 1988 in Lake Erie; then she crossed Lakes Huron and Michigan later that month, and completed a 21-mi arm of Lake Superior Aug 15.

CONQUEROR OF BERING STRAIT: Lynne Cox (b 1957) became the first to swim from the US to Russia across the 2.7-mi channel between Alaska and Siberia. It took her 2 hours 5 min, Aug 7–8, 1987.

The greatest distance covered in a continuous swim is 299 miles by Ricardo Hoffmann (b Oct 5, 1941) from Corrientes to Santa Elena, Argentina, in the River Paraná in 84 hours 37 min, Mar 3–6, 1981.

BACKSTROKE CHAMPION: David Berkoff (US) set a world record in 1988 in Seoul besides getting a gold on the medley team.

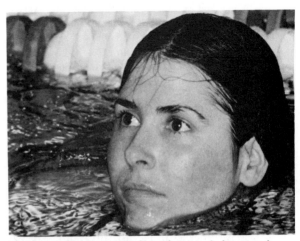

TIME OUT FOR A BITE: Vicki Keith pauses in her record duration swim for a woman—129 hours 45 min in a pool in Kingston, Ont, Canada. She traversed about 78 mi.

SWIMMING □ **183**

SALT-WATER POOL 524 yd long and 82 yd wide in Casablanca, Morocco, is the world's largest.

Bering Straits Swim

The first person to swim across from Alaska to the Soviet Union (2.7 mi), Lynne Cox (b Calif 1957) made the swim in 2 hours 5 min Aug 7–8, 1987. Because of heavy tides and strong currents she had to swim as much as 6 mi from Little Diomede, Alaska to Big Diomede, a military outpost in the Soviet Union. The water was 44°F and her body temperature dropped to 94° during the swim. Cox had previously swum the English Channel in 1972 in 9 hours 57 min, a record at that time.

Fastest Swimmers

The fastest speed measured in a 50 m pool is by Matt Biondi whose best was 5.05 mph in the 1988 Olympics. The women's record is by Yang Wenyi (China), 4.48 mph.

Greatest Lifetime Distance

Gustave Brickner (b Feb 10, 1912) of Charleroi, Pa, recorded 38,512 mi of swimming in the 59 years from 1926 to his retirement in Nov 1986.

Treading Water

The duration record for treading water (vertical posture in an 8-ft square without touching the pool sides or bottom or lane markers) is 98½ hours set by Reginald (Moon) Huffstetler of Belmont, NC, at The Reef in Myrtle Beach, SC, May 20–24, 1986.

Albert Rizzo trod water in the sea at Gzira, Malta, for 108 hours 9 min Sept 7–12, 1983.

Fastest Channel Crossings

The official Channel Swimming Association record is 7 hours 40 min by Penny Dean (b March 21, 1955) of California, who swam from Shakespeare Beach, Dover, England to Cap Gris Nez, France on July 29, 1978.

The fastest crossing by a relay team is 7 hours 17 min by 6 Dover (Eng) lifeguards from England to France on Aug 9, 1981.

Earliest English Channel Swimmers

The first to swim the English Channel (without a life jacket) was the merchant navy captain Matthew Webb (1848–83) (GB), who swam breaststroke from

1988 OLYMPIC SWIMMING GOLD MEDALISTS

MEN

			min sec	
50 m	freestyle:	Matt Biondi (US)	22.14	WR
100 m	freestyle:	Matt Biondi (US)	48.63	OR
100 m	backstroke:	Daichi Suzuki (Japan)	55.05	
100 m	breaststroke:	Adrian Moorhouse (GB)	1:02.04	
100 m	butterfly:	Anthony Nesty (Surinam)	53.00	OR
200 m	freestyle:	Duncan Armstrong (Australia)	1:47.25	WR
200 m	backstroke:	Igor Polianski (USSR)	1:59.37	
200 m	breaststroke:	Jozsef Szabo (Hungary)	2:13.52	
200 m	butterfly:	Michael Gross (W Ger)	1:56.94	OR
200 m	individual medley:	Tamas Darnyi (Hungary)	2:00.17	WR
400 m	freestyle:	Uwe Dassler (E Ger)	3:46.95	WR
400 m	individual medley:	Tamas Darnyi (Hungary)	4:14.75	WR
1,500 m	freestyle:	Vladimir Salnikov (USSR)	15:00.40	
400 m	freestyle relay:	US (Christopher Jacobs, Troy Dalbey, Thomas Jager, Matt Biondi)	3:16.53	WR
400 m	medley relay:	US (David Berkoff, Richard Schroeder, Matt Biondi, Chris Jacobs)	3:36.93	WR
800 m	freestyle relay:	US (Troy Dalbey, Matt Cetlinski, Douglas Gjertsen, Matt Biondi)	7:12.51	WR

WOMEN

			min sec	
50 m	freestyle:	Kristin Otto (E Ger)	25.49	OR
100 m	freestyle:	Kristin Otto (E Ger)	54.93	
100 m	backstroke:	Kristin Otto (E Ger)	1:00.89	
100 m	breaststroke:	Tania Dangalakova (Bulgaria)	1:07.95	OR
100 m	butterfly:	Kristin Otto (E Ger)	59.00	OR
200 m	freestyle:	Heike Friedrich (E Ger)	1:57.65	OR
200 m	backstroke	Krisztina Egerszegi (Hungary)	2:09.29	OR
200 m	breaststroke:	Silke Hoerner (E Ger)	2:26.71	WR
200 m	butterfly:	Kathleen Nord (E Ger)	2:09.51	
200 m	individual medley:	Daniela Hunger (E Ger)	2:12.59	OR
400 m	freestyle:	Janet Evans (US)	4:03.85	WR
400 m	individual medley:	Janet Evans (US)	4:37.76	
800 m	freestyle:	Janet Evans (US)	8:20.20	OR
400 m	freestyle relay:	E Ger (Kristin Otto, Katrin Meissner, Daniela Hunger, Manuela Stellmach)	3:40.63	OR
400 m	medley relay:	E Ger (Kristin Otto, Silke Hoerner, Birte Weigang, Katrin Meissner)	4:03.74	OR

WR = World Record
OR = Olympic Record

Dover, England, to Calais Sands, France, in 21 hours 45 min, Aug 24–25, 1875. Webb swam an estimated 38 miles to make the 21-mile crossing. Paul Boyton (US) had swum from Cap Gris Nez to the South Foreland in his patented lifesaving suit in 23 hours 30 min. May 28–29, 1875. There is good evidence that Jean-Marie Saletti, a French soldier, escaped from a British prison hulk off Dover by swimming to Boulogne in July or Aug 1815. The first crossing from France to England was made by Enrico Tiraboschi, a wealthy Italian living in Argentina, who crossed in 16 hours 33 min on Aug 12, 1923, to win a $5,000 prize. By the end of 1981 the English Channel had been swum by 228 persons on 366 occasions.

The first woman to succeed was Gertrude Ederle (b Oct 23, 1906) (US) who swam from Cap Gris Nez, France, to Deal, England, on Aug 6, 1926, in the then record time of 14 hours 39 min. The first woman to swim from England to France was Florence Chadwick of California, in 16 hours 19 min on Sept 11, 1951.

Youngest and Oldest Channel Swimmers

The youngest conqueror is Thomas Gregory (GB) (b Oct 8, 1976) who swam from Cap Griz Nez (France) to Shakespeare Point, Dover (Eng) in 11 hours 54 min on Sept 8, 1988, when he was 11 years 333 days.

The youngest woman was Samantha Claire Druce (b Apr 21, 1971) aged 12 years 119 days when she swam from England to France in 15 hours 27 min on Aug 18, 1983.

SWIMMING WORLD RECORDS (MEN)

At distances recognized by the Fédération Internationale de Natation Amateur as of July 16, 1983. FINA no longer recognizes any records made for non-metric distances. Only performances in 50-m pools are recognized as World Records.

Distance	min:sec	Name and Nationality	Place	Date
		FREESTYLE		
50 m	22.14	Matthew Biondi (US)	Seoul, S Korea	Sept, 1988
100 m	48.42	Matthew Biondi (US)	Austin, Tex	Aug 10, 1988
200 m	1:47.25	Duncan Armstrong (Australia)	Seoul, S Korea	Sept, 1988
400 m	3:46.95	Uwe Dassler (E Germany)	Seoul, S Korea	Sept, 1988
800 m	7:50.64	Vladimir Salnikov (USSR)	Moscow, USSR	July 4, 1986
1,500 m	14:54.76	Vladimir Salnikov (USSR)	Moscow	Feb 22, 1983
4 × 100 m Relay	3:16.53	US National Team	Seoul, S Korea	Sept, 1988
		(Christopher Jacobs, Troy Dalbey, Thomas Jager, Matt Biondi)		
4 × 200 m Relay	7:12.51	US National Team	Seoul, S Korea	Sept, 1988
		(Troy Dalbey, Matt Cetlinski, Douglas Gjertsen, Matt Biondi)		
		BREASTSTROKE		
100 m	1:01.65	Steve Lundquist (US)	Los Angeles	July 29, 1984
200 m	2:13.34	Victor Davis (Canada)	Los Angeles	Aug 2, 1984
		BUTTERFLY STROKE		
100 m	52.84	Pedro Pablo Morales (US)	Orlando, Fla	June 23, 1986
200 m	1:56.24	Michael Gross (W Ger)	Hanover, W Ger	June 27, 1986
		BACKSTROKE		
100 m	54.51	David Berkoff (US)	Seoul, S Korea	Sept 24, 1988
200 m	1:58.14	Igor Polyansky (USSR)	Erfurt, E Ger	Mar 3, 1985
		INDIVIDUAL MEDLEY		
200 m	2:00.17	Tamas Darnyi (Hungary)	Seoul, S Korea	Sept 25, 1988
400 m	4:14.75	Tamas Darnyi (Hungary)	Seoul, S Korea	Sept 21, 1988
		MEDLEY RELAY		
		(Backstroke, Breaststroke, Butterfly Stroke, Freestyle)		
4 × 100 m	3:36.93	US National Team	Seoul, S Korea	Sept 25, 1988
		(David Berkoff, Richard Schroeder, Matt Biondi, Chris Jacobs)		

Clifford Batt, 68, of Australia, became the oldest man to swim the Channel on Aug 20, 1987.

The oldest woman to conquer the Channel is Stella Ada Rosina Taylor (b Bristol, Avon, England, Dec 20, 1929), aged 45 years 350 days when she swam it in 18 hours 15 min on Aug 26, 1975.

Most Conquests of the English Channel

The greatest number of Channel conquests is 31 by Michael Read (GB), to Aug 19, 1984, including a record 6 in one year. Cindy Nicholas (Canada) (b Aug 20, 1957) made her first crossing of the Channel on July 29, 1975), and her 19th (and fifth 2-way) on Sept 14, 1982.

Double Crossings of the Channel

Antonio Abertondo (Argentina), aged 42, swam from England to France in 18 hours 50 min (8:35 a.m. on Sept 20 to 3:25 a.m. on Sept 21, 1961) and after about 4 minutes' rest returned to England in 24 hours 16 min, landing at St Margaret's Bay at 3:45 a.m. on Sept 22, 1961, to complete the first "double crossing" in 43 hours 10 min.

Philip Rush (NZ) (b Nov 6, 1963), swam two ways in 16 hours 10 min on Aug 17, 1987, for the fastest double crossing, and in the process set a record for one way at 7 hours 55 min.

The fastest by a relay team is 15 hours 36 min 30 sec by the West One International Team on Sept 24, 1985.

Triple Crossing of the Channel

The first triple crossing of the English Channel was by Jon Erikson (b Sept 6, 1954) (US) in 38 hours 27 min, Aug 11–12, 1981.

Bettering the previous record by more than 10 hours, Philip Rush (see above) completed his triple crossing in 28 hours 21 min Aug 17–18, 1987.

Closest Race

In the women's 100 m freestyle final in the 1984 Olympics, Carrie Steinseifer (US) and Nancy Hogs-

SWIMMING WORLD RECORDS (WOMEN)

Distance	min:sec	Name and Nationality	Place	Date
		FREESTYLE		
50 m	24.98	Yang Wenyi (China)	Guangzhou, China	April 10, 1988
100 m	54.73	Kristin Otto (E Ger)	Madrid, Spain	Aug 19, 1986
200 m	1:57.55	Heike Friedrich (E Ger)	E Berlin	June 18, 1986
400 m	4:03.85	Janet Evans (US)	Seoul, S Korea	Sept 22, 1988
800 m	8:17.12	Janet Evans (US)	Orlando, Fla	Mar 22, 1988
1,500 m	15:52.10	Janet Evans (US)	Orlando, Fla	Mar 26, 1988
4 × 100 m Relay	3:40.57	East Germany	Madrid, Spain	Aug 19, 1986
		(Kristin Otto, Manuella Stellmach, Sabina Schulze, Heike Friedrich)		
4 × 200 m Relay	7:55.47	E Germany	Strasbourg, France	Aug 18, 1987
		(Manuella Stellmach, Astrid Strauss, Anke Moehring, Heike Friedrich)		
		BREASTSTROKE		
100 m	1:07.91	Silke Hoerner (E Ger)	Strasbourg, France	Aug 21, 1987
200 m	2:26.71	Silke Hoerner (E Ger)	Seoul, S Korea	Sept 21, 1988
		BUTTERFLY STROKE		
100 m	57.93	Mary Meagher (US)	Milwaukee	Aug 16, 1981
200 m	2:05.96	Mary Meagher (US)	Milwaukee	Aug 13, 1981
		BACKSTROKE		
100 m	1:00.59	Ina Kleber (E Ger)	Moscow	Aug 24, 1984
200 m	2:08.60	Betsy Mitchell (US)	Orlando, Fla	June 27, 1986
		INDIVIDUAL MEDLEY		
200 m	2:11.73	Ute Geweniger (E Ger)	E Berlin	July 4, 1981
400 m	4:36.10	Petra Schneider (E Ger)	Guayaquil, Ecuador	Aug 1, 1982
		MEDLEY RELAY		
		(Backstroke, Breaststroke, Butterfly Stroke, Freestyle)		
4 × 100 m Relay	4:03.69	E German National Team	Moscow	Aug 24, 1984
		(Ina Kleber, Sylvia Gerasch, Ines Geissler, Birgit Meineke)		

head (US) won in a tie at 55.92 sec, and were both awarded gold medals. It was not in record time, but it was the only dead heat in Olympic swimming history.

Most Olympic Medals

The most medals won is 11 by Spitz, who in addition to his 9 golds (see above), won a silver (100 m butterfly) and a bronze (100 m freestyle), both in 1968.

BUTTERFLY CHAMPION: Mary Meagher (US) set 100 m and 200 m butterfly records in 1981 that still stand. She also set Olympic records in these events in 1984. On Jan 12, 1988, she was awarded the Broderick Cup as the outstanding collegiate woman athlete.

KING MEETS DUKE: In the 1912 Olympics in Stockholm, King Gustavus V presented Duke Kahanamoku of Hawaii—his first name was Duke—with the gold medal he won in the 100-m free-style swim. No Games in 1916 but in 1920 Duke won the gold again, and a silver in 1924 when Johnny Weissmuller outswam him.

Most Olympic Gold Medals

The greatest number of Olympic gold medals won is 9 by Mark Andrew Spitz (US) (b Feb 10, 1950), as follows:

100 m freestyle	1972
200 m freestyle	1972
100 m butterfly	1972
200 m butterfly	1972
4 × 100 m freestyle relay	1968 and 1972
4 × 200 m freestyle relay	1968 and 1972
4 × 100 m medley relay	1972

All but one of these performances (the 4 × 200 m relay of 1968) were also world records at the time. He also won a silver (100 m butterfly) and a bronze (100 m freestyle) in 1968 for a record 11 medals.

The record of 7 medals at one Games was tied by Matthew Biondi (US) (b Oct 8, 1965) at Seoul in 1988—5 golds (50m and 100m freestyle and 3 relays), a silver (100m butterfly) and a bronze (200m freestyle).

The record number of gold medals won by a woman is 6 by Kristin Otto (E Ger) (b Feb 7, 1965) at Seoul in 1988: 50m and 100m freestyle, 100m backstroke, 100m butterfly and 2 relays. Four of these were new Olympic records. (See chart.)

Dawn Fraser (Australia) (b Sept 4, 1937) is the only swimmer to win the same event (100m freestyle) on three successive Olympic occasions, 1956, 60 and 64.

Swimming into the Movies

The ability to move well in water has been the key to a movie career for a number of champion swimmers. The first star was Australian Annette Kellerman who made a number of silent films, and was the first woman to wear a one-piece bathing suit. However, it was the 1924 and 1928 Olympic gold medalist, Johnny Weissmuller (US), who became the first major box-office attraction from the swimming world, playing the role of Tarzan in a dozen films. His 1928 Olympic teammate, Clarence "Buster" Crabbe, who later won the 1932 400m freestyle title, also went to Hollywood, where he was the hero in the long-running Buck Rogers and Flash Gordon serials.

A 1932 Olympic champion swimmer, glamorous Eleanor Holm (US) made several movies, although she did not go to Hollywood until she was dropped from the 1936 team for disciplinary reasons. Perhaps the best-known swimming star was Esther Williams, American 100m champion in 1939 and favorite for the cancelled Olympics of 1940. Turning professional she created a new vogue in the cinema, the swimming musical, in which she was supreme throughout the 1940s. One of her co-stars was Fernando Lamas, who had been a national swimming champion in his native Argentina, and whom she later married.

Underwater Swimming

Paul Cryne (UK) and Samir Sawan al Aw swam 49.04 mi underwater in a 24-hour period at Doha, Qatar Feb 21–22, 1985 using sub-aqua equipment. They were swimming underwater for 95.5% of the time.

The first underwater cross-Channel swim was achieved by Fred Baldasare (US), aged 38, who completed a 42-mile swim from France to England with SCUBA in 18 hours 1 min, July 10–11, 1962.

Tony Boyle, Eddie McGettigan, Laurence Thermes and Gearoid Murphy swam a relay of 332.88 mi underwater in 168 hours using sub-aqua equipment at the Mosney Holiday Centre, Co. Meath, Ireland, June 22–29, 1985.

Relay Records

The New Zealand national relay team of 20 swimmers swam a record 113.59 mi in Lower Hutt, NZ in 24 hours, passing 100 mi in 20 hours 47 min 13 sec on Dec 9–10, 1983.

The most participants in a one-day swim relay is

TREADING WATER in the sea at Malta in the Mediterranean for 108 hours 9 min is the record set in 1983 by Albert Rizzo.

2,135, each swimming a length, organized by the Syracuse (NY) YMCA, Apr 11, 1986.

The longest duration swim relay was 216 hours 50 min 16 sec for 373.57 mi by a team of 20 at Katowice, Poland, Feb 17–26, 1987.

The fastest time recorded for 100 miles in a pool by a team of 20 swimmers is 21 hours 41 min 4 sec by the Dropped Sports Swim Club of Indiana State University at Terre Haute, Ind, Mar 12–13, 1982. Four swimmers from the Darien YMCA, Conn, covered 300 miles in relay in 122 hours 59 min 40 sec, Nov 25–30, 1980.

GREATEST MILEAGE IN 24 HOURS: Alyson Gibbons (UK) set the woman's record of 42.05 mi in a 25m pool in Birmingham, Eng, in Sept 1985. The men's record is 60.08 mi by Evan Barry (Aust) in a 50-yd pool on Dec 19–20, 1987, in Brisbane, Australia.

DIVING CHAMPION: Greg Louganis (US) (right and below) proved himself to be the best diver in the world by again winning gold medals in the 1988 Olympic springboard and platform diving contests, repeating his 1984 victories. He is one of two divers to earn perfect 10's from all 7 judges for one dive. He achieved the feat while winning his 2nd and 3rd world championships. (All Sport)

Diving Titles

Greg Louganis (US) (b Jan 29, 1960), has won 4 Olympic golds: springboard and highboard gold medals in the 1988 Seoul Olympics, repeating his unique performance of the 1984 Games. He also has won 5 world diving titles: highboard in 1978, and both highboard and springboard in both 1982 and 1986. At Guayaquil, Ecuador, he became the first to score over 700 points for the 11-dive springboard event with 752.67 on Aug 1, 1982. He went on to be awarded a score of 10.0 by all 7 judges for his highboard inward 1½ somersault in the pike position. In the 1984 Olympics, Louganis set record totals of 754.41 for springboard and 710.91 for highboard.

Mrs Pat McCormick (US) (b May 12, 1930) won golds in the same Olympic events in 1952 and 1956—highboard and springboard—as Louganis did later.

Klaus Dibiasi (Italy, b Austria, Oct 6, 1947) won a total of 5 Olympic diving medals (3 gold, 2 silver) in 4 Games from 1964 to 1976. He is also the only diver to win the same event (highboard) at 3 successive Games (1968, 72 and 76). He also won 4 medals (2 gold, 2 silver) in world events in 1973 and 1975.

Irina Kalinina (USSR) (b Feb 8, 1959) has won 5 medals (3 gold, one silver, one bronze) in 1973, 1975 and 1978. In 1988, the women's gold medals were won by 2 Chinese, Gao Min in the springboard and Xu Yanmei in the highboard.

Perfect Dive

In the 1972 US Olympic Trials, held in Chicago, Michael Finneran (b Sept 21, 1948) was awarded a score of 10 by all seven judges for a backward 1½ somersault 2½ twist (free) from the 10-m platform, an achievement then without precedent. Greg Louganis matched this feat in 1982.

24-Hour Swim

David Goch (US) swam 55.682 mi in a 25-yd pool at Univ of Mich, May 17–18, 1986. In a 50-m pool, Bertrand Malegue swam 54.39 mi at St Etienne, France, May 31–June 1, 1980. The women's record is 42.05 mi in a 25-m pool by Alyson Gibbons (UK) in Birmingham, Eng, Sept 7–8, 1985.

Tony Boyle, Eddie McGettigan, Laurence Thermes and Gearoid Murphy swam a relay of

DIVING RECORD: Pat McCormick (US) won 4 diving events in the 1952 and 1956 Olympics, and shares the record for the most gold medals won by a woman.

332.88 mi underwater in 168 hours using sub-aqua equipment at the Mosney Holiday Centre, Co. Meath, Ireland, June 22–29, 1985.

LONG-TIME CHAMPIONS: No one has been able to beat the record of Petra Schneider of E Germany (left) in the 400 m individual medley since 1982. Cindy Nicholas of Canada (right) was the first woman to make a double crossing of the English Channel in 1977, knocking 10 hours off the men's mark. She beat this by an hour in 1982.

MANHATTAN ROUND-TRIPPERS: Shelley Taylor (left) of Australia came to NY to set a record for swimming around the 28½-mi island in 6 hours 12 min 29 sec in Oct 1985. Here she is under the George Washington Bridge. Julie Ridge (right) a native of NY City, spent 6 days in a row in Aug 1985 in the treacherous waters swimming 20 mi the first day (when she was stopped by a tide turn), and the full 28½ mi circle the other 5 days. (Photos by Luca Del Borgo/Coplan & Assoc)

Synchronized Swimming

Started in 1904 by Annette Kellerman when she swam underwater and performed water ballets on the stage of the NYC Hippodrome, this did not become an Olympic event for women until 1984 at Los Angeles. The contestants are judged on presentation and showmanship as well as the athlete's skill and technique. In the 1988 Olympics, the winners were Carolyn Waldo (Canada) for solo and as one of the duet with Michelle Cameron (Canada).

Largest Pools

The largest swimming pool in the world is the salt-water Orthlieb Pool in Casablanca, Morocco. It is 480m (1,574 ft) long, 75m (246 ft) wide, and has an area of 8.9 acres.

The world's largest competition pool is at Osaka, Japan. It accommodates 13,614 spectators.

TABLE TENNIS

Earliest Reference

In 1879 some Cambridge University students indulged in a diversion in which they hit champagne corks to each other over a pile of books in the center of a table, using cigar boxes as crude bats. Rubber balls soon followed, but it was not until about 1900 that James Gibb, a former English world record-breaking runner, introduced a celluloid ball to the game.

At first the game was called "indoor tennis" and it marked the beginning of the game in the US. In 1902 the game was called Flim-Flam, *Gossima*, Klik-Klak, and Whiff-Whaff. The origin of the word Ping Pong is in doubt. Some claim it came from the use of banjo rackets which had two sides of vellum. The impact of the celluloid ball against this hollow racket made the sound "Ping" and the impact of the ball on the table, the sound "Pong." The game thrived for a period, and in 1902 the first Ping Pong Association was formed in Britain. But the monotony of play due to plain wooden bats soon led to a decline in interest until the 1920s.

The next stage in the history of the game was the use of wooden, cork and sandpaper rackets. In 1920, the studded rubber racket was invented, which allowed a spin to be imparted to the ball. Then, in 1952, sponge rackets were introduced by the Japanese at the world championships in Bombay, India.

The International Table Tennis Federation was founded in 1926 with 7 nations and now there are about 130 nations.

Olympics

Table tennis became an accepted sport in the 1988 Games. The events were dominated by Chinese, who won men's doubles and women's singles, and S Koreans, who were victorious in the men's singles and women's doubles contests.

World Championships

Instituted in 1927, the world championships were held annually until 1957, when the competitions became biennial (rendering most of the following personal records virtually unbreakable).

The most world titles were 25 won by G. Victor Barna (1911–72) (Hungary and England), with 5 men's singles, 8 men's doubles, 2 mixed doubles, 3 Jubilee Cups and 7 men's team titles.

The women's records are 18 titles won by Maria Mednyanszky (1901–79) (Hungary) with 5 women's

"PING" MEETS CHOU: The leading US women's table tennis player of her era, Leah "Ping" Neuberger was the first American to visit China (Apr 14, 1971).

singles, 7 women's doubles and 6 mixed doubles; but Angelica Rozeanu (b Oct 15, 1921) (Romania) has more titles in women's singles (6) but fewer in total (17).

The most victories in the men's team championships (Swaythling Cup) is 12 by Hungary from 1927 through 1979. The women's team title (Marcel Corbillon Cup, instituted in 1934) has been won most often by Japan, with 8 victories from 1952–1971.

Over the years, Hungary has won 10 men's singles, 10 women's singles, 12 men's doubles, 7 women's doubles (plus 4 halves), 13 mixed doubles (plus 4 halves) and 6 men's consolations. Czechoslovakia won 4 women's consolations and England won 4 Jubilee Cups. (Halves are issued when nations share titles as partners.)

In 1937, the US was the first nation to win both Cups, a record that was not broken until 17 years later by Japan. China won all 7 titles in 1983.

US National Titles

In the women's division, Leah Thall (Ping) Neuberger (Columbus, O, and NYC) won a record 9 women's singles plus 12 women's doubles, 8 mixed doubles, one senior women's (for a total of 30 US

170 HITS IN ONE MINUTE is the record these table tennis internationals from Britain, Desmond Douglas (left) and Alan Cooke, set in Eng Feb 28, 1986.

Opens) and one US Closed. In the men's division, Richard Miles has 17 titles (including 10 men's singles victories) for a record. Dal Joon Lee (S Korea and Las Vegas) won 18 titles but only 6 men's US singles, and Dan Seemiller of Pittsburgh won 25 titles but only 5 men's closed singles (US).

Canadian International Open

Leah Thall (Ping) Neuberger won 48 titles, of which 11 were women's singles, 19 women's doubles, 11 mixed doubles and 7 on the women's team.

Youngest International Contestant

The youngest international (in any sport) was Joy Foster, aged 8, when she represented Jamaica in the West Indies Championships at Port of Spain, Trinidad, in Aug 1958.

Longest Match

In the Swaythling Cup final match between Austria and Romania in Prague, Czechoslovakia, in 1936, the play lasted for 11 hours.

Longest Rally

In a Swaythling Cup match in Prague on March 14, 1936, between Alex Ehrlich (Poland) and Farcas Paneth (Romania), the first point was not scored until 2 hours 5 min after play began.

Rick Bowling and Richard De Witt staged a rally lasting 10 hours 9 min at the YWCA in New Haven, Conn, on July 26, 1983.

Fastest Rallying

The record number of hits in 60 sec is an unofficial 170 by Desmond Douglas (GB) (b July 20, 1955) and Alan Cooke (GB) (b Mar 23, 1966) at Scotswood Sports Centre, Newcastle-upon-Tyne, Eng, on Feb 28, 1986. The women's record is 163 by sisters Lisa and Jackie Bellinger at Luton, Eng on June 23, 1985.

With a paddle in each hand, Gary D. Fisher of Olympia, Wash, completed 5,000 consecutive volleys over the net in 44 min 28 sec on June 25, 1979.

Highest Speed

No conclusive measurements have been published, but in a lecture M. Sklorz (W Germany) stated that a smashed ball had been measured at speeds up to 105.6 mph.

Marathon

The longest recorded time for a marathon singles match by two players is 147 hours 47 min by S. Unterslak and J. Boccia at Dewaal Hotel, Cape Town, S Africa, Nov 12–18, 1983.

The longest doubles marathon by 4 players is 101 hours 1 min 11 sec by Lance, Phil and Mark Warren and Bill Weir at Sacramento, Calif, Apr 9–13, 1979.

TENNIS

Origins

The modern game of lawn tennis is generally agreed to have evolved as an outdoor form of the French Royal Tennis or *Jeu de Paume* from the 11th century. "Field Tennis" was mentioned in an English magazine (*Sporting Magazine*) on Sept 29, 1793. In 1858 Major Harry Gem laid out a "court" on the lawn of a friend in Birmingham, Eng, and in 1872 he founded the Leamington Club. In Feb 1874, Major Walter Clopton Wingfield of England (1833–1912) patented a form called "sphairistike," which was nicknamed "sticky," but the game soon became known as lawn tennis. The US Lawn Tennis Association (USLTA) was founded in 1881.

Amateurs were permitted to play with and against professionals in Open tournaments starting in 1968.

"Grand Slams"

The "grand slam" is to hold at the same time all four of the world's major championship titles: Wimbledon, the US Open, Australian and French championships. The first time this occurred was in 1935 when Frederick John Perry (GB) (b 1909) won the French title, having won Wimbledon (1934), the US title (1933–34) and the Australian title (1934).

The first player to hold all four titles in the same calendar year was J. Donald Budge (US) (b June 13, 1915), who won the championships of Wimbledon (1937), the US (1937), Australia (1938), and France

TENNIS IN ITS INFANCY: Leslie's magazine pictured women's entry into the sport in the late 19th century.

(1938). He subsequently retained Wimbledon (1938) and the US (1938). Rodney George Laver (Australia) (b Aug 9, 1938) achieved this grand slam in 1962 as

DOUBLES VISION: "Bunny" Ryan (US) is the all-time Wimbledon doubles champion with 19 titles (12 women's and 7 mixed). Her 19 victories were the overall record until Billie Jean King won the 1979 doubles title. Ryan, who had said she didn't want to live to see her record broken, died the night before Billie Jean's 20th victory.

FIRST "GRAND SLAMMERS": (Left) Fred Perry (GB) won all major titles in 1934–35. Don Budge (US) (right) in 1937–38 held all 4 simultaneously. (Perry photos, AP)

PAST PERFORMERS: (Left) Charlotte "Lottie" Dod (GB) won the first of 5 Wimbledon titles in the late 1800's before she was 16, and also excelled at golf, archery, field hockey, skating and tobogganing. (Right) SUPERSTAR Suzanne Lenglen (France) was unbeaten in US singles 1916–26.

196 □ TENNIS

MOST "GRAND SLAMMERS": In 1962 as an amateur, Rod Laver (Aust) (left) won the Big 4 tournaments and again as a pro in 1969. Martina Navratilova (US) (right) won all the "grand slam" events in 1983–84, and became the woman athlete with the highest earnings—more than $14 million through 1988. (USTA)

STILL MORE "GRAND SLAMMERS": The only women before Martina Navratilova to win the "grand slam" were Maureen Connolly (left) and Margaret Smith Court (right). Connolly (US) performed the feat in 1953; she might well have repeated had she not suffered a serious, career-ending injury in 1954. Court (Australia), who won the "grand slam" in 1970, is the all-time leading title winner. She won 22 titles in the Australian Open (including a record 10 in singles), 18 titles in the US Championships, and 13 titles in the French tournament (including 5 in singles).

Wimbledon Tournament Winners

Men's Singles

1919 Gerald Patterson (Aus)
1920 Bill Tilden (US)
1921 Bill Tilden (US)
1922 Gerald Patterson (Aus)
1923 William Johnston (US)
1924 Jean Borotra (Fra)
1925 René Lacoste (Fra)
1926 Jean Borotra (Fra)
1927 Henri Cochet (Fra)
1928 René Lacoste (Fra)
1929 Henri Cochet (Fra)
1930 Bill Tilden (US)
1931 Sidney Wood (US)
1932 Ellsworth Vines (US)
1933 Jack Crawford (Aus)
1934 Fred Perry (GB)
1935 Fred Perry (GB)
1936 Fred Perry (GB)
1937 Donald Budge (US)
1938 Donald Budge (US)
1939 Bobby Riggs (US)
1940–45 not held
1946 Yvon Petra (Fra)
1947 Jack Kramer (US)
1948 Bob Falkenburg (US)
1949 Ted Schroeder (US)
1950 Budge Patty (US)
1951 Dick Savitt (US)
1952 Frank Sedgman (Aus)
1953 Vic Seixas (US)
1954 Jaroslav Drobny (Cze)
1955 Tony Trabert (US)
1956 Lew Hoad (Aus)
1957 Lew Hoad (Aus)
1958 Ashley Cooper (Aus)
1959 Alex Olmedo (US)
1960 Neale Fraser (Aus)
1961 Rod Laver (Aus)
1962 Rod Laver (Aus)
1963 Chuck McKinley (US)
1964 Roy Emerson (Aus)
1965 Roy Emerson (Aus)
1966 Manuel Santana (Spa)
1967 John Newcombe (Aus)
1968 Rod Laver (Aus)
1969 Rod Laver (Aus)
1970 John Newcombe (Aus)
1971 John Newcombe (Aus)
1972 Stan Smith (US)
1973 Jan Kodes (Cze)
1974 Jimmy Connors (US)
1975 Arthur Ashe (US)
1976 Bjorn Borg (Swe)
1977 Bjorn Borg (Swe)
1978 Bjorn Borg (Swe)
1979 Bjorn Borg (Swe)
1980 Bjorn Borg (Swe)
1981 John McEnroe (US)
1982 Jimmy Connors (US)
1983 John McEnroe (US)
1984 John McEnroe (US)
1985 Boris Becker (W Ger)
1986 Boris Becker (W Ger)
1987 Pat Cash (Aus)
1988 Stefan Edberg (Swe)

Women's Singles

1919 Suzanne Lenglen (Fra)
1920 Suzanne Lenglen (Fra)
1921 Suzanne Lenglen (Fra)
1922 Suzanne Lenglen (Fra)
1923 Suzanne Lenglen (Fra)
1924 Kathleen McKane (GB)
1925 Suzanne Lenglen (Fra)
1926 Kathleen Godfree (GB)
1927 Helen Wills (US)
1928 Helen Wills (US)
1929 Helen Wills (US)
1930 Helen Wills Moody (US)
1931 Cilly Aussem (Ger)
1932 Helen Wills Moody (US)
1933 Helen Wills Moody (US)
1934 Dorothy Round (GB)
1935 Helen Wills Moody (US)
1936 Helen Jacobs (US)
1937 Dorothy Round (GB)
1938 Helen Wills Moody (US)
1939 Alice Marble (US)
1940–45 not held
1946 Pauline Betz (US)
1947 Margaret Osborne (US)
1948 Louise Brough (US)
1949 Louise Brough (US)
1950 Louise Brough (US)
1951 Doris Hart (US)
1952 Maureen Connolly (US)
1953 Maureen Connolly (US)
1954 Maureen Connolly (US)
1955 Louise Brough (US)
1956 Shirley Fry (US)
1957 Althea Gibson (US)
1958 Althea Gibson (US)
1959 Maria Bueno (Bra)
1960 Maria Bueno (Bra)
1961 Angela Mortimer (GB)
1962 Karen Susman (US)
1963 Margaret Smith (Aus)
1964 Maria Bueno (Bra)
1965 Margaret Smith (Aus)
1966 Billie Jean King (US)
1967 Billie Jean King (US)
1968 Billie Jean King (US)
1969 Ann Jones (GB)
1970 Margaret Smith Court (Aus)
1971 Evonne Goolagong (Aus)
1972 Billie Jean King (US)
1973 Billie Jean King (US)
1974 Christine Evert (US)
1975 Billie Jean King (US)
1976 Christine Evert (US)
1977 Virginia Wade (GB)
1978 Martina Navratilova (Cze)
1979 Martina Navratilova (Cze)
1980 Evonne Goolagong Cawley (Aus)
1981 Christine Evert Lloyd (US)
1982 Martina Navratilova (US)
1983 Martina Navratilova (US)
1984 Martina Navratilova (US)
1985 Martina Navratilova (US)
1986 Martina Navratilova (US)
1987 Martina Navratilova (US)
1988 Steffi Graf (W Ger)

Men's Doubles

First held 1884.

Most wins: 8 Laurence Doherty and Reginald Doherty (GB): 1897–1901, 1903–05
Winners since 1965:
1965 John Newcombe, Tony Roche (Aus)
1966 Ken Fletcher, John Newcombe (Aus)
1967 Bob Hewitt, Frew McMillan (S Af)
1968 John Newcombe, Tony Roche (Aus)
1969 John Newcombe, Tony Roche (Aus)
1970 John Newcombe, Tony Roche (Aus)
1971 Roy Emerson, Rod Laver (Aus)
1972 Bob Hewitt, Frew McMillan (S Af)
1973 Jimmy Connors (US), Ilie Nastase (Rom)
1974 John Newcombe, Tony Roche (Aus)
1975 Vitas Gerulaitis, Sandy Mayer (US)
1976 Brian Gottfried (US), Raul Ramirez (Mex)
1977 Ross Case, Geoff Masters (Aus)
1978 Bob Hewitt, Frew McMillan (S Af)
1979 Peter Fleming, John McEnroe (US)
1980 Peter McNamara, Paul McNamee (Aus)
1981 Peter Fleming, John McEnroe (US)
1982 Peter McNamara, Paul McNamee (Aus)
1983 Peter Fleming, John McEnroe (US)
1984 Peter Fleming, John McEnroe (US)
1985 Heinz Gunthardt (Switz) Bela Taroczi (Hungary)
1986 Mats Wilander (Swe) and Joakim Nystram (Swe)
1987 Ken Flach, Robert Seguro (US)
1988 Ken Flach, Robert Seguro (US)

Women's Doubles

First held 1899, but not a championship event until 1913.

Most wins: 12 Elizabeth (Bunny) Ryan (US): 1 with Agatha Morton 1914; 6 with Suzanne Lenglen 1919–23, 1925; 1 with Mary Browne 1926; 2 with Helen Wills Moody 1927, 1930; 2 with Simone Mathieu 1933–34

Winners since 1965:
1965 Maria Bueno (Bra), Billie Jean Moffitt (US)
1966 Maria Bueno (Bra), Nancy Richey (US)
1967 Rosemary Casals, Billie Jean King (*née* Moffitt) (US)
1968 Rosemary Casals, Billie Jean King (US)
1969 Margaret Court, Judy Tegart (Aus)
1970 Rosemary Casals, Billie Jean King (US)
1971 Rosemary Casals, Billie Jean King (US)
1972 Billie Jean King (US), Betty Stove (Hol)
1973 Rosemary Casals, Billie Jean King (US)
1974 Evonne Goolagong (Aus), Peggy Michel (US)
1975 Ann Kiyomura (US), Kazuko Sawamatsu (Japan)
1976 Christine Evert (US), Martina Navratilova (Cze)
1977 Helen Cawley (Aus), Joanne Russell (US)
1978 Kerr Reid, Wendy Turnbull (US)
1979 Billie Jean King (US), Martina Navratilova (Cze)
1980 Kathy Jordan, Anne Smith (US)
1981 Martina Navratilova (Cze), Pam Shriver (US)
1982 Martina Navratilova (US), Pam Shriver (US)
1983 Martina Navratilova (US), Pam Shriver (US)
1984 Martina Navratilova (US), Pam Shriver (US)
1985 Kathy Jordan (US), Liz Smylie (Aus)
1986 Martina Navratilova (US), Pam Shriver (US)
1987 Claudia Kohde-Kilsch (W Ger), Helena Sukova (Czech)
1988 Steffi Graf (W Ger), Gabriella Sabatini (Arg)

WIMBLEDON RECORDS

The first Championship was in 1877. Professionals first played in 1968. From 1971 the tie-break system was introduced, which effectually prevents sets proceeding beyond a 17th game, i.e., 9–8.

The record crowd for one day was 39,813 on June 26, 1986. The record for the whole championship was 400,032 in 1986.

In 1988, Steffi Graf (b June 14, 1969) of W Ger beat Martina Navratilova, 5–7, 6–2, 6–1 to end Navratilova's streak of 6 straight Wimbledon women's singles titles. Stefan Edberg, 22, of Sweden defeated Boris Becker, 4–6, 7–6, 6–4, 6–2, for the men's singles title.

Most Wins

Six-time singles champion Billie Jean King (*née* Moffitt) also won 10 women's doubles and 4 mixed

WIMBLEDON WINNER in 1988: Stefan Edberg (Sweden) beat the top-ranked players for his first major championship. (Michael Baz/Advantage International)

an amateur and repeated as a professional in 1969 to become the first two-time grand slammer.

Four women have achieved the grand slam: Maureen Catherine Connolly (US) (1934–69), in 1953; Margaret Jean Court (*née* Smith) (Australia) (b July 16, 1942) in 1970, Martina Navratilova (US) (b Prague, Czech, Oct 18, 1956) in 1983–4, and Steffi Graf (W Germany) (b June 14, 1969) in 1988. Graf also won the Olympics singles in 1988, to record the first "golden Grand Slam."

The most singles championships in "grand slam" tournaments is 24 by Margaret Court (11 Australian, 5 French, 5 US, 3 Wimbledon), 1960–73. The men's record is 12 by Roy Emerson (Australia) (b Nov 3, 1936) (6 Australian, 2 each French, US, Wimbledon), 1961–67.

In doubles, the only men to win a "grand slam" are Frank Sedgman (Aust) and Ken McGregor (Aust) in 1951. Margaret Smith Court (Aust) and Ken Fletcher (Aust) won it in mixed doubles in 1961. Martina Navratilova (US) and Pam Shriver (US) managed a "grand slam" in doubles in 1983–84, the same year Martina got her "grand slam" in singles.

YOUNGEST WIMBLEDON WINNER: Boris Becker (W Ger) was not yet 18 when he beat the favorites and was victorious in 1985. A year later he won again but was eliminated in the second round in 1987. (Photo by David L. Boehm/Tamron)

doubles during the period 1961 to 1979, to total a record 20 titles.

The greatest number of singles wins was 8 by Helen N. Moody (*née* Wills) (b Oct 6, 1905) (US), who won in 1927–30, 32–33, 35 and 38. This record was tied by Martina Navratilova in 1978, 79, and 82–87.

The greatest number of singles wins by a man since the Challenge Round (wherein the defending champion was given a bye until the final round) was abolished in 1922, is 5 consecutively by Bjorn Borg (Sweden) in 1976–80. The all-time men's record was 7 by William C. Renshaw, 1881–86 and 1889.

The greatest number of doubles wins by men was 8 by the brothers Doherty (GB)—Reginald Frank (1872–1910) and Hugh Lawrence (1875–1919). They won each year from 1897 to 1905 except for 1902. Hugh Doherty also won 5 singles titles (1902–06) and holds the record for most men's titles with 13.

The most wins in women's doubles was 12 by Elizabeth ''Bunny'' Ryan (US) (1894–1979). The greatest number of mixed doubles wins was 7 by Elizabeth Ryan, giving her a record total of 19 doubles wins 1914–34.

The men's mixed doubles record is 4 wins: by Elias Victor Seixas (b Aug 30, 1923) (US) in 1953–56; by Kenneth N. Fletcher (b June 15, 1940) (Australia) in 1963, 65–66 and 68; and by Owen Keir Davidson (Australia) (b Oct 4, 1943) in 1967, 71 and 73–74.

WINNER OF EVERYTHING: Steffi Graf (W Ger) not only won the Grand Slam titles (Australian, French, Wimbledon, and US Open) but she won the Olympics singles for a so-called Golden Slam. She was still only 19 (b June 14, 1969). (Sporting Pictures)

Youngest Champions

The youngest champion ever at Wimbledon was Charlotte (Lottie) Dod (1871–1960), who was 15 years 285 days old when she won in 1887.

The youngest male champion was Boris Becker (W Ger) (b Nov 22, 1967) who won the men's singles title in 1985 at 17 years 227 days.

The youngest-ever player at Wimbledon is reputedly Miss Mita Klima (Austria), who was 13 years old in the 1907 singles competition. The youngest player to win a match at Wimbledon is Kathy Rinaldi (b March 24, 1967) (US), who was 14 years 91 days old on June 23, 1981.

Oldest Champions

The oldest champion was Margaret Evelyn du Pont (*née* Osborne) (b Mar 4, 1918) (US) who was 44 years 125 days old when she won the mixed doubles in 1962 with Neale Fraser (Aust). The oldest singles champion was Arthur Gore (GB, 1868–1928) at 41 years 182 days in 1909.

NEVER A WINNER IN US OPEN: Bjorn Borg (Sweden) won 5 Wimbledon titles and many others though.

US Open Tournament Winners

Most wins:

Men's Singles: 7 Richard D. Sears 1881–87; 7 William A. Larned 1901–02, 1907–11; 7 William T. Tilden 1920–25, 1929

Women's Singles: 7 Molla Mallory 1915–16, 1918, 1920–25, 1926; 7 Helen Wills Moody 1923–25, 1927–29, 1931

Men's Singles
1920 Bill Tilden
1921 Bill Tilden
1922 Bill Tilden
1923 Bill Tilden
1924 Bill Tilden
1925 Bill Tilden
1926 René Lacoste
1927 René Lacoste
1928 Henri Cochet
1929 Bill Tilden
1930 John Doeg
1931 H. Ellsworth Vines
1932 H. Ellsworth Vines
1933 Fred Perry
1934 Fred Perry
1935 Wilmer Allison
1936 Fred Perry
1937 Don Budge
1938 Don Budge
1939 Robert Riggs
1940 Don McNeil
1941 Robert Riggs
1942 F. R. Schroeder Jr.
1943 Joseph Hunt
1944 Frank Parker
1945 Frank Parker
1946 Jack Kramer
1947 Jack Kramer
1948 Pancho Gonzales
1949 Pancho Gonzales
1950 Arthur Larsen
1951 Frank Sedgman
1952 Frank Sedgman
1953 Tony Trabert
1954 E. Victor Seixas Jr
1955 Tony Trabert
1956 Ken Rosewall
1957 Malcolm Anderson
1958 Ashley Cooper
1959 Neale A. Fraser
1960 Neale A. Fraser
1961 Roy Emerson
1962 Rod Laver
1963 Rafael Osuna
1964 Roy Emerson
1965 Manuel Santana
1966 Fred Stolle
1967 John Newcombe
1968 Arthur Ashe
1969 Rod Laver
1970 Ken Rosewall
1971 Stan Smith
1972 Ilie Nastase
1973 John Newcombe
1974 Jimmy Connors
1975 Manuel Orantes
1976 Jimmy Connors
1977 Guillermo Vilas
1978 Jimmy Connors
1979 John McEnroe
1980 John McEnroe
1981 John McEnroe
1982 Jimmy Connors
1983 Jimmy Connors
1984 John McEnroe
1985 Ivan Lendl
1986 Ivan Lendl
1987 Ivan Lendl
1988 Mats Wilander

Women's Singles
1935 Helen Jacobs
1936 Alice Marble
1937 Anita Lizana
1938 Alice Marble
1939 Alice Marble
1940 Alice Marble
1941 Mrs Sarah P. Cooke
1942 Pauline Betz
1943 Pauline Betz
1944 Pauline Betz
1945 Sarah P. Cooke
1946 Pauline Betz
1947 A. Louise Brough
1948 Mrs. Margaret O. duPont
1949 Mrs. Margaret O. duPont
1950 Mrs. Margaret O. duPont
1951 Maureen Connolly
1952 Maureen Connolly
1953 Maureen Connolly
1954 Doris Hart
1955 Doris Hart
1956 Shirley J. Fry
1957 Althea Gibson
1958 Althea Gibson
1959 Maria Bueno
1960 Darlene Hard
1961 Darlene Hard
1962 Margaret Smith
1963 Maria Bueno
1964 Maria Bueno
1965 Margaret Smith
1966 Maria Bueno
1967 Billie Jean King
1968 Virginia Wade
1969 Margaret Smith Court
1970 Margaret Smith Court
1971 Billie Jean King
1972 Billie Jean King
1973 Margaret Smith Court
1974 Billie Jean King
1975 Chris Evert
1976 Chris Evert
1977 Chris Evert
1978 Chris Evert
1979 Tracy Austin
1980 Chris Evert Lloyd
1981 Tracy Austin
1982 Chris Evert Lloyd
1983 Martina Navratilova
1984 Martina Navratilova
1985 Hana Mandlikova
1986 Martina Navratilova
1987 Martina Navratilova
1988 Steffi Graf

Men's Doubles
1922 Bill Tilden—Vincent Richards
1923 Bill Tilden—Brian Norton
1924 Howard Kinsey—Robert Kinsey
1925 R. Norris Williams—Vincent Richards
1926 R. Norris Williams—Vincent Richards
1927 Bill Tilden—Francis Hunter
1928 George Lott—John Hennessey
1929 George Lott—John Doeg
1930 George Lott—John Doeg
1931 Wilmer Allison—John Van Ryn
1932 H. Ellsworth Vines—Keith Gledhill
1933 George Lott—Lester Stoefen
1934 George Lott—Lester Stoefen
1935 Wilmer Allison—John Van Ryn
1936 Don Budge—C. Gene Mako
1937 Baron G. von Cramm—Henner Henkel
1938 Don Budge—C. Gene Mako
1939 Adrian Quist—John Bromwich
1940 Jack Kramer—Frederick Schroeder Jr.
1941 Jack Kramer—Frederick Schroeder Jr.
1942 Gardner Mulloy—William Talbert
1943 Jack Kramer—Frank Parker
1944 Don McNeill—Robert Falkenburg
1945 Gardner Mulloy—William Talbert
1946 Gardner Mulloy—William Talbert
1947 Jack Kramer—Frederick Schroeder Jr.
1948 Gardner Mulloy—William Talbert
1949 John Bromwich—William Sidwell
1950 John Bromwich—Frank Sedgman
1951 Frank Sedgman—Kenneth McGregor
1952 Mervyn Rose—E. Victor Seixas Jr.
1953 Rex Hartwig—Mervyn Rose
1954 E. Victor Seixas Jr—Tony Trabert
1955 Kosel Kamo—Atsushi Miyagi
1956 Lewis Hoad—Ken Rosewall
1957 Ashley Cooper—Neale Fraser
1958 Hamilton Richardson—Alejandro Olmedo
1959 Neale A. Fraser—Roy Emerson
1960 Neale A. Fraser—Roy Emerson
1961 Dennis Ralston—Chuck McKinley
1962 Rafael Osuna—Antonio Palafox
1963 Dennis Ralston—Chuck McKinley

US Open Winners (continued)

1964 Dennis Ralston—Chuck McKinley
1965 Roy Emerson—Fred Stolle
1966 Roy Emerson—Fred Stolle
1967 John Newcombe—Tony Roche
1968 Robert Lutz—Stan Smith
1969 Fred Stolle—Ken Rosewall
1970 Pierre Barthes—Nicki Pilic
1971 John Newcombe—Roger Taylor
1972 Cliff Drysdale—Roger Taylor
1973 John Newcombe—Owen Davidson
1974 Bob Lutz—Stan Smith
1975 Jimmy Connors—Ilie Nastase
1976 Marty Riessen—Tom Okker
1977 Bob Hewitt—Frew McMillan
1978 Stan Smith—Bob Lutz
1979 John McEnroe—Peter Fleming
1980 Stan Smith—Bob Lutz
1981 John McEnroe—Peter Fleming
1982 Kevin Curren—Steve Denton
1983 John McEnroe—Peter Fleming
1984 John Fitzgerald—Tomas Smid
1985 Ken Flach—Robert Seguro
1986 Andres Gomez—Slobodan Zivolinovic
1987 Stefan Edberg—Anders Jarryd
1988 Sergio Casal—Emilio Sanchez

Women's Doubles
1936 Mrs. M. G. Van Ryn—Carolin Babcock
1937 Mrs. Sarah P. Fabyan—Alice Marble
1938 Alice Marble—Mrs. Sarah P. Fabyan
1939 Alice Marble—Mrs. Sarah P. Fabyan
1940 Alice Marble—Mrs. Sarah P. Fabyan
1941 Mrs. S. P. Cooke—Margaret Osborne
1942 A. Louise Brough—Margaret Osborne
1943 A. Louise Brough—Margaret Osborne
1944 A. Louise Brough—Margaret Osborne
1945 A. Louise Brough—Margaret Osborne
1946 A. Louise Brough—Margaret Osborne
1947 A. Louise Brough—Margaret Osborne
1948 A. Louise Brough—Mrs. M. O. duPont
1949 A. Louise Brough—Mrs. M. O. duPont
1950 A. Louise Brough—Mrs. M. O. duPont
1951 Doris Hart—Shirley Fry
1952 Doris Hart—Shirley Fry
1953 Doris Hart—Shirley Fry
1954 Doris Hart—Shirley Fry
1955 A. Louise Brough—Mrs. M. O. duPont
1956 A. Louise Brough—Mrs. M. O. duPont
1957 A. Louise Brough—Mrs. M. O. duPont
1958 Darlene Hard—Jeanne Arth
1959 Darlene Hard—Jeanne Arth
1960 Darlene Hard—Maria Bueno
1961 Darlene Hard—Lesley Turner
1962 Maria Bueno—Darlene Hard
1963 Margaret Smith—Robyn Ebbern
1964 Billie Jean Moffitt—Karen Susman

BIGGEST WINNER in the 1920's: Bill Tilden (US) won only 4 times at Wimbledon (3 singles and one doubles) but 16 times in the US Open (including 7 singles) between 1920 and 1929.

1965 Carole C. Graebner—Nancy Richey
1966 Maria Bueno—Nancy Richey
1967 Rosemary Casals—Billie Jean King
1968 Maria Bueno—Margaret S. Court
1969 Françoise Durr—Darlene Hard
1970 M. S. Court—Judy Tegart Dalton
1971 Rosemary Casals—Judy Tegart Dalton
1972 Françoise Durr—Betty Stove
1973 Margaret S. Court—Virginia Wade
1974 Billie Jean King—Rosemary Casals
1975 Margaret Court—Virginia Wade
1976 Linky Boshoff—Ilana Kloss
1977 Betty Stove—Martina Navratilova
1978 Martina Navratilova—Billie Jean King
1979 Betty Stove—Wendy Turnbull
1980 Martina Navratilova—Billie Jean King
1981 Kathy Jordan—Anne Smith
1982 Rosemary Casals—Wendy Turnbull
1983 Martina Navratilova—Pam Shriver
1984 Martina Navratilova—Pam Shriver
1985 Claudia Kohde-Kilsch—Helena Sukova
1986 Martina Navratilova—Pam Shriver
1987 Martina Navratilova—Pam Shriver
1988 Gigi Fernandez—Robin White

U S CHAMPIONSHIPS

The USTA Championships were first held in 1881 and continued until 1969. The Tournament was superseded in 1970 by the US Open Championships which had first been held in 1968, and is now held at Flushing Meadow, New York.

Most Wins

Margaret Evelyn du Pont (*née* Osborne) won a record 25 titles between 1936 and 1962. She won a record 13 women's doubles (12 with Althea Louise Brough), 9 mixed doubles and 3 singles. The men's record is 16 by William Tatem Tilden, including 7 men's singles, 1920–25, 1929—a record for singles shared with Richard Dudley Sears (1861–1943), 1881–87; William A Larned (1872–1926), 1901–02, 1907–11; and at women's singles by Molla Mallory (*née* Bjurstedt) (1892–1959), 1915–16, 1918, 1920–22, 1926 and Helen Moody (*née* Wills), 1923–25, 1927–29, 1931.

Youngest and Oldest

The youngest champion was Vincent Richards (1903–59) who was 15 years 139 days when he won the doubles with Bill Tilden in 1918. The youngest singles champion was Tracy Ann Austin (b Dec 12, 1962) who was 16 years 271 days when she won the women's singles in 1979.

The oldest champion was Margaret du Pont who won the mixed doubles at 42 years 166 days in 1960.

WHO IS NUMBER ONE? Ivan Lendl (above) was when 1988 began, but Stefan Edberg won Wimbledon, Mats Wilander won the US Open and Lendl won no major tournament. However, he was the man to beat for the title in every match. (David L Boehm/Tamron)

The oldest singles champion was William Larned at 38 years 242 days in 1911.

Fastest Service

The fastest service ever *measured* was one of 163.6 mph by William Tatem Tilden (1893–1953) (US) in 1931.

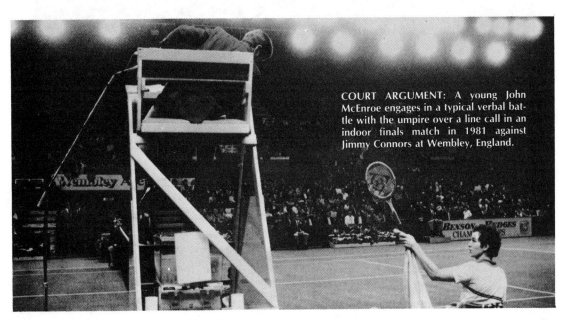

COURT ARGUMENT: A young John McEnroe engages in a typical verbal battle with the umpire over a line call in an indoor finals match in 1981 against Jimmy Connors at Wembley, England.

WIMBLEDON WINNERS: Both Chris Evert Lloyd (left) and Evonne Goolagong Cawley (right) came back with victories after interrupting their successful careers to better enjoy their marriages. Evonne beat Chris in the 1980 Wimbledon finals, but in the following year Chris won at Wimbledon. (Both photos by Leon Serchuk)

THE WINNING MOMENT: Billie Jean King (US) tosses her racket through the air because she just won the championship point from Chris Evert (US) in the 1975 women's singles finals at Wimbledon. The victory was her 19th at Wimbledon (6th in singles). King later won the 1979 doubles title, for her 20th victory, the most in Wimbledon's history.

A serve by Steve Denton (US) (b Sept 5, 1956) was timed at 138 mph at Beaver Creek, Colo on July 29, 1984, and is the record for fastest service timed with modern equipment.

Highest Earnings

Ivan Lendl won the largest single prize of $583,200 in the inaugural 3-day Skins Stakes in W Palm Beach, Fla in 1987, when he beat Pat Cash in the final.

The greatest reward for playing a single match is the $500,000 won by James Scott (Jimmy) Connors (US) (b Sept 2, 1952) when he beat John Newcombe (Australia) (b May 23, 1944) in a challenge match at Caesars Palace Hotel, Las Vegas, Nev, Apr 26, 1975.

The record for career earnings is held by Martina Navratilova, who won $14,058,199 through 1988. The men's record is $12,896,969 by Ivan Lendl through 1988, not including special contests such as the Skins Match (above).

The single season record for men is $2,028,850 by Ivan Lendl in 1982 (and including the Volvo Masters tournament held in January 1983). The women's record is $2,173,556 in 1984 (including a $1 million "Grand Slam" bonus) by Martina Navratilova in 1984.

$500,000 FOR A SINGLE MATCH: This, the greatest reward for one challenge match, was won by Jimmy Connors (right) over John Newcombe in Las Vegas, Nev, in Apr 1975. Connors is shown here playing at Stratton, Vt. (David L. Boehm)

Grand Prix Masters

The first WCT Masters Championships were staged in Tokyo, Japan in 1971 and have been held annually in NYC since 1977. Qualification to this annual event is by relative success in the preceding year's Grand Prix tournaments. John Patrick McEnroe (US) (b Feb 16, 1959) has won a record five titles, 1979, 1981, 1983–5.

Longest Game

The longest known singles game was one of 37 deuces (80 points) between Anthony Fawcett (Rhodesia) and Keith Glass (GB) in the first round of the Surrey championships at Surbiton, Surrey, England, on May 26, 1975. It lasted 31 min.

WIMBLEDON WINNER: Pat Cash, by conquering the #1 seed Ivan Lendl in 1987 in a hard-fought battle replete with volleying, became the first Australian to win the singles title in 16 years. (David L. Boehm)

A junior game lasted 52 min (9 deuces) between Noelle Van Lottum and Sandra Begijn in the semi-finals of the under-13 Dutch National Indoor Championships in Ede, Gelderland, Holland on Feb 12, 1984.

The longest rally in tournament play is one of 643 times over the net between Vicky Nelson and Jean Hepner at Richmond, Va in October 1984. The 6 hour 22 min match was won by Nelson 6–4, 7–6. It concluded with a 1 hour 47 min tiebreaker, 13–11, for which one point took 29 min.

The longest tiebreaker was the 26–24 for the fourth and decisive set of a first round men's doubles at the Wimbledon Championship on July 1, 1985. Jan Gunnarsson (Sweden) and Michael Morterven (Denmark) defeated John Frawley (Australia) and Victor Pecci (Paraguay) 6–3, 6–4, 3–6, 7–6.

Tennis Marathons

The longest recorded tennis singles match is one of 145 hours 44 min by Bobby McWaters and Ed VanTregt at the Kingston Plantation, Myrtle Beach, SC, Sept 25–Oct 1, 1988.

The duration record for doubles is 102 hours by Bobby McWaters, Jim Knapp, Jason Thomas and Ed VanTregt of Myrtle Beach High School, SC, Oct 25–29, 1987, at Kingston Plantation, SC. The organizer and coach was Bob Detwiler.

Davis Cup

The most wins in the Davis Cup (instituted 1900), the men's international team championship, have been (inclusive of 1982) by the US with 28.

Roy Emerson (b Nov 3, 1936) (Australia) played on 8 Cup-winning teams, 1959–62, 1964–67.

Nicola Pietrangeli (Italy) (b Sept 11, 1933) played a record 163 rubbers, 1954 to 1972, winning 120. He played 109 singles (winning 78) and 54 doubles (winning 42). He took part in 66 ties.

Wightman Cup

The most wins in the Wightman Cup, contested annually by women's teams from the US and GB (instituted 1923) have been 50 by the US and 10 by GB through 1988. Virginia Wade (b July 10, 1945) (GB) played in a record 21 ties and 56 rubbers between 1965 and 1985. Christine Evert (b Dec 21, 1954) (US) won all 26 of her singles matches, 1971–85. She was selected by the Women's Sports Foundation in 1985 as the "greatest American Woman Athlete of the last 25 years."

Federation Cup

The most wins in the Federation Cup (instituted 1963), the women's international team championship, is 12 (to 1986) by the US. Virginia Wade (GB) played each year from 1967 to 1983, in a record 57

FIVE-TIME DOUBLES WINNERS at Wimbledon: Rosemary Casals (jumping) and Billie Jean King (US) won in 5 of the 7 years 1967–73. (Leon Serchuk)

ties, playing 100 rubbers, including 56 singles (winning 36) and 44 doubles (winning 30). Christine Evert won her first 29 singles matches, 1977–86. Her overall record from 1977–87 is 35 wins in 37 singles and 15 wins in 19 doubles matches.

Tennis Olympics

Tennis was part of the Olympic program up until 1924 and it was also a demonstration sport at Mexico City in 1968 and LA in 1984. It was reinstated to the Games proper in 1988. The 1988 gold medal winners were:

MEN

Singles: Miloslav Mecir (Czech)
Doubles: Ken Flach, Robert Seguro (US)

WOMEN

Singles: Steffi Graf (W Ger)
Doubles: Pam Shriver, Zina Garrison (US)

TENNIS ON UNICYCLE: Manuel Vargas is the only man to have played 5 consecutive sets of respectable tennis without falling off the 24-inch unicycle. (UNIBALL®)

MILESTONE IN TRACK HISTORY: Breaking the 4-min mile was the outstanding achievement of 1954, and Roger Bannister (GB) was the man who set the record on May 6 of that year at 3:59.4 at Oxford.

(US) who jumped 7 ft 0½ in in June 1956. The breaking of the "4-minute barrier" in the one mile was first achieved by Dr Roger Gilbert Bannister (b Harrow, England, March 23, 1929), when he recorded 3 min 59.4 sec on the Iffley Road track, Oxford, at 6:10 p.m. on May 6, 1954. John Walker (NZ) became the first man to run the mile in less than 4 min 100 times by Feb 17, 1985, in Auckland, NZ. His time was 3:54.57.

Most Records

The greatest number of official world records (in events on the current schedule) broken by one athlete is 14, by Paavo Nurmi (Fin) at various events between 1921 and 1931, and by Iolanda Balas (Rom) in the high jump from 1956 to 1961. Nurmi also set eight marks in events no longer recognized, giving him a grand total of 22.

The only athlete to have his name entered in the record book 6 times in one day (in fact, within one hour) was J. C. "Jesse" Owens (US) (1913–80) who at Ann Arbor, Mich, on May 25, 1935, equaled the 100-yd running record with 9.4 sec at 3:15 p.m.;

TRACK AND FIELD

Earliest References

There is evidence that running was involved in early Egyptian rituals at Memphis c. 3800 BC, but usually track and field athletics date from the ancient Olympic Games. The earliest accurately known Olympiad dates from July 776 BC, at which celebration Coroibos won the foot race of 164–169 yd. The oldest surviving measurements are a long jump of 23 ft 1½ in by Chionis of Sparta c. 656 BC, and a discus throw of 100 cubits (c. 152 ft) by Protesilaus.

Earliest Landmarks

The first time 10 sec ("even time") was bettered for 100 yd under championship conditions was when John Owen, then 30 years old, recorded 9⅘ sec in the AAU Championships at Wash, DC, on Oct 11, 1890. The first recorded instance of 6 ft being cleared in the high jump was when Marshall Jones Brooks (1855–1944) jumped 6 ft 0⅛ in at Marston, near Oxford, England, on March 17, 1876. (He is reputed to have done much of his jumping while wearing a high hat.) The first man over 7 ft was Charlie Dumas

HISTORIC JUMP: Bob Beamon (US) is in midflight of his 29-foot-2½-inch long jump at the 1968 Olympics in Mexico City. The high altitude and a tail wind possibly helped Beamon shatter the record by 1 ft 9 in. The next best jump has been 28 feet 10¼ in by Carl Lewis in 1984.

WORLD-SHAKING SCANDAL: Ben Johnson (Canada) (far right) won the 100 m sprint pictured here in 9.83 sec, beating Carl Lewis (US) (center) in Rome. This still stands as a world record even though Johnson in the 1988 Olympics in Seoul bettered this mark to 9.79. However, the sports world suffered shock when it was revealed that Johnson was found to have used a banned substance, a steroid. He was disqualified, his world record disallowed and the gold medal awarded instead to Carl Lewis who finished second in 9.92 sec. (Claus Anderson)

4 GOLD MEDALS is the record that Carl Lewis (US) set in the 1984 Olympics, emulating Jesse Owens. Lewis is seen jumping 28 ft 0¼ in. (UPI)

long-jumped 26 ft 8¼ in at 3:25 p.m.; ran 220 yd (straight away) in 20.3 sec at 3:45 p.m.; and 220 yd over low hurdles in 22.6 sec at 4 p.m. The two 220-yd runs were ratified as 200-m world records.

Fastest Speed

The fastest speed recorded for a man was 26.95 mph and 22.5 mph for a woman. Analysis of each 10 m of the 100 m final at Seoul on Sept 24, 1988 (which Ben Johnson won but was later disqualified) shows that Johnson and Carl Lewis alongside each other had a peak 10 m interval of 0.83 sec at 26.95 mph.

Evelyn Ashford (US) in the 1984 sprint relay ran the final 100 m leg at a speed of 22.5 mph.

MOST RECORDS IN ONE DAY: Jesse Owens, rated by many as the greatest athlete of the 20th century, and top vote-getter in the inaugural election for the US Olympic Hall of Fame, not only won 4 Olympic golds in one Games (1936), but set 6 world records in one hour at Ann Arbor, Mich (3 to 4PM, May 25, 1935). Here he shows his starting style. (Photo Atlantic Richfield Co—ARCO Jesse Owens Games and Mary Evans)

LONGEST WINNING STREAK: Edwin Moses (US) was finally beaten in May 1987 in the 400 m hurdles after 9 years 281 days. He had won 122 consecutive times. Moses holds the record for the fastest time, 47.02 sec.

THE "FLYING FINN," Paavo Nurmi dominated distance running 1921–31, breaking 14 world records. (Right) Nurmi wins a special 3-mi race at LA Coliseum in 1925. (Wide World) (Left, below) Statue of the hero adorns the entrance to the Helsinki Stadium. (Finnish Tourist Assoc.) (Below, center) Nurmi crosses the finish line in England in a 4-mi invitational race with no competitors in sight. (Below, right) Nurmi has the honor of carrying the flame into the Helsinki Olympics in 1952. (AP wirephoto)

World Championships

The first-ever track and field world championships were staged at Helsinki, Finland, Aug 7–14, 1983. The most gold medals won was 3 by Carl Lewis (US) in the 100 m dash, long jump, and 4 × 100 m relay; and by Marita Koch (E Ger) in the 200 m dash, 4 × 100 m relay, and 4 × 400 m relay. With a silver medal in the 100 m dash, Koch was the top medal winner with 4.

In the 2nd world championships held in Rome in 1987, Lewis won gold medals at long jump and 4 × 100 m relay, also silver at 100 m, so he has won a record 5 gold at the two meets.

Most Olympic Gold Medals in Field and Track

The most Olympic gold medals won in field events is 10 individual medals by Ray C. Ewry (US) (1874–1937) with:

Standing High Jump	1900, 1904, 1906, 1908
Standing Long Jump	1900, 1904, 1906, 1908
Standing Triple Jump	1900, 1904

The most gold medals won by a woman is 4, a record shared by Francina E. Blankers-Koen (Netherlands) (b Apr 26, 1918) with 100 m, 200 m, 80 m hurdles and 4 × 100 m relay (1948); Betty Cuthbert (Australia) (b Apr 20, 1938) with 100 m, 200 m, 4 ×

ALL IN THE FAMILY: Sisters-in-law Jackie Joyner-Kersee (right, throwing the javelin) and Florence Griffith Joyner, both of US, set world records in the US Olympic Trials on the same day (July 16) in 1988. Jackie broke her own mark in the heptathlon, and Flo-Jo set hers in the 100-m dash. Then in the Olympics in Seoul, Korea, in Sept '88, Jackie set a new world mark of 7,291 points and an Olympic record in the long jump of 24 ft 3½ in, while Flo-Jo set a new world record in the 200 m of 21.34 sec and an Olympic record of 10.54 sec in the 100 m.(All Sport, left, and Focus on Sports)

100 m relay (1956) and 400 m (1964); and Barbel Wöckel (*née* Eckert) (b March 21, 1955) (E Germany) with 200 m and 4 × 100 m relay in 1976 and 1980.

The most gold medals at one Olympic celebration is 5 by Nurmi in 1924 and the most individual is 4 by Alvin C. Kraenzlein (US) (1876–1928) in 1900 with 60 m, 110 m hurdles, 200 m hurdles and long jump.

Most Olympic Medals in Track and Field

The most Olympic medals won in track is 12 (9 gold and 3 silver) by Paavo Johannes Nurmi (Finland) (1897–1973) with:

1920   Gold: 10,000 m; Cross-Country, Individual and Team; silver: 5,000 m.
1924   Gold: 1,500 m; 5,000 m; 3,000 m Team; Cross-Country, Individual and Team.
1928   Gold: 10,000 m; silver: 5,000 m; 3,000 m Steeplechase.

The most medals won by a woman athlete is 7 by Shirley de la Hunty (*née* Strickland) (b July 18, 1925)

(Australia) with 3 gold, 1 silver and 3 bronze in the 1948, 1952 and 1956 Games. A recently discovered photo finish indicates that she finished third, not fourth, in the 1948 200 m event, thus unofficially increasing her total to 8. Irena Szewinska (*née* Kirszenstein) of Poland has also won 7 medals (3 gold, 2 silver, 2 bronze) in 1964, 1968, 1972 and 1976. She is the only woman ever to win Olympic medals in track and field in 4 successive Games.

Oldest and Youngest Record Breakers

The greatest age at which anyone has broken a world track and field record is 41 years 196 days in the case of John J. Flanagan (1868–1938), who set a world record in the hammer throw on July 24, 1909. The female record is 36 years 139 days for Marina Stepanova (USSR) (*née* Makeyeva, b May 1, 1950) when she ran 400 m hurdles in 52.94 sec in Tashkent, USSR, Sept 17, 1986.

1988 OLYMPIC GOLD MEDAL WINNERS
WR = World Record   OR = Olympic Record

MEN

		hr min sec	
100 m	Carl Lewis (US)*	9.92	OR
200 m	Joe DeLoach (US)	19.75	
400 m	Steven Lewis (US)	43.87	
800 m	Paul Ereng (Kenya)	1:43.45	
1,500 m	Peter Rono (Kenya)	3:35.96	
5,000 m	John Ngugi (Kenya)	13:11.70	
10,000 m	Brahim Boutayeb (Morocco)	27:21.47	OR
Marathon	Gelindo Bordin (Italy)	2:10.32	
100 m Hurdles	Roger Kingdom (US)	12.98	OR
400 m Hurdles	Andre Phillips (US)	47.19	OR
3,000 m Steeplechase	Julius Kariuki (Kenya)	8:05.51	OR
400 m Relay	USSR	38.19	
	(Victor Bryzgine, Vladimir Krylov, Vladimir Mouraviev, Vitali Savine)		
1,600 m Relay	US	2:56.16 (tie)	WR
	(Danny Everett, Steve Lewis, Kevin Robinzine, Butch Reynolds)		
20 km Road Walk	Jozef Pribilinec (Czech)	1:19.57	OR
50 km Road Walk	Vyacheslav Ivanenko (USSR)	3:38.29	OR

		ft	in	
High Jump	Gennadiy Avdeyenko (USSR)	7	9½	OR
Pole Vault	Sergei Bubka (USSR)	19	4¼	OR
Long Jump	Carl Lewis (US)	28	7½	
Triple Jump	Kristo Markov (Bulgaria)	57	9¼	OR
Shot Put	Ulf Timmerman (E Ger)	73	8¾	OR
Discus	Jurgen Schult (E Ger)	225	9¼	OR
Hammer Throw	Sergei Litvinov (USSR)	278	2	OR
Javelin	Tapio Korjus (Finland)	276	6	OR
Decathlon	Christian Schenk (E Ger)	8,488 pts		

* Ben Johnson (Canada) won in 9.79 sec but was subsequently disqualified on a positive drugs test for steroids.

WOMEN

		hr min sec	
100 m	Florence Griffith Joyner (US)	10.54	OR
200 m	Florence Griffith Joyner (US)	21.34	WR
400 m	Olga Bryzgina (USSR)	48.65	OR
800 m	Sigrun Wodars (E Ger)	1:56.10	
1,500 m	Paula Ivan (Romania)	3:53.96	OR
3,000 m	Tatyana Samolenko (USSR)	8:26.53	OR
10,000 m	Olga Bondarenko (USSR)	31:05.21	OR
Marathon	Rosa Mota (Portugal)	2:25.40	
100 m Hurdles	Jordanka Donkova (Bulgaria)	12.38	OR
400 m Hurdles	Debra Flintoff-King (Australia)	53.17	OR
400 m Relay	US	41.98	
	(Alice Brown, Sheila Echols, Florence Griffith Joyner, Evelyn Ashford)		
1,600 m Relay	USSR	3:15.18	OR
	(Tatiana Ledovskaia, Olga Nazarova, Maria Piniguina, Olga Bryzguina)		

		ft	in	
High Jump	Louise Ritter (US)	6	8	OR
Long Jump	Jackie Joyner-Kersee (US)	24	3½	OR
Shot Put	Natalya Lisovskaya (USSR)	72	11½	
Discus	Martina Hellmann (E Ger)	237	2¼	OR
Javelin	Petra Felke (E Ger)	245	0	OR
Heptathlon	Jackie Joyner-Kersee (US)	7,291 pts		WR

WORLD TRACK AND FIELD RECORDS (MEN)

World Records for the men's events scheduled by the International Amateur Athletic Federation. Note: On July 27, 1976, IAAF eliminated all records for races measured in yards, except for the mile (for sentimental reasons). All distances up to (and including) 400 m must be electrically timed to be records. When a time is given to one-hundredth of a second, it represents the official electrically timed record.

A—These records were set at high altitudes—Mexico City 7,349 ft.

RUNNING

Event	min:sec	Name and Nationality	Place	Date
100 m	9.83	Ben Johnson (Canada)	Rome	Aug 30, 1987
200 m	19.72A	Pietro Mennea (Italy)	Mexico City	Sept 12, 1979
400 m	43.29	Harry Lee (Butch) Reynolds (US)	Zurich	Aug 17, 1988
800 m	1:41.73	Sebastian Coe (GB)	Florence, Italy	June 10, 1981
1,000 m	2:12.18	Sebastian Coe (GB)	Oslo	July 11, 1981
1,500 m	3:29.46	Said Aouita (Morocco)	W Berlin	Aug 23, 1985
1 mile	3:46.32	Steve Cram (GB)	Oslo	July 27, 1985
2,000 m	4:50.81	Said Aouita (Morocco)	Paris	July 16, 1987
3,000 m	7:32.1	Henry Rono (Kenya)	Oslo	June 27, 1978
5,000 m	12:58.39	Said Aouita (Morocco)	Rome	July 22, 1987
10,000 m	27:13.81	Fernando Mamede (Portugal)	Stockholm	July 2, 1984
20,000 m	57:24.2	Josephus Hermens (Neth)	Papendal, Neth	May 1, 1976
25,000 m	1 hr. 13:55.8	Toshihiko Seko (Japan)	Christchurch, NZ	Mar 22, 1981
30,000 m	1 hr. 29:18.8	Toshihiko Seko (Japan)	Christchurch, NZ	Mar 22, 1981
1 hour	13 miles 24 yd 2 ft	Josephus Hermens (Neth)	Papendal, Neth	May 1, 1976

FIELD EVENTS

Event	ft	in	Name and Nationality	Place	Date
High Jump	7	11¼	J.N.P. Sjoberg (Sweden)	Stockholm	June 30, 1987
Pole Vault	19	10½	Sergei Bubka (USSR)	Nice, France	July 10, 1988
Long Jump	29	2½A	Robert Beamon (US)	Mexico City	Oct 18, 1968
Triple Jump	58	11½	Willie Banks (US)	Indianapolis, Ind	June 16, 1985
Shot Put	75	8	Ulf Timmerman (E Ger)	Khania, Greece	May 22, 1988
Discus Throw	243	0	Jurgen Schult (E Ger)	Neubrandenburg, E Ger	June 6, 1986
Hammer Throw	284	7	Yuri Sedykh (USSR)	Stuttgart, W Ger	Aug 30, 1986
Javelin Throw*	343	10	Uwe Hohn (E Ger)	East Berlin	July 20, 1984

HURDLING

Event	min:sec	Name and Nationality	Place	Date
110 m (3'6")	12.93	Renaldo Nehemiah (US)	Zurich	Aug 19, 1981
400 m (3'0")	47.02	Edwin Corley Moses (US)	Coblenz, W Ger	Aug 31, 1983
3,000 m Steeplechase	8:05.4	Henry Rono (Kenya)	Seattle, Wash	May 13, 1978

RELAYS

Event	min:sec	Name and Nationality	Place	Date
4 × 100 m	37.83	US Team	Los Angeles	Aug 11, 1984
		(Sam Graddy, Ron Brown, Calvin Smith, Carl Lewis)		
4 × 200 m	1:20.26†	University of Southern California	Tempe, Ariz	May 27, 1978
		(Joel Andrews, James Sanford, William Mullins, Clancy Edwards)		
4 × 400 m	2:56.16A	US Olympic Team (Vincent Matthews, Ronald Freeman, G. Lawrence James, Lee Edward Evans).	Mexico City	Oct 20, 1968
		Tied by US National Team (Danny Everett, Steve Lewis, Kevin Robinzine, Harry Lee "Butch" Reynolds)	Seoul, S Korea	Sept, 1988
4 × 800 m	7:03.89	Great Britain Team	London	Aug 30, 1982
		(Peter Elliott, Garry Cook, Steve Cram, Sebastian Coe)		
4 × 1,500 m	14:38.8	W German Team	Cologne, W Ger	Aug 17, 1977
		(Thomas Wessinghage, Harald Hudak, Michael Lederer, Karl Fleschen)		

DECATHLON

8,847 points (1985 scoring)		Francis Morgan "Daley" Thompson (GB)	Los Angeles	Aug 8–9, 1984

* Old javelin—new javelin with center of gravity moved forward was introduced in 1986—record under new rules is 287 ft 7 in by Jan Zelezny (Czech) (b June 16, 1966) at Nitra, Czech, on May 31, 1987.
† Texas Christian Univ ran 1:20.20 in Philadelphia Apr 26, 1986, but the time could not be ratified.

WORLD TRACK AND FIELD RECORDS (WOMEN)

RUNNING

Event	min:sec	Name and Nationality	Place	Date
100 m	10.49	Florence Griffith Joyner (US)	Indianapolis, Ind	July 16, 1988
200 m	21.34	Florence Griffith Joyner (US)	Seoul, S Korea	Sept 29, 1988
400 m	47.60	Marita Koch (E Ger)	Canberra, Australia	Oct 6, 1985
800 m	1:53.28	Jarmila Kratochvilova (Czech)	Munich	July 26, 1983
1,000 m	2:30.6	Tanyana Providokhina (USSR)	Podolsk, USSR	Aug 20, 1978
1,500 m	3:52.47	Tatyana Kazankina (USSR)	Zurich, Switz	Aug 13, 1980
1 mile	4:16.71	Mary Decker Slaney (US)	Zurich, Switz	Aug 21, 1985
2,000 m	5:28.69	Maricica Puica (Romania)	London, Eng	July 11, 1986
3,000 m	8:22.62	Tatyana Kazankina (USSR)	Leningrad	Aug 26, 1984
5,000 m	14:37.33	Ingrid Kristiansen (Norway)	Stockholm, Sweden	Aug 5, 1986
10,000 m	30:13.74	Ingrid Kristiansen (Norway)	Oslo, Norway	July 5, 1986

FIELD EVENTS

Event	ft	in	Name and Nationality	Place	Date
High Jump	6	10¼	Stefka Kosadinova (Bulgaria)	Rome	Aug 30, 1987
Long Jump	24	8¼	Galina Christyakova (USSR)	Leningrad, USSR	June 11, 1988
Shot Put	74	3	Natalya Lisovskaya (USSR)	Moscow, USSR	June 7, 1987
Discus Throw	252		Gabriele Reinsch (E Ger)	Neubrandenberg, E Ger	July 9, 1988
Javelin Throw	262	5	Petra Felke (E Ger)	Potsdam, E Ger	Sept 9, 1988

HURDLES

Event	min:sec	Name and Nationality	Place	Date
100 m (2'9")	12.21	Jordanka Donkova (Bulgaria)	Stara Zagora, Bulgaria	Aug 20, 1988
400 m (2'6")	52.94	Marina Stepanova (USSR)	Tashkent, USSR	Sept 17, 1986

RELAYS

Event	min:sec	Name and Nationality	Place	Date
4 × 100 m	41.37	E Germany (Silke Gladisch, Sabine Rieger, Ingrid Auerswold, Marlies Göhr)	Canberra, Australia	Oct 6, 1985
4 × 200 m	1:28.15	E Germany (Marlies Göhr, Romy Müller, Barbel Wöckel, Marita Koch)	Jena, E Ger	Aug 10, 1980
4 × 400 m	3:15.18	USSR (Tatyana Ledovskaya, Olga Nazarova, Maria Piniguina, Olga Bryzguina)	Seoul, S Korea	Oct 1, 1988
4 × 800 m	7:50.17	USSR (Nadezha Olizarenko, Lyubov Gunina, Lyudmila Borisova, Irina Padyalovskaya)	Moscow, USSR	Aug 7, 1984

HEPTATHLON

			Place	Date
7,291 points		Jackie Joyner-Kersee (US)	Seoul, S Korea	Sept 24, 1988

COLLAPSING WITH VICTORY IN HER GRASP: In the Commonwealth Games in Edinburgh, Scotland, a New Zealand schoolteacher, Sylvia Potts, came within 4 yd of winning the gold and setting a record in a 1500 m race, but her stamina gave out, limbs aching, lungs bursting and eyes burning. (London Daily Express)

WORLD INDOOR TRACK AND FIELD RECORDS

MEN

RUNNING

Event	min : sec	Name and Nationality	Place	Date
50 m	5.55	Ben Johnson (Can)	Ottawa, Canada	Jan 31, 1987
60 m	6.41	Ben Johnson (Can)	Indianapolis, Ind	Mar 7, 1987
200 m	20.36	Bruno Marie-Rose (Fra)	Lievin, France	Feb 22, 1987
400 m	45.41	Thomas Schonlebe (E Ger)	Vienna, Austria	Feb 9, 1986
800 m	1:44.91	Sebastian Coe (GB)	Cosford, England	Mar 12, 1983
1,000 m	2:16.62	Robert Druppers (Neth)	The Hague, Neth	Feb 20, 1988
1,500 m	3:35.82	Jose-Luis Gonzalez (Spain)	Oviedo, Spain	Mar 1, 1986
Mile	3:49.78	Eamonn Coghlan (Ire)	E. Rutherford, NJ	Feb 27, 1983
3,000 m	7:39.2	Emiel Puttemans (Bel)	Berlin, W Ger	Feb 18, 1973
5,000 m	13:20.4	Suleiman Nyambui (Tanzania)	New York	Feb 6, 1986
5,000 walk	18:11.41	Roland Weigel (E Ger)	Vienna, Austria	Feb 13, 1988

FIELD EVENTS

Event	ft in	Name and Nationality	Place	Date
High Jump	7 11¼	Carlo Tharnhardt (W Ger)	Berlin, W Ger	Feb 26, 1988
Pole Vault	19 7	Sergei Bubka (USSR)	Turin, Italy	Mar 17, 1987
Long Jump	28 10¼	Carl Lewis (US)	New York	Feb 26, 1984
Triple Jump	58 3¼	Mike Conley (US)	New York	Feb 27, 1987
Shot Put	73 ½	Werner Gunthor (Switz)	Magglingen, Switz	Feb 8, 1987

HURDLING

Event	sec	Name and Nationality	Place	Date
50 m	6.25	Mark McKoy (Can)	Kobe, Japan	Mar 5, 1986
60 m	7.46	Greg Foster (US)	Indianapolis, Ind	Mar 6, 1987

RELAYS

Event	min : sec	Name and Nationality	Place	Date
4 × 200 m	1:22.32	Italy	Turin, Italy	Feb 11, 1984
4 × 400 m	3:05.9	Soviet Union	Vienna, Austria	Mar 14, 1970
4 × 800 m	7:17.8	Soviet Union	Sofia, Bulgaria	Mar 14, 1971

WOMEN

RUNNING

Event	min : sec	Name and Nationality	Place	Date
50 m	6.06	Angella Issajenko (Can)	Ottawa, Canada	Jan 31, 1987
60 m	7.00	Nellie Cooman (Hol)	Madrid, Spain	Feb 23, 1986
200 m	22.27	Heike Drechsler (E Ger)	Indianapolis, Ind	Mar 7, 1987
400 m	49.59	Jarmila Kratochvilova (Czech)	Milan, Italy	Mar 7, 1982
800 m	1:56.40	Christine Wachtel (E Ger)	Vienna, Austria	Feb 13, 1988
1,000 m	2:34.8	Brigitte Kraus (W Ger)	Dortmund, W Ger	Feb 19, 1978
1,500 m	4:00.8	Mary Slaney (US)	New York	Feb 8, 1980
Mile	4:18.86	Doina Melinte (Romania)	E Rutherford, NJ	Feb 13, 1988
3,000 m	8:39.79	Zola Budd (GB)	Cosford, England	Feb 8, 1986
5,000 m	15:25.04	Brenda Webb (US)	Gainesville, Fla	Jan 30, 1988
3,000 walk	12:05.49	Olga Krishtop (USSR)	Indianapolis, Ind	Mar 6, 1987

FIELD EVENTS

Event	ft in	Name and Nationality	Place	Date
High Jump	6 8¾	Stefka Kostadinova (Bul)	Indianapolis, Ind	Mar 8, 1987
Long Jump	24 ¼	Heike Drechsler (E Ger)	New York	Feb 27, 1987
Shot Put	73 10	Helena Fibingerova (Czech)	Jablonec, Czech	Feb 19, 1977

HURDLING

Event	sec	Name and Nationality	Place	Date
50 m	6.71	Cornelia Oschkenat (E Ger)	Berlin, E Ger	Feb 9, 1986
	6.71	Cornelia Oschkenat (E Ger)	Berlin, E Ger	Feb 24, 1987
60 m	7.74	Yordanka Donkova (Bul)	Sofia, Bulgaria	Feb 25, 1987

RELAYS

Event	min :sec	Name and Nationality	Place	Date
4 × 200 m	1:32.55	S. C. Eintracht Hamm (W Ger)	Dortmund, W Ger	Feb 18, 1988
4 × 400 m	3:34.38	West Germany	Dortmund, W Ger	Jan 30, 1981
4 × 800 m	8:24.72	Villanova (US)	Oklahoma City	Mar 14, 1987

OLYMPIC INCIDENT at Los Angeles in 1984 caused Mary Decker (US) (left) to fall down. She later ran the world best mile. Marita Koch (E Ger) (above, #552) holds the 400 m world sprint record. Here, she is running with the great Polish sprinter Irena Szewinska, winner of 7 Olympic medals.

The youngest individual record breaker is Wang Yang (b Apr 9, 1971) (China) who set a women's 3,000 m walk record in 21 min 33.8 sec at Jian, China on Mar 9, 1986, when aged 14 years 334 days. The male record is 17 years 198 days by Thomas Ray (1862–1904) when he pole-vaulted 11 ft 2¼ in on Sept 19, 1879.

Oldest and Youngest Olympic Champions

The oldest athlete to win an Olympic gold was Irish-born Patrick J. "Babe" McDonald (US) (1878–1954) who was aged 42 years 26 days when he won the 56-lb weight throw at Antwerp, Belgium on Aug 21, 1920. The oldest female champion was Lia Manoliu (Romania) (b Apr 25, 1932) aged 36 years

8-FEET HIGH is what Patrek Sjoberg of Sweden will try for next. Here he is leaping 7 ft 11¼ in off the ground in Stockholm on June 30, 1987. The style originated by Fosbury (US) in 1968 allows the jumper's center of gravity to pass beneath the bar as he drapes himself over it in midair.

FASTEST REACTIONS: Seen here in action are Romy Müller (E Ger) (left) and Wilbert Greaves (GB) who recorded the fastest apparent reaction times for sprinters at the 1980 Olympic Games, 0.120 sec in the women's 200-m semi-final and 0.124 sec in the 100-m hurdles heats respectively. (All-Sport)

176 days when she won the discus at Mexico City on Oct 18, 1968.

The oldest Olympic medalist was Tebbs Lloyd Johnson (1900–84), aged 48 years 115 days when he was third in the 1948 50,000 m walk. The oldest woman medalist was Dana Zatopkova aged 37 years 248 days when she was second in the javelin in 1960.

The youngest gold medalist was Barbara Pearl Jones (US) (b March 26, 1937) who was a member of the winning 4 × 100 m relay team, aged 15 years 123 days, at Helsinki, Finland, on July 27, 1952. The youngest male champion was Robert Bruce Mathias (US) (b Nov 17, 1930) aged 17 years 263 days when he won the decathlon at London, Aug 5–6, 1948.

Running Backwards

The fastest time recorded for running 100 yd backwards is 12.8 sec by Ferdie Adoboe (Kenya, now US) in Amherst, Mass, on July 28, 1983.

Yves Pol (France) ran 5 kilometers (3.1 mi) backwards in a record time of 22 min 33 sec on Sept 11, 1988 in NYC, beating the record claimed by Rob Cooper of Toronto, Ohio, of 37 min 16 sec. Pol was advised by policemen enroute that he was running the wrong way. Pol also set a record for running the marathon distance of 26 mi 386 yd backwards in 3 hours 57 min 57 sec in France on Aug 30, 1987 in front of 60 spectators. This was faster than the time recorded by Anthony "Scott" Weiland, 27, who ran the Detroit Marathon backwards in 1982.

Donald Davis (b Feb 10, 1960) (US) ran 1 mi backwards in 6 min 7.1 sec at the University of Hawaii on Feb 21, 1983.

Arvind Pandya (India) ran LA–NY in 107 days, Aug 18–Dec 3, 1984.

Standing Long Jump

Joe Darby (1861–1937), the famous Victorian professional jumper from Dudley, Worcestershire, England, jumped a measured 12 ft 1½ in *without* weights at Dudley Castle, on May 28, 1890. Arne Tverrvaag (Norway) jumped 12 ft 2¼ in in 1968. The best long jump by a woman is 9 ft 7 in by Annelin Mannes (Norway) at Flisa, Norway Mar 7, 1981.

Longest Winning Sequence

Iolanda Balas (Romania) (b Dec 12, 1936) won 140 successive high jump competitions from 1956 to

DECATHLON CHAMPION: (Left) Although he was beaten in the 1988 Olympics in the shot put, Daley Thompson (GB) still holds a world record total of 8,847 points set in the 1984 Olympic Games in LA.

POLE-VAULT RECORDHOLDER: (Above, right) Sergei Bubka (USSR) has broken the world record 9 times. His 19 ft 10½ in leap was made July 10, 1988.

RUNNER/HURDLER RECORDHOLDER: Henry Rono (Kenya) set 4 distance world records between Apr 8 and June 27, 1978—at 3,000m, 5,000m, 10,000m and 3,000m hurdle steeplechase—and two of the marks still stand. (Assoc Sports Photography)

1967. The record for track races is 122 at 400-meter hurdles by Edwin Corley Moses (US) (b July 31, 1955) from 1977 to his defeat by Danny Harris (US) (b Sept 7, 1965) in Madrid on June 4, 1987.

Longest Race

The longest races ever staged were the 1928 (3,422 miles) and 1929 (3,665 miles) transcontinental races from NYC to Los Angeles. The Finnish-born Johnny Salo (1893–1931) was the winner in 1929 in 79 days, from March 31 to June 18. His elapsed time of 525 hours 57 min 20 sec gave a running average of 6.97 mph. His margin of victory was only 2 min 47 sec.

Three-Legged Race

The fastest recorded time for a 100-yd three-legged race is 11.0 sec by Olympic medalists Harry L. Hillman (1881–1945) and Lawson Robertson (1883–1951) in Brooklyn, NYC, on Apr 24, 1909.

RUNNING BACKWARDS: Donald Davis, winner of the 1-mile reverse race in 6 min 7.1 sec, shows how he does it.

24-Hour Record

The greatest distance run on a standard track in 24 hours is 170 miles 974 yd by Dave Dowdle (b Nov 7, 1954) (Gloucester AC) at Blackbridge, Gloucester, England, May 22–23, 1982. The best by a woman is 133 miles 939 yd by Lynn Fitzgerald (b Sept 9, 1947) (Highgate Harriers) in the same race.

GREATEST DISTANCE run in one year is 15,472 mi by Tina Maria Stone (left) who was born in Italy, but is now running in Irvine, Calif. RAN AROUND US: Sarah Fulcher, in a continuous solo run, covered 35 states July–Oct 1988 after running 2,000 mi across Australia previously.

WORLD'S FASTEST HUMAN at 200 meters: Pietro Mennea (Italy) has held the record of 19.72 sec since 1979 when he won in the high-altitude air of Mexico City.

OLDEST RACE RECORD: The 3-legged race record of 100 yards in 11 seconds was set 79 years ago by Harry Hillman (left) and Lawson Robertson (right), both Olympic medalists in 1904.

YOUNGEST OLYMPIC MALE GOLD MEDALIST: Bob Mathias (US) was only 17 years 263 days when he first won the decathlon in London, Aug 5–6, 1948.

TRIPLE JUMPING has never been as popular as today. A major reason is the ebullient enthusiasm and popularity of Willie Banks (left) (US), who holds the world record. LONG DISTANCE RUNNER Said Aouita (right) (Morocco) is the first person in 30 years to hold concurrent world records at 1,500, 2,000, and 5,000 m. (All-Sport)

Mass Relay Record

The record for 100 miles by 100 runners belonging to one club is 7 hours 53 min 52.1 sec by Baltimore Road Runners Club of Towson, Md, on May 17, 1981. The women's mark is 10 hours 47 min 9.3 sec by a team from the San Francisco Dolphins Southend Running Club, on Apr 3, 1977.

The longest relay ever run was 10,524 mi by 2,660 runners at Trondheim, Norway, Aug 26–Oct 20, 1985. Twenty members of the Melbourne Fire Brigade ran around Australia on Highway No. 1 in 43 days 23 hours 58 min, July 10–Aug 23, 1983. The most participants is 4,800 (192 teams of 25), in the Batavierenrace, 103.89 mi from Nijmegen to Enschede, The Netherlands, won in 9 hours 30 min 44 sec on Apr 23, 1983.

Six-Day Race

The greatest distance covered by a man in six days (i.e. the 144 permissible hours between Sundays in Victorian times) was 635 miles 1,385 yards by Yiannis Kouros (Greece) (b Feb 13, 1956) at Colac, Australia on Nov 26–Dec 1, 1984. On the same occasion Eleanor Adams (UK) (b Nov 20, 1947) set the women's record at 500 mi 1,452 yds.

GOLD MEDALISTS: Fanny Blankers-Koen (Neth) (left) and Betty Cuthbert (Aust) (far right) share, with Barbel Wöckel (below) (E Ger), the women's record for most Olympic gold medals with 4 apiece. Blankers-Koen was 30 years old with 2 children when she captured her 4 golds, all in the 1948 Games. Cuthbert won 3 golds in 1956 and picked up her fourth 8 years later.

MILERS: Between them, Britishers Steve Ovett (left) and Sebastian Coe (right, #9) set 5 records for the mile run, including an amazing flurry of 3 records in 10 days during August, 1981. In their 1980 Olympic gold-medal runs, Ovett beat recordholder Coe at 800 meters before Coe beat recordholder Ovett at 1,500 meters. In 1984, Coe won the gold at 1,500 m and the silver at 800 m. Coe still holds the 800m indoor record.

ROAD RUNNER: (Right) Abebe Bikila (Ethiopia) won the 1961 Kosice Marathon in Czechoslovakia. Bikila is the only man to successfully defend the Olympic Marathon title, winning the gold medal in 1960 and 1964. DISTANCE WORLD RECORD HOLDER: (Below) Jos Hermens (Neth), No. 5, ran the fastest time for 20,000 m and the farthest distance for one hour in 1976, and the records still stand.

244-LB SHOT PUT CHAMP: Center of attention was Tamara Andreyevna (Fatty) Tyshkyevich (USSR), the gold medal winner in the 1956 Olympics.

ONE-LEGGED HIGH JUMPER: Arnie Boldt of Canada (below) leaped 6 ft 8¼ in (2.04 m) high in Rome Apr 3, 1981, proving that he is not greatly handicapped.

Pancake Race Record

The annual "Housewives" Pancake Race at Olney, Buckinghamshire, England, was first mentioned in 1445. The record for the winding 415-yd course (three tosses mandatory) is 61.0 sec, set by Sally Ann Faulkner, 16, on Feb 26, 1974. The record for the counterpart race at Liberal, Kansas, is 58.5 sec by Sheila Turner (b July 9, 1953) in 1975.

Dale R. Lyons (b Feb 26, 1937) (GB) has run several marathons during which he tosses a 2-oz pancake repeatedly en route in a 1½ lb pan. His fastest time is 3 hours 6 min 48 sec in London, Apr 20, 1986.

THREE WORLD RECORDS IN 20 DAYS: Steve Cram (GB) set a new record in running 1500 m on July 16, 1985 (3:29.67), in the mile run on July 27 (3:46.32), and 2000 m race on Aug 4 (4:51.39). On Aug 10 he came in with the world's second best time in 1000 m, against a head wind. Shown here, he exults over his victory in the mile. He set a better mark in the 1500 m in 1985. (IAFF Mobil Grand Prix)

DOUBLE WINNER: Valerie Briscoe-Hooks (US) won the 200 m and 400 m races in 1984, setting Olympic records in both events.

FOSBURY FLOPS: This high jump style was originated in 1968 by Dick Fosbury (US) who set the high jump record at 7 ft 4¼ in going over the bar backwards.

Fastest 100 Miles

The fastest recorded time for 100 miles is 11 hours 30 min 51 sec by Donald Ritchie (b July 6, 1944) at Crystal Palace, London, on Oct 15, 1977. The best by a woman is 15 hours 24 min 46 sec by Eleanor Adams (GB) (b Nov 20, 1947) at Honefoss, Norway, July 12–13, 1986.

Blind 100 Meters

The fastest time recorded for 100 m by a blind man is 11.4 sec by Graham Henry Salmon (b Sept 5, 1952) of Loughton, Essex, England, at Grangemouth, Scotland, on Sept 2, 1978.

Fastest 100 Kilometers

Donald Ritchie ran 100 km in a record 6 hours 10 min 20 sec at Crystal Palace, London, on Oct 28,

5,000-METER WORLD RECORDHOLDER, Zola Budd (GB), wearing number 007, heads the field in a cross-country race. A native of South Africa, she is no longer eligible to run for Great Britain.

1978. The women's best, run on the road, is 7 hours 27 min 22 sec by Chantal Langlace (b Jan 6, 1955) (France) at Amiens, France on Sept 6, 1980.

Trans-America Run

The fastest time for the cross-US run is 46 days, 8 hours 36 min by Frank Giannino Jr (b 1952) (US) for the 3,100 miles from San Francisco to NYC, Sept 1–Oct 17, 1980.

When Johnny Salo won the 1929 Trans-America race from NYC to LA, his total elapsed time of 525 hours 57 min 20 sec gave him a margin of only 2 min 47 sec over second-place Peter Gavuzzi—after 3,665 miles.

The women's Trans-America record is 69 days 2 hours 40 min by Mavis Hutchinson (South Africa) (b Nov 25, 1924) Mar 12–May 21, 1978.

Sarah Fulcher of Irvine, Calif, ran 11,134 mi

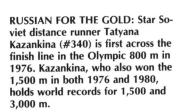

RUSSIAN FOR THE GOLD: Star Soviet distance runner Tatyana Kazankina (#340) is first across the finish line in the Olympic 800 m in 1976. Kazankina, who also won the 1,500 m in both 1976 and 1980, holds world records for 1,500 and 3,000 m.

IN THIN AIR: Helped by the lower air resistance at the US Air Force Academy's high elevation in Colorado Springs, Calvin Smith (far right) broke the world record for the 100-meter dash that Jim Hines had set 15 years earlier under similar conditions in 1968 in the thin air of Mexico City. His mark remains unbeaten. (AP)

around 35 states of the US in a continuous solo run, July 21-Oct 2, 1988. She previously ran 2,000 mi across Australia.

Trans-Canada Run

The only woman to have run across Canada from Victoria, BC, to Halifax, Nova Scotia, a distance of 3,824 mi in 6½ months, touching all 10 provinces, is Kanchan Beryl Stott of Ottawa, Ont. It was probably the longest run ever made by a woman.

Greatest Mileage

Douglas Alistair Gordon Pirie (b Feb 10, 1931) (GB), who set 5 world records in the 1950s, estimated that he had run a total distance of 216,000 miles in 40 years to 1981.

The greatest distance run in one year is 15,472 miles by Tina Maria Stone (b Naples, Italy, Apr 5, 1934) of Irvine, Calif, in 1983.

Ron Grant (Aust) (b Feb 15, 1943) ran around Australia, 8,316 miles in 217 days 3 hours 45 min, running every day Mar 28–Oct 31, 1983.

Ernst Mensen (1799–1846) (Norway), a former seaman in the British Navy, is reputed to have run from Istanbul, Turkey, to Calcutta, in West Bengal, India, and back in 59 days in 1836, so averaging an improbable 92.4 miles per day.

Max Telford (b Hawick, Scotland, Feb 2, 1935) of New Zealand ran 5,110 miles from Anchorage, Alaska, to Halifax, Nova Scotia, in 106 days 18 hours 45 min from July 25 to Nov 9, 1977.

The greatest non-stop run recorded is 352.9 miles in 121 hours 54 min by Bertil Järlåker (Sweden) at Norrköping, Sweden, May 26–31, 1980. He was moving 95.04% of the time.

Standing High Jump

The best high jump from a standing (as opposed to a running) position is 6 ft 2¾ in by Rune Almen (b Oct 20, 1952) (Sweden) at Karlstad, Sweden, on May 30, 1980. The best jump by a woman is 4 ft 11 in by Grete Bjørdalsbakke (b June 23, 1960) (Norway) at Orsta, Norway on Dec 12, 1979.

TRAMPOLINING

Origins

The *sport* of trampolining (from the Spanish word *trampolin*, a springboard) dates from 1936, when the prototype "T" model trampoline was developed by George Nissen (US) in a garage in Cedar Rapids, Iowa. Trampolines were used in show business at least as early as "The Walloons" of the period 1910–12.

World Championships

Instituted in 1964 and since 1968 held biennially:

	Men	Women
1964	Danny Millman (US)	Judy Wills (US)
1965	Gary Irwin (US)	Judy Wills (US)
1966	Wayne Miller (US)	Judy Wills (US)
1967	Dave Jacobs (US)	Judy Wills (US)
1968	Dave Jacobs (US)	Judy Wills (US)
1970	Wayne Miller (US)	Renee Ransom (US)
1972	Paul Luxon (GB)	Alexandra Nicholson (US)
1974	Richard Tisson (Fra)	Alexandra Nicholson (US)
1976	Richard Tisson (Fra)	
	Evgeni Janes (USSR)	Svetlana Levina (USSR)
1978	Evgeni Janes (USSR)	Tatyana Anisimova (USSR)
1980	Stewart Matthews (GB)	Ruth Keller (Switz)
1982	Carl Furrer (GB)	Ruth Keller (Switz)
1984	Lionel Pioline (Fra)	Sue Shotton (GB)
1986	Lionel Pioline (Fra)	Tatyana Luschina (USSR)
1988	Vadim Krasnocaptcha (USSR)	Khoteria Roussoudan (USSR)

Coaching Record

Jeff Hennessy of Lafayette, La, has coached more world champions in trampoline, synchro trampoline, and double mini-trampoline than anyone else.

DOUBLE WINNER INDOORS AND OUT: Heike Drechsler (E Ger) (b Dec 16, 1964) set two indoor world records—running and jumping—in 1987. In the inaugural World Indoor Championships in Indianapolis in the 200-m sprint she set a record of 22.27 sec to go along with her 21.71 sec outdoors world record. In the long jump indoors only a week before, she had jumped 24 ft ¼ in after twice setting an outdoor world jump record of 24 ft 5½ in in 1986. She still holds the indoor records. (Tony Duffy/All-Sport)

Stunts

Septuple twisting back somersault to bed and quintuple twisting back somersault to shoulders were made by Marco Canestrelli to Belmonte Canestrelli at Madison Square Garden, NYC, on Jan 5 and Mar 28, 1979.

Richard Tisson performed a triple twisting triple back somersault for a Guinness TV program near Berchtesgaden, W Germany on June 30, 1981. The first person to perform this was Stuart Ransom of Memphis, Tenn, in 1977 in Lafayette, La.

Richard Cobbing of Gateshead, Eng performed 1,610 consecutive somersaults at Gateshead July 22, 1984. Zoe Finn completed 73 somersaults in 1 min on Nov 21, 1986 at Chatham, Kent, Eng.

TWIST AND TURN: On the shores of the Konigsee, W Germany, Richard Tisson, a 2-time world champion, set a record by landing on his feet after performing a triple back somersault with 3 full twists. The Guinness TV cameras caught the action in 1981.

TRAMPOLINING LEAP: Marco Canestrelli imitates Superman flying through the air over the backs of 4 elephants in the Ringling Bros and Barnum & Bailey Circus.

Marathon Record

The longest recorded trampoline bouncing marathon is one of 1,272 hours (exactly 53 days) on a 13½-ft circular trampoline by 6 members of Tau Kappa Epsilon fraternity, jumping in relays, at the Cleveland State Univ gym, Cleveland, O, Jan 6–Feb 28, 1986. Their names: Nathaniel Cross, Mike Carl, Robert Andrew, Tony Vetturini, Rob Onacila and Ron Trebec.

The solo record is 266 hours 9 min by Jeff Schwartz, 19, at Glenview, Ill, Aug 14–25, 1981.

TRIATHLON

A new type of competition, the Triathlon, began in Feb 1978 in Hawaii when two Navy men challenged each other to a particularly strenuous test of all the major muscles of the body in strength and endurance: a swim of 2.4 miles in the ocean, followed immediately by a 112-mile bike race, and then a full marathon run of 26 miles 385 yd, with no time-outs.

They were joined by 13 others in the first two

1,300 SWIMMERS, representing 40 countries and 49 states, dash into the water for the start of the 1987 Bud Light Ironman Triathlon World Championship, Oct 10 in Kona, Hawaii. This grueling event requires a 2.4-mi ocean swim, followed by a 112-mi bike run and 26.2-mi marathon run to the finish line.

WINNING THE 1988 BUD LIGHT IRONMAN TRIATHLON in Hawaii in the second fastest time was taken coolly by Scott Molina (left) 28, of Boulder, Colo, but for Paula Newby-Frazer, 26, of Zimbabwe (right) it was reason to jump for joy as she finished in record time for a woman, more than 34 min faster than the previous mark.

Triathlons in Feb 1978 and Feb 1979. Then, in 1980 ABC on its ''Wide World of Sports'' began televising what began to be called the Ironman Triathlon and 108 competed. Now there are hundreds of triathlons —but not all are Ironman Triathlons. The ''tinman'' races cut the distances in half or less.

In the Bud Light Ironman Triathlon in Oct 1988, Scott Molina, 28, of Boulder, Colo, captured the championship in a time of 8:31:00—the second-fastest time in the history of the event. Six-time champion Dave Scott holds the course record of 8:28:37, set in 1986.

For the third consecutive year, the women's record was shattered in 1988. Paula Newby-Fraser of Zimbabwe (who now lives in Encinitas, Calif) established a new standard with a time of 9:01:01. She finished 11th overall in the event—the highest finish by a woman ever. Her record time shattered by more than 34 minutes the old mark of 9:35:14 set in 1987 by Erin Baker, of Christchurch, NZ. Baker finished second in the 1988 event.

A total of 1,275 triathletes—representing 48 states and 39 countries—participated in the event. By the 17-hour course closure deadline, 1,189 athletes had crossed the finish line.

In a triathlon of the same distances as the Ironman,

held at Roth, W Germany on July 30, 1988, the men's best was 8 hours 13 min 11 sec by Axel Koenders (The Netherlands). In the 1986 European Championships at Sofia, Bulgaria, a women's record of 9 hours 27 min 36 sec was set by Erin Baker (NZ) (b May 23, 1961).

The largest field in a triathlon of any kind has been 2,362 finishers in the US Triathlon (swim 1500 m, bike 40 km and run 10 km) in Chicago in 1986.

Oldest to Finish

F. Norton Davey of Playa Del Rey, Calif, by age 69, completed five Ironman Triathlons—1982–86—finishing in 1985 in 14 hours 51 min 37 sec.

VOLLEYBALL

Origins

The game was invented as Mintonette in 1895 by William G. Morgan at the YMCA gymnasium at Holyoke, Mass. The International Volleyball Asso-

ciation was formed in Paris in Apr 1947. The ball travels at a speed of up to 70 mph when smashed over the net, which stands 7 ft 11½ in high. In the women's game it is 7 ft 4¼ in high.

World Titles

World Championships were instituted in 1949 for men and 1952 for women. The USSR has won 6 men's titles (1949, 52, 60, 62, 78, and 82). The USSR won the women's championship in 1952, 56, 60 and 70. The record crowd is 90,000 for the 1983 world title matches in Brazil. The US won for the first time in 1986, following victory in the 1984 Olympics. China won the 1986 women's championship.

Most Olympic Medals

In the 1988 Olympics the US won the gold medal in the men's game, and the USSR won in the women's.

The sport was introduced to the Olympic Games for both men and women in 1964. The only volleyball player to win four medals is Inna Ryskal (USSR) (b

ONE-MAN VOLLEYBALL TEAM: (Below) Bob Schaffer of Newark, NJ (see inset) has won over 1,000 games with only 2 losses against 6-man teams.

VOLLEYBALL MARATHON RECORD of 100 hours 3 min was set by these two teams of high school students from Denver, Colo.

June 15, 1944), who won silver medals in 1964 and 76 and golds in 1968 and 72.

The record for medals for men is held jointly by Yuriy Poyarkov (USSR), who won gold medals in 1964 and 68, and a bronze in 1972, and Katsutoshi Nekoda (Japan) (b Feb 1, 1944) who won a gold in 1972, a silver in 1968, and a bronze in 1964.

Collegiate Championships

Since NCAA began sponsoring volleyball, only 4 men's teams have ever won a title. Pepperdine is the (1987) current champion, the other winners being UCLA, San Diego State and Southern Calif. Only twice have schools outside Calif reached the finals: Ohio State in 1977 and Penn State in 1982. UCLA has won more matches than any other college with a record 34 wins and 3 defeats for a .919 percentage.

In the women's division, the Univ of Hawaii has won 3 of the 7 championships: in 1982, 83 and 87.

Marathon

The longest recorded volleyball marathon by two teams of six is 118 hours 30 min by students of Krugersdorf High School, South Africa, Mar 30–Apr 4, 1988.

WALKING

Longest Race

The Paris-Colmar event (until 1980 it was the Strasbourg-Paris event, instituted in 1926 in the reverse direction), now 322 miles, is the world's longest annual walk event. Gilbert Roger (France) has won 6 times (1949, 53–54, 56–58). The fastest performance is by Robert Pietquin (b 1938) (Belgium) who walked 315 miles in the 1980 race in 60 hours 1 min 10 sec (deducting 4 hours of compulsory stops), averaging 5.25 mph. The first woman to complete the race was Annie van den Meer (Neth) (b Feb 24, 1947) who was 10th in 1983 in 82 hours 10 min.

Dumitru Dan (1890–1978) of Romania was the only man out of 200 entrants to succeed in walking 100,000 km (62,137 miles), in a contest organized by the Touring Club de France on Apr 1, 1910. By March 24, 1916, he had covered 96,000 km (59,651 miles), averaging 27.24 miles per day.

Longest Non-Stop Walk

Georges Holtyzer (Belgium) walked 418.49 mi in 6 days 10 hours 58 min at Ninove, Belgium, July 19–27, 1986, making 452 laps of a 1.49 km circuit. He was not permitted any stops for rest and was moving 98.78 percent of the time.

WALKING ACROSS AMERICA: John Lees (Eng) walked the 2,876 miles from LA to NYC in 53½ days in 1972. Lees' time was faster than the then-standing trans-America running record.

Walking Across the Americas, S-N

George Meegen (GB) (b Dec 2, 1952) walked 19,019 mi from Ushuaia, Argentina, at the southern tip of S America to Prudhoe Bay in northern Alaska, taking 2,426 days from Jan 26, 1977 to Sept 18, 1983, and thus completed the longest continuous walk, and the first south-north transverse of the Western Hemisphere.

Walking Around the World

The first person reported to have "walked around the world" is George M. Schilling (US), Aug 3, 1897–1904, but the first verified achievement was by David Kunst (b 1939), who started with his brother John from Waseca, Minn, on June 20, 1970. John

WALK AROUND THE EARTH (below): David Kunst (left) with his brother Pete passing the National Assembly Building in Islamabad, Pakistan, with their 200-year-old Turkish wagon and their Portuguese mule, Willie-Make-It II.

WALK ACROSS THE AMERICAS: Starting from southern Argentina, George Meegan (GB) (b Oct 2, 1952) walked 19,019 mi before planting this British flag at Prudhoe Bay, northern Alaska. He took from Jan 26, 1977 to Sept 18, 1983 for the first complete on-foot transverse south to north of the Western Hemisphere.

was killed in 1972 by Afghan bandits who thought they were carrying UNICEF funds they were soliciting. David was wounded, so another brother, Pete, joined him. David arrived home, after walking 14,500 miles, on Oct 5, 1974.

Tomas Carlos Pereira (b Argentina, Nov 16, 1942) spent 10 years, Apr 6, 1968, through Apr 8, 1978, walking 29,825 miles around all 5 continents.

John Lees, 27, of Brighton, England, Apr 11–June 3, 1972, walked 2,876 miles across the US from City Hall, Los Angeles, to City Hall, NYC, in 53 days 12 hours 15 min (53.746 miles per day).

Sean Eugene Maguire (b Sept 15, 1956) (US) walked 7,327 miles from the Yukon River, north of Livengood, Alaska, to Key West, Fla, in 307 days, from June 6, 1978 to Apr 9, 1979.

The record for the trans-Canada (Halifax to Vancouver) walk of 3,764 miles is 96 days by Clyde McRae, 23, from May 1 to Aug 4, 1973.

Road Walking Records

It should be noted that the severity of road race courses and the accuracy of their measurement may vary, sometimes making comparisons of times unreliable.

MEN

20 km in 1 hour 19 min 8 sec, Mikhail Shchennikov (USSR) (b Dec 24, 1967) at Kiev, USSR, July 30, 1988.

30 km in 2 hours 3 min 6 sec, Daniel Bautista (Mexico) (b Aug 4, 1952) at Cherkassy, USSR on Apr 27, 1980.

50 km in 3 hours 38 min 17 sec, Ronald Weigel (E Ger) (b Aug 8, 1950) at Potsdam, E Ger on May 25, 1986.

WOMEN

10 km in 42:14.2 by Kerry Ann Saxby (Australia) (unofficial as this was in a mixed race). Official record is 43:36.41 by Yelena Nikolayeva (USSR) (b Feb 1, 1966) at Kiev, USSR, July 30, 1988.

20 km in 1 hour 29 min 40 sec, Kerry Ann Saxby (Australia) (b June 2, 1961) at Varnamo, Sweden, May 13, 1988.

50 km in 5 hours 01 min 52 sec, Lillian Millen (GB) (b Mar 5, 1945) at York, Eng on Apr 16, 1983.

Longest in 24 Hours

The greatest distance walked in 24 hours is 140 mi, 1,229 yd by Paul Forthomme (Belgium), on a road

30 KM RECORDHOLDER (left): Daniel Bautista of Mexico (b 1952) has the road walking world record, set in Russia in 1980. He has also won the 20,000 m walk in the 1976 Olympics in Montreal.

course at Woluwé, Belgium Oct 13–14, 1984. The best by a woman is 125.7 miles by Annie van den Meer (Netherlands) at Rouen, France, Apr 30–May 1, 1984, over a 1.185-km-lap road course.

Most Olympic Medals

Walking races have been included in the Olympic schedule since 1906, but walking matches have been known since 1589. The only walker to win 3 gold medals has been Ugo Frigerio (Italy) (1901–68) with the 3,000 m and 10,000 m in 1920 and the 10,000 m in 1920 and 1924. He also holds the record of most medals with 4 (having additionally won the bronze medal in the 50,000 m in 1932), a total shared with Vladimir Golubnichiy (USSR) (b June 2, 1936), who won gold medals for the 20,000 m in 1960 and 1968, the silver in 1972 and the bronze in 1964.

In the 1988 Olympics, Vyacheslav Ivanenko (USSR) won the 50 km walk in 3 hours 38 min 29 sec to set a new world record. Another world record was set at 20 km by Josef Prebilinec (Czech) at 1 hour 19 min 57 sec.

WALKING THE DOG (below): When Sean Maguire says he's taking his dog "Sweden" for a walk, he means it. They set out from the Yukon River, Alaska, and arrived at their destination (Key West, Fla) 10 months and 7,327 miles later.

WALKED 100,000 KM IN 6 YEARS: Dumitru Dan (Romania). WALKED BACKWARDS Calif to Turkey, 8,000 mi in a year: Plennie Wingo (US) carried a mirror in his cane.

Walking Backwards

The greatest exponent of reverse pedestrianism has been Plennie L. Wingo (b Jan 24, 1895) then of Abilene, Tex, who started on his 8,000-mile transcontinental walk on Apr 15, 1931, from Santa Monica, Calif, to Istanbul, Turkey, and arrived on Oct 24, 1932. He celebrated the walk's 45th anniversary by covering the 452 miles from Santa Monica to San Francisco, Calif, backwards, in 85 days, aged 81 years.

The longest distance recorded for walking backwards in 24 hours is 84 mi by Anthony Thornton in Minneapolis, Dec 31, 1985–Jan 1, 1986.

In the quarter-mile Metro Retro race held in Detroit in 1986, Larry Farmer, 26, set a record of 1:16.08.

Most Titles

Four-time Olympian Ronald Owen Laird (b May 31, 1938) of the NYAC, won a total of 65 US National titles from 1958 to 1976, plus 4 Canadian championships.

WATER POLO

Origins

Water polo was developed in England as "Water Soccer" in 1869 and was first included in the Olympic Games in Paris in 1900. The US was introduced to the sport in 1898 but development was slow until after World War II. However, prior to that time the US won three Olympic medals. Since 1946 the popularity of water polo has grown rapidly, especially in California. Women's water polo has never been included in the Olympic program.

Major water polo events include the FINA Cup held every other year, World University Games held every two years for collegiates; Tungsram Cup in Budapest, Hungary, biannually; US Olympic Festival, annually except for the Olympic year; Pan American Games, the Olympics and World Championships every fourth year.

SLAM DUNK: Hungary's Gyorgy Karpati (#7) is one of the 5 players who have won 3 Olympic gold medals in water polo.

Olympic Victories

Yugoslavia won the gold medal in 1984 and 1988.

Hungary has won the Olympic tournament most often with 6 wins, in 1932, 36, 52, 56, 64 and 76. Five players share the record of 3 gold medals: George Wilkinson (1879–1946) in 1900, 08 and 12; Paulo (Paul) Radmilovic (1886–1968) and Charles Sidney Smith (1879–1951) in 1908, 12 and 20—all GB; and the Hungarian Desző Gyarmati (b Oct 23, 1927) and György Kárpáti (b June 23, 1935) in 1952, 56 and 64. Gyarmati's wife (Eva Szekely) and daughter (Andrea) won gold and silver medals respectively in swimming. Radmilovic also won a gold medal for the 4 x 200 m freestyle relay in 1908.

Marathon

Two teams of seven from Shrewsbury School, Shropshire, Eng, played for 25 hours 34 min Nov 29–30, 1986.

Most Goals

The greatest number of goals scored by an individual in an international tournament is 13 by Debbie Handley for Australia (16) vs Canada (10) at the World Championships in Guayaquil, Ecuador, in 1982.

NCAA Championships

Matt Biondi, co-captain of the UCLA water polo team that won a record 7th NCAA championship in 1987, is the same swimmer who starred in the 1984 and 1988 Olympics.

U of Cal at Berkeley won its 8th championship in 1988.

WATER SKIING

Origins

The sport originated with people walking on water with planks attached to their feet, possibly as early as the 14th century. A 19th century treatise on sorcerers refers to Eliseo of Tarentum who, in the 14th century, "walks and dances" on the water. The first report of aquaplaning on large boards behind a motorboat was from the Pacific coast of the US in the early 1900's. A photograph exists of a "plank-riding" contest in a regatta won by a Mr H. Storry at Scarborough, Yorkshire, England, on July 15, 1914. Competitors were towed on a *single* plank by a motor launch.

TWICE A RECORDBREAKER: Deena Brush (US) set the women's jump record at 156 ft on July 9, 1988 at Charlotte, Mich, after setting a slalom record in 1983.

The present-day sport of water skiing was pioneered by Ralph W. Samuelson on Lake Pepin, Minn, on two curved pine boards in the summer of 1922, though claims have been made for the birth of the sport on Lake Annecy (Haute-Savoie), France, in 1920. The first world organization, the United Internationale de Ski Nautique, was formed in Geneva, Switz on July 27, 1946.

Slalom

The world record for slalom is 5 buoys on a 10.75-m line by Bob LaPoint (US) at Shreveport, Fla, 1984. Andy Mapple (GB) tied this record in Sept 1985.

The women's record is 5 buoys, on a 11.25-m line by Jennifer Leachman (US) on Aug 29, 1987, at Fort Worth, Tex, in the MasterCraft International.

Tricks

The tricks or freestyle event involves various maneuvers for which points are awarded according to the degree of difficulty and the speed at which they are performed.

The tricks record is 10,860 points by Cory Pickos (US) at Wapakoneta, Ohio on July 17, 1988.

The women's record is 8,460 points by Tawn Larsen (US) on Lake Holly, Va, July 1988.

Highest Speed

The fastest water skiing speed recorded is 143.08 mph by Christopher Michael Massey (Australia) on the Hawkesbury River, NSW, Australia, Mar 6, 1983. His drag-boat driver was Stanley Charles Sainty. Donna Patterson Brice (US) (b 1953) set a feminine record of 111.11 mph at Long Beach, Calif, on Aug 21, 1977.

Most Titles

World overall championships (instituted 1949) have been won 4 times by Sammy Duvall (US) in 1981, 1983, 1985, and 1987. The women's title has been won three times by Mrs Willa McGuire (*née* Worthington) of the US, in 1949–50 and 55, and Elizabeth Allan-Shetter (US) in 1965, 69, and 75. Allan-Shetter has also won a record 8 individual championship events and is the only person to win all 4 titles (slalom, jumping, tricks and overall) in one year, at Copenhagen, Denmark, in 1969. The US has won the team championship on 20 successive occasions, 1949–87.

Jumps

The first recorded jump on water skis was 50 ft by Ralph W. Samuelson, off a greased ramp at Lake Pepin, Wis, in 1925, and this was not exceeded officially until 1947.

WATERSKI PYRAMID: A team of 17 skiers made a 5-tiered ensemble and was pulled at a speed of 25 mph with special ropes. They remained in formation for more than 20 sec. (Together Again Productions)

The longest jump recorded is one of 205 ft by Sammy Duvall (US) at Shreveport, La on July 24, 1988. The women's record is 156 ft by Deena Brush (US) on July 9, 1988 at Charlotte, Mich.

A high jump record of 5½ ft by 9 men simultaneously over a 14-ft wide ramp was set by the US Water Ski Show Team on July 20, 1986, on the Hudson River at Albany, NY, as part of the city's Tri-Centennial.

Barefoot

The first person to water ski barefoot is reported to be Dick Pope, Jr, at Lake Eloise, Fla, on March 6, 1947. The barefoot duration record is 2 hours 42 min 39 sec by Billy Nichols (US) (b 1964) on Lake Weir, Fla, on Nov 19, 1978. The backwards barefoot record is 39 min by Paul McManus (Australia). The barefoot jump record is 65 ft 11¼ in by Mike Siepel in 1984.

TRICKS RECORDHOLDER Cory Pickos shows the style that won him 10,860 points. (Amer Water Ski Assn)

ROUNDING A BUOY in the record slalom run is Kris LaPoint (US) at the International Cup event in Florida in Apr 1984. (American Water Ski Association)

The official barefoot speed record is 119.36 mph by Scott Michael Pellaton (b Oct 8, 1956) over a quarter-mile course at Chowchilla, Calif on Sept 4, 1983. The fastest by a woman is 73.67 mph by Karen Toms (Australia) on Mar 31, 1984 in New South Wales, Australia. The fastest official speed backward and barefoot is 62 mph by Robert Wing (Australia) on Apr 3, 1982.

Longest Run

The greatest distance traveled continuously on water skis is 1,321.16 mi by Steve Fontaine of Lake Park, Fla Oct 24–25, 1988 at Jupiter Island on Hobe Sound, Fla. He spent 46 hours 3 min 42 sec, including rest breaks, making 81 laps around a course measuring 16.31 mi.

WHO'S THE YOUNGEST? Chrystal Booko (left) of Three Rivers, Mich, barefoot in this photo, is said to have first skied at 3 years 8 months. The parents of Parks Bonifay (right), who are the pros at Cypress Gardens, Fla, say their boy really skied at 6 months 23 days.

SKI JUMP: Nine members of the US Water Ski Show Team leap 5½ ft in the air over a ramp on the Hudson River at Albany, NY. (Photo by Mike Nicholas)

Youngest Water Skier

Two claims have been received claiming the record for youngest. The parents of Parks Bonifay of Lake Alfred, Fla, claim that he first skied at the age of 6 months, 23 days. His parents are professional water skiers at Cypress Gardens, Fla. Also the parents of Chrystal Booko of Three Rivers, Mich, claim that their child is the youngest at 3 years 8 months. Both have submitted photos to prove it.

Biggest Ski Pull

A 19-ft Master Craft Competition Ski Boat pulled 39 water skiers over 1,000 ft on the Mohawk River at Scotia, NY on June 18, 1988, the most pulled by one boat.

KNEEBOARDING, a form of water skiing, has been popular, especially in Florida, for quite a few years. On July 5, 1987, four kneeboarders led by Paul Domb (second from right) went from Bimini to Key Biscayne, leaving at 7:30 AM and arriving 3 hours 45 min later, after traversing 58 mi. The others are Dan Stoll, Steve Constance and Steve McMahon. (Photo by Aixa Montero)

WEIGHTLIFTING
and POWERLIFTING

Origins

Competitions for lifting weights of stone were held in the ancient Olympic Games. The first "world" championship was staged at the Café Monico, Piccadilly, London, on March 28, 1891, and the first official championships were held in Vienna, Austria, July 19–20. 1898, subsequently recognized by the International Weightlifting Federation. Prior to that time, weightlifting consisted of professional exhibitions in which some of the advertised poundages were open to doubt.

The International Weightlifting Federation (IWF) was established in 1920, and their first official championships were held in Tallinn, Estonia on Apr 29–30, 1922.

The first to raise 400 lb was Karl Swoboda (1882–1933) (Austria) in Vienna, with 401¼ lb in 1910, using the continental and jerk style.

In weightlifting, an Olympic sport, there are two types of lifts. One is the "snatch," in which the lifter grips the bar with both hands, palms downward, and with one movement raises the weight to arms' length over his head. In the other lift, called "the clean and jerk," the lifter first brings the weight to his shoulders, pauses, then raises it to arm's length over his head.

Powerlifting is a modern offshoot of weightlifting, popularized by body builders, in which sheer strength and less technique are required. Its three lifts are: (1) the "squat," in which the lifter stands with the bar on his shoulders, squats, and returns to the standing position; (2) the "bench press," in which the competitor, on his back, begins with the weight in outstretched arms, lowers it to his chest, and after a pause, presses it back to arms' length; (3) the "dead lift," in which the lifter removes the weight from the floor and stands erect with the weight hanging at arms' length.

1988 OLYMPIC GOLD MEDAL WINNERS

114.4 lb:	Sevdalin Marinov (Bulgaria) WR
123.2 lb:	Oksen Mirzoyan (USSR)
132 lb:	Naim Suleimanoglou (Turkey)
148.5 lb:	Joachim Kunz (E Ger)
165 lb:	Borislav Gudikov (Bulgaria)
181.5 lb:	Israil Arsamakov (USSR)
198 lb:	Anatoliy Khrapatiy (USSR)
220 lb:	Pavel Kouzyetsov (USSR)
242 lb:	Yuri Zakharevich (USSR)
Over 242 lb:	Aleksandr Kurlovich (USSR)

MOST WORLD RECORDS: Vasili Alexeev (USSR) has 8 world titles, including Olympics, and has set 79 official world records in the heavyweight class, more than any other athlete.

Greatest Lift

The greatest weight known to have been raised by a human being is 6,270 lb in a back lift by the 364-lb Paul Anderson (US) (b Oct 17, 1932), the 1956 Olympic heavyweight champion, at Toccoa, Ga, on June 12, 1957. He lifted a steel safe full of lead on a specially built table loaded in the rest of the space with heavy auto parts.

The greatest by a woman is 3,564 lb with a hip and harness lift by Josephine Blatt (née Schauer) (US) (1869–1923) at the Bijou Theatre, Hoboken, NJ, on Apr 15, 1895.

The greatest overhead lift ever made by a woman is 303 lb by 180-lb Karyn Tarter Marshall (b 1956) in a clean and jerk in NYC Apr 20, 1985. She has been US national champion five times in three separate weight classes. Katie Sandwina, née Brummbach (Germany) (b Jan 21, 1884, d as Mrs Max Haymann in NYC, in 1952) stood 5 ft 11 in tall, weighed 210 lb, and is reputed to have unofficially lifted 312½ lb

Disqualification due to use of drugs has affected this sport more than most with the first cases, gold and silver medalists, being disqualified in the 1976 Olympics. Contestants must pass drug tests nowadays.

GREATEST LIFT BY A WOMAN: Karyn Tarter Marshall of NYC made an overhead lift of 303 lb in a clean-and-jerk on Apr 20, 1985, beating the 286-lb official record set in 1911 by Katie Sandwina. Here Karyn is lifting two gymnates just to show she can lift live weights, too. (Carolyn Vesper)

LIFTING HER BROTHER OVERHEAD (below) was only one feat that Katie Sandwina was known for. She once shouldered a 1,200-lb cannon.

and to have once shouldered a 1,200-lb cannon taken from the tailboard of a Barnum & Bailey circus wagon.

Youngest World Record Holder

Naum Shalamanov (Bulgaria) (b Nov 23, 1967) set 56 kg world records for clean and jerk (160 kg) and total (285 kg) at 15 years 123 days at Allentown, Pa, Mar 26, 1983. He became the youngest world champion at 15 years 334 days.

81-Year-Old Lifts 841 lb

Donat Gadoury of Quebec, Canada at the age of 81 on Oct 1, 1988, lifted a barbell weighing 841 lb (382 kg) in front of 550 people for Camera 88, a television show.

WORLD WEIGHTLIFTING RECORDS

(Through 1988, sanctioned by International Weightlifting Federation, and compiled by Herb Glossbrenner)

Bodyweight class	Lift	kg	lb	Name and country	Place	Date	
52kg 114½ lb FLYWEIGHT	Snatch	120	264½	Sevdalin Marinov (Bulgaria)	Seoul, South Korea	18 Sep	1988
	Jerk	153	337¼	He Zhouqiang (China)	Ostrava, Czechoslovakia	6 Sep	1987
	Total	270	595¼	Sevdalin Marinov (Bulgaria)	Seoul, South Korea	18 Sep	1988
56 kg 123¼ lb BANTAMWEIGHT	Snatch	134	295¼	He Yingqiang (China)	Xilong, China	16 Jun	1988
	Jerk	171	377	Neno Terziiski (Bulgaria)	Ostrava, Czechoslovakia	6 Sep	1987
	Total	300	661¼	Neum Shalamanov (Bulgaria)	Varra, Bulgaria	11 May	1984
60 kg 132¼ lb FEATHERWEIGHT	Snatch	152.5	336	Naim Suleimanoglou (Turkey)*	Seoul, South Korea	20 Sep	1988
	Jerk	190	418¾	Naim Suleimanoglou (Turkey)*	Seoul, South Korea	20 Sep	1988
	Total	342.5	755	Naim Suleimanoglou (Turkey)*	Seoul, South Korea	20 Sep	1988
67.5 kg 148¾ lb † LIGHTWEIGHT	Snatch	158.5	349¼	Israel Militossyan (USSR)	Athens, Greece	24 May	1988
	Jerk	200.5	442	Mikhail Petrov (Bulgaria)	Ostrava, Czechoslovakia	8 Sep	1987
	Total	335	782½	Mikhail Petrov (Bulgaria)	Seoul, South Korea	5 Dec	1987
75 kg 165¼ lb MIDDLEWEIGHT	Snatch	170	374¾	Angel Guenchev (Bulgaria)	Miskolc, Hungary	11 Dec	1987
	Jerk	215½	475	Aleksandr Varbanov (Bulgaria)	Seoul, South Korea	5 Dec	1987
	Total	382.5	843¼	Aleksandr Varbanov (Bulgaria)	Plovdiv, Bulgaria	20 Feb	1988
82.5 kg 181¾ lb LIGHT-HEAVYWEIGHT	Snatch	183	403¼	Asen Zlatev (Bulgaria)	Melbourne, Australia	7 Dec	1986
	Jerk	225	496	Asen Zlatev (Bulgaria)	Sofia, Bulgaria	12 Nov	1986
	Total	405	892½	Yurik Vardanyan (USSR)	Varna, Bulgaria	14 Sep	1984
90 kg 198¼ lb MIDDLE-HEAVYWEIGHT	Snatch	195.5	431	Blagoi Blagoyev (Bulgaria)	Varna, Bulgaria	1 May	1983
	Jerk	235	518	Anatoliy Khrapatiy (USSR)	Cardiff, South Glamorgan	29 Apr	1988
	Total	422.5	931¼	Viktor Solodov (USSR)	Varna, Bulgaria	15 Sep	1984
100 kg 220½ lb	Snatch	200.5	442	Nicu Vlad (Romania)	Sofia, Bulgaria	14 Nov	1986
	Jerk	242.5	532¼	Aleksandr Popov (USSR)	Tallinn, USSR	5 Mar	1988
	Total	440	970	Yuriy Zakharevich (USSR)	Odessa, USSR	4 Mar	1983
110 kg 242½ lb HEAVYWEIGHT	Snatch	210	462¾	Yuriy Zakharevich (USSR)	Seoul, South Korea	27 Sep	1988
	Jerk	250.5	552¼	Yuriy Zakharevich (USSR)	Cardiff, South Glamorgan	30 Apr	1988
	Total	455	1003	Yuriy Zakharevich (USSR)	Seoul, South Korea	27 Sep	1988
Over 110 kg 242½ lb SUPER-HEAVYWEIGHT	Snatch	216	476	Antonio Krastev (Bulgaria)	Ostrava, Czechoslovakia	13 Sep	1987
	Jerk	265.5	585¼	Leonid Taranenko (USSR)	Ostrava, Czechoslovakia	13 Sep	1987
	Total	472.5	1041½	Aleksandr Kurlovich (USSR)	Ostrava, Czechoslovakia	13 Sep	1987

* Formerly Naim Suleimanov or Naum Shalamanov of Bulgaria
† Argel Guenchev (Bulgaria) achieved 160 kg snatch, 202.5 kg jerk for a 262.5 kg total at Seoul, South Korea on 21 Sept 1988 but was subsequently disqualified on a positive drugs test.

WORLD POWERLIFTING RECORDS (Weight in pounds)

(Through 1988, sanctioned by International Powerlifting Federation, courtesy of Mike Lambert, Powerlifting USA magazine.)

Class	Squat		Bench Press		Deadlift		Total	
MEN								
52 kg	535.7	Hideaki Inaba (Jap) 1986	322.9	Joe Cunha (US) 1982	523.6	Hideaki Inaba 1987	1,273.1	Hideaki Inaba 1986
56 kg	529.1	Hideaki Inaba 1987	352.0	Hiro Isagawa (Jap) 1988	638.2	Lamar Gant (US) 1982	1,377.9	Lamar Gant 1982
60 kg	650.4	Joe Bradley (US) 1980	396.8	Joe Bradley 1980	683.0	Lamar Gant 1988	1,559.7	Joe Bradley 1982
67.5 kg	661.4	Jesse Jackson (US) 1987	440.9	Kristhoffer Hulecki (Swe) 1985	690.0	Daniel Austin (US) 1987	1,653.0	Daniel Austin 1988
75 kg	722.1	Roberts Wahl (US) 1980	479.5	James Rouse (US) 1980	733.1	John Inzer (US) 1987	1,873.9	Rick Gaugler (US) 1982
82.5 kg	836.6	Mike Bridges 1982	529.1	Mike Bridges 1981	788.1	Veli Kumpuniemi (Fin) 1980	2,105.4	Mike Bridges 1982
90 kg	826.7	Fred Hatfield (US) 1980	562.1	Mike MacDonald (US) 1980	823.4	Eddie Coppin (Belg) 1987	2,066.8	Mike Bridges 1980
100 kg	903.0	Ed Coan 1988	576.5	Mike MacDonald 1977	832.2	James Cash (US) 1982	2,203.0	Ed Coan 1988
110 kg	867.5	Dan Wohleber (US) 1981	595.2	Jeff Magruder (US) 1982	870.8	John Kuc (US) 1980	2,204.6	John Kuc 1980
125 kg	909.4	Dave Waddington (US) 1982	614.0	Tom Hardman (US) 1982	854.4	Lars Noren (Swe) 1987	2,215.6	Ernie Hackett (US) 1982
125 + kg	981.1	Dwayne Fely (US) 1982	661.4	Bill Kazmaier (US) 1981	892.9	Lars Noren 1987	2,425.1	Bill Kazmaier 1981
WOMEN								
44 kg	314	Delcy Palk (US) 1988	165	Terri Hoyt 1982	364	Nancy Belliveau (US) 1985	777	M. F. Vassart (Bel) 1985
48 kg	325	Majik Jones (US) 1984	182	Michelle Ervis (US) 1981	402	Majik Jones 1984	860	Majik Jones 1984
52 kg	380	Sissy Dolman (Hol) 1984	209	Mary Ryan (US) 1984	434	Diana Rowell (US) 1984	942	Diana Rowell 1984
56 kg	421	Vicki Steenrod (US) 1984	253	Mary Jeffrey 1988	441	Diana Rowell 1984	1,069	Mary Jeffrey 1988
60 kg	442	Ruthi Shafer (US) 1983	232	Vicki Steenrod 1985	470	Ruthi Shafer 1983	1,108	Vicki Steenrod 1985
67.5 kg	509	Ruthi Shafer 1984	233.7	Heidi Wittesch (Aus) 1986	539	Ruthi Shafer 1984	1,246	Ruthi Shafer 1984
75 kg	473.3	Terri Byland (US) 1987	309	Bev Francis (Aus) 1981	468	Marie Geldhof (Belg) 1988	1,212	Bev Francis 1981
82.5 kg	507	Juanita Trujillo (US) 1986	331	Bev Francis 1981	501	Vicki Gagne (US) 1981	1,273	Bev Francis 1983
90 kg	556	Lorraine Costanzo (US) 1988	296	Lorraine Costanzo 1988	501	Lorraine Costanzo 1988	1,339	Lorraine Costanzo 1988
90 + kg	546	Jan Todd (US) 1983	297	Myrtle Augee (GB) 1988	507	Wanda Sander (US) 1983	1,251	Gail Mulhall 1982

Most Weightlifting Titles

The most world title wins, including Olympic Games, is 8 by John Davis (US) (1921–84) in 1938, 46–52; by Tommy Kono (US) (b June 27, 1930) in 1952–9; and by Vasili Alexeev (USSR) (b Jan 7, 1942) 1970–7.

Winner of most Olympic medals in weightlifting is Norbert Schemansky (US) with 4: gold, middle-heavyweight 1952; silver, heavyweight 1948; bronze, heavyweight 1960 and 1964.

POWERLIFTING

Paul Anderson as a professional in 1958 has bench-pressed 627 lb, achieved 1,200 lb in a squat, and deadlifted 820 lb.

Hermann Görner (Germany) performed a one-handed deadlift of 734½ lb in Dresden on July 20, 1920. He once raised 24 men weighing 4,123 lb on a plank with the soles of his feet, in London on Oct 12, 1927, and also carried on his back a 1,444-lb piano for a distance of 52½ ft on June 3, 1921.

GREATEST LIFT: Paul Anderson (364 lb) once raised a loaded steel safe weighing 6,270 lb in a back lift from trestles. A gold medalist in the 1956 Olympics, he later turned professional, switching from weight-lifting to powerlifting, where he succeeded with a squat lift of 1,200 lb.

POWER LIFTER Jan Todd can carry her heavyweight husband, Terry, on her back. She raised 545½ pounds in a squat lift in 1981. Jan has since lost 82 lb, but is still setting records, and has been a leader with Terry Todd in fighting against steroid use.

Lamar Gant (US) was the first to total 12 times his bodyweight (132 lb) with a lift of 1,587 lb at Honolulu, Hawaii on Apr 8, 1988. He also deadlifted five times his body weight (123¼ lb) with 617 lb at Dayton, Ohio on Nov 2, 1979. Mike MacDonald (US) was the first man to hold world records (bench press) in four different classes simultaneously. Dave Waddington (US) was the first powerlifter to squat over 1,000 lb on June 13, 1981. Dan Wohleber (US) was the first to deadlift over 900 lb in official competition on Dec 12, 1982.

The newly instituted two-man deadlift record was raised to 1,448 lb by Clay and Doug Patterson in Arlington, Tex, on Dec 15, 1979.

Peter B. Cortese (US) achieved a one-arm deadlift of 370 lb—22 lb over triple his body weight—at York, Pa, on Sept 4, 1954.

Most World Titles

Hideaki Inaba (Japan) has won 14 world titles in powerlifting.

HEAVIEST SQUAT BY A WOMAN: Lorraine Costanzo of Dayton, Ohio, set a record of 628 lb on Nov 21, 1987. (Mike Lambert, Powerlifting USA Magazine)

WINDSURFING

See Boardsailing

MOST TITLES: Ten-time world champion Aleksandr Medved drives India's Maruti Mane to the mat. Three of Medved's record 10 titles came in Olympic competition, as he moved up in class from light-heavyweight to super-heavyweight.

WRESTLING

Origins

The earliest depictions of wrestling holds and falls on wall plaques and a statue indicate that organized wrestling dates from *c.* 2750–2600 BC. It was the most popular sport in the ancient Olympic Games and victors were recorded from 708 BC. The Greco-Roman style is of French origin and arose about 1860. The International Amateur Wrestling Federation (FILA) was founded in 1912.

Most World Championships

The greatest number of world championships won by a wrestler is 10 by the freestyler Aleksandr Medved (USSR) (b Sept 16, 1937), with the over 97 kg titles in 1962, 63, 64 (Olympic) and 66, the over 97 kg in 1967 and 68 (Olympic) and the over 100 kg title 1969, 70, 71 and 72 (Olympic). The only wrestler to win the same title in 7 successive years has been Valeriy Rezantsev (b Feb 2, 1947) (USSR) in the Greco-Roman 90 kg class, 1970–76, including the Olympic Games of 1972 and 1976.

Three wrestlers have won three Olympic gold medals. They are: Carl Westergren (1895–1958) (Sweden) in 1920, 24 and 32; Ivar Johansson (1903–79) (Sweden) in 1932 (two) and 36; and Medved in 1964, 68 and 72.

Two wrestlers who won more total medals are Imre Polyak (b Apr 16, 1932) (Hungary) who won the silver medal for the Greco-Roman 62 kg in 1952, 56 and 60, and the 63 kg gold in 1964, and Eino Leino (Finland) who won the gold in 1920, silver in 1924, and bronze in 1928 and 1932 as a freestyle at 75, 72, 66, and 72 kg.

Best Records

In international competition, Osamu Watanabe (b Oct 21, 1940) (Japan), the 1964 Olympic freestyle 63 kg champion, was unbeaten and unscored-upon in 187 consecutive matches.

Wade Schalles (US) won 821 bouts from 1964 to 1984, with 530 of these victories by pin. By 1987, Andre Metzger (US) had competed in over 1,500 matches, and had won 95% of them. He finished second in the freestyle championships in 1986 and third in 1987, and was an Olympic alternate in 1988.

Longest Bout

The longest recorded bout was one of 11 hours 40 min between Martin Klein (Estonia, representing

Russia) and Alfred Asikáinen (Finland) in the Greco-Roman 75 kg "A" event for the silver medal in the 1912 Olympic Games in Stockholm, Sweden. Klein won. (Under modern "sudden death" rules, long bouts are disqualified for passivity.) The longest in 1988 was 19 min 58 sec.

Fastest Pin

William R. Kerslake (b Dec 27, 1929) reputedly recorded the fastest fall in national tournament competition when he threw Ralph Bartleman in 4 sec during the 1956 National Amateur Athletic Union (NAAU) Greco-Roman Championships at Tulsa, Okla. Kerslake won 8 consecutive NAAU freestyle championships and 7 consecutive NAAU Greco-Roman championships, 1953–1960, a string of 76 consecutive victories.

Heaviest Heavyweight

The heaviest wrestler in Olympic history is Chris Taylor (1950–79), bronze medalist in 1972, who stood 6 ft 5 in tall and weighed over 420 lb. FILA introduced a top weight limit of 286 lb for international competition in 1985.

1988 OLYMPIC GOLD MEDAL WINNERS

GRECO-ROMAN

106 lb:	Vincenzo Maenza (Italy)
115 lb:	John Ronningen (Norway)
126 lb:	Andras Sike (Hungary)
137 lb:	Kamandar Madzhidov (USSR)
150 lb:	Levon Dzhulfalakyan (USSR)
163 lb:	Kim Young-nam (S Korea)
181 lb:	Mikhail Mamiashvili (USSR)
198 lb:	Atanas Komchev (Bulgaria)
220 lb:	Andrzej Wronski (Poland)
286 lb:	Aleksandr Kareline (USSR)

FREESTYLE

106 lb:	Takashi Kobayashi (Japan)
115 lb:	Mitsuru Sato (Japan)
126 lb:	Sergey Beloglazov (USSR)
137 lb:	John Smith (US)
150 lb:	Arsen Fadzayev (USSR)
163 lb:	Kenneth Monday (US)
181 lb:	Han Myang-woo (S Korea)
198 lb:	Makharbek Khadartsev (USSR)
220 lb:	Vasile Puscasu (Romania)
286 lb:	David Gobedzhichvili (USSR)

YACHTING

Origins

Yachting in England dates from the £100 stake race between King Charles II of England and his brother, James, Duke of York, on the Thames River, on Oct 1, 1661, over 23 miles, from Greenwich to Gravesend. The King won. The earliest club is the Royal Cork Yacht Club (formerly the Cork Harbour Water Club), established in Ireland in 1720, when the first recorded regatta was held.

The word "yacht" is from the Dutch, meaning to hunt or chase. The word "regatta"—meaning a gathering of boats—is Italian and was applied to the proceedings at Ranelagh on the Thames in June 1775. The sport did not really prosper until the seas became safer with the end of the Napoleonic Wars in 1815. That year The Yacht Club (later to become The Royal Yacht Squadron) was formed and organized races at Cowes, Isle of Wight, Eng, which was the beginning of modern yacht racing. In 1844 the New York YC was founded and held its first regatta the following year. The International Yacht Racing Union (IYRU) was established in 1907.

Highest Speed

The highest speed reached under sail on water by any craft over a 500-m timed run is by the boardsailer Pascal Maka (France) at 38.86 knots in a 50-knot wind at Fuerteventura, Canary Islands, on a Gaastra 4 sq-m limited edition speed trial sailboard on July

Transatlantic Recordsetter Loses Race and Record

The man who finished first in record time in a race across the Atlantic Ocean lost the race to a countryman who had stopped to help a troubled sailor.

Philippe Poupon of France thought he had broken a world sailing record by more than one day when he arrived in Newport, RI on June 18, 1985 in 16 days, 11 hours, 56 min in the "Observer Singlehanded Trans-Atlantic Race." Some Marine experts believe that the record breaker should have been Yvon Fauconnier, who finished nearly 11 hours later. Fauconnier, at the helm of the 53-ft-trimaran *Unupro Jardin*, was given a 16-hour handicap for stopping to help Philippe Jeantot, whose boat, *Credit Agricole II*, capsized the week previous.

21, 1986. The women's record was set at the same venue by Britt Dunkerbeke (France) at 33.77 knots

In an unsuccessful attempt on the record in Oct 1978, *Crossbow II* is reported to have momentarily attained a speed of 45 knots (51 mph).

Olympic Victories

The first person ever to win individual gold medals in four successive Olympic Games was Paul B. Elvström (b Feb 24, 1928) (Denmark) in the Firefly class in 1948 and the Finn class in 1952, 56 and 60. He has also won 8 other world titles in a total of 6 classes.

The lowest number of penalty points by the winner of any class in an Olympic regatta is 3 points (5 wins [1 disqualified] and 1 second in 7 starts) by *Superdocious* of the Flying Dutchman class sailed by Lt Rodney Stuart Pattison (b Aug 5, 1943), British Royal Navy, and Ian Somerled Macdonald-Smith (b July 3, 1945), in Acapulco Bay, Mexico, in Oct 1968.

Greatest Distance

The greatest distance covered in a day's run under sail was set by the catamaran *Fleury-Michon VIII* (skipper Philippe Poupon) at 520 nautical mi June 16–17, 1987 during a transatlantic crossing of 7 days 12 hours 50 min.

Longest Race

The longest regular sailing race is the quadrennial Whitbread Round the World race (instituted Aug 1973) organized by the Royal Navy Sailing Association. The distance is 26,180 nautical miles from Portsmouth, England, and return with stops and restarts at Cape Town, Auckland and Mar del Plata.

1988 OLYMPIC GOLD MEDAL WINNERS

OPEN CLASS

Boardsailing: Bruce Kendall (NZ)
Finn: Jose Luis Doreste (Spain)
Flying Dutchman: Jorgen Bojsen-Moller, Christian Gronborg (Den)
Soling: Jochen Schuemann, Thomas Flach, Bernd Jaekel (E Ger)
Star: Michael McIntyre, Bryn Vaile (GB)
Tornado: Jean-Yves Le Deroff, Nicolas Henard (France)

MEN

470 Class: Thierry Peponnet, Luc Pillot (France)

WOMEN

470 Class: Allison Jolly, Lynne Jewell (US)

AMERICA WINS BACK AMERICA'S CUP: Dennis Conner on the "Stars and Stripes" in Feb 1987 off Australia as the San Diego-based yacht beat "Kookaburra III."

The fastest (sailing) time is 117 days 14 hours by *UBS Switzerland* crewed by Pierre Fehlmann (Switz), finishing on May 9, 1986.

Admiral's Cup

The ocean racing series to have attracted the largest number of participating nations (three boats allowed to each nation) is the Admiral's Cup held by the Royal Ocean Racing Club in the English Channel in alternate years. Up to 1981, Britain had a record 8 wins. A record 19 nations competed in the 1975, 77 and 79 competitions.

Largest Marina

The largest marina in the world is that of Marina Del Rey, Los Angeles, Calif, which has 7,500 berths.

Most Competitors

The most competitors ever to start in a single race was 1,947 (of which 1,767 finished) sailing boats in the Round Zeeland (Denmark) race, June 17–20, 1983, over a course of 233 miles.

Most Successful

The most successful racing yacht in history was the British Royal Yacht *Britannia* (1893–1935), owned by King Edward VII while Prince of Wales, and subsequently by King George V, which won 231 races in 625 starts.

America's Cup

The America's Cup was originally won as an outright prize by the schooner *America* on Aug 22, 1851, at Cowes, England, but was later offered by the NY Yacht Club as a challenge trophy. On Aug 8, 1870, J. Ashbury's *Cambria* (GB) failed to capture the trophy from the *Magic*, owned by F. Osgood (US). Since then the Cup was challenged 27 times but the US holders never were defeated, winning 77 races in 132 years and only losing 8, until the 4–3 defeat in Sept 1983 of *Liberty* by *Australia II*, skippered by John Bertrand and owned by a Perth syndicate (headed by Alan Bond) at Newport, RI.

Dennis Conner has been US helmsman for 4 successive challenges, in 1988 retaining the Cup in a challenge match with New Zealand which the US yacht won, 2–0.

The closest race ever was in the trials held on Nov 4, 1986 when *White Crusader* (UK) beat *Canada II* by the margin of 1 sec. The fastest time ever recorded by a 12-m boat for the triangular course of 24.3 miles is 2 hours 27 min 42 sec by *Freedom* on Sept 25, 1980.

LATEST VERIFIED SPORTS RECORDS

Basketball—The most points scored in a college (NCAA) game by two teams was 331 when Loyola Marymount beat US International, 181–150, Jan 31, 1989 in Los Angeles.

Boardsailing—Highest speed: 40.33 knots by Eric Beale (GB) and for a woman 36.66 by Brigitte Gimenez (France) in winds of 35 knots over 500 m at St Maries-de-la-Mer, Camargue, France, Nov 17, 1988.

Bowling—Two perfect games were rolled back-to-back *twice* by Al Spotts of W Reading, Pa on Mar 14, 1982 and again on Feb 1, 1985.

Lacrosse—Largest attendance was 20,007 at the NCAA championship game between Syracuse and Cornell in 1988. Gary Gait (Syracuse) holds the USILA Division I record of 70 goals in one season.

Roller Skating—L. Antoniel of Italy unofficially repeated his record speed of 300 m in 24.99 sec on July 31, 1988. In a marathon race (42 km) at Grenoble, France, G. Cortese of Italy covered the distance in record time of 1 hour 8 min 3 sec on Aug 29, 1987. Jonathan Seutter covered 145.25 mi in 12 hours at Long Beach, Calif, Jan 2, 1988.

Snowmobiling—A speed of 178.144 mph was attained by John K. Deede of Minomenee Falls, Wis in his "Arias Overture" at Lake Hayward, Wis on Jan 24, 1988.

Weightlifting—Over 110 kg category: Leonid Taranenko (USSR) at Canberra, Australia on Nov 26, 1988: jerk 266 kg/586¼ lb, total 475 kg/1047 lb.

SPORTS AND GAMES ENDURANCE MARATHONS

Backgammon—151 hours 11 min by Dick Newcombe and Greg Peterson at Rockford, Ill, June 30–July 6, 1978.

Badminton (singles)—83 hours 25 min by Henry Marais and Jaco Visser at Quartermaster, Pretoria, S Africa, Jan 1–4, 1988. (doubles)—86 hours 22 min by Cameron McMullen, Michael Patterson, Stephen Breuer and Michael Bain at Rhyl, Clywd, Wales, July 18–21, 1987.

Basketball—102 hours by Sigma Nu Fraternity at Indiana U, Indiana, Pa, Apr 13–17, 1983.

Bowling (Ten Pin)—195 hours 1 min by Jim Webb at Gosford City Bowl, NSW, Aust, 1984.

Bridge (Contract)—186 hours 38 min by Johnathan Noad, Jeremy Cohen, Robert Pinder and Andrew Gale at Ariel Hotel, Hayes, Middlesex, Eng, Sept 20–28, 1986.

Checkers—138 hours 28 min by Greg Davis and Mark Schumacher at Denny's Restaurant, Nanuwading, Victoria, Aust, Aug 26–Sept 1, 1985.

Chess—200 hours by Roger Long and Graham Croft at Dingles, Bristol, Eng, May 11–19, 1984.

Cribbage—124 hours 15 min by 4 students from St Anselm's College, Wirral, Merseyside, Eng, July 14–19, 1986.

Croquet—120 hours 25 min by Jane Langan, Miles Harbot, Jo Gill and Daryl Shorthose at Birmingham U, Eng, June 14–19, 1986.

Curling—(4 players) 67 hours 55 min at the Capital Winter Club, Fredericton, NB, Canada, Apr 9–12, 1982. (pair)—43 hours 2 min by Brian Rankin and David Senior at Bradford, W Yorkshire, Eng, July 5–7, 1988.

Darts—168 hours 4 min by David Dingley and Michael Poole at The Three Horseshoes, Malvern, Worcestershire, Eng, Nov 1986.

Dominoes—150 hours 5 min by Neil Thomas and Tim Beesley at St Anselm's College, Wirral, Merseyside, Eng, Aug 5–11, 1985. (4 players)—144 hours by Keith Hannard and Alan, Bob and Ray McKeith at the Cyprus Hotel, S Shields, Eng, Aug 25–31, 1985.

Ice Skating—109 hours 5 min by Austin McKinley at Christchurch, New Zealand, June 21–25, 1977.

Judo—245 hours 30 min by 5 of 6 people at Smithfield RSL Youth Club, NSW, Aust, Jan 3–13, 1984.

Joggling (3 balls)—3 hours 22 min 32.51 sec by Ashrita Furman while competing in a marathon run on July 4, 1988 at Salmon, Idaho. Albert Lucas ran in the 1988 Los Angeles Marathon, alongside more contestants, joggling 3 balls without drop for 3 hours 29 min 17 sec.

Juggling (3 balls without drop)—6 hours 7 min 4 sec by Ashrita Furman in 1987.

Monopoly—660 hours by 4 players in Atlanta, Ga, July 12-Aug 8, 1981.

Pool—363 hours 9 min by Sheena Thompson and Geoff Ham at Carrbrook, Manchester, Eng, Aug 26–Sept 10, 1988.

Roller Skating—344 hours 18 min by Isamu Furugen at Naha Roller Skate Land, Okinawa, Japan, Dec 11–27, 1983.

Scrabble—153 hours by Peter Finan and Neil Smith at St Anselm's College, Wirral, Merseyside, Eng, Aug 18–25, 1984. (Against various opponents)—155 hours 48 min by Ken Cardozo at ''Perfect Pizza,'' Fulham, Eng, Dec 5–11, 1984.

Skiing (Alpine)—138 hours by Luc Labrie at Daie Comeau, Que, Can on Feb 20–25, 1984. (With no waiting for lifts)—87 hours 28 min by John Mordini at Kissing Bridge, NY, Jan 11–14, 1988.

Soccer—75½ hours by two teams of students from Roy High School, Roy, Utah, Aug 8–11, 1988.

Softball (fast pitch)—61 hours 36 min 33 sec by two teams of 9 (no substitutes), Marines of the 2nd Radio Battalion at Camp Lejeune, NC, May 3–5, 1984. (slow pitch)—111 hours 2 min by Brigade Service Support Group-1 and Marine Aircraft Group-24 at Kareohe Marine Corps Air Station, Hawaii, Sept 3–8, 1986.

Squash—126 hours 1 min by P. Etherton and L. Davies at Tannum Sands, Queensland, Aust, July 7–12, 1987.

Table Tennis (singles)—147 hours 47 min by S. Unterslak and J. Boccia at Dewaal Hotel, Cape Town, S Africa, Nov 12–18, 1983. (doubles)—101 hours 1 min 11 sec by Lance, Phil and Mark Warren and Bill Weir at Sacramento, Calif, Apr 9–13, 1979.

Tennis (singles)—72.3 hours by Bob Guerrero, 39, and Dennis Kaufman, 30, of Reno, Nev, Feb 10–12, 1988 at the Reno Athletic Club. (doubles)—102 hours by 4 high school players from Myrtle Beach, SC, Oct 25–29, 1987 at Kingston Plantation, SC.

Trampolining—266 hours 9 min by Jeff Schwartz at Glenview, Ill, Aug 14–25, 1981.

Volleyball—118 hours 30 min by students of Krugersdorp HS, S Africa, Mar 30–Apr 4, 1988.

Water Polo—25 hours 34 min by 2 teams of 7 from Shrewsbury School, Shropshire, Eng, Nov 29–30, 1986.

Index

Aerobatics, earliest, world championships, inverted flight, loops 9

Archery, earliest sport 5, 9, highest 24-hour scores, long-lasting records 9, flight shooting 9, 10, highest championship scores, most titles, Olympic medals, world records, greatest pull 10

Auto Racing, largest crowd 6, earliest races 10–11, fastest races, fastest runs 11, Grand Prix victories 11–12, 16, Indianapolis 500 12, 13–14, 15, 16, youngest and oldest Grand Prix winners and drivers 12–13, Le Mans 13, 15–16, most NASCAR victories, Daytona 500, CART leaders 14, most successful drivers 14–15, fastest stock car 15, fastest pit stop, closest finishes 16, duration record, land speed records, drag racing 17

Automobile, duration test 5

Backgammon 82

Badminton, origins 17, international championships 17–18, most titles, marathons, shortest international game, longest hit and rally 18

Ball Field, largest 5

Baseball, earliest games, night baseball 18, home runs 18, 19, 20, 23, 29, 30, most stolen bases 20–21, 24, most and fewest strikeouts 21, 23, 24, first 40 and 40 23, 24, baseballs in hand, finishing with flourish 23, shortest and tallest players 23–24, youngest and oldest players 24, 27, one-day wonder, fastest base runner 24, most strikeouts in inning, most foul-offs, hit by pitch, catcher's interference 25, consecutive innings 25–26, fastest pitcher, unanimous choice for rookie of year, do-everything record, do-nothing record 26, youngest Cy Young award winner 28, 29, games won by different pitchers, most career strikeouts, longest career, longest throw, longest shutouts, managers 28, most valuable baseball card 28, 31, longest and shortest major league games 28, 30, consecutive games 29, attendances, ball drop from dirigible 30, rained-out game in covered stadium 30–31, running bases in reverse, memorabilia, unearned runs, longest game 31; major league all-time records: individual batting 19–20, 26, 29, 30, stolen bases 20–21, pitching 21, 27, fielding 21–23, World Series records 22, 27

Basketball, origins 31, court 31–32, college individual records, rule change, losing streak 32, individual scoring 33, 34, longest field goal 33, most accurate shooting 33–34, team scoring, Olympic champions, world champions 34, attendances, marathon 36, tallest and shortest players 36–37, youngest and oldest players, college coach 37, NBA regular season records 35–36, 37

Biathlon 171

Billiards 87—88

Blackjack 82

Boardsailing, world championships, highest speed, longest sail across Atlantic 38, endurance, longest line and board 39

Bobsledding 39

Bodybuilding 40–41

Bowling, most participants 6, origins, organizations, lanes, highest score in 24 hours 41, marathon attempts, world championships 42, PBA records 42, 43, ABC league records 42–43, ABC tournament records 43–44, WIBC records 44–45

Boxing, greatest earnings 7, origins 45, longest and shortest fights 45, 47, longest and shortest reigns 45, 48, largest receipts, longest career, tallest boxer 48; world heavyweight champions: oldest and youngest 47, 48, earliest title fight 48, most recaptures 48, 49, heaviest and lightest, tallest and shortest 49, 51, Olympic gold medals 49–50, roster of champions, undefeated 50; world champions (any weight): youngest and oldest 48, 51, most fights without loss, longest and shortest reigns, most recaptures, most simultaneous titles 51, amateur world championships, longest and shortest title fights, most title bouts, most frequent championship fights, most knockdowns in title fights, American champion outside US 52; all fights: highest career earnings, most knockouts, referee counted out, fighter endures plane crash, double knockouts, closest call 52, "real McCoy," greatest "tonnage," smallest champions, most fights 53

Bridge (Contract), origins, most world titles, possible auctions, perfect deals, most durable player, most players 82, most Master Points, youngest Life Masters, oldest active players, marathon 83

Canoeing and Kayaking, origins, Olympic and world titles 53, longest journey 53–54, downstream canoeing 54, 55, longest open sea voyage 54, 55, Eskimo rolls 54, highest speed, fastest 24 hours, greatest lifetime distance, longest race 55

Checkers, origins 83, champions 83–84, most opponents 83–84, longest and shortest games 84

Chess, origins, most opponents 84, longest games 84–85, world champions 84, 85, marathon 85

Cribbage, origins, invention of, rare hands, marathon 84

Croquet 55–56

Cross-Country Running, international championships 56, most appearances, most wins 56, 57, largest field 57

Curling, origins, most titles 57, largest rink, largest bonspiels, largest prizes, "perfect" games, marathon, world championships 58

Cycling, Tour de France 5, 6, 61–62, earliest race 58–59, Olympic gold medals, most world titles 59, 24-hour distance record 59, 60, 62, highest speed 59–60, trans-America cycling, one-hour distance records, human-powered speed record 60, coast-to-coast cycling 61, 62, Triple crown, longest one-day race 62, touring 62–63, human-powered cycling flight, endurance, highest altitude, fastest woman cyclist, bicycle balancing, roller cycling 63, six-day races 63, 64, unicycle records 64

Darts, origins 85, most titles 85–86, fastest 301 match, fastest "round the board," least darts, highest 24-hour score, marathon 86

Disasters, worst, 7

Dog Racing, see Greyhound Racing

Earnings, greatest 7, boxing, women tennis players 7, auto racing 11, 13, 15, bowling 43, golf 92, 95, 97, 102, Greyhound racing 106, harness racing 115–16, horse racing 122, ice skating 126, rodeo 154, tennis 265

Endurance, marathons 251

Equestrian Sports, origin, most Olympic medals, world team championship 64, driving, World Cup, jumping records, world titles, longest ride, first solo transcontinental journey, marathon 65

Fencing, origins, US championships 66, most Olympic titles 66–67, world championships 66, 67, Amateur Fencing Association 67

Field Hockey 68

Fishing, origins, freshwater casting, longest fight, world championships, most fish caught in a season, largemouth bass 69, largest catches 69–71, world records 70, most valuable fish 71, smallest catch, spear-fishing 72

Footbag 72

Football, biggest sports contract 6, heaviest athlete 7, largest stadium 7–8, origins 72–73, college individual records 73, 74, college series records, longest streaks 73, most prolific record-breaker, All-America brothers, first televised football game, statistical leader, worst attendance, highest score 78, coaching records 78–79, 80, NFL champions, shortest touchdown pass, pro playoff heroes 79; all-time NFL records: service 74, scoring 74, 77, rushing 74, 76, 77, passing 74–75, 81, pass reception 75–76, pass interceptions, kickoff returns 76, punting 76, 79, punt returns 76–77, fumbles 77, Super Bowl records 77–78, 80

Game Shooting 164
Games 82–89
Gliding, origins, most world titles, world records 90, hang gliding 90–91
Golf, origins 91, 99, oldest clubs, longest courses and holes, highest and lowest courses, largest green 92, biggest bunkers 92, 93, highest earnings 92, 95, 97, 102, lowest scores for 9 and 18 holes 92–93, women's lowest scores, lowest 36-hole and 72-hole scores, lowest score with one club 93, longest drives 93–94, biggest winning margin 94, most tournament wins 94, 96, 99, 101, 102, longest putt 94, 101, most wins in major tournaments 95, marathon golf 95–96, largest tournament, youngest and oldest champions 96, most shots one hole 103, most balls hit in one hour 104; holes-in-one: longest, consecutive, most eagles in one round 104, most aces 104–05, youngest and oldest 105; national tournaments: US Open 97, British Open 98, US Masters, US PGA championships 100, US Women's Open 102, 104, US Amateur, US Women's Amateur championship 103, Ryder Cup 104
Greyhound Racing, origins, fastest greyhound, fastest speed for 4-bend tracks 105, most wins 105–06, highest earnings 106, longest odds 106
Gymnastics, largest stadium 8, earliest references, American Cup titles, World Cup titles 106, modern rhythmic gymnastics 106, 108, world and Olympic championships 106–07, 108, 109, 112, rope jumping 107, 111, wall press (Samson's chair) 106, 107, youngest international competitors, skip-running 108, rope jumps in one hour, chinning the bar, jumping jacks, parallel bar dips 109, push-ups 109, 110, somersaults 109–10, human suspension bridge, sit-ups and leg raises, pummel horse 110

Handball, US Handball Association national champions, origin, most titles 113; team handball: origins, Olympics and world championships, most championships, highest score, marathon 114
Handball, team 114
Hang Gliding 90–91
Harness Racing, origins 114, records against time 115, most successful driver 115, 116, greatest winnings 115–116, highest prices 116
Heaviest athletes 10
Hockey, origins 116, world championships and Olympic games 116, 118, NHL all-time records 117, Stanley Cup 117, 119, 120, fastest skater, longest season, longest career 118, fastest scoring 118–19, MVP most times 119, team scoring 119–20, longest game, longest streaks 120
Horse Racing, origins 120, largest prizes, speed records 121, jockeys 121, 123–124, victories 121–22, Kentucky Derby winners 122, 123, greatest winning, owners, trainers, topmost tipster, largest grandstand 122, longest race, Triple Crown, most valuable horses, dead heats, most horses in race 123
Horseshoe Pitching 124

Ice and Sand Yachting 124–25
Ice Skating, origins, longest race, largest rink 125, figure skating: most difficult jumps 125–26, highest marks 126, world titles 126–27, Olympic titles, distance 127; speed skating: world titles 127, Olympic titles 127–28, marathon, 24 hours, barrel jumping 128

Jai-Alai (Pelota) 5, 128–29
Joggling 129
Judo, origins, grades, Olympics, throws, world champions, 10-hour record, marathon 130

Karate, origins, oldest and youngest black belts, grades, most titles, Olympic winners 131
Kayaking, see Canoeing and Kayaking

Lacrosse, origin 131–32, world championships, highest score, collegiate, women's championship 132
Luge 40

Marathons (running) 6, 132–33
Marbles, origins, most championships 86, speed record 87
Modern Pentathlon, see Pentathlon (modern)

Monopoly® 87
Motorcycling, earliest motorcycle, earliest races and circuits, longest circuit, fastest circuits 135, speed records 135, 136, fastest race 135–36, smallest motorcycle, longest race 136, world championships, 24-hour distance record 137, cross-US trek 137, 138, youngest and oldest champions, moto-cross (scrambling) 138
Mountaineering, origins, greatest wall 139, Yosemite feats 139, 140, Mount Everest 139, 141, progressive mountaineering altitude records 140, highest bivouac, oldest climber 141

Olympic Games, oldest gold medal winners 5, origins 141, most medals, 141–42, 145, 146, most participations, most and fewest competitors, largest crowds, youngest and oldest medalists 142, Olympic medals restored 143, 146, longest span, most gold medals at one Games 143, largest crowd 147
Orienteering 148

Pelota, see Jai-Alai (Pelota)
Pentathlon (modern), shortest championship reign 7, origins 133–34, Olympic titles 134–35, most world championship titles 135
Poker 87
Polo, largest ball-game field 5, origins, playing field, highest handicap, highest score, largest crowd, most Olympic medals, most internationals 149, elephant polo 149, 150
Polo, Water, see Water Polo
Pool 87
Powerboat Racing, origins 150, highest speeds 150–51, Gold Cup, longest jump, fastest transatlantic crossing 151, longest jump, Cowes International Powerboat Classic 152, longest race 152–53
Powerlifting 242, 245–46

Racquetball 153
Rodeo, origins 153, largest rodeos 153–54, crowds, youngest champion 154, most all-around titles and highest earnings 154, 156, time records 154, 156, steer wrestling champion, barrel-racing champion, bareback champion 155, champion bull, champion bronc 156
Roller Skating, origins, largest rink, marathon 156, free and figure skating 156, 157, endurance 156–57; roller hockey 157–58, speed records 158
Roulette 88
Rowing, youngest champion 5, oldest race 158, Olympic and world championships 158, 160, 161, International Dragon Boat races 160, 162, highest speed, heaviest oarsman, class distinction 161, longest race 161–62, longest in 24 hours, sculling 162
Running, see Cross-country Running; Joggling; Marathons

Sailsurfing, see Surfing
Sand Yachting 124–25
Scrabble® Crossword Game 88
Shooting, oldest Olympic champion, oldest international 5, earliest club, Olympic Games, bench rest shooting 162, clay pigeon shooting, highest 24-hour score, individual world records 163, first woman medalist, small-bore rifle shooting 164; game shooting: record heads, biggest bag 164
Skateboarding 164–65
Skiing, origins 165–66, most Olympic victories 166, 168, 169, most Alpine world titles 166–67, 169, World Cup 167, 168, 169, most Nordic world titles 167–68, duration 168, highest speed—cross country 168–70, closest verdict, longest run, longest jump, longest lift, steepest descent, highest altitude, highest speed—downhill 170, backflip 170, 171, most competitors—Alpine, longest races, biathlon 170, 171
Sky-diving 5
Snowshoe Racing 172
Snowmobiling 172
Soccer, largest crowd 6, largest stadium 7–8, origins, highest team scores 173, World Cup 173–74, marathons 174, ball control 174, 175, individual scoring 174–75, longest matches, goalkeeping, crowds 175
Soccer (table) 88

Softball, origins 175, pitchers 176, 177, slow pitch vs fast pitch 176–77, marathons, world championships 177

Sports World, earliest sports, fastest non-mechanical sports, slowest sports, longest events, youngest and oldest recordbreakers, youngest and oldest champions, youngest and oldest internationals, largest field 5, biggest contract, largest crowd, most participants 6, versatile athletes 6, 7, 8, most athletes 6–7, greatest earnings, heaviest athletes, championship reigns, prolific recordbreakers, disasters 7, largest stadiums 7–8

Squash, earliest champion 177, world titles 177–78, British Open championship 178, longest and shortest championship matches 178–79, marathon 179

Stadiums, largest 7–8, rained-out game in covered stadium 30–31

Surfing, origins, most titles, highest wave ridden, longest paddle 179, longest ride 179–80

Swimming, youngest recordbreaker, youngest diving champion 5, earliest Channel swimmers 180, 184–85, earliest references 180–81, most world records 181, 182, world titles 181, 182, women's world records 181, 182, 187, most Olympic gold medals 181, 188, most individual gold medals 182, long distance swimming 182–83, Bering Straits swim 183, 184, men's world records 183, 186, fastest swimmers, greatest lifetime distance, fastest Channel crossings 184, treading water 184, 189, largest pools 184, 192, 1988 Olympic gold medals 185, youngest and oldest Channel swimmers 185–86, most conquests of English Channel 186, double crossings of Channel 186, 191, triple crossing of Channel 186, closest race 186–87, most Olympic medals 187, swimming into the movies 188–89, underwater swimming, relay records 189, 24-hour swim 189, 191, diving titles 190–91, perfect dive 191, Manhattan round-trippers, synchronized swimming 192

Table Soccer 88

Table Tennis, youngest international 5, earliest references, Olympics, world championships 193, US national titles 193–94, Canadian International Open, youngest international contestant, longest match, longest rally, fastest rallying, highest speed, marathon 194

Team Handball 114

Tennis, greatest women's earnings, longest reign 7, origins 195, "grand slams" 195–97, 199, 200, Grand Prix masters 205, highest earnings 205, longest game 205–06, marathons 206, Olympics, unicycle tennis 207; Wimbledon records: youngest champions 196, 199, 200, tournament winners 195, 198, 204, 205, 207, most wins 199–200, oldest champions 200; US Open winners 201–02; US championships: most wins, youngest and oldest 203, fastest service 203, 205; Davis Cup, Wightman Cup 206, Federation Cup 206–07

Tennis, Real (Royal), longest championship reign 7

Throwing 88–89

Track and Field, shortest championship reign 7, earliest references, earliest landmarks 209, most records 208–09, 210, fastest speed 209, most records in one day 210, longest winning sequence 210, 218–19, world championships 211, most Olympic gold medals 211–12, most Olympic medals 212, oldest and youngest recordbreakers 212, 217, 1988 Olympic gold medal winners 213, men's world records 214, women's world records 215, indoor records 216, oldest and youngest Olympic champions 217–18, 221, running backwards 218, 219, standing long jump 218, longest race, three-legged race 219, 24-hour record, senior-citizen marathon 220, mass relay record, six-day race 222, shotput, pancake race record 225, fastest 100 miles, blind 100 meters 226, fastest 100 kilometers 226–27, trans-America run 227, trans-Canada run, greatest mileage, standing high jump 228

Trampolining, origins 228, stunts, world championships, coaching record 229, marathon 230

Triathlon 230–32

Twister® (game) 89

Tobogganing 39

Versatile Athletes 6, 7, 8

Video Games 89

Volleyball, origins, world titles 232, most Olympic medals 232–33, collegiate championships, marathon 233

Walking, oldest recordbreaker 5, longest race, longest non-stop walk 233, walking across the Americas 234, 235, walking around the world 234–35, road walking records 235, longest in 24 hours 235–36, most Olympic medals 236, walking backwards, most titles 237

Water Polo, origins 237, Olympic victories, marathon, most goals, NCAA championships 238

Water Skiing, origins 238, slalom 238, 240, tricks 238, 239, highest speed, most titles 239, jumps 239, 241, barefoot 239–40, longest run 240, youngest water skier 240, 241, biggest ski pull, kneeboarding 241

Weightlifting and Powerlifting, most prolific recordbreaker 7, origins, Olympic gold medals 242, most titles 242, 245, greatest lift 242–43, 245, youngest world record holder 243, world records 244, powerlifting 246

Windsurfing, see **Boardsailing**

Wrestling, slowest sport 5, earliest references 5, 247, heaviest athlete 7, most world championships, best records 247, longest bout 247–48, fastest pin, heaviest heavyweight, Olympic gold medals 248

Yachting, origins, transatlantic recordsetter loses race and record 248, highest speed 248–49, Olympic victories, greatest distance, longest race, Olympic gold medals, Admiral's Cup, largest marina, most competitors 249, America's Cup 249, 250, most successful 250